T0364944

Rover 600 Series
Service and Repair Manual

Mark Coombs, Spencer Drayton & Andy Legg LAE MIMI

Models covered

(3257-256)

Rover 600 Series Saloon models with normally-aspirated four-cylinder petrol engines, including special/limited editions
1.8 litre (1850 cc), 2.0 litre (1997 cc) & 2.3 litre (2256 cc) petrol engines

Does not cover 620 ti (Turbo) or diesel engine models

ABCDE

© **Haynes Publishing 1997**

A book in the **Haynes Service and Repair Manual Series**

ISBN **978 1 78521 319 9**

British Library Cataloguing in Publication Data
A catalogue record for this book is available from the British Library.

Printed in the UK

Haynes Publishing
Sparkford, Yeovil, Somerset BA22 7JJ, England

Haynes North America, Inc
859 Lawrence Drive, Newbury Park, California 91320, USA

Contents

Contents

REPAIRS & OVERHAUL

Engine and associated systems

Transmission

Brakes and suspension

Body equipment

Wiring diagrams

REFERENCE

Index

The new Rover 600 Saloon was introduced into the UK in early 1993. At its launch, the 600 was offered with a choice of 2.0 litre (1997 cc) or 2.3 litre (2256 cc) engine.

The engine is a well-proven unit which has appeared in many Honda vehicles. The engine is of four-cylinder overhead camshaft design (the 2.0 litre engine being SOHC and the 2.3 litre engine being DOHC), mounted transversely at the front of vehicle with the transmission mounted on its right-hand end. Both engines are fitted with a manual transmission unit as standard with an automatic transmission option.

All models have fully-independent front and rear double wishbone suspension incorporating shock absorbers and coil springs.

A wide range of standard and optional equipment is available within the range to suit most tastes, including central locking, electric windows and an electric sunroof. An air conditioning system was available as an options on certain models.

The model range has remained largely unchanged throughout its life, the only major change being in early 1996 when a 1.8 litre (1850 cc) SOHC engine was introduced into the range (both diesel engine and a 2.0 litre petrol Turbo model were also introduced but are not covered by this manual). Apart from this, only minor detail changes have been made to the vehicle.

Provided that all of the regular servicing is carried out in accordance with the manufacturer's recommendations, the vehicle should prove reliable and very economical. The engine compartment is well-designed, and most of the items requiring frequent attention are easily accessible.

Rover 623 GSi

Rover 620 GSi

The Rover 600 Team

Haynes manuals are produced by dedicated and enthusiastic people working in close co-operation. The team responsible for the creation of this book included:

Authors	**Mark Coombs** **Spencer Drayton** **Andy Legg**
Sub-editor	**Ian Barnes**
Editor & Page Make-up	**Steve Churchill** **Bob Jex**
Workshop manager	**Paul Buckland**
Photo Scans	**John Martin** **Steve Tanswell**
Cover illustration & Line Art	**Roger Healing**
Wiring diagrams	**Matthew Marke**

We hope the book will help you to get the maximum enjoyment from your car. By carrying out routine maintenance as described you will ensure your car's reliability and preserve its resale value.

Your Rover 600 manual

The aim of this manual is to help you get the best value from your vehicle. It can do so in several ways. It can help you decide what work must be done (even should you choose to get it done by a garage). It will also provide information on routine maintenance and servicing, and give a logical course of action and diagnosis when random faults occur. However, it is hoped that you will use the manual by tackling the work yourself. On simpler jobs it may even be quicker than booking the car into a garage and going there twice, to leave and collect it. Perhaps most important, a lot of money can be saved by avoiding the costs a garage must charge to cover its labour and overheads.

The manual has drawings and descriptions to show the function of the various components so that their layout can be understood. Tasks are described and photographed in a clear step-by-step sequence.

Acknowledgements

Thanks are due to Champion Spark Plug, who supplied the illustrations showing spark plug conditions. Thanks are also due to Sykes-Pickavant Limited, who provided some of the workshop tools, and to all those people at Sparkford who helped in the production of this manual.

We take great pride in the accuracy of information given in this manual, but vehicle manufacturers make alterations and design changes during the production run of a particular vehicle of which they do not inform us. No liability can be accepted by the authors or publishers for loss, damage or injury caused by any errors in, or omissions from, the information given.

Working on your car can be dangerous. This page shows just some of the potential risks and hazards, with the aim of creating a safety-conscious attitude.

General hazards

Scalding

• Don't remove the radiator or expansion tank cap while the engine is hot.
• Engine oil, automatic transmission fluid or power steering fluid may also be dangerously hot if the engine has recently been running.

Burning

• Beware of burns from the exhaust system and from any part of the engine. Brake discs and drums can also be extremely hot immediately after use.

Crushing

• When working under or near a raised vehicle, always supplement the jack with axle stands, or use drive-on ramps. **Never venture under a car which is only supported by a jack.**

• Take care if loosening or tightening high-torque nuts when the vehicle is on stands. Initial loosening and final tightening should be done with the wheels on the ground.

Fire

• Fuel is highly flammable; fuel vapour is explosive.
• Don't let fuel spill onto a hot engine.
• Do not smoke or allow naked lights (including pilot lights) anywhere near a vehicle being worked on. Also beware of creating sparks (electrically or by use of tools).
• Fuel vapour is heavier than air, so don't work on the fuel system with the vehicle over an inspection pit.
• Another cause of fire is an electrical overload or short-circuit. Take care when repairing or modifying the vehicle wiring.
• Keep a fire extinguisher handy, of a type suitable for use on fuel and electrical fires.

Electric shock

• Ignition HT voltage can be dangerous, especially to people with heart problems or a pacemaker. Don't work on or near the ignition system with the engine running or the ignition switched on.

• Mains voltage is also dangerous. Make sure that any mains-operated equipment is correctly earthed. Mains power points should be protected by a residual current device (RCD) circuit breaker.

Fume or gas intoxication

• Exhaust fumes are poisonous; they often contain carbon monoxide, which is rapidly fatal if inhaled. Never run the engine in a confined space such as a garage with the doors shut.
• Fuel vapour is also poisonous, as are the vapours from some cleaning solvents and paint thinners.

Poisonous or irritant substances

• Avoid skin contact with battery acid and with any fuel, fluid or lubricant, especially antifreeze, brake hydraulic fluid and Diesel fuel. Don't syphon them by mouth. If such a substance is swallowed or gets into the eyes, seek medical advice.
• Prolonged contact with used engine oil can cause skin cancer. Wear gloves or use a barrier cream if necessary. Change out of oil-soaked clothes and do not keep oily rags in your pocket.
• Air conditioning refrigerant forms a poisonous gas if exposed to a naked flame (including a cigarette). It can also cause skin burns on contact.

Asbestos

• Asbestos dust can cause cancer if inhaled or swallowed. Asbestos may be found in gaskets and in brake and clutch linings. When dealing with such components it is safest to assume that they contain asbestos.

Special hazards

Hydrofluoric acid

• This extremely corrosive acid is formed when certain types of synthetic rubber, found in some O-rings, oil seals, fuel hoses etc, are exposed to temperatures above 400°C. The rubber changes into a charred or sticky substance containing the acid. *Once formed, the acid remains dangerous for years. If it gets onto the skin, it may be necessary to amputate the limb concerned.*
• When dealing with a vehicle which has suffered a fire, or with components salvaged from such a vehicle, wear protective gloves and discard them after use.

The battery

• Batteries contain sulphuric acid, which attacks clothing, eyes and skin. Take care when topping-up or carrying the battery.
• The hydrogen gas given off by the battery is highly explosive. Never cause a spark or allow a naked light nearby. Be careful when connecting and disconnecting battery chargers or jump leads.

Air bags

• Air bags can cause injury if they go off accidentally. Take care when removing the steering wheel and/or facia. Special storage instructions may apply.

Diesel injection equipment

• Diesel injection pumps supply fuel at very high pressure. Take care when working on the fuel injectors and fuel pipes.

⚠ *Warning: Never expose the hands, face or any other part of the body to injector spray; the fuel can penetrate the skin with potentially fatal results.*

Remember...

DO

• Do use eye protection when using power tools, and when working under the vehicle.

• Do wear gloves or use barrier cream to protect your hands when necessary.

• Do get someone to check periodically that all is well when working alone on the vehicle.

• Do keep loose clothing and long hair well out of the way of moving mechanical parts.

• Do remove rings, wristwatch etc, before working on the vehicle – especially the electrical system.

• Do ensure that any lifting or jacking equipment has a safe working load rating adequate for the job.

DON'T

• Don't attempt to lift a heavy component which may be beyond your capability – get assistance.

• Don't rush to finish a job, or take unverified short cuts.

• Don't use ill-fitting tools which may slip and cause injury.

• Don't leave tools or parts lying around where someone can trip over them. Mop up oil and fuel spills at once.

• Don't allow children or pets to play in or near a vehicle being worked on.

The following pages are intended to help in dealing with common roadside emergencies and breakdowns. You will find more detailed fault finding information at the back of the manual, and repair information in the main chapters.

If your car won't start and the starter motor doesn't turn

- ☐ If it's a model with automatic transmission, make sure the selector is in 'P' or 'N'.
- ☐ Open the bonnet and make sure that the battery terminals are clean and tight.
- ☐ Switch on the headlights and try to start the engine. If the headlights go very dim when you're trying to start, the battery is probably flat. Get out of trouble by jump starting (see next page) using a friend's car.

If your car won't start even though the starter motor turns as normal

- ☐ Is there fuel in the tank?
- ☐ Is there moisture on electrical components under the bonnet? Switch off the ignition, then wipe off any obvious dampness with a dry cloth. Spray a water-repellent aerosol product (WD-40 or equivalent) on ignition and fuel system electrical connectors like those shown in the photos. Pay special attention to the ignition coil wiring connector and HT leads.

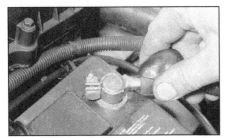

A Check the condition and security of the battery connections.

B Check that the spark plug HT leads are securely connected by pushing them onto the plugs and distributor.

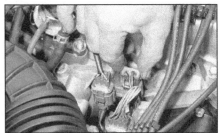

C Check that the distributor wiring connectors are securely connected.

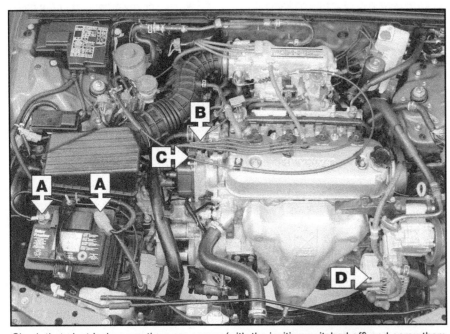

D Check that the wiring connectors are securely connected to the alternator.

Check that electrical connections are secure (with the ignition switched off) and spray them with a water dispersant spray like WD40 if you suspect a problem due to damp

Jump starting

HAYNES HiNT *Jump starting will get you out of trouble, but you must correct whatever made the battery go flat in the first place. There are three possibilities:*

1) *The battery has been drained by repeated attempts to start, or by leaving the lights on.*
2) *The charging system is not working properly (alternator drivebelt slack or broken, alternator wiring fault or alternator itself faulty).*
3) *The battery itself is at fault (electrolyte low, or battery worn out).*

When jump-starting a car using a booster battery, observe the following precautions:

✔ Before connecting the booster battery, make sure that the ignition is switched off.

✔ Ensure that all electrical equipment (lights, heater, wipers, etc) is switched off.

✔ Take note of any special precautions printed on the battery case.

✔ Make sure that the booster battery is the same voltage as the discharged one in the vehicle.

✔ If the battery is being jump-started from the battery in another vehicle, the two vehicles MUST NOT TOUCH each other.

✔ Make sure that the transmission is in neutral (or PARK, in the case of automatic transmission).

1 Connect one end of the red jump lead to the positive (+) terminal of the flat battery

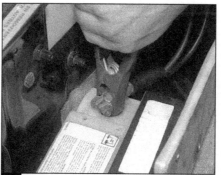

2 Connect the other end of the red lead to the positive (+) terminal of the booster battery

3 Connect one end of the black jump lead to the negative (-) terminal of the booster battery

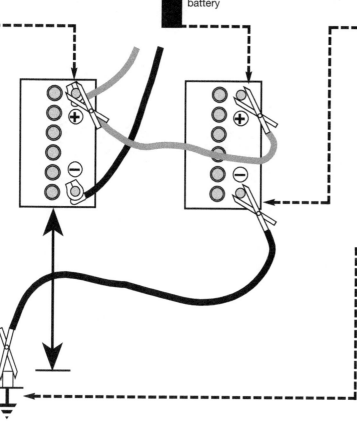

4 Connect the other end of the black jump lead to a bolt or bracket on the engine block, well away from the battery, on the vehicle to be started

5 Make sure that the jump leads will not come into contact with the fan, drivebelts or other moving parts of the engine

6 Start the engine using the booster battery, then with the engine running at idle speed, disconnect the jump leads in the reverse order of connection

Wheel changing

Some of the details shown here will vary according to model. For instance, the location of the spare wheel and jack is not the same on all cars. However, the basic principles apply to all vehicles.

 Warning: Do not change a wheel in a situation where you risk being hit by other traffic. On busy roads, try to stop in a lay-by or a gateway. Be wary of passing traffic while changing the wheel – it is easy to become distracted by the job in hand.

Preparation

- [ ] When a puncture occurs, stop as soon as it is safe to do so.
- [ ] Park on firm level ground, if possible, and well out of the way of other traffic.
- [ ] Use hazard warning lights if necessary.

- [ ] If you have one, use a warning triangle to alert other drivers of your presence.
- [ ] Apply the handbrake and engage first or reverse gear (or Park on models with automatic transmission.

- [ ] Chock the wheel diagonally opposite the one being removed – a couple of large stones will do for this.
- [ ] If the ground is soft, use a flat piece of wood to spread the load under the jack.

Changing the wheel

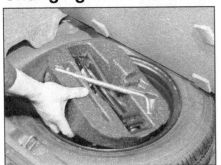

1 The spare wheel and tools are stored in the luggage compartment. Lift up the carpet and remove the tool kit and jack from the centre of the spare wheel.

2 Unscrew the retainer and remove the spare wheel from the luggage compartment.

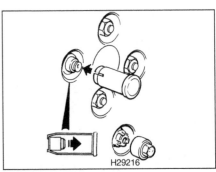

3 Remove the wheel trim/hub cap (as applicable). On models where anti-theft wheel nuts are fitted, use the adaptor in the toolkit to pull off each wheel nut cover then unscrew the wheel nuts using the special socket provided.

4 With the vehicle on the ground, slacken each wheel nut by half a turn.

5 Make sure the jack is located on firm ground and engage the jack head correctly with the sill. Raise the jack until the wheel is raised clear of the ground.

6 Unscrew the nuts and remove the wheel. Fit the spare wheel and screw on the nuts. Lightly tighten the nuts with the wheelbrace then lower the car to the ground.

7 Securely tighten the wheel nuts in a diagonal sequence then refit the wheel trim/hub cap/wheel nut covers (as applicable). Stow the punctured wheel and tools back in the luggage compartment and secure them in position. Note that the wheel nuts should be slackened and retightened to the specified torque at the earliest possible opportunity.

Finally...

- [ ] Remove the wheel chocks.
- [ ] Check the tyre pressure on the wheel just fitted. If it is low, or if you don't have a pressure gauge with you, drive slowly to the nearest garage and inflate the tyre to the right pressure.
- [ ] Have the damaged tyre or wheel repaired as soon as possible.

Identifying leaks

Puddles on the garage floor or drive, or obvious wetness under the bonnet or underneath the car, suggest a leak that needs investigating. It can sometimes be difficult to decide where the leak is coming from, especially if the engine bay is very dirty already. Leaking oil or fluid can also be blown rearwards by the passage of air under the car, giving a false impression of where the problem lies.

 Warning: Most automotive oils and fluids are poisonous. Wash them off skin, and change out of contaminated clothing, without delay.

 The smell of a fluid leaking from the car may provide a clue to what's leaking. Some fluids are distinctively coloured. It may help to clean the car and to park it over some clean paper as an aid to locating the source of the leak. Remember that some leaks may only occur while the engine is running.

Sump oil

Engine oil may leak from the drain plug...

Oil from filter

...or from the base of the oil filter.

Gearbox oil

Gearbox oil can leak from the seals at the inboard ends of the driveshafts.

Antifreeze

Leaking antifreeze often leaves a crystalline deposit like this.

Brake fluid

A leak occurring at a wheel is almost certainly brake fluid.

Power steering fluid

Power steering fluid may leak from the pipe connectors on the steering rack.

Towing

When all else fails, you may find yourself having to get a tow home – or of course you may be helping somebody else. Long-distance recovery should only be done by a garage or breakdown service. For shorter distances, DIY towing using another car is easy enough, but observe the following points:

☐ Use a proper tow-rope – they are not expensive. The vehicle being towed must display an 'ON TOW' sign in its rear window.

☐ Always turn the ignition key to the 'on' position when the vehicle is being towed, so that the steering lock is released, and that the direction indicator and brake lights will work.

☐ Only attach the tow-rope to the towing eyes provided.

☐ Before being towed, release the handbrake and select neutral on the transmission.

☐ Note that greater-than-usual pedal pressure will be required to operate the brakes, since the vacuum servo unit is only operational with the engine running.

☐ On models with power steering, greater-than-usual steering effort will also be required.

☐ The driver of the car being towed must keep the tow-rope taut at all times to avoid snatching.

☐ Make sure that both drivers know the route before setting off.

☐ Only drive at moderate speeds and keep the distance towed to a minimum. Drive smoothly and allow plenty of time for slowing down at junctions.

☐ *Caution: On models with automatic transmission, do not tow the vehicle at speeds in excess of 30 mph (50 kmh) or for a distance of greater than 15 miles (25 km). If the towing speed/distance exceeds these limits, then the vehicle must be towed with its front wheels off the ground.*

Introduction

There are some very simple checks which need only take a few minutes to carry out, but which could save you a lot of inconvenience and expense.

These "Weekly checks" require no great skill or special tools, and the small amount of time they take to perform could prove to be very well spent, for example;

☐ Keeping an eye on tyre condition and pressures, will not only help to stop them wearing out prematurely, but could also save your life.

☐ Many breakdowns are caused by electrical problems. Battery-related faults are particularly common, and a quick check on a regular basis will often prevent the majority of these.

☐ If your car develops a brake fluid leak, the first time you might know about it is when your brakes don't work properly. Checking the level regularly will give advance warning of this kind of problem.

☐ If the oil or coolant levels run low, the cost of repairing any engine damage will be far greater than fixing the leak, for example.

Underbonnet check points

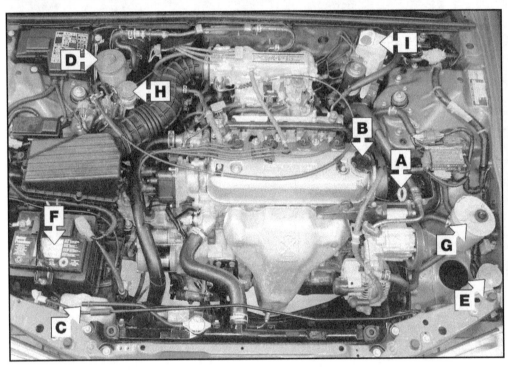

◀ 2.0 litre engine (1.8 litre identical, 2.3 litre similar)

A Engine oil level dipstick
B Engine oil filler cap
C Coolant expansion tank
D Brake fluid reservoir
E Screen washer fluid reservoir
F Battery
G Power steering fluid reservoir
H Clutch fluid reservoir
I ALB modulator high-pressure fluid reservoir

Engine oil level

Before you start
✔ Make sure that your car is on level ground.
✔ Check the oil level before the car is driven, or at least 5 minutes after the engine has been switched off.

 HAYNES HINT *If the oil level is checked immediately after driving the vehicle, some of the oil will remain in the upper engine components, resulting in an inaccurate reading on the dipstick!*

The correct oil
Modern engines place great demands on their oil. It is very important that the correct oil for your car is used (See "Lubricants, fluids and tyre pressures").

Car care
● If you have to add oil frequently, you should check whether you have any oil leaks. Place some clean paper under the car overnight, and check for stains in the morning. If there are no leaks, the engine may be burning oil *(see "Fault finding")*.

● Always maintain the level between the upper and lower dipstick marks (see photo 3). If the level is too low severe engine damage may occur. Oil seal failure may result if the engine is overfilled by adding too much oil.

1 The dipstick is located at the left-hand end of the engine (see *"Underbonnet check points"* on page 0•10 for exact location). Withdraw the dipstick.

2 Using a clean rag or paper towel remove all oil from the dipstick. Insert the clean dipstick into the tube as far as it will go, then withdraw it again.

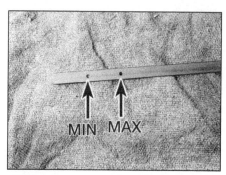
MIN MAX

3 Note the oil level on the end of the dipstick, which should be between the upper ("MAX") mark and lower ("MIN") mark. Approximately 1.0 litre of oil will raise the level from the lower mark to the upper mark.

4 Oil is added through the filler cap. Unscrew the cap and top-up the level; a funnel may help to reduce spillage. Add the oil slowly, checking the level on the dipstick often. Don't overfill (see *"Car care" left*).

Coolant level

 ⚠ **Warning: DO NOT attempt to remove the expansion tank pressure cap when the engine is hot, as there is a very great risk of scalding. Do not leave open containers of coolant about, as it is poisonous.**

Car care
● Adding coolant should not be necessary on a regular basis. If frequent topping-up is required, it is likely there is a leak. Check the radiator, all hoses and joint faces for signs of staining or wetness, and rectify as necessary.

● It is important that antifreeze is used in the cooling system all year round, not just during the winter months. Don't top-up with water alone, as the antifreeze will become too diluted.

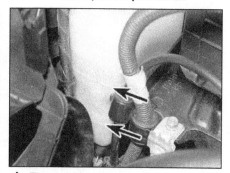
1 The coolant level is checked in the expansion tank on the right-hand side of the engine compartment. When the engine is cold, the coolant level should be between the upper (MAX) and lower (MIN) level markings on the side of the expansion tank.

2 If topping up is necessary, remove the expansion tank cap and add a mixture of water and antifreeze to the expansion tank until the coolant level is between the level marks. Once the level is correct, securely refit the cap.

3 If the expansion tank is completely empty, remove the pressure cap and check the level in the radiator. If necessary top up the radiator until the coolant level is upto the base of the filler neck then refit the cap.

Brake and clutch fluid level

⚠️ **Warning:**
● **Brake fluid can harm your eyes and will damage painted surfaces, so use extreme caution when handling and pouring it.**
● **Do not use fluid that has been standing open for some time, as it absorbs moisture from the air, which can cause a dangerous loss of braking effectiveness.**

Safety first!
● If the reservoir requires repeated topping-up this is an indication of a fluid leak somewhere in the system, which should be investigated immediately.
● If a leak is suspected, the car should not be driven until the braking system has been checked. Never take any risks where brakes are concerned.

HAYNES HiNT
● *Make sure that your car is on level ground.*
● *The fluid level in the reservoir will drop slightly as the brake pads wear down, but the fluid level must never be allowed to drop below the "MIN" mark.*

1 The upper (MAX) and lower (MIN) fluid level markings are on the side of the reservoir, which is located in the right-hand rear corner of the engine compartment. The fluid level must always be kept in between these two marks.

2 If topping up is necessary, first wipe clean the area around the filler cap with a clean cloth then unscrew the cap and remove it along with the rubber diaphragm.

3 Carefully add fluid, avoiding spilling it on the surrounding paintwork. Use only the specified hydraulic fluid. After filling the correct level, refit the cap and diaphragm and tighten it securely. Wipe off any spilt fluid.

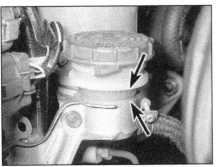

4 Repeat the check on clutch reservoir (level markings arrowed) and, if necessary, top up.

5 On models with equipped with ABS, also check the fluid level in the ABS modulator high pressure reservoir is between the MIN and MAX level markings. If it is noted that the fluid level drops for any reason, the vehicle should be taken to a Rover dealer immediately for inspection.

Power steering fluid level

Before you start:
✔ Park the vehicle on level ground.
✔ Set the steering wheel straight-ahead.
✔ The engine should be turned off.

HAYNES HiNT *For the check to be accurate, the steering must not be turned once the engine has been stopped.*

Safety first!
● The need for frequent topping-up indicates a leak, which should be investigated immediately.

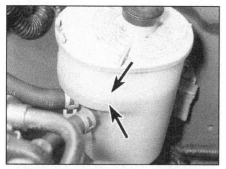

1 The power steering fluid level is checked at the fluid reservoir on the left-hand side of the engine compartment. With the engine cold, the fluid level should be between the upper and lower level markings on the side of the expansion tank.

2 If topping up is necessary, wipe clean the area around the reservoir cap before removing it.

3 Top-up the reservoir with the specified type of the fluid. Once the level is between the level marks, securely refit the reservoir cap. Do not overfill the reservoir.

Screen washer fluid level

Screenwash additives not only keep the winscreen clean during foul weather, they also prevent the washer system freezing in cold weather - which is when you are likely to need it most. Don't top up using plain water as the screenwash will become too diluted, and will freeze during cold weather. *On no account use coolant antifreeze in the washer system - this could discolour or damage paintwork.*

1 The washer fluid reservoir is on the left-hand side of the engine compartment. The filler neck has level markings on it and the float inside the neck indicates how full the reservoir is.

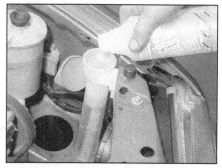

2 If topping up is necessary, add water and a screenwash additive in the quantities recommended by the manufacturer.

Wiper blades

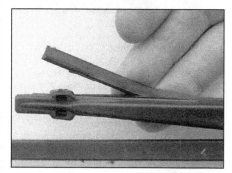

1 Check the condition of the wiper blades: if they are cracked or show signs of deterioration, or if the glass swept area is smeared, renew them.

2 To remove a wiper blade, pull the arm fully away from the screen until it locks. depress the locking clip and swivel the blade through 90°.

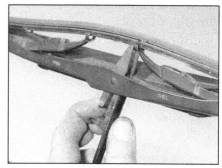

3 Depress the locking clip at the base of the mounting block and disengage the blade from the wiper arm.

Tyre condition and pressure

It is very important that tyres are in good condition, and at the correct pressure - having a tyre failure at any speed is highly dangerous. Tyre wear is influenced by driving style - harsh braking and acceleration, or fast cornering, will all produce more rapid tyre wear. As a general rule, the front tyres wear out faster than the rears. Interchanging the tyres from front to rear ("rotating" the tyres) may result in more even wear. However, if this is completely effective, you may have the expense of replacing all four tyres at once!

Remove any nails or stones embedded in the tread before they penetrate the tyre to cause deflation. If removal of a nail does reveal that the tyre has been punctured, refit the nail so that its point of penetration is marked. Then immediately change the wheel, and have the tyre repaired by a tyre dealer.

Regularly check the tyres for damage in the form of cuts or bulges, especially in the sidewalls. Periodically remove the wheels, and clean any dirt or mud from the inside and outside surfaces. Examine the wheel rims for signs of rusting, corrosion or other damage. Light alloy wheels are easily damaged by "kerbing" whilst parking; steel wheels may also become dented or buckled. A new wheel is very often the only way to overcome severe damage.

New tyres should be balanced when they are fitted, but it may become necessary to re-balance them as they wear, or if the balance weights fitted to the wheel rim should fall off. Unbalanced tyres will wear more quickly, as will the steering and suspension components. Wheel imbalance is normally signified by vibration, particularly at a certain speed (typically around 50 mph). If this vibration is felt only through the steering, then it is likely that just the front wheels need balancing. If, however, the vibration is felt through the whole car, the rear wheels could be out of balance. Wheel balancing should be carried out by a tyre dealer or garage.

1 Tread Depth - visual check
The original tyres have tread wear safety bands (B), which will appear when the tread depth reaches approximately 1.6 mm. The band positions are indicated by a triangular mark on the tyre sidewall (A).

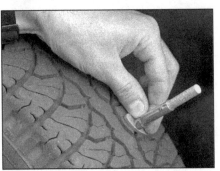

2 Tread Depth - manual check
Alternatively, tread wear can be monitored with a simple, inexpensive device known as a tread depth indicator gauge.

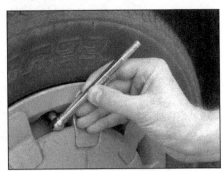

3 Tyre Pressure Check
Check the tyre pressures regularly with the tyres cold. Do not adjust the tyre pressures immediately after the vehicle has been used, or an inaccurate setting will result.

Tyre tread wear patterns

Shoulder Wear

Underinflation (wear on both sides)
Under-inflation will cause overheating of the tyre, because the tyre will flex too much, and the tread will not sit correctly on the road surface. This will cause a loss of grip and excessive wear, not to mention the danger of sudden tyre failure due to heat build-up.
Check and adjust pressures
Incorrect wheel camber (wear on one side)
Repair or renew suspension parts
Hard cornering
Reduce speed!

Centre Wear

Overinflation
Over-inflation will cause rapid wear of the centre part of the tyre tread, coupled with reduced grip, harsher ride, and the danger of shock damage occurring in the tyre casing.
Check and adjust pressures

If you sometimes have to inflate your car's tyres to the higher pressures specified for maximum load or sustained high speed, don't forget to reduce the pressures to normal afterwards.

Uneven Wear

Front tyres may wear unevenly as a result of wheel misalignment. Most tyre dealers and garages can check and adjust the wheel alignment (or "tracking") for a modest charge.
Incorrect camber or castor
Repair or renew suspension parts
Malfunctioning suspension
Repair or renew suspension parts
Unbalanced wheel
Balance tyres
Incorrect toe setting
Adjust front wheel alignment
Note: *The feathered edge of the tread which typifies toe wear is best checked by feel.*

Battery

Caution: *Before carrying out any work on the vehicle battery, read the precautions given in "Safety first" at the start of this manual.*

✔ Make sure that the battery tray is in good condition, and that the clamp is tight. Corrosion on the tray, retaining clamp and the battery itself can be removed with a solution of water and baking soda. Thoroughly rinse all cleaned areas with water. Any metal parts damaged by corrosion should be covered with a zinc-based primer, then painted.

✔ Periodically (approximately every three months), check the charge condition of the battery as described in Chapter 5A.

✔ If the battery is flat, and you need to jump start your vehicle, see **Roadside Repairs**.

1 The battery is located at the front right-hand corner of the engine compartment. The exterior of the battery should be inspected periodically for damage such as a cracked case or cover.

2 Check the battery lead clamps for tightness to ensure good electrical connections and check the leads for signs of damage.

Battery corrosion can be kept to a minimum by applying a layer of petroleum jelly to the clamps and terminals after they are reconnected.

3 If corrosion (white, fluffy deposits) is evident, remove the cables from the battery terminals, clean them with a small wire brush, then refit them. Automotive stores sell a tool for cleaning the battery post . . .

4 . . . as well as the battery cable clamps

Bulbs and fuses

✔ Check all external lights and the horn. Refer to the appropriate Sections of Chapter 12 for details if any of the circuits are found to be inoperative.

✔ Visually check all accessible wiring connectors, harnesses and retaining clips for security, and for signs of chafing or damage.

HAYNES HINT *If you need to check your brake lights and indicators unaided, back up to a wall or garage door and operate the lights. The reflected light should show if they are working properly.*

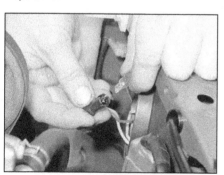

1 If a single indicator light, stop light, sidelight or headlight has failed, it is likely that a bulb has blown and will need to be replaced. Refer to Chapter 12 for details. If both stop lights have failed, it is possible that the switch has failed (see Chapter 9).

2 If more than one indicator light or tail light has failed it is likely that either a fuse has blown or there is a fault in the circuit (see Chapter 12). The fuses are located behind the cover on the driver's side footwell trim panel, and also in the engine compartment fusebox.

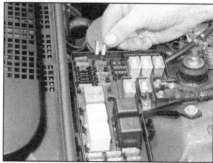

3 To replace a blown fuse, simply pull it out and fit a new fuse of the correct rating (see Chapter 12). If the fuse blows again, it is important that you find out why - a complete checking procedure is given in Chapter 12.

Lubricants and fluids

Engine	Multigrade engine oil, viscosity SAE 10W/30 to 10W/40 to API SF, SG or SH (*Duckhams QS, QXR, Hypergrade Plus, Hypergrade or 10W-40 Motor Oil*)
Cooling system	Ethylene glycol based antifreeze (*Duckhams Antifreeze and Summer Coolant*)
Manual transmission	Multigrade engine oil, viscosity SAE 10W/30 or 10W/40 to API SF, SG or SH (*Duckhams QS, QXR, or 10W-40 Motor Oil*)
Automatic transmission	Dexron type II automatic transmission fluid (ATF) (*Duckhams Uni-Matic*)
Brake and clutch system	Hydraulic fluid DOT 3 or DOT 4 (*Duckhams Universal Brake and Clutch Fluid*)
Power steering	Unipart power steering fluid (*Duckhams Uni-Matic*)

Choosing your engine oil

Oils perform vital tasks in all engines. The higher the engine's performance, the greater the demand on lubricants to minimise wear as well as optimise power and economy. Duckhams tailors lubricants to the highest technical standards, meeting and exceeding the demands of all modern engines.

HOW ENGINE OIL WORKS

• Beating friction

Without oil, the surfaces inside your engine which rub together will heat, fuse and quickly cause engine seizure. Oil, and its special additives, forms a molecular barrier between moving parts, to stop wear and minimise heat build-up.

• Cooling hot spots

Oil cools parts that the engine's water-based coolant cannot reach, bathing the combustion chamber and pistons, where temperatures may exceed 1000°C. The oil assists in transferring the heat to the engine cooling system. Heat in the oil is also lost by air flow over the sump, and via any auxiliary oil cooler.

• Cleaning the inner engine

Oil washes away combustion by-products (mainly carbon) on pistons and cylinders, transporting them to the oil filter, and holding the smallest particles in suspension until they are flushed out by an oil change. Duckhams oils undergo extensive tests in the laboratory, and on the road.

Note: It is antisocial and illegal to dump oil down the drain. To find the location of your local oil recycling bank, call this number free.

OIL BANK LINE
0800 66 33 66

Tyre pressures

Note: *Pressures apply to original-equipment tyres only and may vary if any other make or type of tyre is fitted; check with the tyre manufacturer or supplier for correct pressures if necessary.*
Note: *Tyre pressures must always be checked with the tyres cold to ensure accuracy.*

185/65 R 15 tyres:
    Speeds up to 100 mph:

Front	32 psi (2.2 bar)
Rear	30 psi (2.1 bar)

    Speeds in excess of 100 mph:

Front	38 psi (2.6 bar)
Rear	36 psi (2.5 bar)

195/60 R 15 tyres:
    Speeds upto 100 mph:

Front	33 psi (2.3 bar)
Rear	42 psi (2.9 bar)

    Speeds in excess of 100 mph:

Front	42 psi (2.9 bar)
Rear	41 psi (2.8 bar)

Chapter 1
Routine maintenance and servicing

Contents

Degrees of difficulty

Easy, suitable for novice with little experience	Fairly easy, suitable for beginner with some experience	Fairly difficult, suitable for competent DIY mechanic	Difficult, suitable for experienced DIY mechanic	Very difficult, suitable for expert DIY or professional

Lubricants and fluids .... Refer to 'Weekly checks'

Capacities

Engine oil
After overhaul:
    1.8 and 2.0 litre engines .... 4.9 litres
    2.3 litre engine .... 5.4 litres
At oil change (including oil filter):
    1.8 and 2.0 litre engines .... 3.8 litres
    2.3 litre engine .... 4.3 litres

Cooling system	Total	Coolant change
1.8 litre	6.4 litres	2.7 litres
2.0 litre manual	6.3 litres	2.7 litres
2.0 litre automatic	6.2 litres	2.6 litres
2.3 litre manual	7.0 litres	3.3 litres
2.3 litre automatic	6.9 litres	3.2 litres

Transmission
Manual transmission (approximate) .... 2.0 litres
Automatic transmission (approximate):
    From dry .... 6.0 litres
    At fluid change .... 2.4 litres

Power-assisted steering
All models (approximate) .... 1.8 litres

Engine
Oil filter .... Champion F208
Valve clearances:
    1.8 and 2.0 litre engines:
      Inlet .... 0.26 ± 0.03 mm
      Exhaust .... 0.30 ± 0.03 mm
    2.3 litre engines:
      Inlet .... 0.09 ± 0.03 mm
      Exhaust .... 0.17 ± 0.03 mm

Cooling system
Antifreeze mixture:
    50% antifreeze .... Protection down to -37°C (5°F)
    55% antifreeze .... Protection down to -45°C (-22°F)
Note: *Refer to antifreeze manufacturer for latest recommendations.*

Fuel system
Air filter element .... Champion U661
Fuel filter .... Champion L222
Exhaust CO content .... Less than 0.1%

Ignition system
Ignition timing .... Refer to Chapter 5
Spark plug type (electrode gap) .... Champion RC9MCC (0.9 mm)
The spark plug gap quoted is that recommended by Champion for their specified plug listed above. If spark plugs of any other type are to be fitted, refer to their manufacturers recommendations.

Brakes
Brake pad friction material minimum thickness .... 1.6 mm (front and rear pads)

Torque wrench settings	Nm	lbf ft
Automatic transmission drain plug	50	37
Engine:		
Sump drain plug	45	33
Rocker arm adjusting screw locknut:		
1.8 and 2.0 litre engines	20	15
2.3 litre engines	27	20
Manual transmission:		
Drain plug	40	29
Filler/level plug	45	33
Roadwheel nuts	110	81
Spark plugs	18	13

The maintenance intervals in this manual are provided with the assumption that you, not the dealer, will be carrying out the work. These are the minimum maintenance intervals recommended by us for vehicles driven daily.

If you wish to keep your vehicle in peak condition at all times, you may wish to perform some of these procedures more often. We encourage frequent maintenance, because it enhances the efficiency, performance and resale value of your vehicle.

When the vehicle is new, it should be serviced by a factory-authorised dealer service department, in order to preserve the factory warranty.

Every 250 miles or weekly, whichever comes first

☐ See 'Weekly checks'

Every 6000 miles or 6 months, whichever comes first

☐ Renew the engine oil and filter (Section 3)

Note: *Rover recommend that the engine oil and filter are changed every 12 000 miles or 12 months. However, oil and filter changes are good for the engine and we recommend that the oil and filter are renewed more frequently, especially if the vehicle is used on a lot of short journeys.*

Every 12 000 miles or 12 months, whichever comes first

☐ Check the tension of auxiliary drivebelt(s) (Section 4)
☐ Check all components, pipes and hoses for fluid leaks (Section 5)
☐ Check the front brake pads and discs for wear (Section 6)
☐ Check the manual transmission oil level (Section 7)
☐ Check the automatic transmission fluid level (Section 8)
☐ Check the steering and suspension components for condition and security (Section 9)
☐ Check the condition of the exhaust system and its mountings (Section 10)
☐ Check the underbody and sealant for damage (Section 11)
☐ Check the condition of the seat belts and airbag unit(s) (as applicable) (Section 12)
☐ Lubricate all hinges and locks (Section 13)
☐ Carry out a road test (Section 14)

Every 24 000 miles or 2 years, whichever comes first

☐ Renew air filter element (Section 15)
☐ Renew the spark plugs and check the ignition system components (Section 16)
☐ Renew the automatic transmission fluid (Section 17)
☐ Check and, if necessary, adjust the valve clearances (Section 18)
☐ Check the air conditioning system (Section 19)
☐ Check the rear brake pads and discs for wear (Section 20)
☐ Check the condition of the driveshaft gaiters (Section 21)
☐ Check the operation of the handbrake (Section 22)
☐ Check the exhaust gas emission content (Section 23)

Every 36 000 miles or 3 years, whichever comes first

☐ Renew the fuel filter (Section 24)
☐ Renew the manual transmission oil (Section 25)

Every 60 000 miles

☐ Renew the timing belt and balance shaft belt (Section 26)
☐ Renew the crankcase ventilation (PCV) valve (Section 27)

Every 2 years regardless of mileage

☐ Renew the engine coolant (Section 28)
☐ Renew the brake fluid (Section 29)

Every 4 years regardless of mileage

☐ Renew the anti-lock braking system high-pressure hose (where necessary) (Section 30)

Every 10 years regardless of mileage

☐ Renew the airbag(s) and slip ring/reel (Section 31)

Underbonnet view of a 2.0 litre model
(1.8 litre the same, 2.3 litre model similar)

1   Engine oil filler cap
2   Engine oil level dipstick
3   Battery
4   Brake fluid reservoir
5   Radiator
6   Coolant expansion tank
7   Clutch fluid reservoir
8   Air filter housing
9   Fusebox
10 Starter motor
11 Alternator
12 Distributor
13 Washer fluid reservoir
14 Power steering pump
15 Thermostat housing
16 ABS modulator

Front underbody view

1   Engine oil drain plug
2   Manual transmission
    filler/level plug
3   Manual transmission drain
    plug
4   Oil filter
5   Front suspension lower
    control arm
6   Radius rod
7   Anti-roll bar
8   Track rod
9   Intermediate shaft
10 Exhaust system front pipe
11 Driveshaft

Rear underbody view

1   Fuel tank
2   Rear suspension trailing arm
3   Rear suspension lower control arm
4   Rear suspension anti-roll bar
5   Shock absorber lower mounting
6   Exhaust system tailpipe

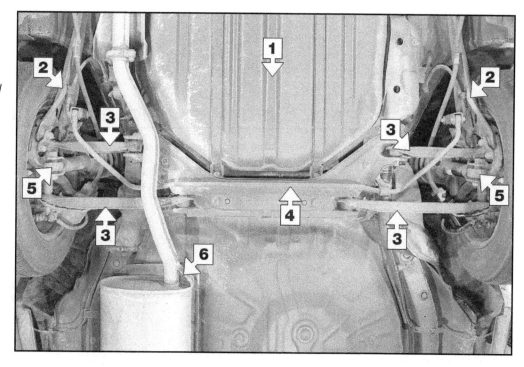

---

1 General information

1 This Chapter is designed to help the home mechanic maintain his/her vehicle for safety, economy, long life and peak performance.

2 The Chapter contains a master maintenance schedule, followed by Sections dealing specifically with each task in the schedule. Visual checks, adjustments, component renewal and other helpful items are included. Refer to the accompanying illustrations of the engine compartment and the underside of the vehicle for the locations of the various components.

3 Servicing your vehicle in accordance with the mileage/time maintenance schedule and the following Sections will provide a planned maintenance programme, which should result in a long and reliable service life. This is a comprehensive plan, so maintaining some items but not others at the specified service intervals, will not produce the same results.

4 As you service your vehicle, you will discover that many of the procedures can - and should - be grouped together, because of

the particular procedure being performed, or because of the proximity of two otherwise-unrelated components to one another. For example, if the vehicle is raised for any reason, the exhaust can be inspected at the same time as the suspension and steering components.

5 The first step in this maintenance programme is to prepare yourself before the actual work begins. Read through all the Sections relevant to the work to be carried out, then make a list and gather all the parts and tools required. If a problem is encountered, seek advice from a parts specialist, or a dealer service department.

Caution: If the radio/cassette in your vehicle is equipped with an anti-theft system, make sure you have the correct activation code before disconnecting the battery.

2 Intensive maintenance

1 If, from the time the vehicle is new, the routine maintenance schedule is followed closely, and frequent checks are made of fluid

levels and high-wear items, as suggested throughout this manual, the engine will be kept in relatively good running condition, and the need for additional work will be minimised.

2 It is possible that there will be times when the engine is running poorly due to the lack of regular maintenance. This is even more likely if a used vehicle, which has not received regular and frequent maintenance checks, is purchased. In such cases, additional work may need to be carried out, outside of the regular maintenance intervals.

3 If engine wear is suspected, a compression test (refer to Chapter 2A) will provide valuable information regarding the overall performance of the main internal components. Such a test can be used as a basis to decide on the extent of the work to be carried out. If, for example, a compression test indicates serious internal engine wear, conventional maintenance as described in this Chapter will not greatly improve the performance of the engine, and may prove a waste of time and money, unless extensive overhaul work is carried out first.

4 The following series of operations are those most often required to improve the performance of a generally poor-running engine:

Primary operations

a) Clean, inspect and test the battery (see 'Weekly checks').
b) Check all the engine-related fluids (see 'Weekly checks').
c) Check the condition and tension of the auxiliary drivebelt (Section 4).
d) Renew the spark plugs (Section 16).
e) Inspect the distributor cap and rotor arm (Section 16).

f) Check the condition of the air filter, and renew if necessary (Section 15).
g) Renew the fuel filter (Section 24).
h) Check the condition of all hoses, and check for fluid leaks (Section 5).
i) Check the exhaust gas emissions (Section 23).

5 If the above operations do not prove fully effective, carry out the following secondary operations:

Secondary operations

All items listed under *Primary operations*, plus the following:

a) Check the charging system (see Chapter 5).
b) Check the ignition system (see Chapter 5).
c) Check the fuel system (refer to Chapter 4).
d) Renew the distributor cap and rotor arm (Section 16).
e) Renew the ignition HT leads (Section 16).

Every 6000 miles or 6 months, whichever comes first

3 Engine oil and filter renewal

1 Frequent oil and filter changes are the most important preventative maintenance procedures which can be undertaken by the DIY owner. As engine oil ages, it becomes diluted and contaminated, which leads to premature engine wear.
2 Before starting this procedure, gather together all the necessary tools and materials. Also make sure that you have plenty of clean rags and newspapers handy, to mop up any spills. Ideally, the engine oil should be warm, as it will drain more easily, and more built-up sludge will be removed with it. Take care not to touch the exhaust or any other hot parts of the engine when working under the vehicle. To avoid any possibility of scalding, and to protect yourself from possible skin irritants and other harmful contaminants in used engine oils, it is advisable to wear gloves when carrying out this work.
3 Firmly apply the handbrake then jack up the front of the vehicle and support it on axle stands.
4 Remove the oil filler cap.

5 Using a spanner, or preferably a suitable socket and bar, slacken the drain plug about half a turn **(see illustration)**. Position the draining container under the drain plug, then remove the plug completely **(see Haynes Hint)**.

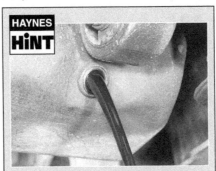

As the drain plug threads release, move it sharply away so the stream of oil issuing from the sump runs into the container, not up your sleeve!

6 Allow some time for the oil to drain, noting that it may be necessary to reposition the container as the oil flow slows to a trickle.
7 After all the oil has drained, wipe the drain plug and the sealing washer with a clean rag.

Examine the condition of the sealing washer, and renew it if it shows signs of scoring or other damage which may prevent an oil-tight seal. Clean the area around the drain plug opening, and refit the plug complete with the washer and tighten it to the specified torque.
8 Move the container into position under the oil filter which is located on the rear of the cylinder block.
9 Use an oil filter removal tool to slacken the filter initially, then unscrew it by hand the rest of the way **(see illustration)**. Empty the oil from the old filter into the container.
10 Use a clean rag to remove all oil, dirt and sludge from the filter sealing area on the engine. Check the old filter to make sure that the rubber sealing ring has not stuck to the engine. If it has, carefully remove it.
11 If a genuine Rover filter is being installed, note whether the filter is a Japanese-made item or a French-made item. Apply a light coating of clean engine oil to the sealing ring on the new filter, then screw the filter into position on the engine until its sealing ring contacts the block/oil cooler surface (as applicable). From this point, the Japanese-made filter must be tightened a further 7/8 of a turn and the French-made filter must be tightened a further 3/4 of a turn. Numbers are marked onto the base of the filter to assist you

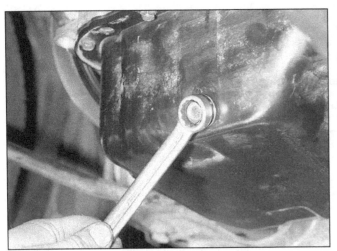

3.5 Slackening the sump drain plug

3.9 Using an oil filter removal tool to slacken the oil filter

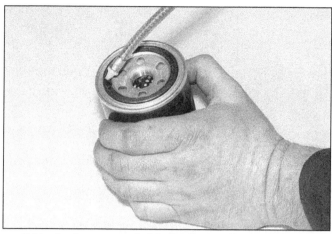

3.11a Apply a smear of oil to the filter sealing ring prior to installation

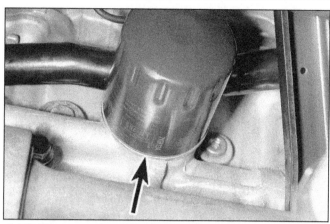

3.11b Where a genuine Rover filter is being installed, refer to the text explanation of the numbers (arrowed) to ensure it is correctly tightened - French-made (Purflux) filter shown

in ensuring the filter is correctly tightened, the Japanese-made filter has the numbers 1 to 8 spaced equally around its circumference and the French-made filter the numbers 1 to 4 **(see illustrations)**. If a pattern filter is being fitted, tighten the filter firmly by hand only - **do not** use any tools.

12 Once the filter is correctly tightened, remove the old oil and all tools from under the vehicle then lower the vehicle to the ground.

13 Fill the engine through the filler hole, using the correct grade and type of oil (refer to

'Weekly checks' for details of topping-up). Pour in half the specified quantity of oil first, then wait a few minutes for the oil to drain into the sump. Continue to add oil, a small quantity at a time, until the level is up to the lower mark on the dipstick. Adding approximately a further 1.0 litre will bring the level up to the upper mark on the dipstick.

14 Start the engine and run it for a few minutes, while checking for leaks around the oil filter seal and the sump drain plug. Note that there may be a delay of a few seconds

before the low oil pressure warning light goes out when the engine is first started, as the oil circulates through the new oil filter and the engine oil galleries before the pressure builds up.

15 Stop the engine, and wait a few minutes for the oil to settle in the sump once more. With the new oil circulated and the filter now completely full, recheck the level on the dipstick, and add more oil as necessary.

16 Dispose of the used engine oil safely, with reference to General repair procedures.

Every 12 000 miles or 12 months, whichever comes first

4 Auxiliary drivebelt check and renewal

Checking

1 Disconnect the battery negative cable and position it away from the terminal.

2 Park the vehicle on a level surface and apply the handbrake and chock the rear wheels.

3 Using a socket and wrench on the crankshaft sprocket bolt, rotate the crankshaft so that the full length of the auxiliary drivebelt(s) can be examined. Look for cracks,

splitting and fraying on the surface of the belt; check also for signs of glazing (shiny patches) and separation of the belt plies. If damage or wear is visible, the belt should be renewed.

Tensioning and renewal

4 Refer to the information given in Chapters 5A or 10, as applicable.

5 Hose and fluid leak check

Coolant

⚠️ **Warning: Refer to the safety information given in Safety First and Chapter 3 before disturbing any of the cooling system components.**

1 Carefully check the radiator and heater coolant hoses along their entire length. Renew any hose which is cracked, swollen or which shows signs of deterioration. Cracks will show up better if the hose is squeezed **(see illustration)**. Pay close attention to the clips that secure the hoses to the cooling system components. Hose clips that have been over-tightened can pinch and puncture hoses, resulting in cooling system leaks.

2 Inspect all the cooling system components (hoses, joint faces etc.) for leaks. Where any problems of this nature are found on system components, renew the component or gasket with reference to Chapter 3.

3 A leak from the cooling system will usually show up as white or rust-coloured deposits, on the area surrounding the leak **(see Haynes Hint)**.

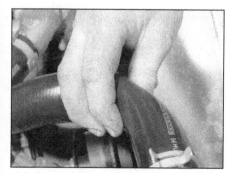

5.1 Cracks in the coolant hoses will show up better if the hose is squeezed

HAYNES HINT

A leak from the cooling system will usually show up as white or rust-coloured deposits, on the area surrounding the leak

5.5 Check the fuel regulator connections for leakage

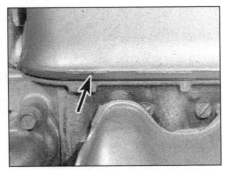

5.8 Inspect the area around the gasket between the camshaft cover and the cylinder head for oil leaks

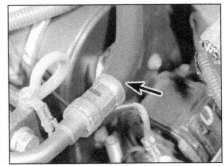

5.11 Examine the high pressure hose between the power steering pump and the steering rack for signs of leakage

Fuel

 Warning: Refer to the safety information given in Safety First and Chapter 4 before disturbing any of the fuel system components.

4 Petrol leaks are difficult to pinpoint, unless the leakage is significant and hence easily visible. Fuel tends to evaporate quickly once it comes into contact with air, especially in a hot engine bay. Small drips can disappear before you get a chance to identify the point of leakage. If you suspect that there is a fuel leak from the area of the engine bay, leave the vehicle overnight then start the engine from cold, with the bonnet open. Metal components tend to shrink when they are cold, and rubber seals and hoses tend to harden, so any leaks will be more apparent whilst the engine is warming up from a cold start.

5 Check all fuel lines at their connections to the fuel rail, fuel pressure regulator and fuel filter **(see illustration)**. Examine each rubber fuel hose along its length for splits or cracks. Check for leakage from the crimped joints between rubber and metal fuel lines. Examine the unions between the metal fuel lines and the fuel filter housing. Also check the area around the fuel injectors for signs of O-ring leakage.

6 To identify fuel leaks between the fuel tank and the engine bay, the vehicle should raised and securely supported on axle stands. Inspect the petrol tank and filler neck for punctures, cracks and other damage. The connection between the filler neck and tank is especially critical. Sometimes a rubber filler neck or connecting hose will leak due to loose retaining clamps or deteriorated rubber.

7 Carefully check all rubber hoses and metal fuel lines leading away from the petrol tank. Check for loose connections, deteriorated hoses, kinked lines, and other damage. Pay particular attention to the vent pipes and hoses, which often loop up around the filler neck and can become blocked or kinked, making tank filling difficult. Follow the fuel supply and return lines to the front of the vehicle, carefully inspecting them all the way for signs of damage or corrosion. Renew damaged sections as necessary.

Engine oil

8 Inspect the area around the camshaft cover, cylinder head, oil filter and sump joint faces **(see illustration)**. Bear in mind that, over a period of time, some very slight seepage from these areas is to be expected - what you are really looking for is any indication of a serious leak caused by gasket failure. Engine oil seeping from the base of the timing belt cover or the transmission bellhousing may be an indication of crankshaft or balance shaft oil seal failure. Should a leak be found, renew the failed gasket or oil seal by referring to the appropriate Chapters in this manual.

9 Where applicable, check the hoses leading to the engine oil cooler at the front of the engine bay for leakage. Look for deterioration caused by corrosion and damage from grounding, or debris thrown up from the road surface.

Automatic transmission fluid

10 Where applicable, check the hoses leading to the transmission fluid cooler at the front of the engine bay for leakage. Look for deterioration caused by corrosion and damage from grounding, or debris thrown up from the road surface. Automatic transmission fluid is a thin oil and is usually red in colour.

Power-assisted steering (PAS) fluid

11 Examine the hose running between the fluid reservoir and the power steering pump, and the return hose running from the steering rack to the fluid reservoir. Also examine the high pressure supply hose between the pump and the steering rack **(see illustration)**.

12 Where applicable, check the hoses leading to the PAS fluid cooler at the front of the engine bay. Look for deterioration caused by corrosion and damage from grounding, or debris thrown up from the road surface.

13 Pay particular attention to crimped unions, and the area surrounding the hoses that are secured with adjustable worm drive clips. Like automatic transmission fluid, PAS fluid is a thin oil, and is usually red in colour.

Air conditioning refrigerant

 Warning: Refer to the safety information given in Safety First and Chapter 3, regarding the dangers of disturbing any of the air conditioning system components.

14 The air conditioning system is filled with a liquid refrigerant, which is retained under high pressure. If the air conditioning system is opened and depressurised without the aid of specialised equipment, the refrigerant will immediately turn into gas and escape into the atmosphere. If the liquid comes into contact with your skin, it can cause severe frostbite. In addition, the refrigerant contains substances which are environmentally damaging; for this reason, it should not be allowed to escape into the atmosphere.

15 Any suspected air conditioning system leaks should be immediately referred to a Rover dealer or air conditioning specialist. Leakage will be shown up as a steady drop in the level of refrigerant in the system.

16 Note that water may drip from the condenser drain pipe, underneath the car, immediately after the air conditioning system has been in use. This is normal, and should not be cause for concern.

Brake/clutch fluid

 Warning: Refer to the safety information given in Safety First and Chapter 9, regarding the dangers of handling brake fluid.

17 With reference to Chapter 9, examine the area surrounding the brake pipe unions at the master cylinder for signs of leakage. Check the area around the base of fluid reservoir, for signs of leakage caused by seal failure. Also examine the brake pipe unions at the ABS hydraulic unit.

18 If fluid loss is evident, but the leak cannot be pinpointed in the engine bay, the brake calipers and underbody brake lines should be carefully checked with the vehicle raised and supported on axle stands **(see illustration)**. Leakage of fluid from the braking system is serious fault that must be rectified immediately.

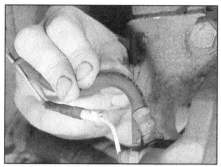

5.18 Examine the brake fluid lines leading to the calipers for signs of leakage

5.19 Check for leakage around the hydraulic fluid pipe connection at the clutch slave cylinder

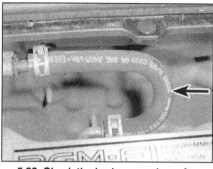

5.22 Check the brake servo hose for vacuum leakage

19 Refer to Chapter 6 and check for leakage around the hydraulic fluid line connections to the clutch master cylinder at the bulkhead, and to the clutch slave cylinder, bolted to the side of the transmission bellhousing **(see illustration)**.
20 Brake/clutch hydraulic fluid is a toxic substance with a watery consistency. New fluid is almost colourless, but it becomes darker with age and use.

Unidentified fluid leaks

21 If there are signs that a fluid of some description is leaking from the vehicle, but you cannot identify the type of fluid or its exact origin, park the vehicle overnight and slide a large piece of card underneath it. Providing that the card is positioned in roughly in the right location, even the smallest leak will show up on the card. Not only will this help you to pinpoint the exact location of the leak, it should be easier to identify the fluid from its colour. Bear in mind, though, that the leak may only be occurring when the engine is running!

Vacuum hoses

22 Although the braking system is hydraulically-operated, the brake servo unit amplifies the effort you apply at the brake pedal by making use of the vacuum in the inlet manifold, generated by the engine. Vacuum is ported to the servo by means of a large-bore, rigid metal pipes and flexible rubber hoses. Any leaks that develop in this hose will reduce the effectiveness of the braking system **(see illustration)**.
23 In addition, many of the underbonnet components, particularly the emission control components, are driven by vacuum supplied from the inlet manifold via narrow-bore hoses. A leak in a vacuum hose means that air is being drawn into the hose (rather than escaping from it) and this makes leakage very difficult to detect. One method is to use an old length of vacuum hose as a kind of stethoscope - hold one end close to (but not in!) your ear and use the other end to probe the area around the suspected leak. When the end of the hose is directly over a vacuum leak, a hissing sound will be heard clearly through the hose. Care must be taken to avoid contacting hot or moving components, as the engine must be running, when testing in this manner. Renew any vacuum hoses that are found to be defective

6 Front brake pad and disc check

Pads

1 Firmly apply the handbrake, then jack up the front of the car and support it securely on axle stands. Remove the front roadwheels.
2 For a quick check, the pad thickness can be carried out via the inspection hole on the front of the caliper **(see Haynes Hint)**. Using a steel rule, measure the thickness of the friction material on the visible brake pad. This must not be less than that indicated in the Specifications.
3 The view through the caliper inspection hole gives a rough indication of the state of the brake pads but only one of the pads will be fully visible. For a comprehensive check, the brake pads should be removed and cleaned, as described in Chapter 9.

⚠️ **Warning: Note that the dust created by wear of the pads may contain asbestos, which is a health hazard. Never blow it out with compressed air, and don't inhale any of it. Douse the braking components with**

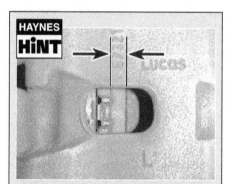

For a quick check, the pad thickness can be carried out via the inspection hole on the front of the caliper. This will give a rough indication of the state of the brake pads but only one pad will be fully visible. For a comprehensive check, the brake pads should be removed and cleaned, as described in Chapter 9

proprietary brake cleaner or methylated spirit before cleaning them, to prevent the dust from becoming airborne. Ideally, an approved filtering mask should be worn when working on the brakes. DO NOT use petrol or petroleum-based solvents to clean brake parts.
4 If any pads friction material is worn to the specified thickness or less, *all four pads must be renewed as a set.* NEVER renew the pads on only one wheel, as uneven braking may result. Likewise, do not be tempted to swap brake pads around to compensate for uneven wear.
5 On completion, refit the roadwheels and lower the car to the ground.

Discs

6 Refer to Chapter 9.

7 Manual transmission oil level check

1 Park the car on a level surface. The oil level must be checked before the car is driven, or at least 5 minutes after the engine has been switched off. If the oil is checked immediately after driving the car, some of the oil will remain distributed around the transmission components, resulting in an inaccurate level reading.
2 Wipe clean the area around the filler/level plug, which is situated on the right-hand side of the transmission, behind the driveshaft inner joint. Unscrew the plug and clean it; discard the sealing washer **(see illustration)**.

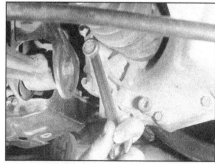

7.2 Removing the manual transmission filler/level plug

3 The oil level should reach the lower edge of the filler/level hole. A certain amount of oil may have gathered behind the filler/level plug, and will trickle out when it is removed; this does **not** necessarily indicate that the level is correct. To ensure that a true level is established, wait until the initial trickle has stopped, then add oil as necessary until a trickle of new oil can be seen emerging. The level will be correct when the flow ceases; use only good-quality oil of the specified type.

4 Filling the transmission with oil is an extremely awkward operation; above all, allow plenty of time for the oil level to settle properly before checking it. If a large amount is added to the transmission, and a large amount flows out on checking the level, refit the filler/level plug and take the vehicle on a short journey so that the new oil is distributed fully around the transmission components, then recheck the level when it has settled again.

5 If the transmission has been overfilled so that oil flows out as soon as the filler/level plug is removed, check that the car is completely level (front-to-rear and side-to-side), and allow the surplus to drain off into a suitable container.

6 When the level is correct, fit a new sealing washer to the filler/level plug. Refit the plug, tightening it to the specified torque wrench setting and wash off any spilt oil.

8 Automatic transmission fluid level check

1 Take the vehicle on a short journey, to warm the transmission up to normal operating temperature, then park the vehicle on level ground and firmly apply the handbrake. The fluid level is checked using the dipstick which is situated on the top of the transmission unit where it is located beside the battery tray.

2 With the engine switched off, withdraw the dipstick from the tube, and wipe all the fluid from its end with a clean rag or paper towel. Insert the clean dipstick back into the tube as far as it will go, then withdraw it once more. Note the fluid level on the end of the dipstick; it should be between the upper and lower marks **(see illustration)**.

3 If topping-up is necessary, add the required quantity of the specified fluid to the transmission via the dipstick tube. Use a funnel with a fine mesh gauze, to avoid spillage, and to ensure that no foreign matter enters the transmission. **Note:** *Never overfill the transmission so that the fluid level is above the upper mark.*

4 After topping-up, take the vehicle on a short run to distribute the fresh fluid, then recheck the level again, topping-up if necessary.

5 Always maintain the level between the two dipstick marks. If the level is allowed to fall below the lower mark, fluid starvation may result, which could lead to severe transmission damage.

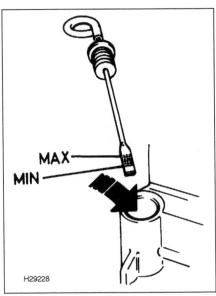

8.2 On automatic transmission models ensure the fluid level is kept between the MIN and MAX marks on the dipstick

6 Frequent need for topping-up indicates that there is a leak, which should be found and corrected before it becomes serious.

9 Steering and suspension component check

Front suspension and steering check

1 Raise the front of the vehicle, and securely support it on axle stands.

2 Visually inspect the balljoint dust covers and the steering rack-and-pinion gaiters for splits, chafing or deterioration. Any wear of these components will cause loss of lubricant, together with dirt and water entry, resulting in rapid deterioration of the balljoints or steering gear.

3 Check the power steering fluid hoses for chafing or deterioration, and the pipe and hose unions for fluid leaks. Also check for signs of fluid leakage under pressure from the steering gear rubber gaiters, which would indicate failed fluid seals within the steering gear.

4 Grasp the roadwheel at the 12 o'clock and 6 o'clock positions, and try to rock it **(see illustration)**. Very slight free play may be felt, but if the movement is appreciable, further investigation is necessary to determine the source. Continue rocking the wheel while an assistant depresses the footbrake. If the movement is now eliminated or significantly reduced, it is likely that the hub bearings are at fault. If the free play is still evident with the footbrake depressed, then there is wear in the suspension joints or mountings.

5 Now grasp the wheel at the 9 o'clock and 3 o'clock positions, and try to rock it as before. Any movement felt now may again be caused

by wear in the hub bearings or the steering track-rod balljoints. If the inner or outer balljoint is worn, the visual movement will be obvious.

6 Using a large screwdriver or flat bar, check for wear in the suspension mounting bushes by levering between the relevant suspension component and its attachment point. Some movement is to be expected as the mountings are made of rubber, but excessive wear should be obvious. Also check the condition of any visible rubber bushes, looking for splits, cracks or contamination of the rubber.

7 With the car standing on its wheels, have an assistant turn the steering wheel back and forth about an eighth of a turn each way. There should be very little, if any, lost movement between the steering wheel and roadwheels. If this is not the case, closely observe the joints and mountings previously described, but in addition, check the steering column universal joints for wear, and the rack-and-pinion steering gear itself.

Rear suspension check

8 Chock the front wheels, then jack up the rear of the vehicle and support securely on axle stands (see *Jacking and Vehicle Support*).

9 Working as described previously for the front suspension, check the rear hub bearings, the suspension bushes and the shock absorber/coil spring assembly mountings for wear.

Suspension shock absorber/coil spring assembly check

10 Check for any signs of fluid leakage around the shock absorber/coil spring assembly body, or from the dust cover around the piston rod. Should any fluid be noticed, the shock absorber/coil spring assembly is defective internally, and should be renewed. **Note:** *Suspension shock absorbers should always be renewed in pairs on the same axle.*

11 The efficiency of the suspension shock absorber may be checked by bouncing the vehicle at each corner. Generally speaking, the body will return to its normal position and stop after being depressed. If it rises and returns on a rebound, the suspension strut/shock absorber is probably suspect. Examine also the suspension shock absorber upper and lower mountings for any signs of wear.

9.4 Check for wear in the hub bearings by grasping the wheel and trying to rock it

10 Exhaust system check

1 Park the vehicle on a level surface and switch off the engine. Chock the front wheels and select first gear, then raise the rear of the vehicle and rest it securely on axle stands - refer to *Jacking and Vehicle Support* in the Reference Chapter of this manual.
2 With the engine cold (wait at least an hour after switching off the engine), check the complete exhaust system from the engine to the end of the tailpipe.
3 Check the exhaust pipes and connections for evidence of leaks, severe corrosion and damage. Make sure that all brackets and mountings are in good condition, and that all relevant nuts and bolts are tight **(see illustration)**. Leakage at any of the joints or in other parts of the system will usually show up as a black, sooty stain in the vicinity of the leak.
4 Rattles and vibrations can often be traced to the exhaust system. Tap the silencer units with a soft mallet and listen for noises caused by corroded or displaced baffle material. **Do not** strike the catalytic converter, as this may damage the ceramic block inside.
5 Carefully rock the pipes and silencers from side to side on their mountings. If the components are able to come into contact with the body or suspension parts, look for broken or worn rubber mountings.
6 Extra clearance can be gained by slackening the clamps between adjacent sections of the exhaust pipe to loosen the joints (where possible - refer to Chapter 4B) and twisting the pipes as necessary to provide the additional clearance. Re-tighten the clamps on completion.

11 Underbody check

1 Jack up the front and rear of the vehicle and support on axle stands (see *Jacking and Vehicle Support*).
2 Working from the front to the rear of the vehicle, check the condition of the entire vehicle structure for signs of corrosion, especially near the load-bearing areas. These include chassis box sections, side sills, cross-members, pillars, and all suspension, steering, braking system and seat belt mountings and anchorages.
3 Check that the anti-corrosion sealing materials on the underbody are intact. Where necessary re-apply the material.
4 In the engine compartment, examine the front suspension upper mountings and inner wing panels, also the lower areas of the front valance for signs of corrosion.
5 Inside the vehicle, lift the carpets where possible and check the floor and inner surfaces of the sills for signs of corrosion.
6 Check the drain holes in the doors for blockages and clear by probing with wire.
7 Where body corrosion is evident, consult a Rover dealer to have it repaired.

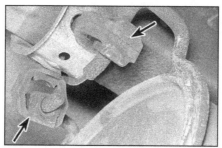

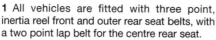

10.3 Check that exhaust pipe mountings are in secure and in good condition

12 Seat belts and airbag unit check

1 All vehicles are fitted with three point, inertia reel front and outer rear seat belts, with a two point lap belt for the centre rear seat.
2 Inspect the belts for signs of fraying or other damage. Also check the operation of the buckles and retractor mechanisms, and ensure that all mounting bolts are securely tightened. Note that the bolts are shouldered so that the belt anchor points are free to rotate.
3 If there is any sign of damage, or any doubt about the condition of a belt, it must be renewed. If the vehicle has been involved in a collision, any belts in use at the time should be renewed as a matter of course, and all other belts should be checked carefully.
4 Use only warm water and non-detergent soap when cleaning the belt webbing. Never use chemicals that could attack the belt fabric and reduce its effectiveness. Keep the belts fully extended until they have dried - do not apply heat to accelerate drying.
5 The airbag unit(s) must be checked by a Rover dealer.

13 Hinge and lock lubrication

1 All hinges and locks (doors, bonnet, bootlid, and fuel filler flap) should be examined for correct operation and any defects rectified.
2 Lubricate the moving parts of the hinges and locks with a little engine oil, and apply a little multipurpose grease to the contact surfaces of the locks and strikers.

14 Road test

Instruments and electrical equipment

1 Check the operation of all instruments and electrical equipment.
2 Make sure that all instruments read correctly, and switch on all electrical equipment in turn, to check that it functions properly.

Steering and suspension

3 Check for any abnormalities in the steering, suspension, handling or road feel.
4 Drive the vehicle, and check that there are no unusual vibrations or noises.
5 Check that the steering feels positive, with no excessive sloppiness, or roughness, and check for any suspension noises when cornering and driving over bumps.

Drivetrain

6 Check the performance of the engine, clutch (where applicable), gearbox/transmission and driveshafts.
7 Listen for any unusual noises from the engine, clutch and gearbox/transmission.
8 Make sure that the engine runs smoothly when idling, and that there is no hesitation when accelerating.
9 Check that, where applicable, the clutch action is smooth and progressive, that the drive is taken up smoothly, and that the pedal travel is not excessive. Also listen for any noises when the clutch pedal is depressed.
10 On manual gearbox models, check that all gears can be engaged smoothly without noise, and that the gear lever action is not abnormally vague or notchy.
11 On automatic transmission models, make sure that all gearchanges occur smoothly, without snatching, and without an increase in engine speed between changes. Check that all the gear positions can be selected with the vehicle at rest. If any problems are found, they should be referred to a Rover dealer.
12 Listen for a metallic clicking sound from the front of the vehicle, as the vehicle is driven slowly in a circle with the steering on full-lock. Carry out this check in both directions. If a clicking noise is heard, this indicates wear in a driveshaft joint, in which case the joint should be renewed.

Check the operation and performance of the braking system

13 Make sure that the vehicle does not pull to one side when braking, and that the wheels do not lock prematurely when braking hard.
14 Check that there is no vibration through the steering when braking.
15 Check that the handbrake operates correctly without excessive movement of the lever, and that it holds the vehicle stationary on a slope.
16 Test the operation of the brake servo unit as follows. With the engine off, depress the footbrake four or five times to exhaust the vacuum. Hold the brake pedal depressed, then start the engine. As the engine starts, there should be a noticeable give in the brake pedal as vacuum builds up. Allow the engine to run for at least two minutes, and then switch it off. If the brake pedal is depressed now, it should be possible to detect a hiss from the servo as the pedal is depressed. After about four or five applications, no further hissing should be heard, and the pedal should feel considerably harder.

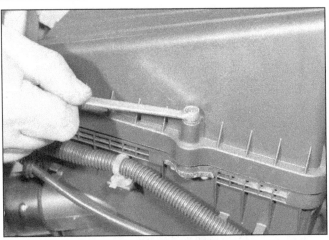

15.1 Remove the each of the securing screws from the outer edge of the air cleaner

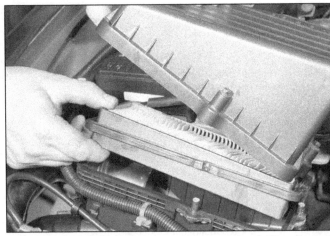

15.2 Lift off the air cleaner cover and remove the air filter element

Every 24 000 miles or 2 years, whichever comes first

15 Air filter element renewal

1 Remove the each of the securing screws from the outer edge of the air cleaner **(see illustration)**.
2 Lift off the air cleaner cover and remove the air filter element **(see illustration)**.
3 Clean out the inside of the air cleaner, removing any debris that may be lodged in the bottom.
4 Lay a new filter element in position, then work around the periphery of the element and press the rubber seal firmly into recessed edge of the air cleaner housing.
5 Refit the air cleaner cover, then insert and tighten the securing screws.

16 Spark plug renewal and ignition system check

Spark plug renewal

1 The correct functioning of the spark plugs is vital for the correct running and efficiency of the engine. It is essential that the plugs fitted are appropriate for the engine (a suitable type is specified at the beginning of this Chapter). If this type is used and the engine is in good condition, the spark plugs should not need attention between scheduled replacement intervals. Spark plug cleaning is rarely necessary, and should not be attempted unless specialised equipment is available, as damage can easily be caused to the firing ends.
2 If the marks on the original-equipment spark plug (HT) leads cannot be seen, mark the leads 1 to 4, to correspond to the cylinder the lead serves (No 1 cylinder is at the timing belt end of the engine).
3 Pull the HT leads from the tops of the spark plugs, by gripping the moulded end fittings. Don't pull on the lead itself, as this may damage the internal connection. Note that the HT leads have long extensions, to allow them to reach the tops of the spark plugs **(see illustration)**.
4 Due to the design of the cylinder head and combustion chambers, access to the spark plugs is via deep access tubes in the top of the cylinder head cover. You will need a long extension bar fitted between your wrench and the spark plug socket, or if you plan to use a dedicated spark plug box spanner, make sure it has a long handle.
5 Unscrew the plugs using the spark plug box spanner, or socket and extension bar. Keep the socket aligned with the spark plug - if it is forcibly moved to one side, the ceramic insulator may crack **(see illustration)**. As each plug is removed, examine it as follows.

16.3 Pull the HT leads from the tops of the spark plugs, by gripping the moulded end fittings. Note that the HT leads have long extensions

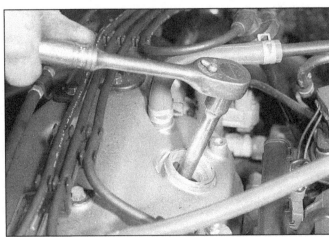

16.5 Removing the spark plugs using a wrench, a long extension bar and a spark plug socket

16.11a Measure the spark plug electrode gap with a feeler blade . . .

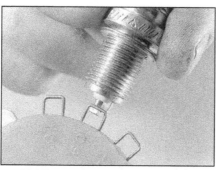

16.11b . . . or spark plug gap gauge

16.12 Using a special tool to adjust the spark plug electrode gap

6 Examination of the spark plugs will give a good indication of the condition of the engine (see the colour page inside the rear cover of this manual). If the insulator nose of the spark plug is clean and white, with no deposits, this is indicative of a weak mixture, or a plug of the wrong heat range (a hot plug transfers heat away from the electrode slowly, a cold plug transfers heat away quickly).

7 If the tip and insulator nose are covered with dry, black-looking carbon deposits, then this is indicative that the mixture is too rich. Should the plug be fouled with oily deposits, then it is likely that oil is entering the combustion chambers, via worn piston rings or valve guides.

8 If the insulator nose is covered with light tan to greyish-brown deposits, then the mixture is roughly correct and it is likely that the engine is in good condition.

9 It is not advisable to try and clean the spark plug electrodes. Many modern plugs have a self-cleaning coating which inhibits the build-up of deposits. If cleaning is attempted with, for example, a wire brush this coating may be removed. When refitted, the plugs may initially perform better, but will become fouled again at an accelerated rate. In addition, cleaning the plug with a wire brush may leave traces of metal on the insulator nose, causing tracking which may then lead to misfiring. Renew the spark plugs if their condition is unsatisfactory.

10 The spark plug electrode gap is of considerable importance. If the gap is too large or too small, the size of the spark and its efficiency will be seriously impaired and it will not perform correctly under all engine speed and load conditions. The gap should be set to the value given in the Specifications at the beginning of this Chapter. Note that manufacturers of certain types of spark plug, particularly plugs with specially-shaped electrodes, supply the plugs pre-gapped. Attempts to adjust the gap on these types of plug may result in electrode damage - always check the manufacturer's information before proceeding.

11 To set the gap, measure it with a feeler blade or spark plug gap gauge and then carefully bend the outer plug electrode until the correct gap is achieved. The centre electrode should never be bent, as this may

crack the insulator and cause plug failure, if nothing worse. If using feeler blades, the gap is correct when the appropriate-size blade is a firm sliding fit **(see illustrations)**.

12 Special spark plug electrode gap adjusting tools are available from most motor accessory shops, or from some spark plug manufacturers **(see illustration)**.

13 Before fitting the spark plugs, check that the threaded connector sleeves are tight, and that the plug exterior surfaces and threads are clean. Apply a smear of anti-seize grease to the threads of each spark plug.

14 If required, use a length of rubber hose to guide the spark plugs into their threaded holes **(see Haynes Hint)**.

HAYNES HINT

It is very often difficult to insert spark plugs into their holes without cross-threading them. To avoid this possibility, fit a short length of 5/16 inch internal diameter rubber hose over the end of the spark plug. The flexible hose acts as a universal joint to help align the plug with the plug hole. Should the plug begin to cross-thread, the hose will slip on the spark plug, preventing thread damage to the aluminium cylinder head

15 Remove the rubber hose (if used), and tighten the plug to the specified torque using the spark plug socket and a torque wrench. Refit the remaining spark plugs in the same manner.

16 Reconnect the HT leads in their correct order, and refit any components that were removed for access.

Ignition system check

17 Label the HT leads and disconnect them from the spark plugs, as described in the previous sub-section.

18 Check the inside of the end fitting of each lead for signs of corrosion, which will look like a white crusty powder. Remove any such deposits with a stiff brush, or fine grade emery paper. Push the end fitting back onto the spark plug, ensuring that it is a tight fit on the plug. If this is not the case, remove the lead again and use long-nosed pliers to carefully shape the metal connector inside the end fitting, until it fits securely on the end of the spark plug.

19 Using a clean rag sprayed with a little penetrating oil, wipe the entire length of the lead to remove any built-up dirt and grease. Once the lead is clean, check for burns, cracks and other damage. Do not bend or kink the lead excessively, or stretch the lead lengthwise, as this may break the conductors inside the lead.

20 Disconnect the other end of the lead from the distributor cap. Again, pull only on the end fitting. Check for corrosion and security as described earlier. If an ohmmeter is available, check the resistance of the lead by connecting the meter between the spark plug end of the lead and the segment inside the distributor cap. Refit the lead securely on completion.

21 Check the remaining leads one at a time, in the same manner.

22 If new HT leads are required, purchase a set for your specific car and engine.

23 With reference to Chapter 5B, remove the distributor cap. Wipe it clean, and carefully inspect it inside and out for signs of cracks, black carbon tracks (tracking) and worn, burned or loose contacts.

24 Check that the cap centre carbon brush is in good condition and is free to move against spring pressure, allowing it to make good contact with the top of the rotor arm.

25 Inspect the metal terminals on the inside the cap. Surface corrosion and light deposits can be removed with fine-grade emery paper, but more serious wear will mean the renewal of the distributor cap.

26 Where applicable, inspect the distributor cap seal and moisture barrier for signs of damage or deterioration. Remove the screw

18.4 On 1.8 and 2.0 litre engines position No 1 cylinder at TDC on its compression stroke check and adjust the clearances of all No 1 cylinder valves

18.5 When the camshaft sprocket UP mark is positioned as shown (arrowed) check and adjust all No 3 cylinder valves

and detach the rotor arm from the distributor shaft and inspect it closely. Light deposits can be removed with fine-grade emery paper, but if the contacts are badly pitted, the rotor arm should be renewed.

 When fitting a new distributor cap, transfer the HT leads from the old cap to the new one in sequence, one at a time, so that the firing order is preserved.

Ignition timing - check and adjustment

27 Descriptions of the ignition timing checking and adjustment procedures are given in Chapter 5B.

17 Automatic transmission fluid renewal

1 Take the vehicle on a short run, to warm the transmission up to normal operating temperature.
2 Park the car on level ground, then switch off the ignition and apply the handbrake firmly. For improved access, jack up the front of the car and support it securely on axle stands. Note that, when refilling and checking the fluid level, the car must be level to ensure accuracy.
3 Remove the dipstick, then position a suitable container under the transmission drain plug which is situated on the right-hand side of the transmission housing.
4 Unscrew the drain plug, and allow the fluid to drain completely into the container. Clean the drain plug, being especially careful to wipe any metallic particles off the magnetic insert. Discard the original sealing washer; it should be renewed whenever it is disturbed.

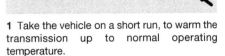 *Warning: If the fluid is hot, take precautions against scalding.*

5 When the fluid has finished draining, clean the drain plug threads and those of the transmission casing. Fit a new sealing washer to the drain plug, and refit the plug to the transmission, tightening it to the specified torque setting.
6 If the car was raised for the draining operation, now lower it to the ground. Make sure that the car is level (front-to-rear and side-to-side).
7 Refilling the transmission is an awkward operation, adding the specified type and amount of fluid to the transmission a little at a time via the dipstick tube. Use a funnel with a fine mesh gauze, to avoid spillage, and to ensure that no foreign matter enters the transmission. Allow plenty of time for the fluid level to settle properly.
8 Start the engine, and allow it to idle for a few minutes whilst moving the selector lever through its various positions. Switch off the engine and add sufficient fluid to bring the level upto the lower mark on the dipstick. Take the car on a short run to fully distribute the new fluid around the transmission, then recheck the fluid level as described in Section 8 with the transmission at normal operating temperature.

18 Valve clearance check and adjustment

Note: *Valve clearances must be checked and adjusted with the engine cold (cylinder head below 38°C).*
1 The importance of having the valve clearances correctly adjusted cannot be overstressed, as they vitally affect the performance of the engine. If the clearances are too big, the engine will be noisy (characteristic rattling or tapping noises) and engine efficiency will be reduced, as the valves open too late and close too early. A more serious problem arises if the clearances are too small, however. If this is the case, the valves may not close fully when the engine is hot, resulting in serious damage to the engine (eg. burnt valve seats and/or cylinder head warping/cracking). The clearances are checked and adjusted as follows.

1.8 and 2.0 litre engines

2 Remove the cylinder head cover and timing belt upper and position the number 1 piston at TDC as described in Chapter 2A. With number 1 piston at TDC, the UP mark on the camshaft sprocket will be at the top and the timing marks on either side of the sprocket rim will be aligned with the cylinder head upper surface.
3 With the engine in this position, check that the clearances of number 1 cylinder's four valves are as given in the Specifications at the start of this Chapter.
4 Clearances are checked by inserting a feeler gauge of the correct thickness between the valve stem and the rocker arm adjusting screw. The feeler gauge should be a light, sliding fit. If adjustment is necessary, slacken the adjusting screw locknut, and turn the screw as necessary **(see illustration)**. Once the correct clearance is obtained, hold the adjusting screw and tighten the locknut to the specified torque. Recheck the valve clearance, and adjust again if necessary.
5 Once all number 1 cylinder valves are correctly adjusted, turn the crankshaft 180° in an anti-clockwise direction to bring number 3 cylinder to TDC. Note that the UP mark on the camshaft will move through 90°, and will now be aligned with the cylinder head surface on the exhaust side of the sprocket **(see illustration)**. Check and, if necessary, adjust the clearances of number 3 cylinder's four valves as described above in paragraph 4.

18.6 Position the camshaft sprocket UP mark and timing marks as shown (arrowed) then adjust all No 4 cylinder valves

18.7 With the camshaft sprocket UP mark positioned as shown (arrowed) check and adjust all No 2 cylinder valves

6 Once all number 3 cylinder valves are correctly adjusted, rotate the crankshaft a further 180°, again in an anti-clockwise direction, to bring number 4 cylinder to TDC; the UP mark on the camshaft sprocket will move a further 90°, and will now be at the bottom and the timing marks will once again be aligned with the cylinder head upper surface **(see illustration)**. Check and, if necessary, adjust the clearances of number 4 cylinder's four valves as described above in paragraph 4.

7 Once all number 4 cylinder valves are correctly adjusted, rotate the crankshaft a further 180°, again in an anti-clockwise direction, to bring number 2 cylinder to TDC. The UP mark will again move through a further 90°, and will now be aligned with the cylinder head upper surface on the inlet side of the sprocket **(see illustration)**. Check and, if necessary, adjust the clearances of number 2 cylinder's four valves as described above in paragraph 4.

8 Once all the valve clearances have been checked, refit the timing belt and cylinder head covers as described in Chapter 2A.

2.3 litre engines

9 Remove the cylinder head cover and timing belt upper cover and position the number 1 piston at TDC as described in Chapter 2A. With number 1 piston at TDC, the UP marks on the camshaft sprockets will be at the top, and the timing marks on each sprocket will align with the cylinder head upper surface **(see illustration)**.

10 With the engine in this position, check the clearances of number 1 cylinder's four valves as described above in paragraph 4, noting that the feeler blade should be inserted between the camshaft lobe and rocker arm bearing surface.

11 Once all number 1 cylinder valves are correctly adjusted, rotate the crankshaft 180° in an anti-clockwise direction to bring number 3 cylinder to TDC. Note that the UP marks on

the camshaft sprockets will move through 90°, and will now be aligned with the cylinder head mating surface on the exhaust side of each sprocket. Check and, if necessary, adjust the clearances of number 3 cylinder's four valves as described above in paragraph 4.

12 Once all number 3 cylinder valves are correctly adjusted, rotate the crankshaft a further 180°, again in an anti-clockwise direction, to bring number 4 cylinder to TDC; the UP marks on the camshaft sprockets will now be at the bottom and the sprocket timing marks will once again be aligned with the cylinder head upper surface. Check and, if necessary, adjust the clearances of number 4 cylinder's four valves as described above in paragraph 4.

13 Once all number 4 cylinder valves are correctly adjusted, rotate the crankshaft a further 180°, again in an anti-clockwise direction, to bring number 2 cylinder to TDC; the UP marks will again move through a further 90°, and will now be aligned with the cylinder head mating surface on the inlet side of each sprocket. Check and, if necessary, adjust the clearances of number 2 cylinders four valves as described above in paragraph 4.

14 Once all the valve clearances have been checked, refit the timing belt and cylinder head covers as described in Chapter 2A.

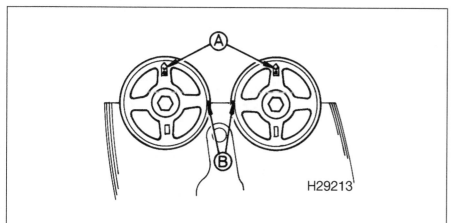

18.9 On 2.3 litre engines, with the camshaft sprocket UP marks (A) and timing marks (B) positioned as shown (No 1 cylinder at TDC on its compression stroke), adjust the clearances of all No 1 cylinder valves

19 Air conditioning system check

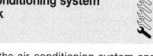

1 Operate the air conditioning system and check that the controls function correctly. During the winter months it is recommended that the air conditioning system is operated once a week in order to circulate the lubricating oil in the compressor.

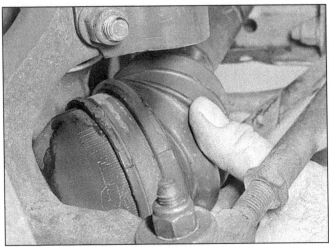

21.1 Inspect the constant velocity joint rubber gaiters for signs of wear or damage

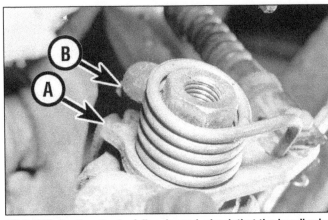

22.5 With the handbrake fully released, check that the handbrake operating lever is in contact with the stop pin on the brake caliper (arrowed)

A Handbrake operating lever   B Brake caliper stop pin

20 Rear brake pad check

1 Park the vehicle on a level surface, then chock the front wheels and select first gear (or PARK on vehicles with automatic transmission). Jack up the rear of the car and support it securely on axle stands. Remove the rear roadwheels.

2 A quick check of the pad thickness can be carried out via the inspection hole on the rear of the caliper, or through the gap between the caliper and the brake disc. Measure the thickness of the friction material on the visible brake pad. This must not be less than that indicated in the Specifications.

3 The view through the caliper gives a rough indication of the state of the brake pads but only one of the pads will be fully visible. For a comprehensive check, the brake pads should be removed and cleaned, as described in Chapter 9.

 Warning: Note that the dust created by wear of the pads may contain asbestos, which is a health hazard. Never blow it out with compressed air, and dont inhale any of it. Douse the braking components with proprietary brake cleaner or methylated spirit before cleaning them, to prevent the dust from becoming airborne. Ideally, an approved filtering mask should be worn when working on the brakes. DO NOT use petrol or petroleum-based solvents to clean brake parts.

4 If any pads friction material is worn to the specified thickness or less, *all four pads must be renewed as a set.* NEVER renew the pads on only one wheel, as uneven braking may result. Likewise, do not be tempted to swap brake pads around to compensate for uneven wear.

5 On completion, refit the roadwheels and lower the car to the ground.

21 Driveshaft gaiter check

1 With the vehicle raised and securely supported on axle stands, turn the steering to full left or right lock, then slowly rotate the roadwheel. Inspect the outer constant velocity (CV) joint rubber gaiters, squeezing the gaiters to open out the folds **(see illustration)**. Check for signs of cracking, splits or deterioration of the rubber, which may allow the grease to escape, or water and grit to enter. Also check the security and condition of the retaining clips. Repeat these checks on the inner CV joints. If any damage or deterioration is found, the gaiters should be renewed (see Chapter 8).

2 At the same time, check the general condition of the CV joints themselves by first holding the driveshaft and attempting to rotate the wheel. Repeat this check whilst holding the inner joint and attempting to rotate the driveshaft. Any appreciable movement indicates wear in the CV joints, wear in the driveshaft splines, or a loose driveshaft retaining nut.

22 Handbrake check

Checking

1 Apply the handbrake by pulling it through between seven to eleven clicks of the ratchet mechanism and check that this locks the rear wheels, holding the vehicle stationary on an incline. In this position, there should be sufficient reserve travel in the handbrake lever to allow for brake shoe wear and cable stretching. If not, the handbrake mechanism is need of adjustment.

Adjustment

2 Park the vehicle on a level surface, select first gear (or Park on models with automatic transmission) and chock the front road wheels. Do not apply the handbrake.

3 Remove the rear passenger ashtray from the back of the centre console - refer to Chapter 11 for details. This allows access to the handbrake cable adjustment nut. Greater access can be gained by removing the centre console completely.

4 Raise the rear of the vehicle and support it securely on axle stands. Remove both rear road wheels.

5 On the rear surface of both brake calipers, identify the handbrake operating lever - this is the spring-loaded lever to which the end of the handbrake cable is attached. Check that, with the handbrake fully released, the handbrake operating lever is in contact with the stop pin on both brake calipers **(see illustration)**.

6 If new rear brake pads, calipers or handbrake cables have been fitted, proceed as described in paragraphs 7 to 8. Otherwise, skip to paragraph 9.

7 Check that with the handbrake lever in the fully-released position, all tension is removed from the handbrake cables. If necessary, slacken the adjustment nut (exposed by the removal of the ashtray from the centre console, as described earlier).

8 Making sure that the front wheels are securely chocked, select neutral, then start the engine and allow it to idle. Pump the brake pedal several times - this will allow the brake caliper self-adjustment mechanism to advance the brake pads towards the disc and then settle correctly and (see Chapter 9 for details). On completion, stop the engine and select first gear (or PARK).

9 From inside the vehicle, pull the handbrake lever up through one click of the ratchet mechanism.

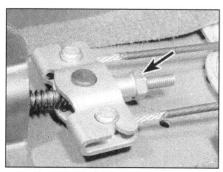

22.10 Location of the handbrake cable adjustment nut (arrowed) - centre console removed for clarity

10 Rotate the handbrake cable adjustment nut through one turn, so that the cables are tensioned **(see illustration)**. Turn both rear roadwheels by hand. Repeat this process, until you feel the rear brakes just begin to bind.

11 Fully release the handbrake lever, and verify that the rear brakes are no longer binding. If this is not the case, slacken off the handbrake cable adjustment nut, then repeat the operation in the previous paragraph.

12 On completion, pull the handbrake lever up through between seven and eleven clicks of the ratchet mechanism and confirm that the rear wheels are fully locked. Release the handbrake lever and confirm that the rear wheels are free to rotate again, without any signs of binding.

13 Refit the rear roadwheels, then lower the vehicle to the ground. Refit the ashtray to centre console.

14 Satisfy yourself that the handbrake is operating correctly, by testing it thoroughly, before bringing the vehicle back into service on the public highway.

23 Exhaust gas emission content check

General information

1 The air:fuel mixture is controlled directly by the PGM-FI engine management system (refer to Chapter 4A for greater detail). As a result, the idle exhaust gas CO content is not manually adjustable, without the aid of special test equipment.

2 However, experienced home mechanics equipped with an accurate tachometer and a calibrated exhaust gas analyser should be able to check the exhaust gas CO content, as described in the following sub-Section.

3 If the results of the test show that the CO content is different to that quoted in the Specifications, this indicates a fault within the fuel delivery, engine management or emission control systems (assuming the vehicle is otherwise in good mechanical order).

4 The engine management system wiring harness incorporates a diagnostic socket. Using this socket, the PGM-FI engine control module can be set in a self-diagnostic mode. In this mode, the ECM will display its stored fault codes by flashing a warning lamp mounted on the instrument panel. See Chapter 4A for details.

5 Testing the PGM-FI system components individually, with standard workshop equipment, in an attempt to locate the fault by elimination is a time consuming operation that is unlikely to be fruitful (particularly if the fault occurs dynamically). It also carries a high risk of damage to the ECM's internal components.

Exhaust gas CO content check

6 Take the vehicle on a short run to allow it to warm up to normal operating temperature. Allow it to idle and wait until the auxiliary cooling fan has cut in and out again, at least twice, before proceeding.

7 Switch on the CO meter and allow it to warm up and stabilise, in accordance with the manufacturers instructions.

8 Insert the CO meter probe into the exhaust tailpipe. Connect a calibrated tachometer to the engine, in accordance with the manufacturer's instructions.

9 Check (and if necessary adjust) the engine idle speed, with reference to Chapter 4A.

10 Ensure that all electrical and mechanical loads (such as headlights, heater blower motor, air conditioning) are switched off. On vehicles with automatic transmission, ensure that Park is selected.

11 Raise the engine speed and maintain it at 2500 to 3000 rpm for at least two minutes. If the auxiliary cooling fan cuts in, wait until it cuts out again.

12 Check the reading on the CO meter, when the display has stabilised.

13 Repeat the test procedure to obtain an average figure, then compare your result with the figure given in the Specifications.

Every 36 000 miles or three years, whichever comes first

24 Fuel filter renewal

Precautions

1 This operation involves the disconnection of fuel lines, which may cause an amount of fuel spillage. Before commencing work, refer to the **Warning** and **Caution** below as well as the information in *Safety First!* at the beginning of this manual

2 Residual fuel pressure always remain in the fuel system, long after the engine has been switched off. This pressure must be relieved in a controlled manner before work can commence on any component in the fuel system.

 Warning: Petrol is extremely flammable - great care must be taken when working on any part of the fuel system. Keep the area well ventilated - open all available doors an windows to create a through-draught. Do not smoke, or allow any naked flames or uncovered light bulbs near the work area. Note that gas powered domestic appliances with pilot flames, such as heaters, boilers and tumble-dryers, also present a fire hazard - bear this in mind if you are working in an area where such appliances are installed. Always keep a suitable fire extinguisher close to the work area and familiarise yourself with its operation before starting work. Wear eye protection when working on fuel systems and wash off any fuel spilt on bare skin immediately with soap and plenty of water. Note that fuel vapour is just as dangerous as liquid fuel; a vessel that has been emptied of liquid fuel will still contain vapour and could be potentially explosive.
Caution: When working with fuel system components, pay particular attention to cleanliness - dirt entering the fuel system may cause blockages which could lead to poor running or even failure.

Renewal

3 Disconnect the battery negative cable and position it away from the terminal.

4 Pad the area surrounding the fuel filter with wads of absorbent rag, to soak up any fuel spills.

5 Refer to Chapter 4A and depressurise the fuel system.

6 Slacken and withdraw the large banjo bolt from the top of the fuel filter canister. Discard both sealing washers - new items must be used on refitting **(see illustrations)**.

24.6a Slacken and withdraw the large banjo bolt from the top of the fuel filter canister

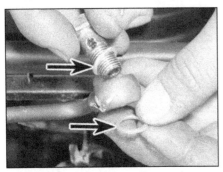

24.6b Discard both sealing washers (arrowed) - new items must be used on refitting

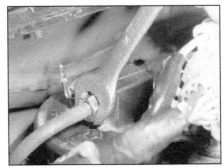

24.7 Unscrew the union nut and withdraw the rigid fuel pipe from the top of the filter canister

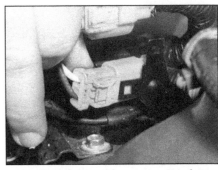

24.8 Detach the wiring connectors from the lugs at the top of the filter bracket

7 Unscrew the union nut and withdraw the rigid fuel pipe from the top of the filter canister **(see illustration)**.

8 Detach the wiring connectors from the lugs at the top of the filter bracket **(see illustration)**.

9 Unclip the wiring harness from the side of the filter bracket **(see illustration)**

10 Remove the securing screws, then lift the filter canister, together with its mounting bracket, from the bodywork **(see illustrations)**.

11 Detach the filter from the bracket by removing the securing screws. Note the direction of flow markings on the top of the filter casing **(see illustrations)**.

12 Fit the new filter canister by following the removal procedure in reverse, noting the following points:

(a) *Ensure that all fuel pipe connections are clean before reassembly.*

(b) *Use new sealing washers when refitting the large banjo bolt.*

(c) *Ensure that all fixings are tightened to the specified torque.*

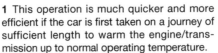

25 Manual transmission oil renewal

1 This operation is much quicker and more efficient if the car is first taken on a journey of sufficient length to warm the engine/transmission up to normal operating temperature.

2 Park the car on level ground, switch off the ignition and apply the handbrake firmly. For improved access, jack up the front of the car

and support it securely on axle stands. Note that the car must be level, to ensure accuracy, when refilling and checking the oil level.

3 Wipe clean the area around the filler/level plug, which is situated on the right-hand side of the transmission, behind the driveshaft inner joint. Unscrew the plug and remove it.

4 Position a container under the drain plug situated on the right-hand side of the transmission housing, directly below the driveshaft joint.

5 Unscrew the drain plug and allow the oil to drain into the container **(see illustration)**. If the oil is hot, take precautions against scalding. Clean both the filler/level and the drain plugs, being especially careful to wipe any metallic particles off the magnetic inserts. Discard the original sealing washers; they should be renewed whenever they are disturbed.

24.9 Unclip the wiring harness from the side of the filter bracket

24.10a Remove the securing screws (arrowed) . . .

24.10b . . . then lift the filter canister, together with its mounting bracket, from the bodywork

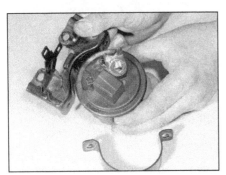

24.11a Detach the filter from the bracket by removing the securing screws

24.11b Note the direction of flow markings on the top of the filter casing (arrowed)

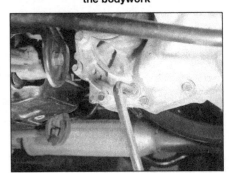

25.5 Removing the manual transmission drain plug

6 When the oil has finished draining, clean the drain plug threads and those of the transmission casing, fit a new sealing washer and refit the drain plug, tightening it to the specified torque setting. It the car was raised for the draining operation, now lower it to the ground.

7 Refilling the transmission is an extremely awkward operation. Above all, allow plenty of time for the oil level to settle properly before checking it. Note that the car must be parked on flat level ground when checking the oil level.

8 Refill the transmission via the filler/level plug hole with the exact amount of the specified type of oil then check the oil level as described in Section 7. When the level is correct, refit filler/level plug with a new sealing washer and tighten it to the specified torque. **Note:** *If the correct amount was poured into the transmission and a large amount flows out on checking the level, refit the filler or filler/level plug and take the car on a short journey so that the new oil is distributed fully around the transmission components, then check the level again on your return.*

Every 60 000 miles

26 Timing belt and balance shaft belt renewal

Refer to Chapter 2A

27 Crankcase ventilation (PCV) valve renewal

1 Using a flat bladed screwdriver, prise the PCV valve from the top of the cylinder head cover **(see illustration)**.

2 Release the hose clip, then pull the breather hose from the port on the top of the valve.

3 Clean off all traces of oil from the grommet in the cylinder head cover, then press the new valve into position.

4 Fit the breather hose onto the port at the top of the new valve, then secure it position with the clip.

5 Check the operation of the valve as follows. Start the engine and allow it to idle. Crimp the hose that runs between the PCV valve and the inlet manifold, then release it. With a hand resting on the valve, it should be possible to feel the valve click as it closes and opens, when the breather hose is crimped and released.

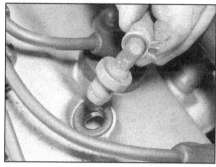

27.1 Prise the PCV valve from the top of the cylinder head cover

Every 2 years regardless of mileage

28 Coolant renewal

Warning: Wait until the engine is cold before starting this procedure. Do not allow antifreeze to come in contact with your skin, or with the painted surfaces of the vehicle. Rinse off spills immediately with plenty of water. Never leave antifreeze lying around in an open container, or in a puddle in the driveway or on the garage floor. Children and pets are attracted by its sweet smell, but antifreeze can be fatal if ingested.

Draining

1 If the engine is cold, unscrew and remove the pressure cap from the radiator. If it is not possible to wait until the engine is cold, place a cloth over the pressure cap and slowly unscrew it. Wait until all pressure has escaped, then remove the cap.

2 Set the heater temperature to maximum heat in order to open the coolant tap located on the bulkhead in the engine compartment.

3 Drain plugs are provided in the centre of the radiator lower tank and on the rear of the cylinder block by the oil filter, and suitable containers should be placed beneath these to catch the flow of escaping coolant prior to removing them. Refer to Chapter 3 for more information.

4 With all the coolant drained into the containers refit and tighten the drain plugs. Note that a new washer must be fitted to the cylinder block drain plug and suitable sealant must be applied to its threads before inserting. If the system needs to be flushed after draining refer to the following sub-section.

5 When draining the cooling system, do not forget to drain the coolant from the expansion tank.

Cooling system flushing

6 If coolant renewal has been neglected, or if the antifreeze mixture has become diluted, then in time, the cooling system may gradually lose efficiency, as the coolant passages become restricted due to rust, scale deposits, and other sediment. The cooling system efficiency can be restored by flushing the system clean.

7 The radiator should be flushed independently of the engine, to avoid unnecessary contamination.

Radiator flushing

8 To flush the radiator disconnect the top and bottom hoses from the radiator.

9 Insert a garden hose into the radiator top inlet. Direct a flow of clean water through the radiator, and continue flushing until clean water emerges from the radiator bottom outlet.

10 If after a reasonable period, the water still does not run clear, the radiator can be flushed with a good proprietary cooling system cleaning agent. It is important that the manufacturer's instructions are followed carefully. If the contamination is particularly bad, remove the radiator then insert the hose in the radiator bottom outlet, and reverse-flush the radiator.

Engine flushing

11 To flush the engine, remove the thermostat as described in Chapter 3 then temporarily refit the thermostat cover to enable the water to run out through the disconnected bottom hose. Disconnect the radiator top hose at the radiator and also remove the cylinder block drain plug.

12 With the top and bottom hoses disconnected from the radiator, insert a garden hose into the radiator top hose. Direct a clean flow of water through the engine, and continue flushing until clean water emerges from the radiator bottom hose.

13 On completion of flushing, refit the thermostat and drain plug and reconnect the hoses with reference to Chapter 3.

Cooling system filling

14 Before attempting to fill the cooling system, reconnect all hoses and make sure that all clips are in good condition and tight, and the drain plugs are also tight. Note that an antifreeze mixture must be used all year round, to prevent corrosion of the engine components (see following sub-Section).

15 Fill the expansion tank halfway with water, then top up the level to the MAX mark with antifreeze.

16 Loosen the air bleed screw on top of the thermostat housing on the right-hand side of the inlet manifold.

17 Mix the correct quantity of antifreeze to a slightly less amount of water in a container, then fill the system slowly through the radiator filler. Keep an eye on the air bleed screw and tighten it as soon as coolant emerges from it. Top up the coolant with water until the level reaches the bottom of the filler neck. While filling, compress the radiator hoses frequently to purge air locks from the system.

18 With the radiator cap still removed, start the engine and allow it to idle for one minute then top up the coolant to the bottom of the filler neck. Refit the cap and allow the engine to idle until heat can be felt through the radiator top hose and the electric cooling fan operates. Accelerate the engine briefly several times, then switch off the ignition and allow the engine to cool (preferably for an hour).

19 With the engine completely cool, check and top up the level in the radiator then refit the radiator cap. Top up the level in the expansion tank to the MAX mark.

20 Check for leaks, particularly around disturbed components.

Antifreeze mixture

21 The antifreeze should always be renewed at the specified intervals. This is necessary not only to maintain the antifreeze properties, but also to prevent corrosion which would otherwise occur as the corrosion inhibitors become progressively less effective.

22 Always use an ethylene-glycol based antifreeze which is suitable for use in mixed-metal cooling systems. The quantity of antifreeze and levels of protection are indicated in the Specifications.

23 Before adding antifreeze, the cooling system should be completely drained, preferably flushed, and all hoses checked for condition and security.

24 After filling with antifreeze, a label should be attached to the expansion tank, stating the type and concentration of antifreeze used, and the date installed. Any subsequent topping-up should be made with the same type and concentration of antifreeze.

25 Do not use engine antifreeze in the windscreen/headlamp washer system, as it will cause damage to the vehicle paintwork. A screenwash additive should be added to the washer system in the quantities stated on the bottle.

29 Brake fluid renewal

⚠️ *Warning: Brake hydraulic fluid can harm your eyes and damage painted surfaces, so exercise extreme caution when handling and pouring it. Do not use fluid that has been standing in an open container for some time, as it absorbs moisture from the air. Brake fluid containing moisture can cause a sudden, dangerous loss of braking efficiency.*

1 The brake fluid renewal procedure is very similar to the brake system bleeding procedure, described in Chapter 9, in that the old fluid is bled from each brake caliper in a pre-determined sequence, whilst the level in the brake master cylinder reservoir is maintained with new brake fluid.

2 The difference is that instead of just ejecting air bubbles from the caliper bleed nipples, the bleeding is allowed to continue until new brake fluid can be seen flowing out. Old brake fluid is usually much darker in colour than new fluid, making them easy to distinguish.

3 Note that before starting the renewal procedure, the majority of the old fluid should be emptied from the brake master cylinder reservoir, using an old syringe or a clean poultry baster.

4 Working as described in Chapter 9, open the bleed screw at the first caliper in the sequence, and pump the brake pedal gently until nearly all the old fluid has been emptied from the brake master cylinder reservoir. However, do not allow the level to drop so low that air is drawn into the master cylinder.

5 Top-up the fluid reservoir to the MAX level with new fluid, and continue pumping the brake pedal new fluid can be seen emerging from the bleed screw. Tighten the screw, and top the reservoir level up to the MAX level line.

6 Work through all the remaining calipers in the given sequence, until new brake fluid emerges from each bleed nipple. Be careful to keep the master cylinder reservoir topped-up to above the MIN level at all times. If the level is allowed to drop too low, air may enter the system and the whole process will have to be restarted.

7 When the operation is complete, check that all bleed screws are securely tightened, and that their dust caps are refitted. Wash off all traces of spilt fluid, and re-check the master cylinder reservoir fluid level.

8 Without starting the engine, assess the feel of the brake pedal - any sponginess or excess travel will probably be due to air bubbles, trapped in the brake lines. Repeat the bleeding process to expel the air, until normal pedal feel is restored.

9 Test the braking system exhaustively, to satisfy yourself that it is working correctly, before bringing the vehicle back into service on the public highway.

Every 4 years regardless of mileage

30 Anti-lock braking system high-pressure hose renewal

1 This operation involves disturbing the high pressure section of the anti-lock braking hydraulic system. Access to specialised tools and test equipment is required, to ensure that the operation is carried out correctly.

2 Because of this, and the safety-critical nature of the components involved, the operation is deemed to be beyond the scope of this manual. It is recommended that this task is entrusted to a Rover dealer or braking system specialist.

Every 10 years regardless of mileage

31 Airbag and the slip ring/reel renewal

1 Refer to Chapter 10, Section 14, for renewal of the driver's airbag, Chapter 11, Section 26, for renewal of the passenger's airbag, and Chapter 10, Section 14, for renewal of the slip ring or reel (as applicable). Considering the safety aspect involved, it is recommended that a Rover dealer carries out the work.

Chapter 2 Part A
Engine in-car overhaul procedures

Contents

Degrees of difficulty

| Easy, suitable for novice with little experience | Fairly easy, suitable for beginner with some experience | Fairly difficult, suitable for competent DIY mechanic  | Difficult, suitable for experienced DIY mechanic | Very difficult, suitable for expert DIY or professional |

Specifications

General

Type:
1.8 and 2.0 litre engine . . . . Four-cylinder, in-line, single overhead camshaft (SOHC)
2.3 litre engine . . . . Four-cylinder, in-line, double overhead camshaft (DOHC)
Designation:
1.8 litre engine F18A3
2.0 litre engine:
   Base (i) model F20Z2
   All other models F20Z1
2.3 litre engine H23A3
Capacity:
1.8 litre engine . . . . 1850 cc
2.0 litre engine . . . . 1997 cc
2.3 litre engine . . . . 2259 cc
Bore:
1.8 and 2.0 engine . . . . 85.0 mm
2.3 litre engine . . . . 87.0 mm
Stroke:
1.8 litre engine . . . . 81.5 mm
2.0 litre engine . . . . 88.0 mm
2.3 litre engine . . . . 95.0 mm
Firing order . . . . 1-3-4-2 (No 1 cylinder at timing belt end of engine)
Direction of crankshaft rotation . . . . Anti-clockwise, viewed from timing belt end

Compression pressures

Standard . . . . 12.5 bar (181 psi)
Minimum . . . . 9.5 bar (138 psi)
Maximum difference between any two cylinders . . . . . 2 bar (29 psi)

Rocker arms and shafts - 1.8 and 2.0 litre engine

Rocker arm to shaft running clearance:
Standard:
   Inlet . . . . 0.017 to 0.050 mm
   Exhaust . . . . 0.018 to 0.054 mm
Service limit . . . . 0.08 mm

Camshaft

Endfloat:
   Standard . . . . 0.05 to 0.15 mm
   Service limit . . . . 0.5 mm
Lobe height (standard):
   1.8 litre engine:
      Inlet . . . . 38.095 mm
      Exhaust . . . . 38.387 mm
   2.0 litre engine:
      F20Z1 engine:
         Inlet . . . . 38.741 mm
         Exhaust . . . . 38.972 mm
      F20Z2 engine:
         Inlet . . . . 38.095 mm
         Exhaust . . . . 38.890 mm
   2.3 litre engine:
      Inlet . . . . 33.661 mm
      Exhaust . . . . 33.725 mm
Camshaft bearing running clearance:
   Standard . . . . 0.050 to 0.089 mm
   Service limit . . . . 0.15 mm
Camshaft runout:
   Standard . . . . less than 0.03 mm
   Service limit . . . . 0.04 mm

Lubrication system

Minimum oil pressure (engine hot):
   At idle . . . . 0.7 bar (10 psi)
   At 3000 rpm . . . . 3.5 bar (51 psi)
Oil pump clearances:
   Outer rotor-to-body:
      Standard . . . . 0.10 to 0.19 mm
      Service limit . . . . 0.21 mm
   Inner rotor tip-to-outer rotor:
      Standard . . . . 0.02 to 0.16 mm
      Service limit . . . . 0.20 mm
   Rotor endfloat:
      Standard . . . . 0.02 to 0.07 mm
      Service limit . . . . 0.12 mm

Torque wrench settings

	Nm	lbf ft
Camshaft bearing cap bolts:		
1.8 and 2.0 litre engine:		
M6 bolts	12	9
M8 bolts	22	16
2.3 litre engine:		
M6 bolts:		
Ordinary bolts	10	7
Bolts incorporating cover studs	12	9
M8 bolts	22	16
Camshaft sprocket bolt	38	28
Connecting rod (big-end) cap nuts	32	24
Crankshaft pulley bolt	220	162
Crankshaft rear oil seal housing bolts	12	9
Cylinder head bolts:		
Stage 1	40	30
Stage 2	70	52
Stage 3	100	74
Cylinder head cover nuts	10	7
Driveplate bolts	75	55
Engine/transmission mountings:		
Left-hand mounting:		
Through-bolt	65	48
Mounting to bracket nut and bolt	55	41
Mounting bracket to engine bolts:		
M8 bolts	22	16
M10 bolts	48	35

Torque wrench settings (continued)

	Nm	lbf ft
Engine/transmission mountings (continued):		
Right-hand mounting:		
Through-bolt	65	48
Mounting to transmission nut	39	29
Front mounting:		
Upper and lower through-bolt	65	48
Mounting bracket to cylinder block bolts	39	29
Rear mounting:		
Through-bolt	65	48
Mounting to crossmember bolts	39	29
Mounting bracket bolts	55	41
Support bracket (where fitted):		
Retaining nut	22	16
Mounting bolt	39	29
Flywheel/driveplate cover plate bolts	12	9
Flywheel bolts	105	77
Front balance shaft:		
Sprocket bolt	30	22
Thrust plate bolts	12	9
Main bearing cap bolts:		
Stage 1	30	22
Stage 2	75	55
Main bearing cap bridge baffle plate bolts	12	9
Oil pump:		
Pick-up/strainer bolts	12	9
Housing bolts	12	9
Cover screws	7	5
Rear balance shaft:		
Drive gear bolt	25	18
Sprocket housing bolts and nut	25	18
Timing hole access plug	30	22
Roadwheel nuts	110	81
Sump drain plug	45	33
Sump bolts	12	9
Timing belt cover bolts	12	9
Timing/balance shaft belt tensioner pulley nut	45	33

1 General information

How to use this Chapter

1 This Part of Chapter 2 is devoted to in-car repair procedures for the engine. All procedures concerning engine removal and refitting, and engine block/cylinder head overhaul can be found in Chapter 2B.

2 Most of the operations included in Chapter 2A are based on the assumption that the engine is still installed in the car. Therefore, if this information is being used during a complete engine overhaul, with the engine already removed, many of the steps included here will not apply.

Engine description

3 The engine is a four-cylinder, in-line unit, mounted transversely at the front of the car, with the clutch and transmission on its right-hand end. The engine is available in three different capacities; 1.8 litre, 2.0 litre and 2.3 litre. The 1.8 litre and 2.0 litre engines are single overhead camshaft (SOHC) sixteen-valve units whereas the 2.3 litre engine is a double overhead camshaft (DOHC) sixteen-valve unit. Apart from the different cylinder head designs, all engines are of identical construction.

4 The aluminium alloy cylinder block is of the dry-liner type. The crankshaft is supported within the cylinder block on five shell-type main bearings. Thrustwashers are fitted to number 4 main bearing, to control crankshaft endfloat. Balance shafts are fitted to the cylinder block to dampen engine vibration, the shafts are driven off of the crankshaft by a toothed belt.

5 The connecting rods are attached to the crankshaft by horizontally split shell-type big-end bearings, and to the pistons by interference-fit gudgeon pins. The aluminium alloy pistons are of the slipper type, and are fitted with three piston rings, comprising two compression rings and a scraper-type oil control ring.

6 The camshaft(s) is/are mounted directly in the cylinder head, and driven by the crankshaft via a toothed rubber timing belt (which also drives the water pump). The camshaft(s) operates each valve via a rocker arm. On the 1.8 and 2.0 litre engine, the rocker arms are mounted on a shaft above the camshaft; on 2.3 litre engines, the rocker arms are located below the camshafts, and are mounted directly into the cylinder head via a balljoint type arrangement.

7 Lubrication is by pressure-feed from a gear-type oil pump, which is mounted on the left-hand end of the crankshaft. It draws oil through a strainer located in the sump, and then forces it through an externally-mounted full-flow cartridge-type filter. The oil flows into galleries in the main bearing cap bridge arrangement and cylinder block/crankcase, from where it is distributed to the crankshaft (main bearings) and camshaft(s). The big-end bearings are supplied with oil via internal drillings in the crankshaft, while the camshaft bearings also receive a pressurised supply. The camshaft lobes and valves are lubricated by splash, as are all other engine components.

8 On 2.3 litre engines, an oil cooler is mounted between the oil filter and cylinder block, to cool the oil as it passes through the filter. The oil cooler is cooled by the engine coolant.

9 A semi-closed crankcase ventilation system is employed; crankcase fumes are drawn from cylinder head cover, through the PCV valve, and passed via a hose to the inlet manifold.

Repair operations possible with the engine in the car

10 The following operations can be carried out without having to remove the engine from the vehicle:

a) *Removal and refitting of the cylinder head.*
b) *Removal and refitting of the balance shaft belt, timing belt and sprockets.*
c) *Renewal of the camshaft oil seal(s).*
d) *Removal and refitting of the camshaft(s).*
e) *Removal and refitting of the sump.*
f) *Removal and refitting of the connecting rods and pistons*.*
g) *Removal and refitting of the oil pump.*
h) *Renewal of the crankshaft oil seals.*
i) *Renewal of the engine mountings.*
j) *Removal and refitting of the flywheel/driveplate.*

* Although the operation marked with an asterisk can be carried out with the engine in the car after removal of the sump, it is better for the engine to be removed, in the interests of cleanliness and improved access. For this reason, the procedure is described in Chapter 2B.

Caution: If the radio/cassette in your vehicle is equipped with an anti-theft system, make sure you have the correct activation code before disconnecting the battery.

2 Compression test – description and interpretation

1 When engine performance is down, or if misfiring occurs which cannot be attributed to the ignition or fuel systems, a compression test can provide diagnostic clues as to the engines condition. If the test is performed regularly, it can give warning of trouble before any other symptoms become apparent.

2 The engine must be fully warmed-up to normal operating temperature, the battery must be fully charged, and the spark plugs must be removed (see Chapter 1). The aid of an assistant will also be required.

3 Disable the ignition system by removing the engine management/ignition system fuse (number 2) from the passenger compartment fusebox (see Chapter 12).

4 Fit a compression tester to the number 1 cylinder spark plug hole the type of tester which screws into the plug thread is to be preferred.

5 Have the assistant hold the throttle wide open and crank the engine on the starter motor; after one or two revolutions, the compression pressure should build up to a maximum figure, and then stabilise. Record the highest reading obtained.

6 Repeat the test on the remaining cylinders, recording the pressure in each.

7 All cylinders should produce very similar pressures; any difference greater than that specified indicates the existence of a fault. Note that the compression should build up quickly in a healthy engine; low compression on the first stroke, followed by gradually-increasing pressure on successive strokes, indicates worn piston rings. A low compression reading on the first stroke, which does not build up during successive strokes, indicates leaking valves or a blown head gasket (a cracked head could also be the cause). Deposits on the undersides of the valve heads can also cause low compression.

8 If the pressure in any cylinder is reduced to the specified minimum or less, carry out the following test to isolate the cause. Introduce a teaspoonful of clean oil into that cylinder through its spark plug hole, and repeat the test.

9 If the addition of oil temporarily improves the compression pressure, this indicates that bore or piston wear is responsible for the pressure loss. No improvement suggests that leaking or burnt valves, or a blown head gasket, may be to blame.

10 A low reading from two adjacent cylinders is almost certainly due to the head gasket having blown between them; the presence of coolant in the engine oil will confirm this.

11 If one cylinder is about 20 per cent lower than the others, and the engine has a slightly rough idle, a worn camshaft lobe could be the cause.

12 If the compression reading is unusually high, the combustion chambers are probably coated with carbon deposits. If this is the case, the cylinder head should be removed and decarbonised.

13 On completion of the test, refit the spark plugs, and refit the engine management/ignition fuse to the fusebox.

3 Top Dead Centre (TDC) for number 1 piston – locating

Note: *If the crankshaft pulley bolt slackens while the crankshaft is being rotated, it must be tightened to the specified torque (referring to Section 5 for further information) before proceeding further.*

1 In its travel up and down its cylinder bore, Top Dead Centre (TDC) is the highest point that each piston reaches as the crankshaft rotates. While each piston reaches TDC both at the top of the compression stroke and again at the top of the exhaust stroke, for the purpose of timing the engine, TDC refers to the piston position (usually number 1) at the top of its compression stroke.

2 Number 1 piston (and cylinder) is at the left-hand (timing belt) end of the engine, and its TDC position is located as follows. Note that the crankshaft rotates anti-clockwise when viewed from the left-hand side of the car.

3 Disconnect the battery negative terminal, and remove all the spark plugs as described in Chapter 1.

4 To view the camshaft sprocket timing marks, remove the cylinder head cover as described in Section 4. On 1.8 and 2.0 litre models it will also be necessary to remove the timing belt upper cover as described in Section 6.

5 Turn the steering onto full left lock. Access to the crankshaft pulley retaining bolt can then be gained through the hole in the left-hand side of the plastic undercover.

3.6a On 1.8 and 2.0 litre engines position the camshaft sprocket so that the UP mark (A) is at the top and the timing marks (B) align with the cylinder head surface

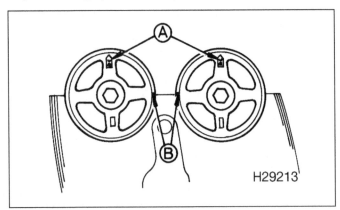

3.6b On 2.3 litre engines position the camshaft sprockets with the UP marks (A) at the top so that the timing marks (B) are aligned with the cylinder head surface

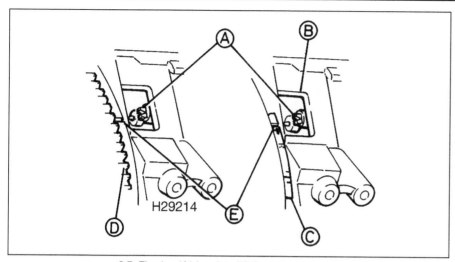

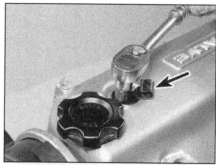

4.4 Slacken and remove the head cover retaining nuts noting the correct fitted location of all retaining clips (arrowed) - 2.0 litre model shown

3.7 Flywheel/driveplate TDC marking details

A   *Pointer arrangement*
B   *Transmission housing aperture*
C   *Driveplate (models with automatic transmission)*
D   *Flywheel (models with manual transmission)*
E   *TDC mark*

6 Turn the crankshaft whilst keeping an eye on the camshaft sprocket(s). Rotate the crankshaft until the UP mark on the camshaft sprocket(s) is/are at the top and the timing mark on each side of the sprocket rim(s) are correctly aligned with the cylinder head upper surface **(see illustrations)**.

7 Remove the rubber bung from the front of the transmission housing to gain access to the flywheel/driveplate timing marks. Check that the pointer on the transmission unit is correctly aligned with the TDC mark on the flywheel/driveplate (the mark should be highlighted with white paint). The pointer on the transmission housing is in the form of a set of sights; the sights work in the same way as the sights on a rifle do; the lower pointer aligns with the notch on the transmission lug **(see illustration)**. Rotate the crankshaft as necessary.

8 With the flywheel/driveplate TDC mark and camshaft sprocket timing marks positioned as described, the engine is positioned with No1 piston at TDC on its compression stroke.

4   Cylinder head cover –
    removal and refitting

Removal

1 Disconnect the battery negative terminal. On 2.3 litre models, undo the retaining screws and remove the wiring harness cover from the left-hand end of the cylinder head cover.

2 Using a suitable pair of pliers, release the retaining clip, and disconnect the breather hose and crankcase ventilation hoses from the cylinder head cover.

3 Carefully disconnect the ignition HT leads from the spark plugs, then free the leads from their retaining clips, and position them clear of the cylinder head cover. Also free the accelerator cable from its retaining clip(s) and undo the retaining screw and detach the earth lead (where fitted) from the cover.

4 Slacken and remove the cylinder head cover retaining nuts and lift off the retaining clips (where fitted), noting each ones correct fitted location **(see illustration)**. Remove all

the sealing washers from the cover studs.

5 Carefully lift off the cylinder head cover, and remove it from the engine along with its rubber seals. Inspect the cover seals, spark plug hole sealing rings and cover retaining nut sealing washers for signs of wear or damage, and renew as required.

Refitting

6 Ensure the cover and cylinder head mating surfaces are clean and dry. Fit the main cover seal and the spark plug hole sealing rings to the cylinder head cover ensuring each one is correctly located in the cover groove. Apply a smear of sealant to the cylinder head cover gasket on each side of all the camshaft cut-outs **(see illustrations)**.

7 Refit the cylinder head cover to the engine, taking great care to ensure that all the sealing rings remain in position on the cover.

8 Once the cover is correctly seated, refit all the sealing washers and the retaining clips (where fitted). Refit the cover retaining nuts and tighten them to the specified torque.

9 Reconnect the HT leads to the relevant plugs, then refit the leads to all their retaining clips. Refit the accelerator cable to its retaining clips and reconnect the earth lead (where fitted).

10 Reconnect the breather hose and ventilation hose to the cylinder head cover and reconnect the battery negative terminal. On 2.3 litre models ensure the wiring harness is correct routed then refit the harness cover.

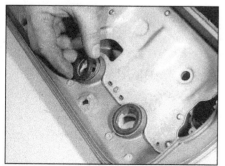

4.6a Fit the new spark plug hole sealing rings . . .

4.6b . . . and the main seal to the cylinder head cover grooves . . .

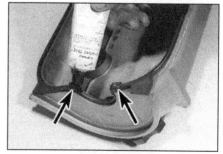

4.6c . . . and apply sealant to the areas of the main seal on each side of the camshaft cut-outs (arrowed) - 2.0 litre model shown

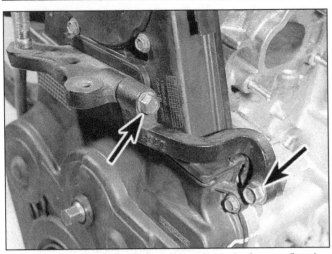

6.2 On 1.8 and 2.0 litre engines undo the bolts (arrowed) and remove the mounting bracket . . .

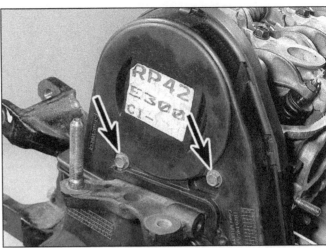

6.3 . . . then undo the retaining bolts and lift off the timing belt upper cover

5 Crankshaft pulley – removal and refitting

Removal

1 Apply the handbrake, then jack up the front of the car and support it on axle stands. Remove the left-hand roadwheel.

2 From underneath the front of the vehicle, slacken and remove the retaining screws and fasteners and remove the undercover from beneath the engine/transmission unit.

3 Remove the auxiliary drivebelt(s) as described in Chapter 1.

4 Slacken the crankshaft pulley retaining bolt. On manual transmission models, to prevent crankshaft rotation whilst the retaining bolt is slackened, have an assistant select top gear and apply the brakes firmly; if the engine is removed from the vehicle it will be necessary to lock the flywheel (see Section 17). On automatic transmission models, unbolt the lower cover plate from the base of the transmission then remove one of the torque converter retaining bolts and bolt the driveplate to the transmission housing using a metal bar and suitable bolts.

5 Unscrew the retaining bolt and washer and remove the crankshaft pulley from the end of the crankshaft. **Note:** *On some models it may prove necessary to lower the engine unit slightly to gain the necessary clearance required to remove the crankshaft pulley. If this is the case, remove the left-hand mounting assembly (see Section 18) and lower the engine unit.*

Refitting

6 Align the crankshaft pulley centre notch with the Woodruff key, and slide the pulley onto the crankshaft end. Apply a few drops of oil to the pulley retaining bolt threads, then refit the bolt and washer. Where necessary, refit the left-hand engine mounting assembly.

7 Lock the crankshaft by the method used on removal, and tighten the pulley retaining bolt to the specified torque setting.

8 Refit the auxiliary drivebelt(s) as described in Chapter 1.

9 Refit the undercover panel and roadwheel, and lower the car to the ground and tighten the wheel nuts to the specified torque.

6 Timing belt covers – removal and refitting

Removal

Upper cover

1 Remove the cylinder head cover as described in Section 4.

2 Unscrew the retaining bolts and remove the support bracket from the rear of the left-hand engine mounting **(see illustration)**.

3 Unscrew the retaining bolts then lift the upper cover away from the engine and recover the sealing strip which is fitted around the engine mounting bracket **(see illustration)**.

Lower cover

4 Remove the crankshaft pulley as described in Section 5.

5 Remove the upper cover as described earlier in this Section.

6 Slacken and remove the dipstick tube retaining bolt then ease the tube out of position and remove it from the engine, along with its sealing ring **(see illustration)**.

7 Remove the rubber seal from around the belt tensioner pulley nut which protrudes out of the centre of the lower cover **(see illustration)**. **Note:** *Do not slacken the tensioner pulley nut.*

8 Slacken and remove the bolts securing the cover in position then manoeuvre the cover downwards and out of position **(see illustration)**. **Note:** *On some models it may prove necessary to lower the engine unit slightly to gain the necessary clearance required to remove the lower cover. If this is the case, remove the left-hand mounting assembly (see Section 18) and lower the engine unit.*

9 Recover the sealing strip which is fitted to the top of the cover and seal which is fitted between the cover and cylinder block.

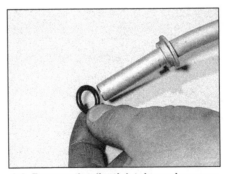

6.6 Remove the dipstick tube and recover the sealing ring

6.7 Remove the sealing from around the tensioner pulley nut: do not slacken the nut

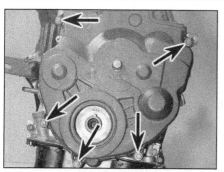

6.8 Timing belt lower cover retaining bolts (arrowed)

6.10 On refitting, ensure all the sealing strips are correctly located in the cover grooves

7.3 Prior to slackening the tensioner pulley nut lock the timing belt tensioner in position with one of the cover bolts

Refitting

10 Refitting is the reverse of removal, noting the following.
  a) Examine all the rubber seals for signs of damage or deterioration and renew as necessary (see illustration).
  b) Tighten the cover retaining bolts and the engine support bracket bolts to the specified torque.
  c) When refitting the lower cover, take care to ensure the rubber seal is correctly located in the belt tensioner pulley nut recess. Refit the crankshaft pulley as described in Section 5.

7.4 Slacken the nut then move the tensioner pulley away from the belt and secure it in position by retightening the nut . . .

7.5 . . . then slip the belt off of its pulleys

7 Balance shaft belt - removal and refitting

TOOL TiP A locking tool will be required on refitting to ensure the balance shafts are correctly timed. The special Rover tool (18G1671) is 7 mm in diameter, to locate in the cylinder block, with its end stepped down to 6 mm to engage with the rear balance shaft. To simulate this, use a long 6 mm diameter drill/bolt and wrap insulation tape around the drill/bolt to build it up until it is a snug fit in the cylinder block. Bear in mind that the tool will have to be fairly strong if it is to be used to lock the balance shaft in position whilst the drivegear bolt is slackened/tightened.

Removal

1 Position number 1 cylinder at TDC on its compression stroke as described in Section 3. To enable the engine to turn over easier, remove the spark plugs as described in Chapter 1.
2 Remove the timing belt lower cover as described in Section 6.
3 Lock the timing belt tensioner pulley in position by screwing one of the timing belt cover bolts into the threaded hole behind the

7.8a Unscrew the access plug from the rear of the cylinder block . . .

slot in the tensioner pulley backplate (see illustration).
4 Slacken the belt tensioner pulley nut by one complete turn then pivot the balance shaft belt tensioner away from the belt (see illustration). Lock the tensioner in position by securely tightening the pulley nut.
5 If the belt is to be re-used, use white paint or similar to mark the direction of rotation on the belt, then slip the belt off its sprockets (see illustration).
6 Check the belt carefully for any signs of uneven wear, splitting or oil contamination, and renew it if there is the slightest doubt about its condition. If the engine is undergoing an overhaul and has covered 60 000 miles since the original belt was fitted, renew the belt as a matter of course, regardless of its apparent condition. If signs of oil contamination are found, trace the source of the oil leak and rectify it, then wash down the engine timing belt area and all related components to remove all traces of oil.

Refitting

7 Ensure that the crankshaft is still correctly positioned with number 1 cylinder at TDC on its compression stroke (see Section 3).
8 To time the rear balance shaft, unscrew the access plug and washer from the rear of the cylinder block; renew the washer if it shows signs of damage. Rotate the shaft until its locating hole is correctly aligned with the cylinder block hole and lock the shaft in position using the special tool (see Tool Tip at the start of this Section) (see illustrations).

7.8b . . . and lock the rear balance shaft

7.9 Align the mark on the front balance shaft sprocket with the mark on the oil pump housing (arrowed)

7.11 Slacken the pulley nut and check the tensioner moves in to tension the belt under the pressure of the spring (arrowed) before retightening the nut securely

9 Position the front balance shaft so that the timing mark on the sprocket rim is correctly aligned with the mark on the front of the oil pump housing **(see illustration)**.
10 With the balance shafts and crankshaft correctly positioned, manoeuvre the belt into position ensuring all slack is on the tensioner pulley side of the belt. Do not twist the belt sharply while refitting it. Ensure that the belt teeth are correctly seated centrally in the sprockets, and that the timing marks remain in alignment. If a used belt is being refitted, ensure that the arrow mark made on removal points in the normal direction of rotation, as before.
11 Slacken the tensioner pulley nut, check that the tensioner pulley moves to tension the belt, then tighten it securely **(see illustration)**. If the tensioner assembly is not free to move

under spring tension, rectify the fault, or the belt will not be correctly tensioned.
12 Ensure the timing marks are correctly positioned then remove the balance shaft locking pin. Refit the access plug and sealing washer and tighten it to the specified torque setting **(see illustration)**.
13 Temporarily refit the crankshaft pulley bolt and tighten securely. Rotate the crankshaft through one complete rotation in an anti-clockwise direction to settle the belt in position then slacken the tensioner pulley nut one complete turn before tightening it to the specified torque setting **(see illustration)**.
14 Slacken and remove the bolt which was used to lock the timing belt tensioner in position then refit the timing belt covers as described in Section 6. Refit the spark plugs as described in Chapter 1.

8 Timing belt – removal and refitting

Removal

1 Position number 1 cylinder at TDC on its compression stroke as described in Section 3. On 2.3 litre engines, the camshafts can be held in the correct position by inserting two suitably-sized pegs or bolts through the holes in the top of the left-hand end camshaft bearing caps and into the camshafts; this will prevent the shafts moving under valve spring pressure when the timing belt is removed.
2 Remove the balance shaft belt as described in Section 7, ignoring the remark about locking the timing belt tensioner pulley in

7.12 Ensure the timing marks are correctly positioned then remove the locking tool from the rear balance shaft and refit the access plug and sealing washer

7.13 Rotate the crankshaft through one complete turn then slacken the tensioner nut one complete turn before tightening it to the specified torque

8.2 Removing the balance shaft belt sprocket from the crankshaft

8.4 Slacken the nut then move the tensioner pulley away from the timing belt before retightening the nut to hold it in position

position. Slide the balance shaft belt pulley off the end of the crankshaft, noting which way around it is fitted (see illustration).

3 If not already having done so, support the engine and remove the left-hand engine/transmission mounting assembly (see Section 18).

4 Slacken the belt tensioner pulley nut then pivot the pulley fully away from the belt and retighten the nut to hold it in position (see illustration).

5 If the timing belt is to be re-used, use white paint or similar to mark the direction of rotation on the belt, then slip the belt off its sprocket(s). Do not rotate the crankshaft until the timing belt has been refitted.

6 Check the timing belt carefully for any signs of uneven wear, splitting or oil contamination, and renew it if there is the slightest doubt about its condition. If the engine is undergoing an overhaul and has covered 60 000 miles since the original belt was fitted, renew the belt as a matter of course, regardless of its apparent condition. If signs of oil contamination are found, trace the source of the oil leak and rectify it, then wash down the engine timing belt area and all related components to remove all traces of oil.

Refitting

7 On reassembly, thoroughly clean the timing belt sprockets, and check that the camshaft sprocket timing marks and the flywheel/driveplate TDC mark are still correctly positioned (see Section 3).

8 Fit the timing belt over the crankshaft and camshaft sprockets, ensuring that the belt front run (and, on 2.3 litre engines, the top run) is taut (ie, all slack is on the tensioner pulley side of the belt), then fit the belt over the coolant pump sprocket and tensioner pulley (see illustration). Do not twist the belt sharply while refitting it. Ensure that the belt teeth are correctly seated centrally in the sprockets, and that the timing marks remain in alignment.

If a used belt is being refitted, ensure that the arrow mark made on removal points in the normal direction of rotation, as before. On 2.3 litre engines, remove the camshaft retaining pins/bolts from the camshaft bearing caps (where fitted).

9 Slacken the tensioner pulley nut, making sure the pulley moves to tension the belt under spring pressure, then tighten the nut securely. If the tensioner assembly is not free to move under spring tension, rectify the fault, or the timing belt will not be correctly tensioned.

10 Temporarily refit the crankshaft pulley bolt and tighten securely. Rotate the crankshaft approximately 45° in an anti-clockwise direction so that the camshaft sprocket moves through approximately 3 teeth of movement. Slacken the tensioner pulley adjuster nut by one complete turn, to allow the spring to tension the timing belt then tighten the pulley nut securely (there is no need to tighten it to the specified torque setting since it will be slackened again when the balance shaft belt is refitted).

11 Lock the timing belt tensioner pulley in position by screwing one of the timing belt cover bolts into the threaded hole behind the slot in the tensioner pulley backplate.

8.8 Fit the new timing belt ensuring it is located centrally in the sprocket teeth

12 Rotate the crankshaft through a further one and three-quarter rotations to bring number 1 cylinder back to TDC on its compression stroke (see Section 3) then refit the balance shaft belt sprocket to the crankshaft, making sure its flanged face is outermost.

13 Refit the balance shaft belt as described in Section 7.

9 Timing/balance shaft belt tensioner and sprockets – removal, inspection and refitting

Removal

1 Firmly apply the handbrake, then jack up the front of the car and support it on axle stands. Remove the left-hand roadwheel. From underneath the front of the vehicle, slacken and remove the retaining screws and fasteners and remove the undercover from beneath the engine/transmission unit.

2 Position number 1 cylinder at TDC on its compression stroke as described in Section 3, then proceed as described under the relevant sub-heading.

Camshaft sprocket – 1.8 and 2.0 litre engine

3 Remove the rubber seal from around the belt tensioner pulley nut which protrudes out of the timing belt lower cover then slacken the nut through one complete turn. Using a long flat-bladed screwdriver, carefully push down on the tensioner pulley backplate from above, to move the pulley away from the belt and relieve the timing belt tension. Hold the pulley in this position while an assistant tightens the pulley nut securely. Note: To avoid damaging the timing belt ensure the screwdriver is resting on the tensioner assembly and not the timing belt, before exerting any pressure on the screwdriver.

9.6a On 1.8 and 2.0 litre engines, unscrew the retaining bolt then remove the sprocket . . .

9.6b . . . and Woodruff key, noting which way around it is fitted

4 Disengage the belt from the camshaft sprocket, taking care not to twist it too sharply. **Do not** rotate the crankshaft until the timing belt is refitted.

5 Slacken the sprocket retaining bolt and washer and remove. To prevent rotation as the bolt is slackened, a sprocket-holding tool will be required. In the absence of the special Rover tool, an acceptable substitute can be fabricated as follows. Use two lengths of steel strip (one long, the other short), and three nuts and bolts; one nut and bolt forms the pivot of a forked tool, with the remaining two nuts and

bolts at the tips of the forks to engage with the sprocket spokes as shown **(see illustration 9.30)**.

6 With the retaining bolt removed, slide off the sprocket and recover the Woodruff key from the end of the camshaft **(see illustrations)**. Examine the oil seal for signs of oil leakage and, if necessary, renew it as described in Section 10.

Camshaft sprocket(s) – 2.3 litre engine

7 Remove the timing belt upper cover as described in Section 6.

8 Release the timing belt tension as described in paragraph 3. Disengage the belt from the camshaft sprockets, taking care not to twist it too sharply. **Do not** rotate the crankshaft until the timing belt is refitted.

9 Using a suitable open-ended spanner fitted to the hexagonal section of the camshaft, hold the camshaft and slacken the camshaft sprocket retaining bolt(s) **(see illustration)**.

10 Realign the camshaft sprocket timing marks with the cylinder head surface and insert two suitably-sized pegs or bolts through the holes in the top of the left-hand end camshaft bearing caps and into the camshafts; this will prevent the camshafts from moving under valve spring pressure whilst the sprockets are removed **(see illustration)**.

11 Remove the bolt and washer, and slide the sprocket off the camshaft end. Remove the Woodruff key from the camshaft groove, and store it with the sprocket for safe keeping **(see illustrations)**.

Crankshaft balance shaft belt sprocket

12 Remove the balance shaft belt as described in Section 7.

13 Slide the balance shaft belt sprocket off the end of the crankshaft, noting which way around the sprocket is fitted.

9.9 On 2.3 litre engines, slacken the camshaft sprocket bolt while holding the camshaft with an open-ended spanner

9.10 Return the camshaft to its original position and peg it in position with a suitable pin (arrowed)

9.11a Slide the sprocket off the end of the camshaft . . .

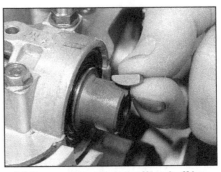

9.11b . . . and remove the Woodruff key

9.15a Remove the crankshaft sprocket (timing mark arrowed) . . .

9.15b . . . then remove the Woodruff key . . .

9.15c . . . and inner timing belt guide, noting which way around all components are fitted

Crankshaft timing belt sprocket

14 Remove the timing belt, (see Section 8).

15 Slide the crankshaft sprocket off the end of the crankshaft and remove the Woodruff key; if the sprocket is tight, carefully lever it off using a large flat-bladed screwdriver. If necessary, remove the timing belt inner guide, noting which way around that it is fitted (see illustrations). Examine the oil seal for signs of oil leakage and, if necessary renew as described in Section 17.

Front balance shaft sprocket

16 Remove the balance shaft belt as described in Section 7.

17 Slacken the sprocket retaining bolt and washer and remove. To prevent rotation, insert a screwdriver through the hole in shaft and use it to retain the shaft whilst the sprocket bolt is slackened (see illustration 9.47).

18 With the retaining bolt removed, slide off the sprocket from the end of the balance shaft (see illustration). Examine the oil seal for signs of oil leakage and, if necessary, renew it as described in Section 10.

Rear balance shaft sprocket

19 Remove the balance shaft belt as described in Section 7.

20 Using pliers, carefully unhook the spring from the end of the balance shaft pulley tensioner arm and remove it from the engine unit. Unscrew the pivot bolt and remove the tensioner arm from the engine (see illustrations).

21 Slacken and remove the sprocket housing retaining bolts, noting each ones correct fitted location, and nut. Remove the sprocket housing assembly, along with the protective cover (where fitted) and discard the sealing

ring (see illustration). If the locating dowels are a loose fit, remove them and store them safely with the housing. Note: Do not try to dismantle the housing and sprocket; the drivegear, housing and sprocket must be treated as a sealed unit.

Balance shaft belt tensioner pulley

22 Remove the balance shaft belt as described in Section 7.

23 Using pliers, carefully unhook the spring from the end of the belt tensioner arm and remove it from the engine unit. Unscrew the pivot bolt and remove the tensioner arm from the engine (see illustration).

24 Ensure the timing belt tensioner pulley is securely locked in position then slacken and remove the retaining nut and washer and slide the pulley off its mounting stud.

Timing belt tensioner pulley

25 Remove the timing belt as described in Section 8.

26 Using pliers, carefully unhook the timing belt tensioner spring and remove it from the engine.

27 Remove the balance shaft belt tensioner pulley as described in paragraphs 23 and 24 then slide the timing belt tensioner pulley off of the mounting stud.

Inspection

28 Clean thoroughly the camshaft/ crankshaft/balance shaft sprockets, and renew any that show signs of wear, damage or cracks.

29 Clean the tensioner pulleys, but do not use any strong solvent which may enter the pulley

9.18 Unscrew the retaining bolt and slide off the front balance shaft sprocket

9.20a Unhook the tensioner spring . . .

9.20b . . . then unscrew the pivot bolt and remove the tensioner arm from the engine

9.21 Slacken and remove the retaining bolts and remove the rear balance shaft sprocket housing from the engine

9.23 Removing the tensioner arm

9.30 Using a home-made tool to hold the camshaft sprocket stationary whilst the retaining bolt is tightened to the specified torque

9.44 On refitting, ensure the crankshaft timing belt sprocket is fitted with its timing mark (arrowed) facing outwards

bearings. Check that each pulley rotates freely, with no sign of stiffness or of free play. Renew the assembly if there is any doubt about its condition, or if there are any obvious signs of wear or damage. It is recommended that the tensioner springs are renewed regardless of their apparent condition since their condition is critical for the correct tensioning of the timing belt/ balance shaft belt.

Refitting

Camshaft sprocket – 1.8 and 2.0 litre engine

30 Refit the Woodruff key to the groove in the camshaft, ensuring its tapered end is innermost. Slide the sprocket onto the camshaft, ensuring that the sprocket markings are facing outwards. Refit the sprocket retaining bolt and washer, and tighten it to the specified torque while using the method employed on removal to retain the sprocket **(see illustration)**.

31 Ensure the flywheel/driveplate TDC mark is still aligned with the pointer, then position the camshaft sprocket so the UP mark is at the top and the timing mark on each side of the sprocket rim is correctly aligned with the cylinder head upper surface (see Section 3).

32 Fit the timing belt over the camshaft sprocket, ensuring that the belt front run is taut (ie, all slack is on the tensioner pulley side of the belt). Do not twist the belt sharply while refitting it. Ensure that the belt teeth are correctly seated centrally in the sprockets, and that the timing marks remain in alignment.

33 Slacken the tensioner pulley nut, making sure the pulley moves to tension the belt under spring pressure, then tighten the nut securely. If the tensioner assembly is not free to move under spring tension, rectify the fault, or the timing belt will not be correctly tensioned.

34 If all is well, rotate the crankshaft approximately 45° in an anti-clockwise direction so that the camshaft sprocket moves through

approximately 3 teeth of movement. Slacken the tensioner pulley adjuster nut by one complete turn, to allow the spring to tension the timing belt then tighten the pulley nut to the specified torque. Carry on rotating the pulley anti-clockwise until number 1 piston is back at TDC on compression, and make a final check that the sprocket and flywheel/driveplate marks are correctly positioned. If all is well, refit the rubber seal to the tensioner nut groove.

35 Refit the timing belt upper cover as described in Section 6. Once all components are correctly installed, refit the undercover panel and roadwheel. Lower the car to the ground and tighten the wheel nuts to the specified torque.

Camshaft sprocket – 2.3 litre engine

36 Refit the Woodruff key to the groove in the camshaft, then slide the sprocket onto the camshaft, ensuring that the sprocket markings are facing outwards. Refit the sprocket retaining bolt and washer, and tighten it to the specified torque while holding the camshaft with an open-ended spanner.

37 Check that the flywheel/driveplate TDC mark is still aligned with pointer (see Section 3), then fit the timing belt over the camshaft sprockets. Ensure that the belt front and top runs are taut (ie, all slack is on the tensioner pulley side of the belt). Do not twist the belt sharply while refitting it. Ensure that the belt teeth are correctly seated centrally in the sprockets, and that the timing marks remain in alignment.

38 Slacken the tensioner pulley retaining nut by one complete rotation, and check that the tensioner pulley moves to tension the belt; if the tensioner assembly is not free to move under spring tension, rectify the fault, or the timing belt will not be correctly tensioned. Check that the flywheel/driveplate mark is still correctly aligned, then securely tighten the tensioner pulley nut and remove the locating pins or bolts from the camshaft bearing caps.

39 Rotate the crankshaft through 45° in an anti-clockwise direction so that the camshaft sprockets move through approximately 3 teeth of movement. Slacken the tensioner pulley nut by one complete turn, to allow the spring to tension the timing belt, then tighten the pulley nut to the specified torque. Carry on rotating the pulley anti-clockwise until number 1 piston is back at TDC on compression, and make a final check that the sprocket marks and flywheel/driveplate mark are correctly positioned. If all is well, refit the rubber seal to the groove in the tensioner pulley nut.

40 Refit the timing belt upper cover and the cylinder head cover as described in Sections 4 and 6, then refit the undercover panel and roadwheel. Lower the car to the ground and tighten the wheel nuts to the specified torque.

Crankshaft balance shaft belt sprocket

41 Slide the sprocket onto the crankshaft, making sure it is fitted with its flanged face outermost, and engage it with the Woodruff key.

42 Refit the balance shaft belt (Section 7).

Crankshaft timing belt sprocket

43 Refit the timing belt inner guide to the crankshaft, ensuring it is fitted the correct way around with its concave surface facing inwards (towards the engine).

44 Refit the Woodruff key to the crankshaft groove, ensuring its tapered end is innermost. Slide the sprocket into position making sure its timing mark is facing outwards **(see illustration)**.

45 Refit the timing belt, (Section 8).

Front balance shaft sprocket

46 Align the sprocket key with the balance shaft groove and locate the sprocket on the end of the shaft **(see illustration)**.

47 Refit the sprocket retaining bolt and washer and tighten it to the specified torque setting whilst retaining the balance shaft with a screwdriver **(see illustration)**.

9.46 Refit the front balance shaft sprocket, aligning its key (arrowed) with the shaft slot

9.47 Use a screwdriver to retain the balance shaft whilst tightening the bolt to the specified torque

9.49a Fit a new sprocket housing sealing ring to the oil pump housing groove (locating dowels arrowed) . . .

9.49b . . . and lubricate the faces of the driveshaft gears with molybdenum disulphide grease

48 Refit the balance shaft belt, (see Section 7).

Rear balance shaft sprocket

49 Ensure the mating surfaces are clean and dry and fit a new sealing ring to the groove in the oil pump housing. Ensure that the balance shaft is correctly locked in position (see Section 7) and lubricate the faces of the balance shaft drive gears with molybdenum disulphide grease **(see illustrations)**.

50 Align the cut-out on the rim of the sprocket with the left-hand timing mark on the housing. Refit the locating dowels and manoeuvre the housing assembly into position, taking care to ensure the balance shaft drive gears engage correctly. With the housing fully located on the dowels, check that the timing mark on the sprocket outer

face aligns with the mark on the oil pump housing; the notch on the sprocket rim should now align with the second mark on the sprocket housing **(see illustrations)**.

51 Refit the protective cover (where fitted) and insert the housing retaining bolts and nut, tightening them to the specified torque.

52 Engage the tensioner arm with the pulley and securely tighten the pivot bolt. Refit the tensioner spring ensuring it is correctly engaged with the arm and engine.

53 Refit the balance shaft belt as described in Section 7.

Balance shaft belt tensioner pulley

54 Slide the pulley onto the mounting stud, ensuring it is the correct way around, then refit the washer and retaining nut.

55 Engage the tensioner arm with the pulley and securely tighten the pivot bolt. Refit the tensioner spring ensuring it is correctly engaged with the arm and engine.

56 Refit the balance shaft belt as described in Section 7.

Timing belt tensioner pulley

57 Slide the timing belt tensioner pulley onto the mounting stud, aligning the backplate hole with the lug on the cylinder block. Refit the spring making sure it is correctly engaged with the pulley backplate and locating stud **(see illustrations)**.

58 Refit the balance shaft belt pulley, arm and spring as described in paragraphs 54 and 55.

59 Refit the timing belt as described in Section 8.

9.50a Align the cut-out on the sprocket rim with the left-hand timing mark (arrowed) on the housing . . .

9.50b . . . then refit the housing. With the housing fully located check that the sprocket timing mark is correctly aligned with the lower mark (arrowed) . . .

9.50c . . . and the cutout is aligned with the second mark on the top of the housing (arrowed)

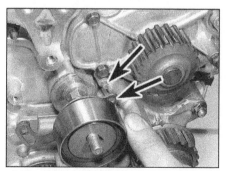

9.57a Slide the timing belt tensioner into position aligning its backplate hole with the cylinder block lug (arrowed)

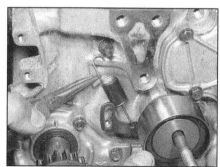

9.57b Engage the tensioner spring with the backplate and hook it over the locating stud

10.2 Removing a camshaft oil seal (2.0 litre engine shown)

10.4 Fitting a camshaft oil seal (2.3 litre engine shown)

11.6 Removing the camshaft bearing cap/rocker arm assembly (2.0 litre engine shown)

10 Camshaft and balance shaft oil seal – renewal

Note: *If an oil seal is to be renewed with the timing belt still in place, check first that the belt is free from oil contamination (renew the belt as a matter of course if signs of oil contamination are found; see Section 8). Cover the belt to protect it from contamination by oil while work is in progress, and ensure that all traces of oil are removed from the area before the belt is refitted.*

Camshaft oil seal

1 Remove the camshaft sprocket, as described in Section 9.
2 Carefully punch or drill two small holes opposite each other in the oil seal. Screw a self-tapping screw into each, and pull on the screws with pliers to extract the seal **(see illustration)**.
3 Clean the seal housing, and polish off any burrs or raised edges which may have caused the seal to fail in the first place.
4 Lubricate the lips of the new seal with clean engine oil, and drive it into position using a suitable tubular drift (such as a socket) which bears only on the hard outer edge of the seal **(see illustration)**. Take care not to damage the seal lips during fitting; note that the seal lips should face inwards.
5 Refit the camshaft sprocket as described in Section 9.

Front balance shaft seal

6 Remove the balance shaft sprocket as described in Section 9.
7 Note the correct fitted depth of the oil seal then carefully punch or drill two small holes opposite each other in the oil seal. Screw a self-tapping screw into each and pull on the screws with pliers to extract the seal.
8 Clean the seal housing and polish off any burrs or raised edges which may have caused the seal to fail in the first place.
9 Lubricate the lips of the new seal with clean engine oil and ease it into position on the end of the shaft. Press the seal squarely into position until it is flush with the oil pump

housing. If necessary, a suitable tubular drift, such as a socket, which bears only on the hard outer edge of the seal can be used to tap the seal into position. Take great care not to damage the seal lips during fitting and ensure that the seal lips face inwards.
10 Wash off any traces of oil, then refit the crankshaft sprockets as described in Section 9.
11 Refit the sprocket as described in Section 9.

Rear balance shaft oil seal

12 If oil is leaking from the rear balance shaft sprocket shaft, the complete sprocket housing assembly will have to renewed; it is not possible to renew the sprocket oil seal individually. If the oil is leaking from the housing seal, remove the sprocket housing and renewing the sealing ring. Refer to Section 9 for sprocket housing removal and refitting details.

11 Camshaft(s) and rocker arms – removal, inspection and refitting

Removal

1.8 and 2.0 litre engine

1 Remove the distributor, (see Chapter 5).
2 Remove the camshaft sprocket, as described in Section 9.
3 Slacken all the rocker arm adjusting screw locknuts, then unscrew the adjusting screws until all valve spring pressure has been relieved from the camshaft.

11.8a Slide out the retaining bolt and remove the bearing cap . . .

4 Set up a dial gauge on one end of the camshaft, and measure the camshaft endfloat while moving the camshaft to and fro. If the endfloat exceeds the specified service limit, expert advice should be sought from a Rover dealer or an engine repair specialist.
5 Working in reverse of the tightening sequence **(see illustration 11.26)**, evenly and progressively slacken the camshaft bearing cap retaining bolts. **Note:** *Fully unscrew all the bolts from the cylinder head, but do not remove any bolts from the bearing caps.*
6 Lift the camshaft bearing cap/rocker arm assembly clear of the cylinder head, ensuring that all retaining bolts remain in position in the caps. Remove the spark plug hole sealing rings from the underside of the bearing caps, and discard them; new ones should be used on refitting. Note the correct fitted positions of bearing cap locating dowels, and remove any that are loose **(see illustration)**.
7 Lift the camshaft out of the cylinder head and discard the oil seal; a new one must be used on refitting.
8 If necessary, the camshaft bearing cap/rocker arm assembly can be dismantled by removing the retaining bolts one at a time, and sliding the various components off the end of the shafts. Keeping all components in their correct fitted order, make a note of each components correct fitted position as it is removed, to ensure it is positioned correctly on reassembly. Note that each bearing cap has an identification number, 1 to 6, cast onto its upper surface, and each inlet rocker arm

11.8b . . . then slide off the washers, rocker arms and springs noting each components correct fitted locations

11.8c Each camshaft bearing cap has an identification number (arrowed) stamped onto its upper surface . . .

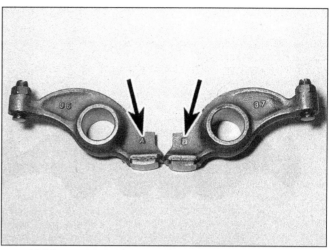

11.8d . . . and the inlet rocker arms are also marked for identification purposes (arrowed)

has an identification letter, A or B, cast onto its side **(see illustrations for this paragraph and also illustration 11.23)**.

2.3 litre engine

9 Remove the distributor (see Chapter 5).

10 Remove the camshaft sprockets, as described in Section 9.

11 Remove the locating pins or bolts from the left-hand bearing caps, then slacken all the rocker arm adjusting screw locknuts, and unscrew the adjusting screws until all valve spring pressure is relieved from the camshafts.

11.12 Measuring camshaft endfloat (2.3 litre engine shown)

12 Set up a dial gauge on one end of the inlet camshaft, and measure the camshaft endfloat while moving the camshaft to and fro. Repeat the procedure and measure the exhaust camshaft endfloat **(see illustration)**. If the endfloat of either camshaft exceeds the specified service limit, expert advice should be sought from a Rover dealer or an engine repair specialist.

13 The bearing caps are marked for identification I1 to I6, and E1 to E6; the caps marked I are the inlet camshaft bearing caps, and the caps marked E are the exhaust camshaft bearing caps **(see illustration)**. For both sets of caps, number 1 cap is the left-hand cap and number 6 the right-hand bearing cap (ie. bearing cap I1 is the left-hand inlet camshaft cap, and cap E6 is the right-hand exhaust camshaft cap). All caps must be installed with the arrow cast on the top of the cap (next to the identification mark) pointing towards the timing belt (left-hand) end of the engine.

14 Working in the reverse of the tightening sequence **(see illustration 11.35)**, evenly and progressively slacken all the inlet camshaft bearing cap retaining bolts. Remove the bearing caps from the cylinder head, noting the identification marks cast onto the top surface of each cap (see paragraph 33). To avoid confusion on refitting, store the retaining bolts

with their relevant bearing caps. Note the locating dowels which are fitted to each cap; remove any that are loose, and store them with the bearing caps for safe keeping.

15 Lift the inlet camshaft out of the cylinder head, and store it with the bearing caps. Remove the sealing cap from the right-hand end of the cylinder head and slide the oil seal off the camshaft. Discard the oil seal, a new one should be used on refitting.

16 Remove the exhaust camshaft and bearing caps as described in paragraphs 13 and 14, noting that there is no sealing cap. Note that the inlet and exhaust camshafts are not interchangeable, and must be kept separate; the shafts are marked to avoid confusion **(see illustration)**.

17 Take a small box and divide it into sixteen separate compartments, or make up a cardboard template of the cylinder head. Remove each rocker arm from the cylinder head one at a time, and store it in its correct fitted position in the container or template (as applicable) **(see illustration)**. This is necessary to ensure that the rocker arms are refitted to their original positions on reassembly; if the rocker arms are interchanged, the rate of wear between the rocker arms and camshaft will be dramatically increased.

11.13 On 2.3 litre engines all bearing caps are stamped with an identification marking and arrow to indicate their correct fitment

11.16 On 2.3 litre engines the camshafts are marked to avoid confusion (exhaust camshaft shown)

11.17 Rocker arm assemblies can be lifted out from the cylinder head once the camshafts have been removed

Inspection

18 Examine the camshaft bearing surfaces and cam lobes for signs of wear ridges and scoring. Renew the camshaft if any of these conditions are apparent. Examine the condition of the bearing surfaces both on the camshaft journals and in the cylinder head. If the head bearing surfaces are worn excessively, the cylinder head will need to be renewed.

19 If the necessary measuring equipment is available, measure the outside diameter of each camshaft journal, then bolt the camshaft bearing caps onto the cylinder head and measure the inside diameter of the camshaft bearing journals. Subtract the camshaft journal outside diameter from the bearing inside diameter, and calculate the camshaft journal running clearance. Also measure the height of each cam lobe. If any of the measurements exceed the wear limits given in the Specifications, renew the camshaft and/or cylinder head **(see illustration)**.

20 Support the camshaft end journals on V-blocks, and measure the run-out at the centre

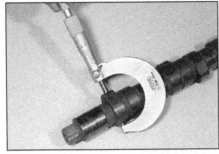

11.19 Measuring a camshaft lobe height

journal using a dial gauge. If the run-out exceeds the specified limit, the camshaft should be renewed. Examine the rocker arm bearing surfaces which contact the camshaft lobes for wear ridges and scoring. Renew any rocker arms on which these conditions are apparent.

21 On 1.8 and 2.0 litre engines, if the camshaft bearing cap/rocker arm assembly has been dismantled, examine the rocker arm and shaft bearing surfaces for wear ridges and scoring. If the necessary measuring

equipment is available, measure the inside diameter of the rocker arm and the outside diameter of the rocker shaft at the point where the rocker pivots, and calculate the running clearance. If the clearance exceeds the figure given in the Specifications at the start of this Chapter (or if there are obvious signs of wear), the rocker arm and/or shaft must be renewed.

22 On 2.3 litre engines, inspect the rocker arm adjusting screw pivots for signs of wear or damage. If wear is found, then the adjusting screw must be renewed, along with its pivot seat, which is a screw fit in the cylinder head.

Refitting

1.8 and 2.0 litre engine

23 If the camshaft bearing cap/rocker arm assembly was dismantled, reassemble it by reversing the dismantling sequence, noting that the exhaust rocker shaft oilways must be facing downwards. If difficulties arise, use the rocker arm and bearing cap identification marks for reference **(see illustration)**. Prior to

**11.23 Exploded view of camshaft bearing cap/rocker arm assemblies -
1.8 and 2.0 litre engine**

A Number 6 bearing cap
B Inlet rocker shaft (short)
C Number 5 bearing cap
D Inlet rocker shaft (long)
E Number 4 bearing cap
F Wave washer
G Number 3 bearing cap
H Inlet rocker arm (B)
J Number 2 bearing cap
K Inlet rocker arm (A)
L Number 1 bearing cap
M Exhaust rocker arm
N Exhaust rocker shaft
O Spring (long)
P Spring (short)

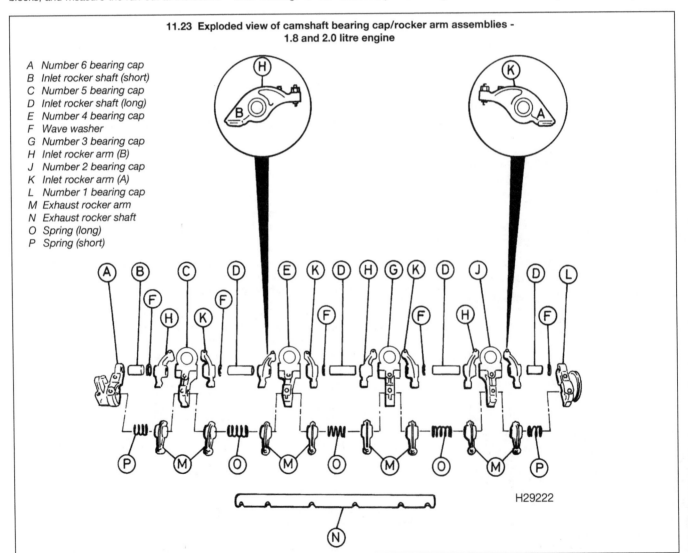

H29222

11.24a Lubricate the bearings with clean engine oil . . .

11.24b . . . then refit the camshaft, positioning it with its sprocket Woodruff key slot (arrowed) at the top

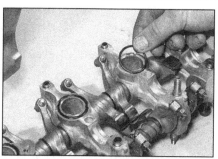

11.25a Fit the new spark plug hole sealing rings to the recesses on the base of the bearing caps . . .

reassembly, apply a smear of clean engine oil to the shaft and rocker arm bearing surfaces.

24 Ensure the cylinder head and camshaft bearing surfaces are clean, then liberally oil the camshaft bearings and lobes, and refit the camshaft. Position the shaft so that its sprocket keyway is in the 12 o'clock position (uppermost) and check that flywheel/ driveplate TDC mark is still correctly aligned with its pointer (see Section 3) **(see illustrations)**.

25 Check that all bearing cap locating dowels are in position, and fit new spark plug hole sealing rings to the recesses in the base of the camshaft bearing caps. Ensure the bearing cap mating surfaces are clean and dry and apply sealant to the specified areas of number 1 and 6 bearing cap surfaces **(see illustrations)**.

26 Carefully refit the camshaft bearing cap/rocker arm assembly to the cylinder head, taking great care to ensure that the sealing rings remain in position. Once the assembly is correctly seated, refit the camshaft bearing cap bolts, tightening them all by hand only. Working in the sequence shown, tighten the camshaft bearing cap retaining bolts evenly and progressively to their specified torque settings **(see illustration)**.

27 Lubricate the lips of a new camshaft oil seal with clean engine oil, and drive it into position using a suitable tubular drift (such as a socket) which bears only on the hard outer edge of the seal. Take care not to damage the seal lips during fitting; note that the seal lips should face inwards.

28 Refit the camshaft sprocket as described in Section 9, noting that the valve clearances must be adjusted as described in Chapter 1

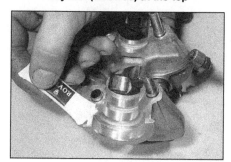

11.25b . . . and apply a smear of suitable sealant . . .

before the upper timing belt and cylinder head covers are installed.

29 Refit the distributor, (see Chapter 5).

2.3 litre engine

30 Apply a drop of oil to the rocker arm adjusting screw pivots, then refit all the rocker arms to their original locations in the cylinder head. Once installed, ensure all the rocker arm grooves are correctly engaged with the valve stem ends.

31 Ensure the cylinder head and camshaft bearing surfaces are clean, then liberally oil the camshaft bearings and lobes. Refit both the camshafts to the cylinder head, ensuring that the inlet and exhaust camshafts are fitted in the correct locations. Position each shaft so that its sprocket keyway is in the 12 o'clock position (uppermost) and check that the flywheel/driveplate TDC mark is still correctly aligned with its pointer (see Section 3).

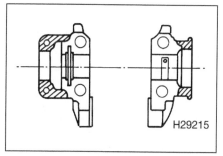

11.25c . . . to the shaded areas of number 1 and 6 bearing caps

32 Ensure all the locating dowels are in position, and that the cylinder head and camshaft bearing cap mating surfaces are clean and dry.

33 The bearing caps are marked for identification I1 to I6, and E1 to E6; the caps marked I are the inlet camshaft bearing caps, and the caps marked E are the exhaust camshaft bearing caps. For both sets of caps, number 1 cap is the left-hand cap and number 6 the right-hand bearing cap (ie. bearing cap I1 is the left-hand inlet camshaft cap, and cap E6 is the right-hand exhaust camshaft cap). All caps must be installed with the arrow cast on the top of the cap (next to the identification mark) pointing towards the timing belt (left-hand) end of the engine.

34 Apply a smear of sealant to the mating surfaces of number 1 and number 6 bearing caps (both inlet and exhaust) prior to refitting as shown **(see illustration)**.

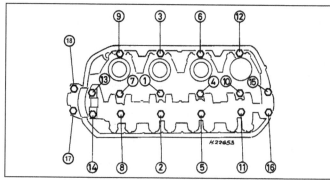

11.26 Camshaft bearing cap bolt tightening sequence - 1.8 and 2.0 litre engine

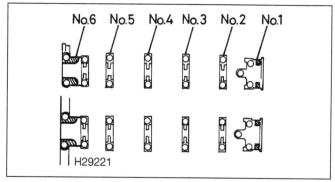

11.34 On 2.3 litre engines, apply sealant to the shaded areas of number 1 and 6 inlet and exhaust camshaft bearing caps

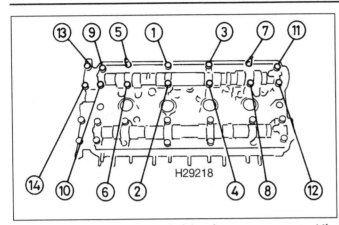

11.35 Camshaft bearing cap bolt tightening sequence - repeat the sequence on the second camshaft

12.12 Using a timing belt cover bolt to extract the oil control jet from the cylinder block

35 Using the identification marks, refit the caps and bolts to their original locations on the cylinder head. Evenly and progressively tighten the bearing cap bolts so that each camshaft is pulled squarely down onto cylinder head. Once all caps are correctly seated, go around in the specified sequence, and tighten the cap retaining bolts to their specified torque settings **(see illustration)**.
36 Lubricate the lips of a new inlet camshaft oil seal with clean engine oil, and drive it into position using a suitable tubular drift (such as a socket) which bears only on the hard outer edge of the seal. Take care not to damage the seal lips during fitting; note that the seal lips should face inwards. Fit a new exhaust camshaft oil seal in the same way.
37 Using an open-ended spanner on the hexagonal section of each camshaft, position both shafts so that their sprocket keyways are in the 12 o'clock position, then insert two suitably-sized pegs or bolts through the holes in the left-hand bearing caps and into the camshafts, to hold the shafts in this position.
38 Refit the camshaft sprockets as described in Section 9, noting that the valve clearances must be adjusted as described in Chapter 1 before the cylinder head cover is installed.
39 Refit the distributor as described in Chapter 5.

12 Cylinder head – removal and refitting

Removal

1 Disconnect the battery negative terminal. Firmly apply the handbrake, then jack up the front of the car and support it on axle stands. Remove the left-hand roadwheel. From underneath the front of the vehicle, slacken and remove the retaining screws and fasteners and remove the undercover from beneath the engine/transmission unit.
2 Drain the cooling system and remove the spark plugs, as described in Chapter 1.

3 Referring to Chapter 10, unbolt the power steering pump and position it clear of the cylinder head with its hydraulic hoses still attached.
4 Remove the inlet and exhaust manifolds as described in Chapter 4.
5 On 1.8 and 2.0 litre engines, if the cylinder head is to be dismantled, remove the rocker arms and camshaft as described in Section 11. If the head is not being dismantled, disengage the timing belt from the camshaft sprocket as described in paragraphs 1 to 4 of Section 9.
6 On 2.3 litre engines remove the camshafts and rocker arms as described in Section 11. Slacken the retaining bolts and unbolt the left-hand engine/transmission mounting support bracket from the end of the cylinder head. Unbolt the timing belt inner cover and remove it from the cylinder head along with its sealing strips.
7 On all engines disconnect the wiring connectors from the distributor (where still fitted) and coolant temperature sensor(s) which are fitted to the right-hand end of the cylinder head. Free the wiring harness from all the relevant retaining clips and position it clear of the head.
8 Release the retaining clips and disconnect the radiator and heater coolant hoses from the cylinder head.
9 Working in the **reverse** of the tightening sequence **(see illustrations 12.24a and 12.24b)**, progressively slacken the cylinder head bolts by a third of a turn at a time until all bolts can be unscrewed by hand. Remove each bolt in turn, along with its washer, noting the correct fitted location of the longer bolt.
10 Once all the cylinder head bolts are removed, gently rock the head to break the gasket joint. If necessary, the joint can be broken by carefully levering between the cylinder head and block using a flat-bladed screwdriver at the pry points located at each corner of the head.
Caution: Only lever the cylinder head off using the pry points provided. Do not force a screwdriver in between the head and

block at any other point as this will damage the mating surface(s), which could lead to leakage when the head is refitted.
11 When the joint is broken, lift the cylinder head upwards and away from the engine. Remove the gasket and discard it. Note the fitted positions of the two locating dowels, and remove them for safe keeping if they are loose.
12 Carefully screw a M6 bolt into the threads in the centre of oil control jet and remove the jet from the rear of the cylinder block mating surface, noting which way around it is fitted **(see illustration)**. Discard its sealing ring; the sealing ring **must** be renewed whenever it is disturbed.

Inspection

13 The mating faces of the cylinder head and block must be perfectly clean before refitting the head. Use a scraper to remove all traces of gasket and carbon, and also clean the tops of the pistons. Take particular care with the aluminium surfaces, as the soft metal is damaged easily. Also, make sure that debris is not allowed to enter the oil and water channels - this is particularly important for the oil circuit, as carbon could block the oil supply to the camshaft or crankshaft bearings. Using adhesive tape and paper, seal the water, oil and bolt holes in the cylinder block. To prevent carbon entering the gap between the pistons and bores, smear a little grease in the gap. After cleaning the piston, rotate the crankshaft so that the piston moves down the bore, then wipe out the grease and carbon with a cloth rag. Clean the piston crowns in the same way.
14 Check the block and head for nicks, deep scratches and other damage. If slight, they may be removed carefully with a file. More serious damage may be repaired by machining, but this is a specialist job.
15 If warpage of the cylinder head is suspected, use a straight-edge to check it for distortion. Refer to Chapter 2B if necessary.
16 Ensure that the cylinder head bolt holes in the crankcase are clean and free of oil.

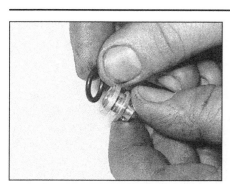

12.20a Fit a new sealing ring . . .

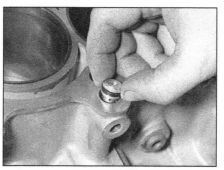

12.20b . . . and refit the oil control jet to the cylinder block

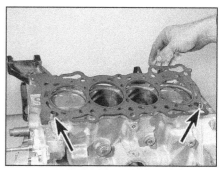

12.21 Locate the new gasket on the locating dowels (arrowed) . . .

Syringe or soak up any oil left in the bolt holes. This is most important in order that the correct bolt tightening torque can be applied and to prevent the possibility of the block being cracked by hydraulic pressure when the bolts are tightened.

17 Examine the cylinder head bolt threads in the cylinder block for damage. If necessary, use the correct-size tap to chase out the threads in the block and renew any damaged bolts. Although Rover do not actually specify that the cylinder head bolts must be renewed, it is highly recommended that new bolts are used on refitting.

Refitting

18 Position number 1 piston at TDC, and wipe clean the mating faces of the head and block.

19 Ensure that the two locating dowels are in position at each end of the cylinder block/crankcase surface.

20 Fit a new O-ring to the oil control jet, then apply a smear of clean engine oil to the jet, and (ensuring it is the correct way around) fit it to the cylinder block **(see illustrations)**.

21 Fit a new cylinder head gasket to the block, ensuring that all the coolant passages and oilways align correctly with those of the gasket **(see illustration)**.

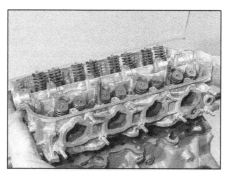

12.22 . . . and carefully lower the cylinder head into position

22 Carefully refit the cylinder head, locating it on the dowels **(see illustration)**.

23 Wash all the bolts in a suitable solvent, then wipe them dry, leaving them to dry fully before oiling and fitting. Very lightly oil under the head and on the threads of each bolt, then carefully insert them into their original holes (**do not drop**) and screw them in, finger-tight only at this stage **(see illustration)**.

24 Working progressively, in the sequence shown, first tighten all the cylinder head bolts to the stage 1 torque setting. Once all bolts have been tightened to the stage 1 torque, again working in the sequence shown, progress-

12.23 Lightly oil the threads and heads of the cylinder bolts prior to installation

ively tighten all the bolts to the stage 2 torque setting. Finally go around in the specified sequence and tighten all bolts to the specified stage 3 torque setting **(see illustrations)**.

25 Reconnect the coolant hoses to the cylinder head and secure them in position with the retaining clips. Reconnect the wiring to the coolant temperature sensor(s) and distributor making sure the wiring is correctly routed.

26 On 1.8 and 2.0 litre engines, refit the camshaft and rocker arms (if removed) as described in Section 11, or refit the timing belt to the camshaft sprocket as described in paragraphs 31 to 35 of Section 9.

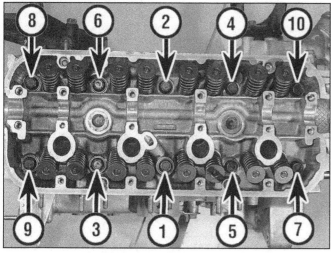

12.24a Cylinder head bolt tightening sequence - 1.8 and 2.0 litre engine

12.24b Cylinder head bolt tightening sequence - 2.3 litre engine

13.6a Slacken and remove the retaining nuts and bolts . . .

13.6b . . . then remove the sump from the engine and discard the gasket

13.7a Slacken and remove the retaining nuts and bolts (arrowed) then remove the pick-up/strainer . . .

27 On 2.3 litre engines ensure the sealing strips are correctly positioned then refit the timing belt inner cover, tightening its retaining bolts securely. Refit the mounting support bracket, tightening its mounting bolts to the specified torque then install the rocker arms and camshafts as described in Section 11.
28 Refit the inlet and exhaust manifolds as described in Chapter 4.
29 Refit the power steering pump as described in Chapter 10.
30 Refit the undercover and roadwheel then lower the vehicle to the floor and tighten the wheel nuts to the specified torque.
31 Refill the cooling system as described in Chapter 1 and refit the spark plugs.

13 Sump – removal and refitting

Removal

1 Disconnect the battery negative terminal.
2 Drain the engine oil as described in Chapter 1, then fit a new sealing washer and refit the drain plug, tightening it to the specified torque.
3 Apply the handbrake, then jack up the front of the car and support it on axle stands.
4 Referring to Chapter 4, unbolt the exhaust system front pipe from the manifold and support bracket to gain the clearance necessary to remove the sump.

5 Slacken and remove the flywheel/driveplate lower cover retaining bolts and remove the cover from the base of the transmission unit.
6 Progressively slacken and remove all the sump retaining nuts and bolts. Break the sump joint by striking the sump with the palm of the hand, then lower the sump away from the engine and withdraw it. Remove the gasket and discard it **(see illustrations)**.
7 While the sump is removed, take the opportunity to check the oil pump pick-up/strainer for signs of clogging or splitting. If necessary, unbolt the pick-up/strainer and remove it from the base of the oil pump housing along with its gasket **(see illustrations)**. The strainer can then be cleaned easily in solvent or renewed.

Refitting

8 Remove all traces of dirt and oil from the mating surfaces of the sump and cylinder block and (where removed) the pick-up/strainer and oil pump housing.
9 Where necessary, position a new gasket on top of the oil pump pick-up/strainer and fit the strainer, tightening its retaining nuts and bolts to the specified torque.
10 Apply a suitable sealant to the areas of the sump on each side of the semi-circular crankshaft cut-out, then fit a new gasket to the sump. Apply the sealant to the same areas of the gasket upper surface **(see illustrations)**.
11 Offer up the sump to the cylinder block/crankcase, then refit the sump retaining

nuts and bolts. Working out from the centre in a diagonal sequence, progressively tighten the sump retaining nuts and bolts to their specified torque setting.
12 Refit the flywheel/driveplate cover, and tighten its retaining bolts to the specified torque setting.
13 Refit the exhaust system front pipe as described in Chapter 4.
14 Lower the vehicle to the ground then fill the engine with fresh oil, with reference to Chapter 1.

14 Oil pump – removal, overhaul and refitting

Removal

1 Remove crankshaft and both front and rear balance shaft sprockets as described in Section 9.
2 Remove the sump and oil pump pick-up/strainer as described in Section 13. Undo the retaining bolts and remove the baffle plate (where fitted) from the base of the main bearing cap bridge.
3 With the rear balance shaft still locked in position, slacken and remove the retaining bolt and washer then slide off the drivegear and thrust washer from the shaft end **(see illustration)**.

13.7b . . . along with its gasket

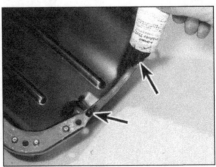

13.10a Apply sealant to the areas of the sump on each side of the crankshaft cutout (arrowed) . . .

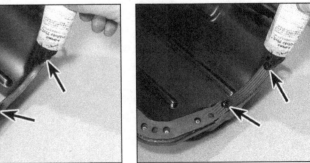

13.10b . . . then fit the gasket to sump and apply sealant to the same areas of the gasket (arrowed)

14.3 Unscrew the retaining bolt and washer and remove the rear balance shaft drive gear

14.4 Unscrew the retaining bolts (arrowed) and remove the oil pump housing from the cylinder block

4 Slacken and remove the retaining bolts then slide the oil pump housing assembly off of the end of the crankshaft, taking great care not to lose the locating dowels **(see illustration)**. Remove the housing sealing rings and discard them.

Overhaul

5 Undo the retaining screws and lift off the pump cover from the rear of the housing **(see illustration)**.
6 Using a suitable marker pen, mark the surface of both the pump inner and outer rotors; the marks can then be used to ensure the rotors are refitted the correct way around.

7 Lift out the inner and outer rotors from the pump housing **(see illustration)**.
8 Unscrew the oil pressure relief valve bolt from the base of the housing and withdraw the spring and plunger from the housing, noting which way around the plunger is fitted.
9 Clean the components, and carefully examine the rotors, pump body and relief valve plunger for any signs of scoring or wear. No individual components are available so if any component shows signs of wear or damage the complete pump assembly must be renewed.
10 If the components appear serviceable, measure the clearance between the pump

body and the outer rotor, and the inner rotor tip to outer rotor clearance using feeler blades. Also measure the rotor endfloat, and check the flatness of the end cover **(see illustrations)**. If the clearances exceed the specified tolerances, the pump must be renewed.
11 If the pump is satisfactory, reassemble the components in the reverse order of removal, applying sealant to the threads of the oil pressure relief valve bolt and tightening the cover screws to the specified torque **(see illustrations)**. Prime the oil pump by filling it with clean engine oil whilst rotating the inner rotor.

14.5 Undo the retaining screws and lift off the oil pump cover

14.7 Remove the inner and outer rotors from the pump housing, noting which way around they are fitted

14.10a Measuring outer rotor-to-pump body clearance

14.10b Measuring inner rotor tip-to-outer rotor clearance

14.10c Measuring rotor endfloat

14.11a Refit the pressure relief valve piston and spring . . .

14.12a Carefully lever the crankshaft seal out of position . . .

14.12b . . . and tap the new seal into the housing using a socket which bears only on the hard outer edge of the seal

Refitting

12 Prior to refitting, note the correct fitted depth of the crankshaft oil seal and the then carefully lever out the seal using a flat-bladed screwdriver. Fit the new oil seal, ensuring its sealing lip is facing inwards, and press it squarely into the housing using a tubular drift which bears only on the hard outer edge of the seal. Press the seal into position so that it is flush with the housing **(see illustrations)**. Renew the front balance shaft oil seal in the same way.

13 Ensure the locating dowels are in position then wipe clean the mating faces of the oil pump and cylinder block. Apply a thin coating of sealant to the cylinder block mating surface of the oil pump housing and locate the sealing rings in the cover recesses **(see illustrations)**.

14 Carefully manoeuvre the oil pump into position, engaging the inner rotor with the crankshaft, taking great care not damage the oil seal lips. Ensure the sealing rings remain correctly positioned and locate the pump housing on its dowels.

15 Refit the pump housing retaining bolts in their original locations and tighten them to the specified torque.

16 Apply molybdenum disulphide grease to the contact surfaces of the rear balance shaft drive gear and refit the thrust washer and gear, aligning its slot with the shaft locating pin, to the end of the shaft. Refit the sprocket retaining bolt and washer and tighten it to the specified torque **(see illustrations)**.

17 Refit the baffle plate (where fitted), tightening its retaining bolts securely.

18 Refit the oil pump pick-up/strainer and sump as described in Section 13.

19 Refit the balance shaft and crankshaft sprockets as described in Section 9.

20 On completion refill the engine with clean oil as described in Chapter 1.

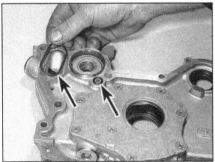

14.13a Fit the sealing rings (arrowed) to the rear of the pump housing . . .

14.13b . . . and apply sealant to the pump housing mating surface

15 Oil cooler (2.3 litre engine only) – removal and refitting

Removal

1 Apply the handbrake, then jack up the front of the car and support it on axle stands.

2 Position a suitable container beneath the oil filter, then remove the filter as described in Chapter 1. If the engine is nearing its service interval when the oil and filter are due for renewal, it is recommended that the engine oil is also drained. After reassembly, the engine can then be replenished with fresh engine oil, and a new oil filter fitted. Refer to Chapter 1 for further information.

3 Either drain the cooling system as described in Chapter 1, or be prepared for some coolant spillage during the following operation. Release the retaining clips and disconnect the coolant hoses from the oil cooler. Plug both the hose ends to prevent the entry of dirt into the cooling system. Work quickly to minimise coolant loss if the system has not been drained.

4 Unscrew the oil cooler centre bolt, and remove the cooler from the rear of the cylinder block. Remove the oil cooler sealing ring and discard it; it must be renewed whenever it is disturbed.

Refitting

5 Fit a new sealing ring to the recess in the oil cooler and locate the cooler on the cylinder block. Refit the centre bolt and tighten it securely.

6 Refit the coolant hoses to the oil cooler, and secure them in position with their retaining clips. Work quickly again to minimise coolant loss if the cooling system was not drained. Top-up or refill the cooling system as described in Chapter 1.

7 Working as described in Chapter 1, fit the oil filter, then lower the car to the ground and top-up or refill (as applicable) the cooling system and engine oil.

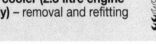

14.16a Refit the thrust washer then install the drivegear aligning its slot with the rear balance shaft pin (arrowed)

14.16b Retain the balance shaft with the locking tool and tighten the drivegear bolt to the specified torque

14.11b . . . and securely tighten the valve bolt having applied sealant to its threads prior to refitting

16 Flywheel/driveplate –
removal, inspection and refitting

Removal

Manual transmission models

1 Remove the transmission as described in Chapter 7A then remove the clutch assembly as described in Chapter 6.
2 Prevent the flywheel from turning by locking the ring gear teeth with a similar arrangement to that shown **(see illustration)**. Alternatively, bolt a strap between the flywheel and the cylinder block/crankcase. Make alignment marks between the flywheel and crankshaft using paint or a suitable marker pen.
3 Slacken and remove the flywheel retaining bolts and remove the flywheel. Do not drop it, as it is very heavy.

Automatic transmission models

4 Remove the transmission as described in Chapter 7B.
5 Prevent the driveplate from turning by bolting it to the cylinder block/crankcase with a metal strap. Make alignment marks between the driveplate and crankshaft using paint or a suitable marker pen.
6 Slacken and remove the retaining bolts and spacer then remove the driveplate, noting which way around it is fitted.

Inspection

7 On models with manual transmission, examine the flywheel for scoring of the clutch face, and for wear or chipping of the ring gear teeth. If the clutch face is scored, the flywheel may be surface-ground, but renewal is preferable. Seek the advice of a Rover dealer or engine reconditioning specialist to see if machining is possible.
8 On models with automatic transmission, check the torque converter driveplate carefully for signs of distortion. Look for any hairline cracks around the bolt holes or radiating outwards from the centre. If any sign of wear or damage is found, the driveplate must be renewed.

Refitting

Manual transmission models

9 Clean the mating surfaces of the flywheel and crankshaft.
10 Offer up the flywheel and refit the retaining bolts. If the original is being refitted align the marks made prior to removal.
11 Lock the flywheel using the method employed on dismantling then, working in a diagonal sequence, evenly and progressively tighten the retaining bolts to the specified torque **(see illustration)**.
12 Refit the clutch as described in Chapter 6 then remove the locking tool, and refit the transmission as described in Chapter 7A.

16.2 Home-made flywheel locking tool in position

Automatic transmission models

13 Clean the mating surfaces of the driveplate, spacer and crankshaft.
14 Offer up the driveplate, ensuring it is the correct way around. Align the marks made on removal (if the original is being refitted) then refit the spacer and screw in the retaining bolts.
15 Lock the driveplate using the method employed on dismantling then, working in a diagonal sequence, evenly and progressively tighten the bolts to the specified torque.
16 Refit the transmission (see Chapter 7B).

17 Crankshaft oil seals –
renewal

Left-hand (timing belt end) oil seal

1 Remove the crankshaft sprockets as described in Section 9.
2 Carefully punch or drill two small holes opposite each other in the oil seal. Screw a self-tapping screw into each and pull on the screws with pliers to extract the seal.
Caution: Great care must be taken to avoid damage to the oil pump.
3 Clean the seal housing and polish off any burrs or raised edges which may have caused the seal to fail in the first place.
4 Lubricate the lips of the new seal with clean engine oil and ease it into position on the end of the shaft. Press the seal squarely into position until it is flush with the oil pump housing. If necessary, a suitable tubular drift, such as a socket, which bears only on the hard outer edge of the seal can be used to tap the seal into position. Take great care not to damage the seal lips during fitting and ensure that the seal lips face inwards.
5 Wash off any traces of oil, then refit the crankshaft sprockets as described in Section 9.

Right-hand (flywheel/driveplate) oil seal

Note: *Although it is possible to renew the oil seal with the housing in position on the engine, the position of the oil seal in its housing is critical. Without access to Rover special tool 18G 1485 to install the new seal it will be very difficult to ensure that the seal is*

16.11 Tighten the flywheel bolts to the specified torque whilst preventing rotation using the home-made tool (arrowed)

correctly positioned. For this reason, it is recommended that the oil seal housing is removed from the engine for oil seal renewal.
6 Remove the flywheel/driveplate, as described in Section 16.
7 Remove the sump, as described in Section 13.
8 Slacken and remove the retaining bolts and slide the seal housing off the end of the crankshaft, noting its two locating dowels.
9 Using a large flat-bladed screwdriver, carefully lever the old seal out of the housing. Clean the seal housing, and polish off any burrs or raised edges which may have caused the seal to fail in the first place.
10 Lubricate the outer edge of the new seal, and tap the seal gently into place in the housing until the chamfer of the seal outer surface is correctly lined up with the inner chamfer of the oil seal housing. Note that its sealing lip must be facing inwards. With the seal in this position, use feeler gauges to check that the clearance between the inner edge of the seal and the locating shoulder of the seal housing is 0.5 to 0.8 mm. Note that the gap must also be equal all the way around the circumference of the seal. If necessary, carefully adjust the position of the seal by gently levering it out or tapping it into the housing (as applicable) until the seal is correctly fitted **(see illustrations)**.

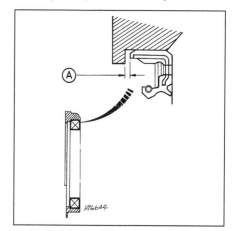

17.10a Crankshaft right-hand oil seal installation - ensure the gap (A) between the inner edge of the seal and cover is 0.5 to 0.8 mm

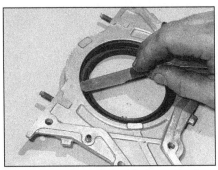

17.10b Using a feeler blade to check crankshaft right-hand oil seal-to-cover gap

17.12 Apply sealant to the oil seal housing mating surface (locating dowels arrowed) . . .

17.13 . . . then refit the housing to the cylinder block and tighten its retaining bolts to the specified torque

11 Remove all traces of sealant from the cylinder block and housing mating surfaces, and ensure the surfaces are clean and dry.
12 Apply a thin coating of a suitable sealant to the housing mating surface, and lubricate the oil seal lip with a smear of engine oil (see illustration).
13 Check that the locating dowels are in position, then carefully ease the oil seal housing over the crankshaft end, and push it fully into position on the cylinder block. Refit the housing retaining bolts, and tighten them to the specified torque setting (see illustration).
14 Refit the sump as described in Section 13.
15 Refit the flywheel/driveplate as described in Section 16.

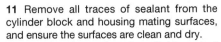

18 Engine/transmission mountings – inspection and renewal

Inspection

1 If improved access is required, raise the front of the car and support it securely on axle stands.
2 Check the mounting rubber to see if it is cracked, hardened or separated from the metal at any point; renew the mounting if any such damage or deterioration is evident.
3 Check that all the mounting's fasteners are securely tightened; use a torque wrench to check if possible.

4 Using a large screwdriver or a pry bar, check for wear in the mounting by carefully levering against it to check for free play; where this is not possible, enlist the aid of an assistant to move the engine/transmission unit back and forth, or from side to side, while you watch the mounting. While some free play is to be expected, even from new components, excessive wear should be obvious. If excessive free play is found, check first that the fasteners are correctly secured, then renew any worn components as described below.

Renewal

Right-hand mounting

5 Disconnect the battery negative terminal. To improve access to the mounting remove the battery and mounting plate (see Chapter 5).
6 Support the weight of the engine/transmission using a trolley jack with a block of wood placed on its head.
7 Slacken and remove the mounting through-bolt and mounting nuts and remove the assembly from the top of the transmission unit (see illustrations). If necessary, undo the retaining nuts and separate the mounting rubber from its mounting plate.
8 Check all components for signs of wear or damage, and renew as necessary.
9 On reassembly, refit the rubber mounting to the mounting plate (where separated) and tighten the nuts to the specified torque.

Manoeuvre the mounting assembly into position and tighten its mounting nuts to the specified torque.
10 Align the mounting with the body bracket then refit the through-bolt and tighten it to the specified torque setting.
11 Remove the trolley jack from underneath the car and (where removed) refit the mounting plate and battery.

Left-hand mounting

12 Disconnect the battery negative terminal.
13 Support the weight of the engine/transmission using a trolley jack, with a wooden spacer to prevent damage to the sump. Slacken and remove the mounting through-bolt, then undo the nut and bolt securing the mounting to its engine mounting bracket, and remove the mounting from the car (see illustrations).
14 To dismantle the engine mounting bracket, first remove the lower timing belt cover as described in Section 6. The bracket assembly can then be unbolted from the cylinder block.
15 Check all components for signs of wear or damage, and renew as necessary.
16 On reassembly, refit the engine mounting bracket assembly (if removed), tightening all its fasteners to the specified torque, and refit the timing belt covers as described in Section 6.
17 Manoeuvre the mounting into position, then refit its retaining nut and bolt, and tighten them to the specified torque setting.

18.7a Slacken and remove the through-bolt . . .

18.7b . . . then unscrew the mounting nuts (arrowed) . . .

18.7c . . . and remove the right-hand engine/transmission mounting

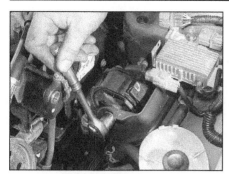

18.13a Slacken and remove the through-bolt . . .

18.13b . . . then unscrew the mounting nut and bolt (arrowed) . . .

18.13c . . . and lift off the left-hand engine/transmission mounting

18 Use the trolley jack to raise the engine to the correct height, then refit the mounting through-bolt, tightening it to the specified torque setting. Remove the trolley jack and reconnect the battery.

Front mounting

19 Disconnect the battery negative terminal.
20 Support the weight of the engine/ transmission using a trolley jack, with a wooden spacer to prevent damage to the sump.
21 Unscrew the through-bolt securing the upper end of the mounting to the engine and remove the special nut **(see illustration)**. Unscrew the bolt securing the lower end of the mounting to the subframe and remove the mounting link from the vehicle. If necessary, the mounting bracket can be unbolted and removed from the engine.
22 Check the mounting link rubbers for signs of wear or deterioration, and renew if necessary. Refit the mounting bracket to the cylinder block (where removed) tightening its mounting bolts to the specified torque.
23 Manoeuvre the mounting link into position and refit the lower through-bolt. Refit the upper through-bolt nut, ensuring it is correct engaged with the mounting bracket, and refit the through-bolt **(see illustration)**. Remove

the jack from beneath the engine unit and tighten both through-bolts to the specified torque setting. Reconnect the battery.

Rear mounting - manual transmission models

24 Disconnect the battery negative terminal. To gain access to the rear mounting, remove the air cleaner housing as described in Chapter 4.
25 Support the weight of the engine/ transmission using a trolley jack, with a wooden spacer to prevent damage to the transmission casing.
26 Slacken and remove the mounting through-bolt then undo the bolts securing mounting to the subframe and manoeuvre it out of position.
27 If necessary, the mounting bracket can then be unbolted and removed from the transmission unit.
28 Check all components for signs of wear or damage, and renew as necessary.
29 Refit the mounting bracket (where removed) tightening its mounting bolts to the specified torque.
30 Manoeuvre the mounting into position and refit the bolts securing it to the subframe, tightening them to the specified torque. Insert the through-bolt and tighten it to the specified torque then reconnect the battery.

Rear mounting - automatic transmission models

31 On models with an automatic transmission unit, and engine mounting control system is fitted to the rear mounting assembly to minimise engine vibration at idle. The system is controlled by the engine mounting ECU (which is situated in the passenger footwell) via an electrically-operated solenoid valve. the rear mounting incorporates two liquid-filled chambers and has a vacuum diaphragm unit fitted to it. At idle speed, the ECU opens the solenoid valve which allows vacuum to act on the mounting diaphragm unit. This changes the flow of liquid between the fluid chambers of the mounting assembly and cancels out engine vibration. At engine speeds above 920 rpm, the ECU closes the solenoid valve which shuts off the vacuum supply to the diaphragm; the engine mounting then acts just like a normal mounting rubber.
32 Removal and refitting of the mounting is as described in paragraphs 24 to 30 noting that it will be necessary to disconnect/ reconnect the vacuum hose from the mounting diaphragm unit. Also note that a rubber insulating washer is position on either side of the link upper end; renew these washers if they show signs of damage or deterioration.

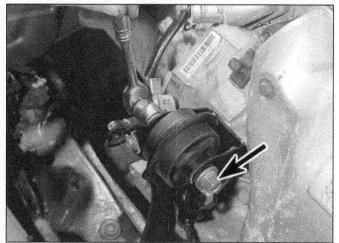

18.21 Slacken and remove the through-bolt and recover the nut (arrowed) from the upper end of the front mounting link

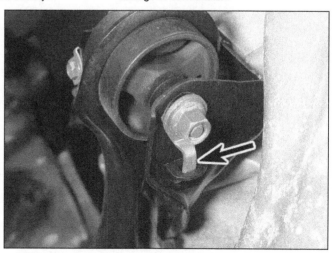

18.23 On refitting ensure the mounting link upper bolt nut tab (arrowed) is correctly engaged with the mounting bracket

Notes

Chapter 2 Part B
General engine overhaul procedures

Contents

Degrees of difficulty

Easy, suitable for novice with little experience		Fairly easy, suitable for beginner with some experience		Fairly difficult, suitable for competent DIY mechanic		Difficult, suitable for experienced DIY mechanic		Very difficult, suitable for expert DIY or professional	

Specifications

Cylinder head

Maximum gasket face distortion	0.05 mm
Cylinder head height:	
1.8 and 2.0 litre engine	99.95 to 100.05 mm
2.3 litre engine	131.95 to 132.05 mm

Balance shafts

	Standard	Service limit
Endfloat:		
Front shaft	0.10 to 0.35 mm	
Rear shaft	0.06 to 0.18 mm	
Journal diameter:		
No.1 journal:		
Front shaft	42.722 to 42.734 mm	42.71 mm
Rear shaft	20.938 to 20.950 mm	20.92 mm
No.2 journal	38.712 to 38.724 mm	38.70 mm
No.3 journal	34.722 to 34.734 mm	34.71 mm
Maximum allowable journal taper	0.005 mm	
Balance shaft run-out	Less than 0.02 mm	0.03 mm
Cylinder block bearing diameter:		
No.1 journal:		
Front shaft	42.800 to 42.820 mm	42.83 mm
Rear shaft	21.000 to 21.013 mm	21.02 mm
No.2 journal	38.800 to 38.820 mm	38.83 mm
No.3 journal	34.800 to 34.820 mm	34.83 mm
Journal running clearance:		
No.1 journal:		
Front shaft	0.066 to 0.098 mm	0.12 mm
Rear shaft	0.050 to 0.075 mm	0.09 mm
No.2 journal	0.076 to 0.108 mm	0.13 mm
No.3 journal	0.066 to 0.098 mm	0.12 mm

Valves, valve springs and guides

	Standard	Service limit
Valve stem diameter:		
1.8 and 2.0 litre engine:		
Inlet	5.485 to 5.495 mm	5.455 mm
Exhaust	5.450 to 5.460 mm	5.420 mm
2.3 litre engine:		
Inlet	6.580 to 6.590 mm	6.550 mm
Exhaust	6.550 to 6.560 mm	6.520 mm

	Inlet	Exhaust
Valve length (new):		
1.8 and 2.0 litre engine	110.88 to 111.18 mm	122.15 to 122.45 mm
2.3 litre engine	102.50 to 102.80 mm	101.40 to 101.70 mm
Valve head diameter (new)	33.9 to 34.1 mm	28.9 to 29.1 mm

	Standard	Service limit
Valve head thickness:		
Inlet	0.85 to 1.15 mm	0.65 mm
Exhaust	1.05 to 1.35 mm	0.95 mm
Stem-to-guide clearance:		
Inlet	0.02 to 0.05 mm	0.08 mm
Exhaust:	0.05 to 0.08 mm	0.11 mm
Valve head movement when installed in guide (see text):		
Inlet	0.04 to 0.10 mm	0.16 mm
Exhaust	0.10 to 0.16 mm	0.24 mm
Valve stem fitted height:		
1.8 and 2.0 litre engine:		
Inlet	48.245 to 48.715 mm	48.965 mm
Exhaust	50.315 to 50.785 mm	51.035 mm
2.3 litre engine:		
Inlet	39.365 to 39.835 mm	40.085 mm
Exhaust	39.165 to 39.635 mm	39.885 mm
Valve seat width:		
Standard	1.25 to 1.55 mm	
Service limit	2.00 mm	

	Inlet	Exhaust
Valve spring free length (approximate):		
1.8 and 2.0 litre engines	53.42 mm	54.66 mm
2.3 litre engine	47.14 mm	47.14 mm
Valve guide projection above cylinder head:		
1.8 and 2.0 litre engines	24.00 mm	15.30 mm
2.3 litre engine	13.25 to 13.75 mm	13.75 to 14.25 mm
Valve clearances	See Chapter 1	

Cylinder block

	Standard	Service limit
Maximum gasket face distortion	0.10 mm	
Cylinder bore diameter:		
1.8 and 2.0 litre engine:		
Size group A	85.010 to 85.020 mm	85.070 mm
Size group B	85.000 to 85.010 mm	85.070 mm
2.3 litre engine:		
Size group A	87.010 to 87.020 mm	87.070 mm
Size group B	87.000 to 87.010 mm	87.070 mm
Oversize pistons available:		
1.8 and 2.0 litre engines	0.25 and 0.50 mm	
2.3 litre engine	0.25 mm	
Maximum cylinder bore ovality	N/A	
Maximum cylinder bore taper	0.05 mm	

Gudgeon pins

Diameter	21.994 to 22.000 mm
Gudgeon pin-to-piston clearance	0.012 to 0.024 mm

Connecting rod

Big-end side clearance:	
Standard	0.15 to 0.30 mm
Service limit	0.40 mm
Small-end bore diameter	21.968 to 21.981 mm
Big-end bore diameter (nominal):	
1.8 and 2.0 litre engines	48 mm
2.3 litre engine	51 mm

Pistons and rings

	Standard	Service limit
Piston diameter:		
Size group A	84.98 to 84.99 mm	84.97 mm
Size group B	84.97 to 84.98 mm	84.96 mm
Piston-to-bore clearance:		
1.8 and 2.0 litre engine	0.020 to 0.040 mm	0.05 mm
2.3 litre engine	0.007 to 0.030 mm	0.04 mm
Piston ring end gaps (fitted in bore):		
1.8 and 2.0 litre engine:		
Top compression ring	0.20 to 0.35 mm	0.6 mm
Second compression ring	0.40 to 0.55 mm	0.7 mm
Oil control ring	0.2 to 0.7 mm	0.8 mm
2.3 litre engine:		
Top compression ring	0.25 to 0.35 mm	0.6 mm
Second compression ring	0.60 to 0.75 mm	0.9 mm
Oil control ring	0.2 to 0.6 mm	0.7 mm
Piston ring-to-groove clearance:		
1.8 and 2.0 litre engine:		
Top compression ring	0.035 to 0.060 mm	0.13 mm
Second compression ring	0.030 to 0.055 mm	0.13 mm
Oil control ring	N/A	
2.3 litre engine:		
Top compression ring	0.045 to 0.075 mm	0.13 mm
Second compression ring	0.040 to 0.070 mm	0.13 mm
Oil control ring	N/A	

Crankshaft

Main bearing journal diameter:		
1.8 and 2.0 litre engines:		
No.1 and 4 journals	49.984 to 50.008 mm	
No.2 journal	49.976 to 50.000 mm	
No.3 journal	49.972 to 49.996 mm	
No.5 journal	49.988 to 50.012 mm	
2.3 litre engine:		
No.1 and 2 journals	49.976 to 50.000 mm	
No.3 journal	49.972 to 49.996 mm	
No.4 journal	49.984 to 50.008 mm	
No.5 journal	49.988 to 50.012 mm	
Big-end bearing journal (crankpin) diameter:		
1.8 and 2.0 litre engine	44.976 to 45.000 mm	
2.3 litre engine	47.976 to 48.000 mm	

	Standard	Service limit
Journal out-of round	Less than 0.005 mm	0.006 mm
Journal taper	Less than 0.005 mm	0.006 mm
Endfloat	0.10 to 0.35 mm	0.45 mm
Crankshaft run-out	Less than 0.003 mm	0.004 mm
Main bearing running clearance:		
1.8 and 2.0 litre engines:		
No.1 and 4 journals	0.013 to 0.037 mm	0.050 mm
No.2 journal	0.021 to 0.045 mm	0.050 mm
No.3 journal	0.025 to 0.049 mm	0.055 mm
No.5 journal	0.009 to 0.033 mm	0.040 mm
2.3 litre engine:		
No.1 and 2 journals	0.021 to 0.045 mm	0.050 mm
No.3 journal	0.025 to 0.049 mm	0.055 mm
No.4 journal	0.013 to 0.037 mm	0.050 mm
No.5 journal	0.009 to 0.033 mm	0.040 mm
Big-end bearing (crankpin) running clearance:		
1.8 and 2.0 litre engine	0.015 to 0.043 mm	0.050 mm
2.3 litre engine	0.027 to 0.055 mm	0.060 mm

Torque wrench settings

Refer to Chapter 2A Specifications

1 General information

1 Included in this Part of Chapter 2 are details of removing the engine/transmission from the car and general overhaul procedures for the cylinder head, cylinder block and all other engine internal components.

2 The information given ranges from advice concerning preparation for an overhaul and the purchase of replacement parts, to detailed step-by-step procedures covering removal, inspection, renovation and refitting of engine internal components.

3 After Section 6, all instructions are based on the assumption that the engine has been removed from the car. For information concerning in-car engine repair, as well as the removal and refitting of those external components necessary for full overhaul, refer to Part A of this Chapter and to Section 6. Ignore any preliminary dismantling operations described in Part A that are no longer relevant once the engine has been removed from the car.

4 Apart from torque wrench settings, which are given at the beginning of Part A, all specifications relating to engine overhaul are at the beginning of this Part of Chapter 2.

2 Engine overhaul - general information

1 It is not always easy to determine when, or if, an engine should be completely overhauled, as a number of factors must be considered.

2 High mileage is not necessarily an indication that an overhaul is needed, while low mileage does not preclude the need for an overhaul. Frequency of servicing is probably the most important consideration. An engine which has had regular and frequent oil and filter changes, as well as other required maintenance, should give many thousands of miles of reliable service. Conversely, a neglected engine may require an overhaul very early in its life.

3 Excessive oil consumption is an indication that piston rings, valve seals and/or valve guides are in need of attention. Make sure that oil leaks are not responsible before deciding that the rings and/or guides are worn. Perform a compression test, as described in Part A of this Chapter, to determine the likely cause of the problem.

4 Check the oil pressure with a gauge fitted in place of the oil pressure switch, and compare it with that specified in Part A of this Chapter. If it is extremely low, the main and big-end bearings, and/or the oil pump, are probably worn out.

5 Loss of power, rough running, knocking or metallic engine noises, excessive valve gear noise, and high fuel consumption may also point to the need for an overhaul, especially if they are all present at the same time. If a complete service does not remedy the situation, major mechanical work is the only solution.

6 An engine overhaul involves restoring all internal parts to the specification of a new engine. During an overhaul, the pistons and the piston rings are renewed. New main and big-end bearings are generally fitted; if necessary, the crankshaft may be renewed, to restore the journals. The valves are also serviced as well, since they are usually in less-than-perfect condition at this point. While the engine is being overhauled, other components, such as the starter and alternator, can be overhauled as well. The end result should be an as-new engine that will give many trouble-free miles. **Note:** *Critical cooling system components such as the hoses, thermostat and water pump should be renewed when an engine is overhauled. The radiator should be checked carefully, to ensure that it is not clogged or leaking. Also, it is a good idea to renew the oil pump whenever the engine is overhauled.*

7 Before beginning the engine overhaul, read through the entire procedure, to familiarise yourself with the scope and requirements of the job. Overhauling an engine is not difficult if you carefully follow all of the instructions, have the necessary tools and equipment, and pay close attention to all specifications. It can, however, be time-consuming. Plan on the car being off the road for a minimum of two weeks, especially if parts must be taken to an engineering works for repair or reconditioning. Check on the availability of parts and make sure that any necessary special tools and equipment are obtained in advance. Most work can be done with typical hand tools, although a number of precision measuring tools are required for inspecting parts to determine if they must be renewed. Often the engineering works will handle the inspection of parts and offer advice concerning reconditioning and renewal. **Note:** *Always wait until the engine has been completely dismantled, and until all components (especially the cylinder block and the crankshaft) have been inspected, before deciding what service and repair operations must be performed by an engineering works. The condition of these components will be the major factor to consider when determining whether to overhaul the original engine, or to buy a reconditioned unit. Do not, therefore, purchase parts or have overhaul work done on other components until they have been thoroughly inspected.* As a general rule, time is the primary cost of an overhaul, so it does not pay to fit worn or sub-standard parts.

8 As a final note, to ensure maximum life and minimum trouble from a reconditioned engine, everything must be assembled with care, in a spotlessly-clean environment.

Caution: If the radio/cassette in your vehicle is equipped with an anti-theft system, make sure you have the correct activation code before disconnecting the battery.

3 Engine removal - methods and precautions

1 If you have decided that the engine must be removed for overhaul or major repair work, several preliminary steps should be taken.

2 Locating a suitable place to work is extremely important. Adequate work space, along with storage space for the car, will be needed. If a workshop or garage is not available, at the very least, a flat, level, clean work surface is required.

3 Cleaning the engine compartment and engine/transmission before beginning the removal procedure will help keep tools clean and organised.

4 An engine hoist or A-frame will also be necessary. Make sure the equipment is rated in excess of the combined weight of the engine and transmission. Safety is of primary importance, considering the potential hazards involved in lifting the engine/transmission out of the car.

5 If this is the first time you have removed an engine, an assistant should ideally be available. Advice and aid from someone more experienced would also be helpful. There are many instances when one person cannot simultaneously perform all of the operations required when lifting the engine out of the vehicle.

6 Plan the operation ahead of time. Before starting work, arrange for the hire of or obtain all of the tools and equipment you will need. Some of the equipment necessary to perform engine/transmission removal and installation safely and with relative ease (in addition to an engine hoist) is as follows: a heavy duty trolley jack, complete sets of spanners and sockets as described in the end of this manual, wooden blocks, and plenty of rags and cleaning solvent for mopping up spilled oil, coolant and fuel. If the hoist must be hired, make sure that you arrange for it in advance, and perform all of the operations possible without it beforehand. This will save you money and time.

7 Plan for the car to be out of use for quite a while. An engineering works will be required to perform some of the work which the do-it-yourselfer cannot accomplish without special equipment. These places often have a busy schedule, so it would be a good idea to consult them before removing the engine, in order to accurately estimate the amount of time required to rebuild or repair components that may need work.

8 Always be extremely careful when removing and refitting the engine/transmission. Serious injury can result from careless actions. Plan ahead and take your time, and a job of this nature, although major, can be accomplished successfully.

4 Engine/manual transmission unit - removal, separation and refitting

Removal

Note: *The engine can be removed from the car only as a complete unit with the transmission; the two are then separated for overhaul.*

1 Park the vehicle on firm, level ground. Chock the rear wheels, then firmly apply the handbrake. Jack up the front of the vehicle, and securely support it on axle stands. Remove both front roadwheels.
2 Remove the bonnet (see Chapter 11).
3 Undo the retaining screws and fasteners and remove the plastic undercover from beneath the engine/transmission unit.
4 If the engine is to be dismantled, working as described in Chapter 1, first drain the oil and remove the oil filter. Clean and refit the drain plug, using a new sealing washer, and tighten it to the specified torque.
5 Drain the transmission oil as described in Chapter 1. Refit the drain and filler plugs, and tighten them to the specified torque.
6 Remove the battery and mounting tray as described in Chapter 5.
7 Remove the crankshaft pulley as described in Chapter 2A.

4.10 Undo the retaining bolt and disconnect the cylinder head earth lead (2.0 litre engine shown)

4.8a Disconnect the braking system servo vacuum hose . . .

8 Referring to Chapter 4, carry out the following procedures.
a) *Remove the air cleaner housing and associated components.*
b) *Depressurise the fuel system and disconnect the fuel feed and return hoses from the fuel rail.*
c) *Disconnect the accelerator cable from the throttle housing and position it clear of the engine.*
d) *Disconnect the brake servo hose and various vacuum hoses and from the inlet manifold, noting each hoses correct fitted location* **(see illustration)**.

4.11a Disconnect the engine wiring harness connectors (arrowed) on the left-hand side of the engine compartment . . .

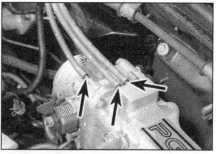
4.8b . . . and the emission control system vacuum box hoses (arrowed) from the inlet manifold

e) *Unbolt the emission system vacuum control box and remove it from the engine compartment bulkhead* **(see illustration)**.
f) *Unbolt the exhaust system front pipe from the manifold and undo the bolts securing the front pipe to its mounting bracket.*

9 Remove the radiator as described in Chapter 3. Slacken the retaining clips and disconnect the heater hoses from their unions on the cylinder head.
10 Unscrew the retaining nut and disconnect the main electrical feed cable from the starter motor solenoid (see Chapter 5). Unbolt the cable retaining clip(s) from the transmission unit and position the cable clear. Undo the retaining bolts and disconnect the cylinder head and transmission housing earth leads **(see illustration)**.
11 Trace the engine/transmission wiring back to the connectors on the left-hand side of the engine compartment. Disconnect the various wiring connectors and unscrew the earth cable retaining bolt. Unbolt the harness retaining clips from the body then free the harness so the wiring is free to be removed with the engine/transmission unit. Repeat the operation on the right-hand side noting it will be necessary to remove the fusebox cover to gain access to the earth lead retaining bolt **(see illustrations)**.

4.11b . . . then undo the retaining bolt and free the harness from the body

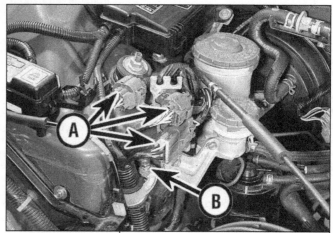
4.11c Disconnect the three engine wiring connectors (A) on the right-hand side of the engine compartment then undo the retaining bolt (B) . . .

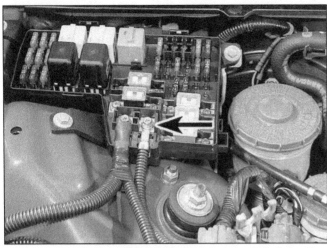

4.11d . . . then remove the fusebox cover and unbolt the earth lead (arrowed)

4.24 Removing the engine/transmission unit from the vehicle

12 Referring to Chapter 10, unbolt the power steering pump and position it clear of the engine unit with its hoses still attached. Undo the retaining bolt and free the power steering hose retaining clip from the side of the inlet manifold.

13 On early models where the speedometer drive is connected into the power steering hydraulic circuit, release the retaining clips and disconnect the hoses from the drive (see Chapter 7). Plug the hose ends and drive unions to minimise fluid loss and prevent the entry of dirt.

14 On models equipped with air conditioning, remove the auxiliary drivebelt (see Chapter 1) then unbolt the compressor, and position it clear of the engine unit. Support the weight of the compressor by tying it to the vehicle body, to prevent any excess strain being placed on the compressor lines whilst the engine is removed. *Do not disconnect the refrigerant lines from the compressor (refer to the warnings given in Chapter 3).*

15 Remove the split pins and washers securing the gearchange cables to the transmission levers (see Chapter 7) then undo the retaining bolts and free the cable mounting bracket from the top of the transmission.

16 Starting at the master cylinder, work along the clutch hydraulic hose/pipe unscrewing all the mounting bracket bolts and free the pipe/hose from all the relevant clips (see Chapter 6). Slacken and remove the slave cylinder retaining bolts and position the pipe/hose and cylinder assembly clear of the transmission unit. Fully retract the pushrod into the slave cylinder and secure it in position with a stout elastic band or cable tie (to prevent the piston being accidentally expelled by spring pressure).
Caution: Whilst the cylinder is removed from the transmission, do not depress the clutch pedal.

17 Referring to Chapter 8, disconnect the driveshaft inner ends from the intermediate shaft and transmission unit. Note that it is not necessary to remove the driveshafts completely, they can be left attached to the hub assemblies and released as the hub is pulled outwards. **Note:** *Do not allow the shafts to hang down under their own weight as this could damage the constant velocity joints/gaiters.*

18 Manoeuvre the engine hoist into position, and attach it to the lifting brackets bolted onto the engine/transmission. Raise the hoist until it is supporting the weight of the engine.

19 Slacken and remove the through-bolt from the rear engine/transmission mounting. Where necessary, also unbolt the support bracket from the right-hand side of the mounting.

20 Unscrew the through-bolt and washer securing the front mounting link to the engine/transmission and recover its special nut from the mounting bracket.

21 Slacken and remove the through-bolt from the left-hand mounting then undo the retaining nut and bolt and remove the mounting assembly.

22 Unscrew the through-bolt then undo the retaining nuts and remove the right-hand mounting assembly from the top of the transmission housing.

23 Make a final check that any components which would prevent the removal of the engine/transmission from the car have been removed or disconnected. Ensure that components such as the driveshafts are secured so that they cannot be damaged on removal.

24 Lift the engine/transmission out of the car, ensuring that nothing is trapped or damaged. Enlist the help of an assistant during this procedure, as it will be necessary to tilt the engine assembly to clear the body panels **(see illustration)**.

25 Once the engine is high enough, lift it out over the front of the body, and lower the unit to the ground.

Separation

26 With the engine/transmission assembly removed, support the assembly on suitable blocks of wood, on a workbench (or, failing that, on a clean area of the workshop floor).

27 Slacken and remove the mounting bolts and remove the intermediate shaft from the rear of the cylinder block (see Chapter 8).

28 Undo the retaining bolts, and remove the flywheel lower cover plate from the transmission.

29 Undo the retaining bolts and remove the starter motor from the transmission (see Chapter 5).

30 Ensure that both engine and transmission are adequately supported, then slacken and remove the remaining bolts securing the transmission housing to the engine. Note the correct fitted positions of each bolt (and the relevant brackets) as they are removed, to use as a reference on refitting.

31 Carefully withdraw the transmission from the engine, ensuring that the weight of the transmission is not allowed to hang on the input shaft while it is engaged with the clutch friction disc.

32 If they are loose, remove the locating dowels from the engine or transmission, and keep them in a safe place.

Refitting

33 If the engine and transmission have been separated, perform the operations described below in paragraphs 34 to 40. If not, proceed as described from paragraph 41 onwards.

34 Ensure the clutch plate and transmission input shaft splines are clean and dry. Apply a smear of high-melting point grease (Rover recommend the use of Urea Grease UM264 - available from your Rover dealer) to the release fork pivot and the contact surfaces of the release fork, bearing and transmission housing. Do not apply too much, otherwise there is a possibility of the grease contaminating the clutch friction plate.

35 Ensure the locating dowels are correctly positioned prior to installation and make sure the clutch release mechanism components are correctly fitted (see Chapter 6).

36 Carefully offer the transmission to the engine, until the locating dowels are engaged. Ensure that the weight of the transmission is not allowed to hang on the input shaft as it is engaged with the clutch friction disc.

37 Refit the transmission housing-to-engine bolts, ensuring that all the necessary brackets are correctly positioned, and tighten them to the specified torque setting.

38 Refit the starter motor and tighten its mounting bolts to the specified torque (see Chapter 5).

39 Refit the flywheel lower cover plate to the transmission, and tighten its retaining bolts to the specified torque.

40 Referring to Chapter 8, refit the intermediate shaft and tighten its mounting bracket bolts to the specified torque. **Note:** *It is recommended that the driveshaft oil seal is renewed before the shaft is refitted (see Chapter 7).*

41 Reconnect the hoist and lifting tackle to the engine lifting brackets. With the aid of an assistant, lift the assembly over the engine compartment.

42 The assembly should be tilted as necessary to clear the surrounding components, as during removal; lower the assembly into position in the engine compartment, manipulating the hoist and lifting tackle as necessary.

43 Lower the engine/transmission assembly into position, aligning it with the front and rear mountings.

44 Refit the right-hand mounting assembly to the transmission unit and insert the through-bolts, tightening both mounting nuts and through-bolt by hand only at this stage.

45 Refit the left-hand mounting assembly and tighten its retaining nut and bolt and through-bolt by hand only.

46 Engage the front mounting link special nut with the bracket slot then refit the through-bolt and washer tightening it lightly only at this stage.

47 Refit the rear mounting through-bolt and tighten by hand. Where necessary refit the support bracket to the side of the mounting.

48 Rock the engine to settle it on its mountings then go around and tighten all the mounting nuts and bolts to their specified torque settings in the following sequence.

1 Left-hand mounting to bracket nut and bolt.
2 Right-hand mounting to transmission nuts.
3 Left-hand mounting through-bolt.
4 Right-hand mounting through-bolt.
5 Rear mounting through-bolt and (where fitted) support bracket nut and bolt.
6 Front mounting through-bolt.

49 Once all mounting nuts and bolts are tightened to the specified torque, detach the hoist from the engine.

50 The remainder of the refitting procedure is a direct reversal of the removal sequence, noting the following points:

a) Ensure that all wiring is correctly routed and retained by all the relevant retaining clips and that all connectors are correctly and securely reconnected.
b) Prior to refitting the right-hand driveshaft to the transmission, renew the driveshaft oil seal as described in Chapter 7.
c) Ensure that all disturbed hoses are correctly reconnected, and securely retained by their retaining clips.
d) Refit the slave cylinder and ensure the hydraulic pipe/hose is securely retained by all the necessary clips. On completion, check the operation of the clutch as described in Chapter 6.
e) Reconnect the gearchange cables to the transmission using new split pins and adjust as described in Chapter 7.
f) Adjust the accelerator cable as described in the Chapter 4.
g) Refill the engine and transmission with correct quantity and type of oil, as described in Chapter 1.
h) Refill the cooling system as described in Chapter 1.
i) On early models where the speedometer drive is connected into the power steering system, on completion bleed the hydraulic system (see Chapter 10).

5 Engine/automatic transmission unit - removal, separation and refitting

Removal

Note: *The engine can be removed from the car only as a complete unit with the transmission; the two are then separated for overhaul.*

1 Carry out the operations described in paragraphs 1 to 14 of Section 4.

2 Make identification marks between the oil cooler hoses and their unions on the front of the transmission housing. Clamp the hoses to minimise fluid loss then slacken the hose clamps and disconnect the hoses from the transmission. Plug the hose and transmission union ends to prevent the entry of dirt into the hydraulic system.

3 Referring to Chapter 7, undo the retaining screws and remove the selector cable retaining plate from the base of the transmission unit. Bend back the locking plate tabs then unscrew the retaining bolt and free the selector lever from the transmission shaft. Discard the locking plate, a new one should be used on refitting, and position the cable clear of the transmission unit.

4 Remove the engine/transmission unit as described in paragraphs 17 to 25 of Section 4, taking care to lose the rubber insulating washers which are fitted to the upper end of the front mounting link.

Separation

5 With the engine/transmission assembly removed, support the assembly on suitable blocks of wood, on a workbench (or failing that, on a clean area of the workshop floor).

6 Slacken and remove the mounting bolts and remove the intermediate shaft from the rear of the cylinder block (see Chapter 8).

7 Undo the retaining bolts and remove the driveplate lower cover plate from the base of the transmission housing.

8 Undo the retaining bolts and remove the starter motor from the transmission (see Chapter 5).

9 Slacken and remove the bolts securing the torque converter to the engine driveplate. The bolts are accessible through the cover plate aperture. Unscrew the visible bolt(s) then, using a socket and extension bar to rotate the crankshaft pulley, undo the remaining bolts securing the torque converter to the driveplate as they become accessible. There are eight bolts in total.

10 Ensure that both the engine and transmission are adequately supported, then slacken and remove the remaining bolts securing the transmission housing to the engine. Note the correct fitted positions of each bolt (and any relevant brackets) as they are removed, to use as a reference on refitting.

11 With the bolts removed, make the torque converter is pushed fully onto the transmission unit shaft, then carefully withdraw the transmission from the engine. If the locating dowels are a loose fit in the engine/transmission, remove them and keep them in a safe place. Secure the torque converter in position by bolting a length of metal bar to one of the housing holes.

Refitting

12 If the engine and transmission have been separated, perform the operations described below in paragraphs 13 to 20. If not, proceed as described from paragraph 21 onwards.

13 Ensure that the locating dowels are correctly positioned in the engine or transmission.

14 Remove the retaining strap (where fitted) and make sure the torque converter is pushed fully into position.

15 Carefully offer the transmission to the engine, aligning the torque converter with the driveplate holes, until the locating dowels are correctly engaged.

16 Refit the transmission housing-to-engine bolts, ensuring that all the necessary brackets are correctly positioned, and tighten them to the specified torque setting.

17 Refit the torque converter retaining bolts and tighten them to the specified torque (see Chapter 7).

18 Refit the driveplate lower cover plate and tighten its retaining bolts to the specified torque.

19 Refit the starter motor and tighten its mounting bolts to the specified torque setting (see Chapter 5).

20 Referring to Chapter 8, refit the intermediate shaft and tighten its mounting bracket bolts to the specified torque. **Note:** *It is recommended that the driveshaft oil seal is renewed before the shaft is refitted (see Chapter 7).*

21 Reconnect the hoist and lifting tackle to the engine lifting brackets. With the aid of an assistant, lift the assembly over the engine compartment.

22 The assembly should be tilted as necessary to clear the surrounding components, as during removal; lower the assembly into position in the engine compartment, manipulating the hoist and lifting tackle as necessary.

23 Ensure the rubber insulating washers are correctly fitted to the upper end of the front mounting link then lower the engine/transmission assembly into position, aligning it with the front and rear mountings.

24 Refit the right-hand mounting assembly to the transmission unit and insert the through-bolts, tightening both mounting nuts and through-bolt by hand only at this stage.

25 Refit the left-hand mounting assembly and tighten its retaining nut and bolt and through-bolt by hand only.

26 Engage the front mounting link special nut with the bracket slot then refit the through-bolt and washer tightening it lightly only at this stage.

27 Refit the rear mounting through-bolt and tighten by hand. Where necessary refit the support bracket to the side of the mounting.

28 Rock the engine to settle it on its mountings then go around and tighten all the mounting nuts and bolts to their specified torque settings in the following sequence.

1 *Left-hand mounting to bracket nut and bolt.*
2 *Right-hand mounting to transmission nuts.*
3 *Left-hand mounting through-bolt.*
4 *Right-hand mounting through-bolt.*
5 *Rear mounting through-bolt and (where fitted) support bracket nut and bolt.*
6 *Front mounting through-bolt.*

29 Once all mounting nuts and bolts are tightened to the specified torque, detach the hoist from the engine.

30 The remainder of the refitting procedure is a direct reversal of the removal sequence, noting the following points:

a) *Ensure that all wiring is correctly routed and retained by all the relevant retaining clips and that all connectors are correctly and securely reconnected.*
b) *Prior to refitting the right-hand driveshaft to the transmission, renew the driveshaft oil seal as described in Chapter 7.*
c) *Ensure that all disturbed hoses are correctly reconnected, and securely retained by their retaining clips.*
d) *Reconnect and adjust the selector cable as described in Chapter 7.*
e) *Adjust the accelerator cable (Chapter 4) then adjust the kickdown cable (Chapter 7).*

f) *Refill the engine and transmission with correct quantity and type of oil, and refill the cooling system as described in Chapter 1.*
g) *On early models where the speedometer drive is connected into the power steering system, on completion bleed the hydraulic system as described in Chapter 10.*

6 Engine overhaul - dismantling sequence

1 It is much easier to dismantle and work on the engine if it is mounted on a portable engine stand. These stands can often be hired from a tool hire shop. Before the engine is mounted on a stand, the flywheel/driveplate should be removed, so that the stand bolts can be tightened into the end of the cylinder block.

2 If a stand is not available, it is possible to dismantle the engine with it blocked up on a sturdy workbench, or on the floor. Be extra-careful not to tip or drop the engine when working without a stand.

3 If you are going to obtain a reconditioned engine, all the external components must be removed first, to be transferred to the replacement engine (just as they will if you are doing a complete engine overhaul yourself). These components include the following:

a) *Inlet and exhaust manifolds (Chapter 4).*
b) *Alternator/power steering pump/air conditioning compressor bracket(s) (as applicable).*
c) *Coolant pump (Chapter 3).*
d) *Fuel system components (Chapter 4).*
e) *Wiring harness and all electrical switches and sensors.*
f) *Oil filter (Chapter 1).*
g) *Flywheel/driveplate (Part A of this Chapter).*

Note: *When removing the external components from the engine, pay close attention to details that may be helpful or important during refitting. Note the fitted position of gaskets, seals, spacers, pins, washers, bolts, and other small items.*

4 If you are obtaining a short engine (which consists of the engine cylinder block,

crankshaft, pistons and connecting rods all assembled), then the cylinder head, sump, oil pump, and timing belt will have to be removed also.

5 If you are planning a complete overhaul, the engine can be dismantled, and the internal components removed, in the order given below, referring to Part A of this Chapter unless otherwise stated.

a) *Inlet and exhaust manifolds (Chapter 4).*
b) *Balance shaft belt, timing belt, sprockets and tensioner.*
c) *Cylinder head.*
d) *Flywheel/driveplate.*
e) *Sump.*
f) *Oil pump.*
g) *Balance shafts.*
h) *Piston/connecting rod assemblies.*
i) *Crankshaft.*

6 Before beginning the dismantling and overhaul procedures, make sure that you have all of the correct tools necessary. Refer to the *Tools and working facilities* Section of this manual for further information.

7 Cylinder head - dismantling

Note: *New and reconditioned cylinder heads are available from the manufacturer, and from engine overhaul specialists. Be aware that some specialist tools are required for the dismantling and inspection procedures, and new components may not be readily available. It may therefore be more practical and economical for the home mechanic to purchase a reconditioned head, rather than dismantle, inspect and recondition the original head.*

1 Remove the camshaft(s) and rocker arms as described in Part A of this Chapter.

2 Remove the cylinder head as described in Part A of this Chapter.

3 Using a valve spring compressor, compress each valve spring in turn until the split collets can be removed. Release the compressor, and lift off the spring retainer and spring. Using a pair of pliers, carefully extract the valve stem seal from the top of the guide then slide off the spring seat **(see illustration)**.

7.3 Using suitable pliers, pull off the seal from the top of the valve guide

7.6 Use a labelled plastic bag to keep together and identify valve components

4 If, when the valve spring compressor is screwed down, the spring retainer refuses to free and expose the split collets, gently tap the top of the tool, directly over the retainer, with a light hammer. This will free the retainer.

5 Withdraw the valve through the combustion chamber.

6 It is essential that each valve is stored together with its collets, retainer, spring, and spring seat. The valves should also be kept in their correct sequence, unless they are so badly worn that they are to be renewed. If they are going to be kept and used again, place each valve assembly in a labelled polythene bag or similar small container **(see illustration)**.

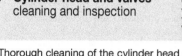

8 Cylinder head and valves - cleaning and inspection

1 Thorough cleaning of the cylinder head and valve components, followed by a detailed inspection, will enable you to decide how much valve service work must be carried out during the engine overhaul. **Note:** *If the engine has been severely overheated, it is best to assume that the cylinder head is warped - check carefully for signs of this.*

Cleaning

2 Scrape away all traces of old gasket material from the cylinder head.

3 Scrape away the carbon from the combustion chambers and ports, then wash the cylinder head thoroughly with paraffin or a suitable solvent.

4 Scrape off any heavy carbon deposits that may have formed on the valves, then use a power-operated wire brush to remove deposits from the valve heads and stems.

Inspection

Note: *Be sure to perform all the following inspection procedures before concluding that the services of a machine shop or engine overhaul specialist are required. Make a list of all items that require attention.*

Cylinder head

5 Inspect the head very carefully for cracks, evidence of coolant leakage, and other damage. If cracks are found, a new cylinder head should be obtained.

6 Use a straight-edge and feeler gauge blade to check that the cylinder head surface is not distorted **(see illustration)**. If it is, it may be possible to resurface it, provided that the cylinder head is not reduced to less than the minimum specified height.

7 Examine the valve seats in each of the combustion chambers. If they are severely pitted, cracked or burned, then they will need to be renewed or recut by an engine overhaul specialist. If they are only slightly pitted, this can be removed by grinding-in the valve heads and seats with fine valve-grinding

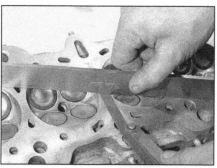

8.6 Measuring cylinder head gasket surface warpage

compound, as described below. To check whether they are excessively worn, refit the valve and measure the installed height of its stem tip above the cylinder head upper surface; if the measurement is above the specified limit, repeat the test using a new valve **(see illustration)**. If the measurement is still excessive, the valve seat is excessively worn, and the cylinder head must be renewed.

8 If the valve guides are worn (indicated by a side-to-side motion of the valve, and accompanied by excessive blue smoke in the exhaust when running) new guides must be fitted. Measure the diameter of the existing valve stems (see below) and the bore of the guides, then calculate the clearance and compare the result with the specified value. An alternative method is to measure the amount of side play there is with the valve installed in its guide using a dial gauge. To do this, refit the valve to its original position in the cylinder head, and hold it approximately 10 mm above the cylinder head surface. Position the dial gauge on the edge of the valve head, and measure the side play while moving valve to and fro **(see illustration)**. If either method shows valve stem/guide wear to be excessive, renew the valves or guides as necessary.

9 The renewal of valve guides is best carried out by an engine overhaul specialist. If the work is to be carried out at home, however, use a stepped, double-diameter drift to drive out the worn guide towards the combustion chamber. On fitting the new guide, place it first in a deep-freeze for one hour, then drive it into its cylinder head bore from the camshaft

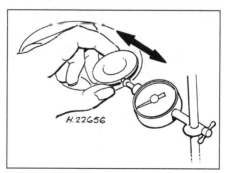

8.8 Checking valve guide wear using a dial gauge

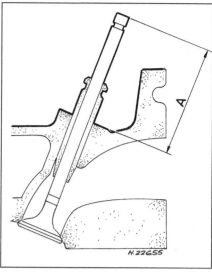

8.7 Check valve seat wear by measuring valve stem installed height (A)

side until it projects the specified amount above the cylinder head surface.

10 If the valve seats are to be re-cut this must be done only after the guides have been renewed.

Valves

11 Examine the head of each valve for pitting, burning, cracks and general wear, and check the valve stem for scoring and wear ridges. Rotate the valve, and check for any obvious indication that it is bent. Look for pitting and excessive wear on the tip of each valve stem. Renew any valve that shows any such signs of wear or damage.

12 If the valve appears satisfactory at this stage, measure the dimensions of the valve as shown, using a micrometer and vernier calipers, noting that the valve stem diameter should be measured at several points along its length **(see illustration)**. If any of the measurements obtained exceed the specified service limit, or are significantly different to the measurements for a new valve, the valve(s) must be renewed.

13 If the valves are in satisfactory condition, they should be ground (lapped) into their respective seats, to ensure a smooth gas-tight seal. If the seat is only lightly pitted, or if

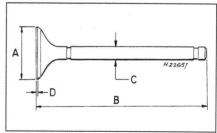

8.12 Valve measurement points

A Head diameter	C Stem diameter
B Length	D Head thickness

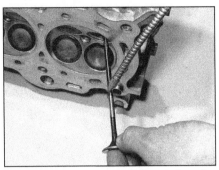

9.1 Lubricate the stem and insert the valve into the correct guide

9.2a Fit the spring seat over the valve guide

9.2b Note that inlet and exhaust valve stem oil seals are not interchangeable. The inlet valve seals are fitted with a white spring (A) and the exhaust valve seals a black spring (B)

it has been re-cut, fine grinding compound **only** should be used to produce the required finish. Coarse valve-grinding compound should **not** be used unless a seat is badly burned or deeply pitted; if this is the case, the cylinder head and valves should be inspected by an expert to decide whether seat re-cutting, or even the renewal of the valve or seat insert, is required.

14 Valve grinding is carried out as follows. Place the cylinder head upside-down on a bench.

15 Smear a trace of the appropriate grade of valve-grinding compound on the seat face, and press a suction grinding tool onto the valve head. With a semi-rotary action, grind the valve head to its seat, lifting the valve occasionally to redistribute the grinding compound. A light spring placed under the valve head will greatly ease this operation.

16 If coarse grinding compound is being used, work only until a dull, matt even surface is produced on both the valve seat and the valve, then wipe off the used compound and repeat the process with fine compound. When a smooth unbroken ring of light grey matt finish is produced on both the valve and seat, the grinding operation is complete. **Do not** grind in the valves any further than absolutely necessary, or the seat will be prematurely sunk into the cylinder head.

17 To check that the seat has not been over-ground, measure the valve stem installed height, as described in paragraph 7 above.

18 When all the valves have been ground-in,

carefully wash off all traces of grinding compound using paraffin or a suitable solvent before reassembly of the cylinder head.

Valve components

19 Examine the valve springs for signs of damage and discoloration; if possible; also compare the existing spring free length with new components.

20 Stand each spring on a flat surface, and check it for squareness. If any of the springs are damaged, distorted or have lost their tension, obtain a complete new set of springs.

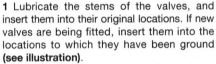

9 Cylinder head - reassembly

1 Lubricate the stems of the valves, and insert them into their original locations. If new valves are being fitted, insert them into the locations to which they have been ground **(see illustration)**.

2 Working on the first valve, refit the lower spring seat. Dip the correct valve stem seal in fresh engine oil, then carefully locate it over the valve and onto the guide. **Note:** *The inlet and exhaust valve stem oil seals are different (not interchangeable); the inlet valve seals are fitted with a white spring and the exhaust valve seals are fitted with a black spring.* Take care not to damage the seal as it is passed over the valve stem. Use a suitable socket or metal tube to press the seal firmly onto the guide **(see illustrations)**.

3 Locate the spring on the seat, ensuring its closest-wound coils are at the bottom, and fit the spring retainer **(see illustration)**.

4 Compress the valve spring, and locate the split collets in the recess in the valve stem **(see illustration)**. Release the compressor, then repeat the procedure on the remaining valves.

 HAYNES HINT *Use a little dab of grease to hold the collets in position on the valve stem while the spring compressor is released.*

5 With all the valves installed, place the cylinder head flat on the bench and, using a hammer and interposed block of wood, tap the end of each valve stem to settle the components.

6 Refit the cylinder head as described in Part A of this Chapter and install the camshaft(s) and rocker arms.

10 Balance shafts - removal, inspection and refitting

Removal

1 Remove the sump as described in Part A of this Chapter.

9.2c Press the valve stem seal onto the guide using a socket

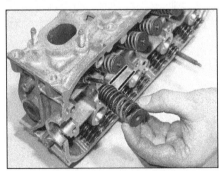

9.3 Refit the valve spring, ensuring its closest-wound coils are at the bottom, and spring retainer . . .

9.4 . . . then compress the spring and refit the collets, using grease to hold them in position

10.2a To check balance shaft endfloat, remove the crankshaft rear oil seal housing . . .

10.2b . . . then check the endfloat using a dial gauge in contact with the rear end of the shaft

10.4 Removing the rear balance shaft

2 To check the balance shaft endfloat, remove the flywheel/driveplate then unbolt the rear oil seal housing from the end of the cylinder block (see Part A). Position a dial gauge in contact with the end of one of the balance shafts. Push the shaft fully one way, and then zero the gauge. Pull the shaft fully the other way, and check the endfloat **(see illustrations)**. Repeat the procedure on the other shaft. Compare the results with those given in the Specifications. If the front balance shaft endfloat is excessive, renew the thrust plate; if the rear balance shaft endfloat is excessive then it is likely that the thrust surfaces of the oil pump/sprocket housing are worn and will require renewal. **Note:** *It is not necessary to remove the flywheel/driveplate and oil seal housing if it is not wished to check the endfloat.*

3 Remove the oil pump housing as described in Part A of this Chapter.

4 The rear balance shaft can then be slid out from the cylinder block, once its locking pin has been removed **(see illustration)**.

5 To remove the front balance shaft, undo the two retaining bolts securing the thrust plate in position then slide the thrust plate and balance shaft out from the cylinder block **(see illustration)**.

Inspection

6 Examine the balance shaft bearing surfaces for signs of wear ridges and scoring. Using a micrometer, measure the outside diameter of each journal at each edge (number 1 journal is at the timing belt end of each shaft) **(see illustration)**.

7 Support the balance end journals on V-blocks, and measure the run-out at the centre journal using a dial gauge. If the run-out exceeds the specified limit, the camshaft should be renewed.

8 If the balance shaft is bent or if any journal is tapered or worn to beyond the specified minimum then the shaft must be renewed.

9 Inspect the balance shaft bearing surfaces in the cylinder block. If the necessary measuring equipment is available, measure the internal diameter of each bearing. Subtract the balance shaft journal outside diameter from the bearing inside diameter, and calculate the bearing running clearance. If any of the measurements exceed the wear limits given in the Specifications, the bearings must be renewed. Renewal of the bearings is a complex task requiring the use of several special tools and, for this reason, should be entrusted to a Rover dealer or other suitably-equipped engineering works.

10 If the endfloat of either shaft was found to exceed the specified limits (see paragraph 2), carefully examine the thrust plate (front shaft) or the oil pump and sprocket housing thrust faces (rear shaft) and renew any components which show signs of wear or damage.

Refitting

11 Lubricate the balance shaft bearings with clean engine oil and slide the shafts into position in the cylinder block. Engage the thrustplate with the groove in the front balance shaft then refit the retaining bolts, tightening them to the specified torque **(see illustrations)**.

12 Refit the oil pump housing to the cylinder block as described in Part A of this Chapter.

13 If the endfloat was checked prior to removal, renew the crankshaft oil seal then refit the oil seal housing and flywheel/ driveplate as described in Part A of this Chapter.

14 Refit the sump as described in Part A.

10.5 Unbolt the thrust plate and slide the front balance shaft out of the cylinder block

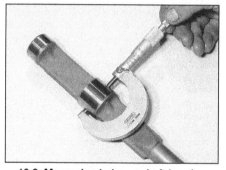

10.6 Measuring balance shaft bearing journal diameter

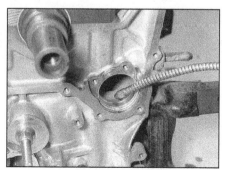

10.11a Lubricate the bearings with clean engine oil . . .

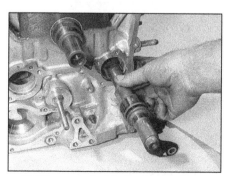

10.11b . . . and slide the front balance shaft into position

10.11c Engage the thrust plate with the shaft groove and tighten its retaining bolts to the specified torque

11.4 Always mark big-end caps and connecting rods prior to removal (see text)

11 Piston/connecting rod assembly - removal

Note: *Access to the connecting rod big-end bearing cap nuts (number 4 cylinder in particular) is restricted with the main bearing cap bridge casting in position, to improve access, remove the casting as described in Section 12.*

1 Working as described in Part A of this Chapter, remove the cylinder head and sump then unbolt the pick-up/strainer from the base of the oil pump. On models where a baffle plate is fitted to the base of the main bearing cap casting, unbolt and remove the plate.

2 If there is a pronounced wear ridge at the top of any bore, it may be necessary to remove it, with a scraper or ridge reamer, to avoid piston damage during removal. Such a ridge indicates excessive wear of the cylinder bore.

3 Prior to removal, using feeler blades, measuring the connecting rod big-end side clearance of each rod. If any rod exceeds the specified clearance, it must be renewed.

4 Using a hammer and centre-punch, paint or similar, mark each connecting rod and its bearing cap with its respective cylinder number on the flat machined surface provided; if the engine has been dismantled before, note carefully any identifying marks made previously **(see illustration)**. Note that No 1 cylinder is at the timing belt end of the engine.

5 Turn the crankshaft to bring pistons 1 and 4 to BDC (bottom dead centre). If the main bearing cap casting is still fitted, position the crankshaft so that access to the connecting rod nuts can be gained through the casting apertures.

6 Unscrew the nuts from No 1 piston big-end bearing cap. Take off the cap and recover the bottom half bearing shell. If the bearing shells are to be re-used, tape the cap and the shell together.

7 Using a hammer handle, push the piston up through the bore, and remove it from the top of the cylinder block. Recover the bearing shell, and tape it to the connecting rod for safe-keeping.

8 Loosely refit the big-end cap to the connecting rod, and secure with the nuts - this will help to keep the components in their correct order.

9 Remove No 4 piston assembly in the same way.

10 Turn the crankshaft through 180° to bring pistons 2 and 3 to BDC (bottom dead centre), and remove them in the same way.

12 Crankshaft - removal

1 Remove the oil pump and the flywheel/driveplate as described in Part A of this Chapter. If the piston and connecting rod assemblies are also to be removed, remove the cylinder head.

2 Check the crankshaft endfloat as described in Section 15, then proceed as follows.

3 Remove the piston and connecting rod assemblies as described in Section 10. If no work is to be done on the pistons and connecting rods, unbolt the caps and push the pistons far enough up the bores that the connecting rods are positioned clear of the crankshaft journals.

4 Slacken and remove the retaining bolts securing the crankshaft rear oil seal housing to the cylinder block and remove the housing from the crankshaft. If the cover locating dowels are a loose fit, remove and store them with the cover for safe-keeping.

5 Working in the **reverse** of the tightening sequence **(see illustration 19.23b)**, evenly and progressively slacken the ten main bearing cap retaining bolts by half a turn at a time **(see illustration)**. Remove the bolts along with their washers.

6 Carefully free the main bearing cap bridge from the caps, and remove it from the engine, noting the fitted positions of its locating dowels **(see illustration)**. Remove the O-ring from the centre of the bridge, and discard it; the O-ring **must** be renewed whenever it is disturbed.

7 The main bearing caps should be numbered 1 to 5 from the timing belt end of the engine and have an arrow stamped on them indicating their correct fitted direction. If not, mark them accordingly using a centre-punch or paint in the same way as the connecting rods.

8 Carefully remove each cap from the cylinder block, ensuring that the lower main bearing shell remains in position in the cap. Note the fitted positions of the cap locating dowels; remove any that are loose, and store them with the relevant cap for safe keeping **(see illustration)**.

9 Carefully lift out the crankshaft, taking care not to displace the upper main bearing shells, and remove the thrustwasher halves from the sides of number 4 main bearing.

10 Recover the upper bearing shells from the cylinder block, and tape them to their respective caps for safe-keeping.

13 Cylinder block - cleaning and inspection

Cleaning

1 Remove all external components and electrical switches/sensors from the block. For complete cleaning, the core plugs should ideally be removed. Drill a small hole in the plugs, then insert a self-tapping screw into the hole. Pull out the plugs by pulling on the screw with a pair of grips, or by using a slide hammer.

12.5 Evenly and progressively slacken the main bearing cap bolts in the reverse of the tightening sequence

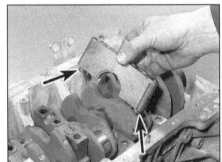

12.6 Lift off the main bearing cap bridge . . .

12.8 . . . and remove the bearing caps (locating dowels arrowed)

13.11 Cylinder bore diameter size group markings (arrowed)

2 Scrape all traces of gasket from the cylinder block, and from the main bearing casting (where fitted), taking care not to damage the gasket/sealing surfaces.

3 Remove all oil gallery plugs (where fitted). The plugs are usually very tight - they may have to be drilled out, and the holes re-tapped. Use new plugs when the engine is reassembled.

4 If any of the castings are extremely dirty, all should be steam-cleaned.

5 After the castings are returned, clean all oil holes and oil galleries one more time. Flush all internal passages with warm water until the water runs clear. Dry thoroughly, and apply a light film of oil to all mating surfaces to prevent rusting. Also oil the cylinder bores. If you have access to compressed air, use it to speed up the drying process, and to blow out all the oil holes and galleries.

 Warning: Wear eye protection when using compressed air!

6 If the castings are not very dirty, you can do an adequate cleaning job with hot (as hot as you can stand!), soapy water and a stiff brush. Take plenty of time, and do a thorough job. Regardless of the cleaning method used, be sure to clean all oil holes and galleries very thoroughly, and to dry all components well. Protect the cylinder bores as described above, to prevent rusting.

7 All threaded holes must be clean, to ensure accurate torque readings during reassembly. To clean the threads, run the correct-size tap into each of the holes to remove rust, corrosion, thread sealant or sludge, and to restore damaged threads. If possible, use compressed air to clear the holes of debris produced by this operation.

8 Apply suitable sealant to the new oil gallery plugs, and insert them into the holes in the block. Tighten them securely.

9 If the engine is not going to be reassembled right away, cover it with a large plastic bag to keep it clean; protect all mating surfaces and the cylinder bores as described above, to prevent rusting.

Inspection

10 Visually check the castings for cracks and corrosion. Look for stripped threads in the threaded holes. If there has been any history of internal water leakage, it may be worthwhile having an engine overhaul specialist check the cylinder block/crankcase with special equipment. If defects are found, have them repaired if possible, or renew the assembly.

11 Check the bore of each cylinder liner for scuffing and scoring. Note that there are two different size groups of standard bore diameter to allow for manufacturing tolerances; size group A and B. The relevant size group of each bore is stamped on the front, right-hand end of the cylinder block top surface; the first letter in the sequence is number 1 (timing belt end) cylinder and the last letter number 4 (flywheel/driveplate end) cylinder (see illustration). Note: *On some engines the letters on the cylinder block may be replaced with symbols; I in place of A and iI in place of B.*

12 Measure the diameter of each cylinder bore at the top (just below the wear ridge), centre and bottom of the bore, both parallel to the crankshaft axis and at right angles to it, so that a total of six measurements are taken.

13 Compare the results with the Specifications at the beginning of this Chapter; if any measurement exceeds the service limit specified, the cylinder block must be rebored if possible, or renewed and new piston assemblies fitted.

14 If the cylinder bores are badly scuffed or scored, or if they are excessively worn, out-of-round or tapered, or if the piston-to-bore clearances is excessive (see Section 14), the cylinder block must be rebored (if possible) or renewed and new pistons fitted. Two sizes of oversize pistons are available oversize for 1.8 and 2.0 litre engines (0.25 mm and 0.5 mm) and one size for 2.3 litre engines (0.25 mm).

15 If the bores are in reasonably good condition and not worn to the specified limits, then the piston rings should be renewed. If this is the case, the bores should be honed to allow the new rings to bed in correctly and provide the best possible seal. The conventional type of hone has spring-loaded stones, and is used with a power drill. You will also need some paraffin (or honing oil) and rags. The hone should be moved up and down the bore to produce a crosshatch pattern, and plenty of honing oil should be used. Ideally, the crosshatch lines should intersect at approximately a 60° angle. Do not take off more material than is necessary to produce the required finish. If new pistons are being fitted, the piston manufacturers may specify a finish with a different angle, so their instructions should be followed. Do not withdraw the hone from the bore while it is still being turned – stop it first. After honing a bore, wipe out all traces of the honing oil. If equipment of this type is not available, or if you are not sure whether you are competent to undertake the task yourself, an engine overhaul specialist will carry out the work at moderate cost.

14 Piston/connecting rod assembly - inspection

1 Before the inspection process can begin, the piston/connecting rod assemblies must be cleaned, and the original piston rings removed from the pistons.

2 Carefully expand the old rings over the top of the pistons. The use of two or three old feeler blades will be helpful in preventing the rings dropping into empty grooves (see illustration). Be careful not to scratch the piston with the ends of the ring. The rings are brittle, and will snap if they are spread too far. Note that the third (oil control) ring consists of a spacer and two side rails. Always remove the rings from the top of the piston. Keep each set of rings with its piston if the old rings are to be re-used.

3 Scrape away all traces of carbon from the top of the piston. A hand-held wire brush (or a piece of fine emery cloth) can be used, once the majority of the deposits have been scraped away. The piston identification markings should now be visible.

4 Remove the carbon from the ring grooves in the piston, using an old ring. Break the ring in half to do this (be careful not to cut your fingers - piston rings are sharp). Be careful to remove only the carbon deposits - do not remove any metal, and do not nick or scratch the sides of the ring grooves.

5 Once the deposits have been removed, clean the piston/connecting rod assembly with paraffin or a suitable solvent, and dry thoroughly. Make sure that the oil return holes in the ring grooves are clear.

6 If the cylinder bores are not damaged or worn excessively, and if the cylinder block does not need to be rebored (see Section 13), check the pistons as follows.

7 Carefully inspect each piston for cracks around the skirt, around the gudgeon pin holes, and at the piston ring lands (between the ring grooves).

8 Look for scoring and scuffing on the piston skirt, holes in the piston crown, and burned areas at the edge of the crown. If the skirt is scored or scuffed, the engine may have been suffering from overheating, and/or abnormal

14.2 Using a feeler blade to remove a piston ring

15.2 Measuring crankshaft endfloat using a dial gauge

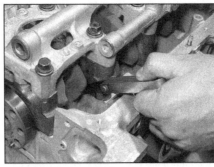

15.3 Measuring crankshaft endfloat using a feeler gauge

15.10 Measuring crankshaft main bearing diameter with a micrometer

combustion which caused excessively high operating temperatures. The cooling and lubrication systems should be checked thoroughly. Scorch marks on the sides of the pistons show that blow-by has occurred. A hole in the piston crown, or burned areas at the edge of the piston crown, indicates that abnormal combustion (pre-ignition, knocking, or detonation) has been occurring. If any of the above problems exist, the causes must be investigated and corrected, or the damage will occur again. The causes may include incorrect ignition timing, or a faulty injector.

9 Corrosion of the piston, in the form of pitting, indicates that coolant has been leaking into the combustion chamber and/or the crankcase. Again, the cause must be corrected, or the problem may persist in the rebuilt engine.

10 Measure the piston diameter at right angles to the gudgeon pin axis, 21 mm up from the bottom of the skirt; compare the results with the Specifications at the beginning of this Chapter.

11 To measure the piston-to-bore clearance, either measure the bore (see Section 13) and piston skirt as described and subtract the skirt diameter from the bore measurement, or insert each piston into its original bore, then select a feeler gauge blade and slip it into the bore along with the piston. The piston must be aligned exactly in its normal attitude, and the feeler gauge blade must be between the piston and bore, on one of the thrust faces, approximately 20 mm up from the bottom of the bore. If the clearance is excessive, a new piston will be required. If the piston binds at the lower end of the bore and is loose towards the top, the bore is tapered. If tight spots are encountered as the piston/feeler gauge blade is rotated in the bore, the bore is out-of-round.

12 Repeat this procedure for the remaining pistons and cylinder bores. Any piston which is worn beyond the specified limits must be renewed.

13 Examine each connecting rod carefully for signs of damage, such as cracks around the big-end and small-end bearings. Check that the rod is not bent or distorted. Damage is highly unlikely, unless the engine has been seized or badly overheated. Detailed checking of the connecting rod assembly can only be carried out by a Rover dealer or engine repair specialist with the necessary equipment.

14 The gudgeon pins are an interference fit in the connecting rod small-end bearing. Therefore, piston and/or connecting rod renewal should be entrusted to a Rover dealer or engine repair specialist, who will have the necessary tooling to remove and install the gudgeon pins. If new pistons are to be fitted, ensure that the correct size pistons are fitted to each bore (see Section 13); size group A standard pistons have no marking on the piston crown whereas size group B pistons have the letter B stamped on their crowns.

15 Crankshaft - inspection

Checking crankshaft endfloat

1 If the crankshaft endfloat is to be checked, this must be done when the crankshaft is still installed in the cylinder block, but is free to move (see Section 12).

2 Check the endfloat using a dial gauge in contact with the end of the crankshaft. Push the crankshaft fully one way, and then zero the gauge. Push the crankshaft fully the other way, and check the endfloat **(see illustration)**. The result can be compared with the specified amount, and will give an indication as to whether new main bearing shells are required.

3 If a dial gauge is not available, feeler gauges can be used. First push the crankshaft fully towards the flywheel/driveplate end of the engine, then use feeler gauges to measure the gap between the web of the crankpin and the side of number 4 bearing shell **(see illustration)**.

Inspection

4 Clean the crankshaft using paraffin or a suitable solvent, and dry it, preferably with compressed air if available. Be sure to clean the oil holes with a pipe cleaner or similar probe, to ensure that they are not obstructed.

 Warning: Wear eye protection when using compressed air.

5 Check the main and big-end bearing journals for uneven wear, scoring, pitting and cracking.

6 Big-end bearing wear is accompanied by distinct metallic knocking when the engine is running (particularly noticeable when the engine is pulling from low speed) and some loss of oil pressure.

7 Main bearing wear is accompanied by severe engine vibration and rumble - getting progressively worse as engine speed increases - and again by loss of oil pressure.

8 Check the bearing journal for roughness by running a finger lightly over the bearing surface. Any roughness (which will be accompanied by obvious bearing wear) indicates that the crankshaft requires regrinding (where possible) or renewal.

9 Check for burrs around the crankshaft oil holes (the holes are usually chamfered, so burrs should not be a problem unless regrinding has been carried out carelessly). Remove any burrs with a fine file or scraper, and thoroughly clean the oil holes as described previously.

10 Using a micrometer, measure the diameter of the main and big-end bearing journals, and compare the results with the Specifications **(see illustration)**. By measuring the diameter at a number of points around each journals circumference, you will be able to determine whether or not the journal is out-of-round. Take the measurement at each end of the journal, near the webs, to determine if the journal is tapered. Compare the results obtained with those given in the Specifications.

11 Check the oil seal contact surfaces at each end of the crankshaft for wear and damage. If the seal has worn a deep groove in the surface of the crankshaft, consult an engine overhaul specialist; repair may be possible, but otherwise a new crankshaft will be required.

12 Set the crankshaft up in V-blocks, and position a dial gauge on the top of the crankshaft number 1 main bearing journal. Zero the dial gauge, then slowly rotate the crankshaft through two complete revolutions, noting the journal run-out. Repeat the procedure on the remaining four main bearing journals, so that a run-out measurement is available for all main bearing journals. If the difference between the run-out of any two journals exceeds the service limit given in the Specifications, the crankshaft must be renewed.

13 At the time of writing, no oversize shells are produced by Rover and, if the crankshaft has worn beyond the specified limits, it will have to be renewed. Seek the advice of a Rover dealer or engine overhaul specialist for further information.

16 Main and big-end bearings - inspection

1 Even though the main and big-end bearings should be renewed during the engine overhaul, the old bearings should be retained for close examination, as they may reveal valuable information about the condition of the engine.

2 Bearing failure can occur due to lack of lubrication, the presence of dirt or other foreign particles, overloading the engine, or corrosion **(see illustration)**. Regardless of the cause of bearing failure, the cause must be corrected (where applicable) before the engine is reassembled, to prevent it from happening again.

3 When examining the bearing shells, remove them from the cylinder block, the main bearing caps, the connecting rods and the connecting rod big-end bearing caps. Lay them out on a clean surface in the same general position as their location in the engine. This will enable you to match any bearing problems with the corresponding crankshaft journal.

4 Dirt and other foreign matter gets into the engine in a variety of ways. It may be left in the engine during assembly, or it may pass through filters or the crankcase ventilation system. It may get into the oil, and from there into the bearings. Metal chips from machining operations and normal engine wear are often present. Abrasives are sometimes left in engine components after reconditioning, especially when parts are not thoroughly cleaned using the proper cleaning methods. Whatever the source, these foreign objects often end up embedded in the soft bearing material, and are easily recognized. Large particles will not embed in the bearing, and will score or gouge the bearing and journal. The best prevention for this cause of bearing failure is to clean all parts thoroughly, and keep everything spotlessly-clean during engine assembly. Frequent and regular engine oil and filter changes are also recommended.

5 Lack of lubrication (or lubrication breakdown) has a number of interrelated causes. Excessive heat (which thins the oil), overloading (which squeezes the oil from the bearing face) and oil leakage (from excessive bearing clearances, worn oil pump or high engine speeds) all contribute to lubrication

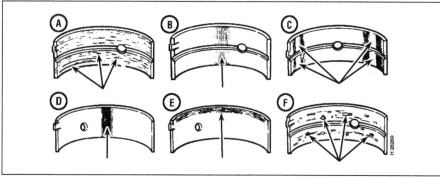

16.2 Typical bearing failures

A *Scratched by dirt; dirt embedded in bearing material*
B *Lack of oil; overlay wiped out*
C *Improper seating; bright (polished) sections*
D *Tapered journal; overlay gone from entire surface*
E *Radius ride*
F *Fatigue failure; craters or pockets*

breakdown. Blocked oil passages, which usually are the result of misaligned oil holes in a bearing shell, will also oil-starve a bearing, and destroy it. When lack of lubrication is the cause of bearing failure, the bearing material is wiped or extruded from the steel backing of the bearing. Temperatures may increase to the point where the steel backing turns blue from overheating.

6 Driving habits can have a definite effect on bearing life. Full-throttle, low-speed operation (labouring the engine) puts very high loads on bearings, tending to squeeze out the oil film. These loads cause the bearings to flex, which produces fine cracks in the bearing face (fatigue failure). Eventually, the bearing material will loosen in pieces, and tear away from the steel backing.

7 Short-distance driving leads to corrosion of bearings, because insufficient engine heat is produced to drive off the condensed water and corrosive gases. These products collect in the engine oil, forming acid and sludge. As the oil is carried to the engine bearings, the acid attacks and corrodes the bearing material.

8 Incorrect bearing installation during engine assembly will lead to bearing failure as well. Tight-fitting bearings leave insufficient bearing running clearance, and will result in oil starvation. Dirt or foreign particles trapped behind a bearing shell result in high spots on the bearing, which lead to failure.

9 As mentioned at the beginning of this Section, the bearing shells should be renewed as a matter of course during engine overhaul; to do otherwise is false economy.

17 Engine overhaul - reassembly sequence

1 Before reassembly begins, ensure that all new parts have been obtained, and that all necessary tools are available. Read through the entire procedure to familiarise yourself with the work involved, and to ensure that all items necessary for reassembly of the engine are at hand. In addition to all normal tools and materials, thread-locking compound will be needed. A good quality tube of liquid sealant will also be required for the joint faces that are fitted without gaskets.

2 In order to save time and avoid problems, engine reassembly can be carried out in the following order:
  a) *Crankshaft.*
  b) *Piston/connecting rod assemblies.*
  c) *Oil pump.*
  d) *Sump.*
  e) *Flywheel/driveplate.*
  f) *Cylinder head.*
  g) *Balance shaft/timing belt tensioner and sprockets, and belts.*
  h) *Engine external components.*

3 At this stage, all engine components should be absolutely clean and dry, with all faults repaired. The components should be laid out (or in individual containers) on a completely clean work surface.

18 Piston rings - refitting

1 Before fitting new piston rings, the ring end gaps must be checked as follows.

2 Lay out the piston/connecting rod assemblies and the new piston ring sets, so that the ring sets will be matched with the same piston and cylinder during the end gap measurement and subsequent engine reassembly.

3 Insert the top ring into the first cylinder, and push it down the bore using the top of the piston. This will ensure that the ring remains square with the cylinder walls. Push the ring down into the bore until it is positioned 15 to 20 mm up from the bottom edge of the bore, then withdraw the piston.

4 Measure the end gap using feeler gauges, and compare the measurements with the figures given in the Specifications **(see illustration)**.

18.4 Measuring piston ring end gap (see text)

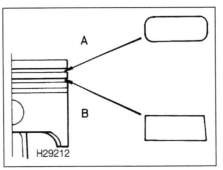

18.9a Ensure the top (A) and second (B) compression rings are fitted in the correct locations . . .

18.9b . . . and that they are installed with their markings (arrowed) uppermost

5 If the gap is too small (unlikely if genuine Rover parts are used), it must be enlarged, or the ring ends may contact each other during engine operation, causing serious damage. Ideally, new piston rings providing the correct end gap should be fitted. As a last resort, the end gap can be increased by filing the ring ends very carefully with a fine file. Mount the file in a vice with soft jaws, slip the ring over the file with the ends contacting the file face, and slowly move the ring to remove material from the ends. Take care, as piston rings are sharp, and are easily broken.

6 With new piston rings, it is unlikely that the end gap will be too large. If the gaps are too large, check that you have the correct rings for your engine and for the particular cylinder bore size.

7 Repeat the checking procedure for each ring in the first cylinder, and then for the rings in the remaining cylinders. Remember to keep rings, pistons and cylinders matched up.

8 Once the ring end gaps have been checked and if necessary corrected, the rings can be fitted to the pistons.

9 Fit the piston rings using the same technique as for removal. Fit the bottom (oil control) spacer first then install both the side rails, noting that both the spacer and side rails can be installed either way up. Fit the second and top compression rings ensuring that each ring is fitted the correct way up with its identification mark uppermost **(see illustrations)**. **Note:** *Always follow any instructions supplied with the new piston ring sets - different manufacturers may specify different procedures. Do not mix up the top and second compression rings, as they have different cross-sections.*

10 With the piston rings correctly installed, check that each ring is free to rotate easily in its groove. Check the ring-to-groove clearance of each ring using feeler gauges and check that the clearance is within the specified range then position the ring end gaps as shown **(see illustrations)**.

19 Crankshaft - refitting and main bearing running clearance check

Note: *It is recommended that new main bearing shells are fitted regardless of the condition of the original ones.*

Selection of bearing shells

1 The main bearing running clearance is controlled in production by selecting one of

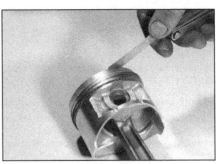

18.10a Using a feeler gauge to check the piston ring-to-groove clearance

five grades of bearing shell. The grades are indicated by a colour-coding marked on the edge of each shell which governs the shells thickness **(see illustration)**. In order, from the thinnest to the thickest, the shell grades are: Pink, Yellow, Green, Brown and Black.

2 If the bearing shells are to be renewed, first check and record the identification number stamped on the crankshaft adjacent to each main bearing journal. The number, between 1 and 6, is the size code of the adjacent main bearing journal outside diameter; 1 indicates the largest-possible outside diameter, and 4 the smallest. Number 1 (timing belt end of the engine) bearing code is situated to the right of the journal, whereas all other codes are on the left-hand side of the relevant journal **(see illustration)**. **Note:** *On some engines the numbers may be replaced with symbols; the number of lines in the symbol indicates the journal size group ie. I indicates size group 1 and iiiiil indicates size group 6.*

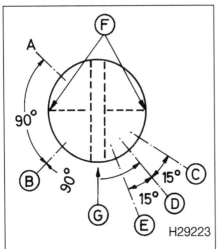

18.10b Piston ring end gap spacing

   A *Second compression ring*
   B *Top compression ring*
   C *Oil control ring upper side rail*
   D *Oil control ring spacer*
   E *Oil control ring lower side rail*
   F *Piston thrust surfaces*
   G *Gudgeon pin axis*

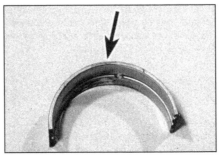

19.1 Bearing shell size group is indicated by the paint marking (arrowed) on the edge of the shell

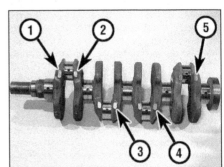

19.2 Crankshaft main bearing journal size code locations

19.3 Cylinder block main bearing bore size identification markings (arrowed)

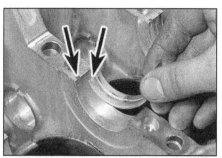

19.6 Fit the upper bearing shells ensuring their tabs locate correctly in the cylinder block cut-outs (arrowed)

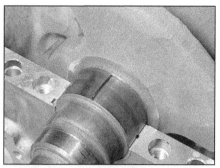

19.10 Lay a strip of Plastigauge on each cleaned main bearing journal . . .

19.11 . . . then refit the main bearing caps and bridge casting and tighten the bolts (see text)

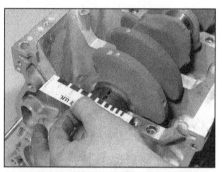

19.12 Remove the main bearing bridge and caps and measure the width of the crushed Plastigauge using the gauge provided

3 Secondly, check and record the main bearing bore size code identification markings which are stamped on the right-hand, rear end of the cylinder block lower mating surface (see illustration). The markings are in the form of numbers (1 to 4), letters (A to D) or symbols (I to iiii - see note in previous paragraph). The first marking indicates the size group of number 1 (timing belt end) main bearing bore and the last number 5.

4 Match the relevant main bearing bore code with its crankshaft journal code, and select a new set of bearing shells using the table shown at the foot of this page. The crankshaft codes are listed down the left-hand side, and the main bearing bore codes along the top; the required bearing grade is indicated in the box where the two columns intersect.

Main bearing running clearance check

5 Clean the backs of the bearing shells and the bearing locations in both the cylinder block and the main bearing caps.

6 Press the bearing shells into their locations, ensuring that the tab on each shell engages in the notch in the cylinder block or main bearing cap (see illustration). If the original bearing shells are being used for the check ensure they are refitted in their original locations. The clearance can be checked in either of two ways.

7 One method (which will be difficult to achieve without a range of internal micrometers or internal/external expanding calipers) is to refit the main bearing caps to the cylinder block, with bearing shells in place. Refit the bearing cap bridge and with the cap retaining bolts correctly tightened, measure the internal diameter of each assembled pair of bearing shells. If the diameter of each corresponding crankshaft journal is measured and then subtracted from

the bearing internal diameter, the result will be the main bearing running clearance.

8 The second (and more accurate) method is to use a product known as Plastigauge. This consists of a fine thread of perfectly round plastic which is compressed between the bearing shell and the journal. When the shell is removed, the plastic is deformed and its width can be measured with a special card gauge supplied with the kit. The running clearance is determined from this gauge. Plastigauge is sometimes difficult to obtain but enquiries at one of the larger specialist quality motor factors should produce the name of a stockist in your area. The procedure for using Plastigauge is as follows.

9 With the main bearing upper shells in place, carefully lay the crankshaft in position. Do not use any lubricant; the crankshaft journals and bearing shells must be perfectly clean and dry.

10 Cut several lengths of the appropriate size Plastigauge (they should be slightly shorter than the width of the main bearings) and place one length on each crankshaft journal axis (see illustration).

11 With the main bearing lower shells in position, ensure the locating dowels are in position and refit the main bearing caps (see illustration). Ensure all the locating dowels are correctly fitted then refit the main bearing cap bridge casting and tighten the bolts as described in paragraph 23. Take care not to disturb the Plastigauge and do not rotate the crankshaft at any time during this operation. Working in the reverse of the tightening sequence, evenly and progressively slacken and remove the main bearing bolts then lift off the bridge casting and caps again taking great care not to disturb the Plastigauge, or rotate the crankshaft.

12 Compare the width of the crushed Plastigauge on each journal to the scale printed on the Plastigauge envelope to obtain the main bearing running clearance (see illustration). Compare the clearance measured with that given in the Specifications at the start of this Chapter.

13 If the clearance is significantly different from that expected, the bearing shells may be the wrong size (or excessively worn if the original shells are being re-used). Before deciding that the crankshaft is worn, make sure that no dirt or oil was trapped between the bearing shells and the caps or block when the clearance was measured. If the Plastigauge was wider at one end than at the other, the crankshaft journal may be tapered.

14 Before condemning the components concerned, seek the advice of your Rover dealer or suitable engine repair specialist.

Main bearing shell selection table

	1, A or I	2, B or iI	3, C or iii	4, D or iiii
1 or I	Red	Pink/Yellow	Yellow	Yellow/Green
2 or iI	Pink/Yellow	Yellow	Yellow/Green	Green
3 or iii	Yellow	Yellow/Green	Green	Green/Brown
4 or iiii	Yellow/Green	Green	Green/Brown	Brown
5 or iiiii	Green	Green/Brown	Brown	Brown/Black
6 or iiiiii	Green/Brown	Brown	Brown/Black	Black

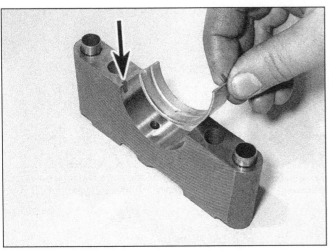

19.18 Fit the lower bearing shells engaging their tabs in the main bearing cap slots (arrowed)

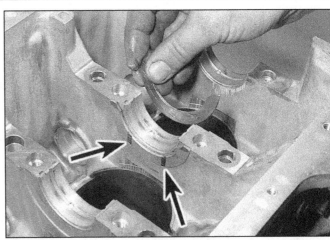

19.19a Using grease, stick the thrustwashers to each side of number 4 main bearing ensuring the washer grooves (arrowed) are facing outwards

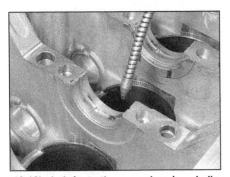

19.19b Lubricate the upper bearing shells with clean engine oil . . .

19.19c . . . and carefully refit the crankshaft

19 Using a little grease, stick the thrustwashers to each side of the number 4 main bearing upper location; ensure that the oilway grooves on each thrustwasher face outwards. Wipe the shells and crankshaft journals dry with a lint-free cloth. Liberally lubricate each bearing shell in the cylinder block with clean engine oil then lower the crankshaft into position ensuring that the bearing shells and thrust washers remain correctly seated **(see illustrations)**.

20 Check the crankshaft endfloat as described in Section 14.

21 Ensure the locating dowels and bearing shells are correctly located in the caps and refit the caps to the cylinder block. Ensure the caps are fitted in their correct locations, with No 1 cap at the timing belt end, and are fitted the correct way around so that all the arrows point towards the timing belt end of the engine **(see illustration)**.

22 Fit a new sealing ring to the recess in the centre of the main bearing cap bridge, using a smear of grease to hold it in position **(see illustration)**. Ensure all the locating dowels

They will also be able to inform as to the best course of action or if renewal will be necessary.

15 Where necessary, obtain the correct size of bearing shell and repeat the running clearance checking procedure as described above.

16 On completion, carefully scrape away all traces of the Plastigauge material from the crankshaft and bearing shells using a fingernail or other object which is unlikely to score the bearing surfaces.

Final crankshaft refitting

17 Carefully lift the crankshaft out of the cylinder block once more.

18 Place the bearing shells in their locations as described above in paragraphs 5 and 6 **(see illustration)**. If new shells are being fitted, ensure that all traces of the protective grease are cleaned off using paraffin. Wipe dry the shells and caps with a lint-free cloth.

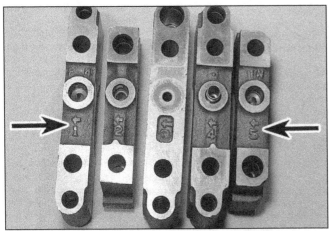

19.21 Refit the main bearing caps using the identification markings to ensure each is correctly fitted

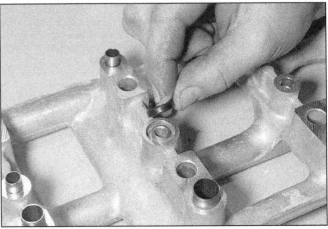

19.22 Fit a new sealing ring to the recess in the centre of the main bearing cap bridge prior to refitting

19.23a Lightly oil the threads and underside of the heads of the main bearing cap bolts prior to refitting

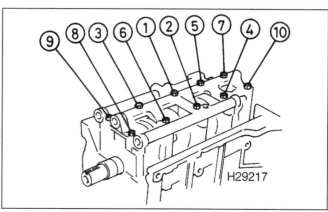

19.23b Main bearing cap bolt tightening sequence

are correctly positioned, then refit the bridge to the bearing caps, taking great care to ensure that the sealing ring remains firmly seated in its recess.

23 Apply a smear of clean engine to oil to the threads and underneath the heads of the main bearing cap bolts. Refit the bolts and washers to their original positions and tighten them all by hand. Working in the specified sequence, tighten the main bearing cap bolts first to the specified Stage 1 torque setting. Once all bolts are tightened to the specified Stage 1 torque, go around again in the specified sequence and tighten them to the specified Stage 2 torque setting **(see illustrations)**. Check that the crankshaft is free to rotate smoothly; if excessive pressure is required to turn the crankshaft, investigate the cause before proceeding further.

24 Refit/reconnect the piston connecting rod assemblies to the crankshaft as described in Section 20.

25 Renew the right-hand crankshaft oil seal, and refit the seal housing as described in Part A of this Chapter.

26 Refit the oil pump, flywheel/driveplate, cylinder head, timing belt sprockets (as applicable) and fit a new timing belt as described in Part A.

20 Piston/connecting rod assembly - refitting and big-end running clearance check

Note: *It is recommended that new piston rings and big-end bearing shells are fitted regardless of the condition of the original ones.*

Selection of bearing shells

1 The big-end bearing running clearance is controlled in production by selecting one of seven grades of bearing shell. The grades are indicated by a colour-coding marked on the edge of each shell which governs the shells thickness **(see illustration 19.1)**. In order, from the thinnest to the thickest, the shell grades are: Red, Pink, Yellow, Green, Brown, Black and Blue.

2 If the bearing shells are to be renewed, first check and record the number stamped across one face of each big-end bearing cap and connecting rod **(see illustration)**. The number, between 1 and 4, is the size code of the connecting rod big-end bore inside diameter; 1 indicates the smallest-possible inside diameter,

and 4 the largest. **Note:** *On some engines the numbers may be replaced with symbols; the number of lines in the symbol indicates the journal size group ie. I indicates size group 1 and iiil indicates size group 4.*

3 Secondly, check and record the crankpin/big-end journal code letters stamped on the crankshafts web on the left-hand side of each big-end journal **(see illustration)**. The letter, between A and D, indicates the outside diameter of the crankpin/big-end journal; A indicates the largest-possible outside diameter, and D the smallest. **Note:** *On some engines the numbers may be replaced with symbols; the number of lines in the symbol indicates the journal size group ie. I indicates size group A and iiil indicates size group D.*

4 Match the relevant connecting rod bearing bore code with its crankshaft journal code, and select a new set of bearing shells using the table below. The crankshaft codes are listed down the left-hand side, and the connecting rod bearing bore codes along the top; the required bearing grade is indicated in the box where the two columns intersect.

Connecting rod (big-end) bearing shell selection table

	1 or I	2 or iI	3 or iiI	4 or iiiI
A or I	Red	Pink	Yellow	Green
B or iI	Pink	Yellow	Green	Brown
C or iiI	Yellow	Green	Brown	Black
D or iiiI	Green	Brown	Black	Blue

19.23c Tighten the main bearing cap bolts in the specified sequence through the stages described in text

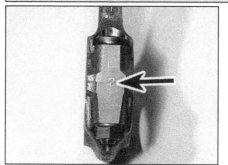

20.2 Connecting rod big-end bearing bore size code marking (arrowed)

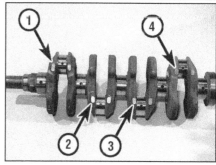

20.3 Crankshaft big-end (crankpin) journal size code markings

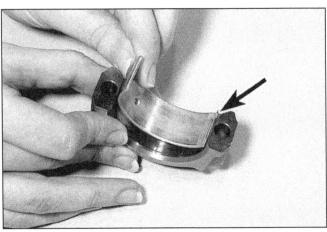

20.6 Fit the bearing shells to the connecting rods/caps engaging the shell tab with the cut-out (arrowed)

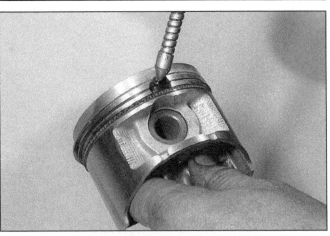

20.10 Lubricate the piston rings with clean engine oil ...

Big-end bearing running clearance check

5 Clean the backs of the bearing shells and the bearing locations in both the connecting rod and bearing cap.

20.11 ... then space the end gaps correctly and clamp the rings in position with a compressor

6 Press the bearing shells into their locations, ensuring that the tab on each shell engages in the notch in the connecting rod and cap **(see illustration)**. If the original bearing shells are being used for the check ensure they are refitted in their original locations. The clearance can be checked in either of two ways.

7 One method is to refit the big-end bearing cap to the connecting rod, with bearing shells in place. With the cap retaining nuts correctly tightened, use an internal micrometer or vernier caliper to measure the internal diameter of each assembled pair of bearing shells. If the diameter of each corresponding crankshaft journal is measured and then subtracted from the bearing internal diameter, the result will be the big-end bearing running clearance.

8 The second method is to use Plastigauge as described in Section 19, paragraphs 8 to 16. Place a strand of Plastigauge on each (cleaned) crankpin journal and refit the (clean) piston/connecting rod assemblies, shells and big-end bearing caps. Tighten the nuts to the specified torque wrench setting taking care not to disturb the Plastigauge. Dismantle the

assemblies without rotating the crankshaft and use the scale printed on the Plastigauge envelope to obtain the big-end bearing running clearance. On completion of the measurement, carefully scrape off all traces of Plastigauge from the journal and shells using a fingernail or other object which will not score the components.

Final piston/connecting rod assembly refitting

9 Ensure the bearing shells are correctly refitted as described above in paragraphs 5 and 6. If new shells are being fitted, ensure that all traces of the protective grease are cleaned off using paraffin. Wipe dry the shells and connecting rods with a lint-free cloth.

10 Lubricate the bores, the pistons and piston rings then lay out each piston/connecting rod assembly in its respective position **(see illustration)**.

11 Starting with assembly number 1, make sure that the piston rings are still spaced as described in Section 18, then clamp them in position with a piston ring compressor **(see illustration)**.

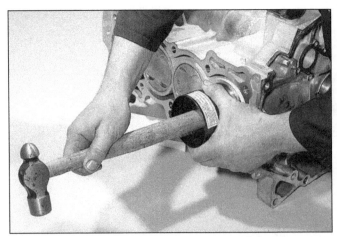

20.12a Insert the piston/connecting rod assembly into the correct bore and tap it into position using a hammer handle ...

20.12b ... ensuring it is correctly positioned with the arrow (arrowed) on the piston crown pointing towards the timing belt end of the engine

20.13 Refit the connecting rod bearing cap . . .

20.14 . . . and tighten the nuts evenly and progressively to the specified torque

12 Insert the piston/connecting rod assembly into the top of cylinder No 1, ensuring that the arrow marking on the piston crown is pointing towards the timing belt end of the engine. Using a block of wood or hammer handle against the piston crown, tap the assembly into the cylinder until the piston crown is flush with the top of the cylinder **(see illustrations)**.

13 Taking care not to mark the cylinder bore, liberally lubricate the crankpin and both bearing shells, then pull the piston/connecting rod assembly down the bore and onto the crankpin and refit the big-end bearing cap using the markings to ensure it is fitted the correct way around (the upper and lower bearing shells locating tabs should be on the same side) **(see illustration)**.

14 Refit the bearing cap nuts and tighten them evenly and progressively to the specified torque setting **(see illustration)**.

15 Refit the remaining three piston and connecting rod assemblies in the same way.

16 Rotate the crankshaft, and check that it turns freely, with no signs of binding or tight spots.

17 Refit oil pump, sump and the cylinder head as described in Part A of this Chapter.

21 Engine - initial start up after overhaul

1 With the engine refitted in the vehicle, double-check the engine oil and coolant levels. Make a final check that everything has been reconnected, and that there are no tools or rags left in the engine compartment.

2 Disable the ignition system by removing the engine management/ignition system fuse (number 2) from the passenger compartment fusebox (see Chapter 12).

3 Turn the engine on the starter until the oil pressure warning light goes out. Refit the spark plugs, and reconnect the spark plug (HT) leads, referring to Chapter 1 for further information. Refit the fuse to the fusebox and refit the cover.

4 Start the engine, noting that this may take a little longer than usual, due to the fuel system components having been disturbed.

5 While the engine is idling, check for fuel, water and oil leaks. Dont be alarmed if there are some odd smells and smoke from parts getting hot and burning off oil deposits.

6 Assuming all is well, keep the engine idling until hot water is felt circulating through the top hose, then switch off the engine. **Note:** *Rover state that if the big-end and/or main bearing shells have been replaced, the engine should be run at idle speed for 15 minutes to allow the shells to bed in before the vehicle is used.*

7 Check the ignition timing, and the idle speed settings (as appropriate), then switch the engine off.

8 After a few minutes, recheck the oil and coolant levels as described in 'Weekly checks', and top-up as necessary.

9 If new pistons, rings or crankshaft bearings have been fitted, the engine must be treated as new, and run-in for the first 500 miles (800 km). *Do not* use full-throttle, or allow the engine to labour at low engine speeds in any gear. It is recommended that the oil and filter be changed at the end of this period.

Notes

Chapter 3
Cooling, heating and ventilation systems

Contents

Degrees of difficulty

Easy, suitable for novice with little experience	Fairly easy, suitable for beginner with some experience	Fairly difficult, suitable for competent DIY mechanic	Difficult, suitable for experienced DIY mechanic 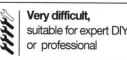	Very difficult, suitable for expert DIY or professional

Specifications

General
Radiator cap opening pressure . . . . 0.95 to 1.25 bars (14.0 to 18.38 psi)

Thermostat
Opening temperature . . . . 76° to 80°C
Fully open temperature . . . . 90°C
Minimum valve lift at 90°C . . . . 8.0 mm

Cooling fan temperature switch
Switch-on temperature . . . . 90°C to 96°C
Switch-off temperature . . . . 2° to 7° lower than switch-on temperature

Cooling fan timer
Switch-on temperature . . . . 103°C to 109°C
Switch-off temperature . . . . 2° to 5° lower than switch-on temperature

Coolant temperature gauge sender
Resistance:
    At 56°C (or engine cold) . . . . 142 ohms
    At 85° to 100°C . . . . 49 to 32 ohms

Torque wrench settings

	Nm	lbf ft
A/C compressor bracket	50	37
A/C compressor drivebelt adjustment bolt	22	16
A/C compressor mounting bolts	22	16
Bleed screw to thermostat housing	10	7
Coolant inlet housing to cylinder head	22	16
Coolant temperature gauge sender (RH end of cylinder head)	9	7
Cooling fan shroud to radiator	10	7
Cooling fan temperature switch	28	21
Cooling fan to motor spindle	5	4
Engine temperature sensor (RH end of cylinder head)	18	13
Heater assembly mounting nuts	10	7
Heater blower motor assembly mounting nuts	10	7
Radiator mounting bolts	10	7
Thermostat cover to housing	12	9
Thermostat housing to inlet manifold	12	9
Water pump	12	9
Water pump/thermostat housing pipe to cylinder block	22	16

1 General information and precautions

General information

1 The cooling system is of pressurised type, comprising a water pump, a radiator, a coolant expansion tank (at atmospheric pressure), an electric cooling fan, a thermostat, heater matrix, and all associated hoses and switches. The water pump is driven by the timing belt.

2 The system functions as follows. The water pump pumps cold water around the cylinder block and head passages, and through the fast idle thermo valve and heater matrix.

3 When the engine is cold, the coolant circulates through the engine only, and the thermostat is closed. When the coolant reaches a predetermined temperature, the thermostat opens, and the coolant passes through the radiator. As the coolant circulates through the radiator, it is cooled by the inrush of air when the car is in forward motion. The airflow is supplemented by the action of the electric cooling fan when necessary.

4 The thermostat is located in the rear right-hand end of the inlet manifold, in the return circuit from the radiator lower hose, and therefore a certain amount of heat will find its way into the top of the radiator even when the thermostat is closed. The thermostat element senses engine coolant temperature via a bypass hose connected to the housing at the right-hand end of the water pump connecting pipe. Without the bypass hose it would not be possible for the coolant to reach the (closed) thermostat since it is located in the return circuit to the water pump.

5 When the engine is at normal operating temperature, the coolant expands, and some of it is released through the valve in the radiator pressure cap and displaced into the expansion tank. Coolant collects in the tank, and is returned to the radiator when the system cools. The expansion tank is not pressurised.

6 The electric cooling fan is mounted on the rear of the radiator. At a predetermined coolant temperature, the coolant temperature switch contacts close and the fan is actuated via a relay. If the engine is switched off and the coolant temperature is above 106°C, the cooling fan will continue to operate via the timer for approximately 15 minutes. On models with air conditioning, an additional fan is located on the rear of the radiator.

7 On automatic transmission models the radiator lower tank incorporates a cooler for the automatic transmission hydraulic fluid.

Precautions

> ⚠ **Warning: Do not attempt to remove the radiator pressure cap, or to disturb any part of the cooling system, while the engine**

is hot, as there is a high risk of scalding. If the radiator pressure cap must be removed before the engine and radiator have fully cooled (even though this is not recommended), the pressure in the cooling system must first be relieved. Cover the cap with a thick layer of cloth, to avoid scalding, and slowly unscrew the pressure cap until a hissing sound is heard. When the hissing has stopped, indicating that the pressure has reduced, slowly unscrew the pressure cap until it can be removed; if more hissing sounds are heard, wait until they have stopped before unscrewing the cap completely. At all times, keep your face well away from the pressure cap opening, and protect your hands.

> ⚠ **Warning: Do not allow antifreeze to come into contact with your skin, or with the painted surfaces of the vehicle. Rinse off** spills immediately, with plenty of water. Never leave antifreeze lying around in an open container, or in a puddle in the driveway or on the garage floor. Children and pets are attracted by its sweet smell, but antifreeze can be fatal if ingested.

> ⚠ **Warning: Refer to Section 10 for precautions to be observed when working on models equipped with air conditioning.**

Caution: If the radio/cassette in your vehicle is equipped with an anti-theft system, make sure you have the correct activation code before disconnecting the battery.

2 Cooling system hoses - disconnection and renewal

Note: Refer to the warnings given in Section 1 of this Chapter before proceeding. Hoses should only be disconnected once the engine has cooled sufficiently to avoid scalding.

1 If the checks described in Chapter 1 reveal a faulty hose, it must be renewed as follows.

2 First drain the cooling system (see Chapter 1). If the coolant is not due for renewal, it may be re-used if it is collected in a clean container. Squirt a little penetrating oil onto the hose clips if they are corroded.

3 To disconnect a hose, release its retaining clips, then move them along the hose, clear of the stubs. Carefully work the hose free. **Do not** attempt to disconnect any part of the system while it is still hot.

4 Note that the radiator stubs are fragile; do not use excessive force when attempting to remove the hoses. If a hose proves difficult to remove, try to release it by twisting it.

> **If all else fails, cut the hose with a sharp knife, then slit it so that it can be peeled off in two pieces. Although this** may prove expensive if the hose is otherwise undamaged, it is preferable to buying a new radiator.

5 When fitting a hose, first slide the clips onto the centre of the hose, then work the hose into position. If clamp type clips were originally fitted and they have lost their tension, it is a good idea to replace them with screw type clips when refitting the hose. If the hose is stiff, use a little soapy water as a lubricant.

6 Work the hose into position, checking that it is correctly routed, then slide each clip along the hose until it passes over the flared end of the relevant outlet, before securing it in position with the retaining clip.

7 Refill the cooling system with reference to Chapter 1.

8 Check thoroughly for leaks as soon as possible after disturbing any part of the cooling system.

3 Radiator - removal, inspection and refitting

Removal

Note: If leakage is the reason for removing the radiator, bear in mind that minor leaks can often be cured using a radiator sealant with the radiator in situ.

1 Disconnect the battery negative lead.

2 Drain the cooling system as described in Chapter 1.

3 Disconnect the top and bottom hoses from the radiator **(see illustration)**.

4 On automatic transmission models, clamp the hydraulic fluid hoses then disconnect them from the radiator bottom tank.

5 Disconnect the wiring from the electric fan(s) on the rear of the radiator **(see illustration)**.

6 Disconnect the expansion tank hose from the top of the radiator **(see illustration)**, and pull the expansion tank from its mounting bracket. Place the tank to one side making sure that the hose is positioned so that the coolant does not syphon from the tank.

3.3 Disconnecting the top hose from the radiator

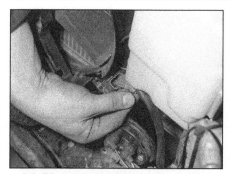

3.5 Disconnecting the electric cooling fan wiring

3.6 Disconnecting the expansion tank hose

3.7 Removing the radiator upper mountings

3.8a Lifting the radiator from the engine compartment

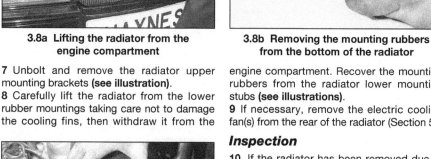

3.8b Removing the mounting rubbers from the bottom of the radiator

7 Unbolt and remove the radiator upper mounting brackets **(see illustration)**.

8 Carefully lift the radiator from the lower rubber mountings taking care not to damage the cooling fins, then withdraw it from the engine compartment. Recover the mounting rubbers from the radiator lower mounting stubs **(see illustrations)**.

9 If necessary, remove the electric cooling fan(s) from the rear of the radiator (Section 5).

Inspection

10 If the radiator has been removed due to suspected blockage, reverse flush it as described in Chapter 1. Clean dirt and debris from the radiator fins, using an air line (in which case, wear eye protection) or a soft brush. Be careful, as the fins are sharp, and easily damaged.

11 If necessary, a radiator specialist can perform a flow test on the radiator, to establish whether an internal blockage exists.

12 A leaking radiator must be referred to a specialist for permanent repair. Do not attempt to weld or solder a leaking radiator, as damage to the plastic components may result.

13 If the radiator is to be sent for repair, or is to be renewed, remove all hoses first.

14 Inspect the condition of the upper and lower radiator mounting rubbers, and renew them if necessary.

Refitting

15 Refitting is a reversal of removal, but on completion, refill and bleed the cooling system as described in Chapter 1.

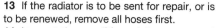

4 Thermostat - removal, testing and refitting

Removal

1 The thermostat is located in a housing on the rear right-hand end of the inlet manifold. The housing is attached to a connecting pipe leading to the water pump inlet.

2 Drain the cooling system as described in Chapter 1.

3 Remove the air cleaner cover and air duct with reference to Chapter 4A **(see illustration)**.

4 Loosen the clip and disconnect the radiator lower hose from the thermostat housing cover **(see illustration)**.

5 Unbolt the earth lead from the thermostat housing cover **(see illustration)**.

6 Disconnect the wiring from the temperature sensor in the thermostat housing cover **(see illustration)**.

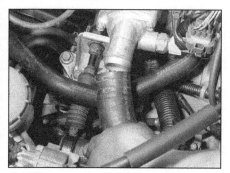

4.3 Removing the air cleaner cover and air duct

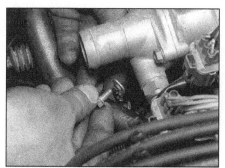

4.4 Disconnecting the radiator lower hose from the thermostat housing cover

4.5 Unbolting the earth lead from the thermostat housing cover

4.6 Disconnecting the wiring from the temperature sensor

4.7a Unscrew the bolts . . .

4.7b . . . and remove the thermostat housing cover

4.8 Removing the thermostat from its housing

7 Unbolt and remove the cover **(see illustrations)**.

8 Note that the jiggle pin is positioned at the top of the thermostat, then remove the thermostat from its housing together with the sealing rubber **(see illustration)**.

9 If required, the thermostat housing may be unbolted and removed from the inlet manifold and connecting pipe after disconnecting the hoses. Recover the O-ring.

Testing

10 A rough test of the thermostat may be made by suspending it with a piece of string in a container full of water. Heat the water - the thermostat must open by the time the water boils. If not, renew it.

11 If a thermometer is available, the precise opening and fully open temperatures of the thermostat may be determined; compare with the figures given in the Specifications. The opening temperature is also marked on the thermostat.

12 If the thermostat fails to close as the water cools, it must be renewed.

Refitting

13 Commence refitting by thoroughly cleaning the mating faces and seating of the cover and housing.

14 If removed, fit a new O-ring to the connecting pipe then locate the housing on the inlet manifold and tighten the mounting bolt to the specified torque. Reconnect the hoses and tighten the clips.

15 Fit a new sealing rubber to the thermostat, then locate the thermostat and rubber in the housing with the jiggle pin facing upwards.

16 Refit the cover and tighten the mounting bolts to the specified torque.

17 Reconnect the wiring to the temperature sensor.

18 Reconnect the earth lead the the thermostat housing cover.

19 Reconnect the lower hose to the radiator and tighten the clip.

20 Refit the air cleaner cover and air duct with reference to Chapter 4A.

21 Refill the cooling system as described in Chapter 1.

5 Electric cooling fan - testing, removal and refitting

Testing

1 Current supply to the cooling fan is via the radiator fan relay which is triggered by the engine temperature switch located on the thermostat cover. The relay is located in the fusebox on the right-hand side of the engine compartment.

2 Detailed fault diagnosis can be carried out by a Rover dealer using suitable test equipment, but basic diagnosis can be carried out as follows.

3 If the fan does not appear to work, run the engine until normal operating temperature is reached, then allow it to idle. The fan should cut in within a few minutes (before the temperature gauge needle enters the red section).

4 The motor can be tested by disconnecting it from the wiring loom, and connecting a 12-volt supply directly to it, or by disconnecting the wires from the temperature switch and connecting the wires together. The motor should operate - if not, the motor or wiring is faulty.

5 If the motor operates when tested as described in paragraph 4, the fault must lie in the engine wiring harness, the relay, or the temperature switch. The temperature switch can be tested as described in Section 6. Any further fault diagnosis should be referred to a suitably-equipped Rover dealer.

5.7 Unbolting the cooling fan assembly from the radiator

Removal

6 The electric cooling fan can be removed leaving the radiator in position, however if necessary remove the radiator first as described in Section 3.

7 Unscrew the mounting bolts securing the cooling fan assembly to the rear of the radiator, then withdraw the assembly taking care not to damage the radiator fins **(see illustration)**.

8 If necessary, unscrew the nut and remove the fan, then unbolt and remove the motor.

Refitting

9 Refitting is a reversal of removal, but take care not to damage the radiator fins. Refer to Section 3 if the radiator has been removed.

6 Cooling system electrical sensors - testing, removal and refitting

Cooling fan temperature switch

Testing

1 The cooling fan temperature switch controls the electric cooling fan located on the rear of the radiator (refer to Section 5 for more details). The switch is located on the thermostat cover on the right-hand end of the inlet manifold.

2 Testing may be carried out (after the switch has been removed with the engine cold) by immersing its temperature sensing end, with a thermometer, in a pan of cold water and testing for continuity as the water is heated. Connect an ohmmeter to the switch terminals. Check that the internal contacts operate in accordance with the information given in Specifications.

Removal

3 Drain the cooling system as described in Chapter 1.

4 Disconnect the wiring, then unscrew the switch from the thermostat cover. Recover the O-ring.

Refitting

5 Refitting is a reversal of removal but tighten the switch to the specified torque. Refill the cooling system with reference to Chapter 1.

6.10 Removing the engine temperature sensor from the right-hand end of the cylinder head

7.4 Water pump mounting bolt locations

Engine temperature sensor

Testing

6 The engine temperature sensor is located on the right-hand end of the cylinder head, and provides information to the engine management system. It contains a thermistor - an electronic component whose electrical resistance decreases at a predetermined rate as its temperature rises.

7 Refer to Chapter 4A for more details of testing and checking the engine temperature sensor.

Removal

8 Drain the cooling system as described in Chapter 1.

9 Disconnect the wiring plug from the sensor.

10 Unscrew the sensor from the right-hand end of the cylinder head (see illustration).

Refitting

11 Refitting is a reversal of removal, but tighten the sensor to the specified torque and refill the cooling system as described in Chapter 1.

Coolant temperature gauge sender

Testing

12 The sender is located on the right-hand end of the cylinder head, in front of the engine coolant temperature sensor.

13 With the engine cold, disconnect the red wire from the sender then connect an ohmmeter between the sender terminal and a good earthing point on the engine (eg the inlet manifold).

14 Check that the resistance of the sender is as given in the Specifications.

15 Run the engine to normal operating temperature (ie until the cooling fan comes on), then check that the resistance of the sender is as given in the Specifications.

16 If the readings are not as given in the Specifications, renew the sender unit.

17 To check the gauge, disconnect the red wire from the sender unit and earth it to the inlet manifold. Switch on the ignition and check that the pointer on the gauge moves towards the red zone.

Caution: Switch off the ignition before the pointer enters the red zone, otherwise the gauge may be damaged.

18 If the pointer remains in the cold section on the gauge, check the sender wire for an open circuit. If the wire is good, the gauge is faulty.

Removal and refitting

19 The procedure is similar to that described previously in this Section for the engine temperature sensor.

---

7 Water pump - removal, inspection and refitting

Note: *The water pump incorporates two holes in the rear-facing edge of its body, for the escape of any small amounts of coolant which pass the internal seal. A minimal amount of coolant from these holes is acceptable, however, more than this indicates a worn seal requiring renewal of the water pump.*

Removal

1 Disconnect the battery earth lead.

2 Drain the cooling system as described in Chapter 1.

3 Remove the timing belt (and balancer shaft belt) as described in Chapter 2A.

4 Unscrew the water pump mounting bolts noting that the long bolt is located at the bottom (see illustration).

5 Remove the water pump from the cylinder block and recover the O-ring (see illustrations).

Inspection

6 Check the pump body and impeller for signs of excessive corrosion. Turn the impeller, and check for stiffness due to corrosion, or roughness due to excessive end play.

7 Thoroughly clean the contact surfaces of the water pump and cylinder block.

Refitting

8 Refitting is a reversal of removal, but always fit a new O-ring and tighten the mounting bolts to the specified torque. Refer to Chapter 2A when refitting the timing belt and balancer shaft belt, and refer to Chapter 1 to refill the cooling system.

7.5a Remove the water pump from the cylinder block . . .

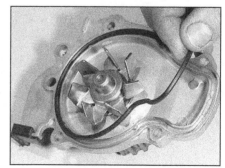

7.5b . . . and recover the O-ring

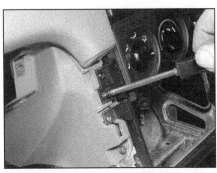

9.2 Removing the heater control panel mounting screws

9.4a Control cables on the right-hand side of the heater assembly

9.4b Disconnecting the heater/ventilation control cables

8 Heating and ventilation system - general information

1 The heater/ventilation system consists of a blower motor (housed beneath the left-hand side of the facia), face level vents in the centre and at each end of the facia, and air ducts to the front and rear footwells.

2 The control unit is located in the centre of the facia, and the controls operate flap valves to deflect and mix the air flowing through the various parts of the heating/ventilation system. The flap valves are contained in the air distribution housing, which acts as a central distribution unit, passing air to the various ducts and vents.

3 Cold air enters the system through the grille at the rear of the engine compartment. If

9.5a Disconnect the wiring . . .

required, the airflow is boosted by the blower fan, and then flows through the various ducts, according to the settings of the controls. Stale air is expelled through ducts at the rear of the vehicle. If warm air is required, the cold air is passed over the heater matrix, which is heated by the engine coolant.

4 On models fitted with air conditioning, a recirculation switch enables the outside air supply to be closed off, while the air inside the vehicle is recirculated. This can be useful to prevent unpleasant odours entering from outside the vehicle, but should only be used briefly, as the recirculated air inside the vehicle will soon become stale.

9 Heating and ventilation system components - removal and refitting

Heater/ventilation control panel

Removal

1 Remove the surround panel from the facia with reference to Chapter 11.

2 Unscrew the screws securing the control panel to the facia (see illustration).

3 Remove the centre console with reference to Chapter 11.

4 Note the setting positions of the control cables on the heater unit, then release the clips and disconnect the cables (see illustrations).

5 Withdraw the control panel from the facia and disconnect the wiring (see illustrations).

If necessary, remove the screws and separate the clock/hazard switch from the control panel.

Refitting

6 Refitting is a reversal of removal, but reconnect the control cables in their previously noted positions. Check the operation of the control panel before refitting the surround panel.

Heater assembly

> ⚠️ **Warning: It is not recommended that the heater unit is removed on models fitted with air conditioning, as the evaporator must be removed which entails evacuating the air conditioning system. This work cannot be carried out by the home mechanic.**

Removal

7 Drain the cooling system as described in Chapter 1. Position cloth rags or absorbent material in the front footwells to catch spilt coolant from the heater.

8 Working in the engine compartment, loosen the clips and disconnect the heater hoses from the matrix pipes on the bulkhead. Note the position of the hoses for correct refitting (see illustration).

9 Disconnect the heater temperature control cable from the heater valve.

10 Working inside the vehicle, remove the facia panel as described in Chapter 11.

11 Unbolt and remove the air duct from the heater assembly (see illustrations).

9.5b . . . and withdraw the heater/ventilation control panel

9.8 Heater hoses on the bulkhead in the engine compartment

9.11a Unscrew the bolts . . .

9.11b ... and remove the air duct

12 Detach the wiring holder from the heater.
13 Unscrew the mounting nuts, then carefully withdraw the heater assembly from inside the vehicle.

Refitting

14 Refitting is a reversal of removal, but note the following:
  a) Apply suitable sealant to the bulkhead rubber grommets.
  b) Make sure that all wiring and cables are routed as noted during dismantling.
  c) Make sure that all air ducts are securely reconnected.
  d) Refit the facia panel with reference to Chapter 11.
  e) On completion, refill and bleed the cooling system as described in Chapter 1.

Heater matrix

Removal

15 Remove the heater assembly as described in paragraphs 6 to 13.
16 Unscrew the screws and remove the inlet air duct then the air duct and matrix cover from the side of the heater.
17 Withdraw the matrix from the heater.

Refitting

18 Refitting is a reversal of removal, but refer to paragraph 14 when refitting the heater assembly.

Blower motor (models without air conditioning)

Removal

19 Remove the glovebox as described in Chapter 11, Section 26.
20 Unscrew the screws and remove the cross-bar from the glovebox aperture.
21 Disconnect the wiring from the heater air duct, then unscrew the screws and withdraw the duct from between the heater assembly and the heater blower motor.
22 Disconnect and unclip the wiring, then unscrew the mounting nuts and remove the blower motor housing (see illustrations).
23 The motor may be removed from its housing by prising off the clips and removing the screws. The heater resistor may be unclipped from the housing and the wiring disconnected (see illustration).

Refitting

24 Refitting is a reversal of removal.

Blower motor (models with air conditioning)

Removal

25 Remove the glovebox as described in Chapter 11, Section 26.
26 Unscrew the screws and remove the cross-bar from the glovebox aperture.
27 Remove the passenger side footwell kickplate and pull back the carpet for access to the engine management ECM. Remove the ECM with reference to Chapter 4A.
28 Disconnect the air conditioning wiring from its holder, then remove the holder.
29 Remove the screws and withdraw the bracket from the blower motor.
30 Unscrew the mounting screws and nuts and disconnect the wiring, then withdraw the blower motor housing and tilt it to remove.
31 The motor may be removed from its housing by prising off the clips and removing the screws.

Refitting

32 Refitting is a reversal of removal.

10 Air conditioning system - general information and precautions

General information

1 An air conditioning system is fitted as standard equipment on 623GSi models and is available as an option on other models. The system enables the temperature of incoming air to be lowered, and it also dehumidifies the air, which makes for rapid demisting and increased comfort.
2 The cooling side of the system works in the same way as a domestic refrigerator. Refrigerant gas is drawn into a belt-driven compressor, and passes into a condenser mounted on the front of the radiator, where it loses heat and becomes liquid. The liquid passes through an expansion valve to an evaporator, where it changes from liquid under high pressure to gas under low

9.22a Disconnect the wiring ...

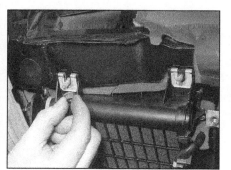

9.22c ... unscrew the mounting nuts ...

9.22d ... and remove the blower motor housing

9.23 The heater resistor

9.22b ... unclip the wiring support ...

pressure. This change is accompanied by a drop in temperature, which cools the evaporator. The refrigerant returns to the compressor, and the cycle begins again.

3 Air blown through the evaporator passes to the air distribution unit and then into the passenger compartment.

4 The heating side of the system works in the same way as on models without air conditioning.

5 The system is electronically-controlled. Any problems with the system should be referred to a Rover dealer.

Precautions

6 With an air conditioning system, it is necessary to observe special precautions whenever dealing with any part of the system, or its associated components. If for any reason the system must be disconnected, entrust this task to your Rover dealer or a refrigeration engineer.

 Warning: The refrigeration circuit contains a liquid refrigerant (Freon). The refrigerant is potentially dangerous, and should only be handled by qualified persons. If it is splashed onto the skin, it can cause frostbite. It is not itself poisonous, but in the presence of a naked flame (including a cigarette), it forms a poisonous gas. Uncontrolled discharging of the refrigerant is dangerous, and

potentially damaging to the environment. For all these reasons, it is dangerous to disconnect any part of the system without specialised knowledge and equipment.

7 Do not operate the air conditioning system if it is known to be short of refrigerant, as this may damage the compressor.

---

11 Air conditioning system components - removal and refitting

 Warning: Do not attempt to open the refrigerant circuit. Refer to the precautions given in Section 10.

1 The only operation which can be carried out easily without discharging the refrigerant is renewal of the compressor drivebelt. All other operations must be referred to a Rover dealer or an air conditioning specialist.

2 If necessary for access to other components, the compressor can be unbolted and moved aside, *without disconnecting its flexible hoses,* after removing the drivebelt. The following paragraphs described this procedure.

Compressor

Removal (leaving hoses connected)

3 Remove the compressor drivebelt as described in Chapter 1.

4 Remove the alternator as described in Chapter 5A.

5 Disconnect the wiring from the condenser fan motor and remove the connector from the fan shroud. Disconnect the wiring from the compressor.

6 Unbolt and remove the condenser fan shroud from the radiator.

7 Unscrew the mounting bolts and withdraw the compressor from its mounting bracket. Support the compressor to one side taking care not to damage the radiator fins.

8 If necessary, unscrew the bolt from the heater insulator, then unbolt and remove the compressor mounting bracket from the cylinder block.

Refitting

9 Refitting is a reversal of removal, but refit the alternator with reference to Chapter 5A and refit and adjust the compressor drivebelt as described in Chapter 1. Tighten all nuts and bolts to the specified torque.

Compressor drivebelt

Removal, refitting and adjustment

10 Where fitted, the air condioning compressor is located below the alternator on the front left-hand side of the engine. The drivebelt is shared by the alternator, and its removal, refitting and adjustment procedure is as described in Chapter 5A.

Chapter 4 Part A
PGM-FI fuel injection system

Contents

Degrees of difficulty

Easy, suitable for novice with little experience	**Fairly easy,** suitable for beginner with some experience	**Fairly difficult,** suitable for competent DIY mechanic	**Difficult,** suitable for experienced DIY mechanic	**Very difficult,** suitable for expert DIY or professional

Specifications

General

Fuel pump type	Electric, contact impeller-type, immersed in fuel tank
Fuel pump delivery rate:	
New	0.23 litres in 10 sec
Service limit	0.11 litres in 10 sec
Fuel pressure:	
Regulated	220 to 270 kPa
Maximum	280 to 330 kPa
Engine idle speed:	
Normal	770 ± 50 rpm
With IAC valve disconnected	620 ± 50 rpm
Fast idle	1400 ± 200 rpm
Injector electrical resistance	1.5 to 2.5 Ω
Injector resistors	5 to 7 Ω
Accelerator cable deflection	10 to 12 mm
Fuel gauge sender unit, electrical resistance:	
Full position	2 to 5 Ω
Half-full position	26 to 40 Ω
Empty position	105 to 110 Ω

Torque wrench settings

	Nm	lbf ft
Accelerator cable locknut	10	7
ECT sensor to cylinder head	18	13
EGR valve nuts	22	16
Fast idle thermo valve bolts	22	16
Fuel delivery banjo bolt to fuel rail	22	16
Fuel pressure regulator screws	12	9
Fuel pump delivery union banjo bolt	28	21
Fuel pump mounting nuts	6	4
Fuel rail securing nuts	12	9
Fuel rail service port drain bolt	12	9
Fuel rail to inlet manifold	25	18
Fuel tank drain bolt	50	37
Fuel tank strap bolts	38	28
IAC valve bolts	12	9
IAT sensor screws	12	9
Inlet manifold-to-cylinder head bolts	25	18
Lambda sensor	55	41
Lower inlet manifold-to-cylinder head bolts	22	16
Oxygen sensor to exhaust downpipe	45	33
Throttle body securing nuts	22	16
Upper-to-lower inlet manifold nuts and bolts	22	16

1 General information and precautions

1 PGM-FI is an integrated electronic engine management system that primarily controls the fuel injection and ignition. This chapter deals with the fuel system components only; the ignition system components are dealt with in Chapter 5B.

2 The major components comprise a fuel tank, an electric fuel pump, a fuel filter, fuel supply and return lines, a throttle body, a fuel rail, a fuel pressure regulator, four electronic fuel injectors, and an Electronic Control Module (ECM), together with its associated sensors, actuators and wiring. The overall function of each of these components is outlined below.

3 On all models, the fuel tank is mounted horizontally underneath the loadspace floorpan. The fuel level sender unit, mounted on the top of the tank, can be accessed without removing the fuel tank from the vehicle.

4 The fuel pump is of the electric, contact impeller type and is mounted inside the fuel tank. The pump motor is cooled by the fuel, in which both the pump impeller and motor are permanently immersed. The pump contains a check valve, which prevents the fuel supply line from draining when the engine is switched off and also isolates the fuel tank from the rest of the fuel system. The pump also contains pressure relief valve, to prevent excessive fuel pressure build-up in the event of a restriction occurring the fuel delivery line.

5 The fuel pump delivers a constant supply of fuel through a cartridge filter to the fuel rail, at a slightly higher pressure than required. A fuel pressure regulator maintains a constant fuel pressure to the fuel injectors and returns excess fuel to the tank via the return line. As well as providing sufficient fuel pressure for all operating conditions, this constant flow system also helps to lower fuel temperature, which inhibits vapourisation.

6 The fuel injectors are electromagnetic valves, opened and closed by the ECM. The ECM calculates the injection timing and duration according to information received electronically from sensors mounted on and around the engine. This information includes engine speed, crankshaft angular position, throttle position, intake manifold depression, ambient atmospheric pressure, intake air temperature, coolant temperature and exhaust gas oxygen content. The current supplied to each injector is limited by means of a resistor pack, to prevent overheating during continuous periods of high engine speed or repeated hard acceleration.

7 Intake air is drawn into the engine through the air cleaner, which contains a renewable paper filter element. See Chapter 1 for details of the fiter element renewal.

8 The engine idle speed is controlled, during normal operation, by an Idle Air Control (IAC) valve mounted on the side of the intake manifold. When the engine is started from cold, the idle speed is raised by additional air flow, supplied by a fast idle thermo valve, which is also mounted on the intake manifold. The thermo valve is controlled by an internal wax capsule, which expands and contracts with temperature. The IAC is controlled by the ECM, which varies the valve opening to maintain the optimum engine idle speed. The ECM also reacts to engine load signals from the alternator and air conditioning system by increasing the IAC valve opening accordingly.

9 The exhaust gas oxygen content is constantly monitored by the ECM via the Lambda sensor, which is mounted in the exhaust pipe. The ECM then uses this information to modify the injection timing and duration to maintain the optimum air:fuel ratio - a result of this is that manual adjustment of the idle exhaust CO content is not neccessary or possible. In addition, all models are fitted with an exhaust catalytic converter - see Chapter 4B for details.

10 The ECM controls the operation of the activated charcoal filter evaporative loss and Exhaust Gas Recirculation (EGR) systems - refer to Chapter 4B for further details.

11 It should be noted that fault diagnosis of the PGM-FI engine management system can be carried out without the need for dedicated electronic test equipment. The engine management system wiring harness incorporates a diagnostic socket, which can be used to set the PGM-FI ECM in a self-diagnostic mode. In this mode, the ECM will display any stored fault codes by flashing a warning lamp mounted on the instrument panel. See Section 4 for details.

12 Testing the PGM-FI system components individually, with standard workshop equipment, in an attempt to locate a fault by elimination is a time consuming operation that is unlikely to be fruitful (particularly if the fault occurs dynamically). It also carries a high risk of damage to the ECM's internal components. Problems with the systems operation that cannot be pinpointed by reference to Section 4 should be referred to a Rover dealer or fuel injection system specialist for assessment. Once the fault has has been identified, the removal/refitting sequences detailed in the following Sections will then allow the appropriate component(s) to renewed as required.

Precautions

13 Many of the operations described in this Chapter involve the disconnection of fuel lines, which may cause an amount of fuel spillage. Before commencing work, refer to the **Warning** and **Caution** below as well as the information in *Safety First!* at the beginning of this manual.

14 Residual fuel pressure always remain in the fuel system, long after the engine has been switched off. This pressure must be relieved in a controlled manner before work can commence on any component in the fuel system - refer to Section 11 for details.

15 In the interests of personal safety and equipment protection, many of the procedures in this Chapter suggest that the negative cable should be removed from the battery terminal. This firstly eliminates the possiblity of accidental short circuits being caused as the vehicle is being worked upon, and secondly prevents damage to electronic components (eg sensors, actuators, electronic control units) which are particularly sensitive to the power surges caused by disconnection or reconnection of the wiring harness whilst they are still live.

16 It should be noted, however, that many of the engine management system described in this Chapter (and Chapter 5B) have a learning capability that allows the system to adapt to the engine's running charaterristics as it wears with use. This learnt information is lost when the battery is disconnected and the system will then take a short period of time to re-learn the engine's characteristics - this may be manifested (temporarily) as rough idling, reduced throttle response and possibly a slight increase in fuel consumption, until the system re-adapts. The re-adaption time will depend on how often the vehicle is used and the driving conditions encountered.

Warning: Care must be exercised when working on any part of the fuel system. Keep the area well ventilated - open all available doors an windows to create a through-draught. Do not smoke, or allow any naked flames or uncovered light bulbs near the work area. Note that gas powered domestic appliances with pilot flames, such as heaters, boilers and tumble-dryers, also present a fire hazard - bear this in mind if you are working in an area where such appliances are installed. Always keep a suitable fire extinguisher close to the work area and familiarise yourself with its operation before starting work. Wear eye protection when working on fuel systems and wash off any fuel spilt on bare skin immediately with soap and plenty of water.

Warning: Great care must be taken to avoid disturbing any of the airbag (SRS) system wiring and components when working on the fuel system. The airbag inflation mechanism may be accidentally detonated if the wiring is disconnected in an uncontrolled manner. Refer to Chapter 12 for greater detail.

Caution: When working with fuel system components, pay particular attention to cleanliness - dirt entering the fuel system may cause blockages which could lead to poor running or even failure.

Caution: If the radio/cassette in your vehicle is equipped with an anti-theft system, make sure you have the correct activation code before disconnecting the battery.

2.1 Slacken the locknut and release the cable outer sheath from the support bracket

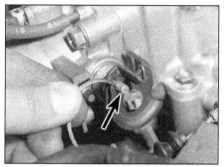

2.2 Disconnect the nipple (arrowed) from the throttle valve spindle plate

2.6 Release the cable from its securing clips

2 Accelerator cable - removal, refitting and adjustment

Removal

1 Slacken the locknut and release the cable outer sheath from the support bracket. The locknut is the one on the throttle body side of the support bracket (see illustration).
2 At the throttle body, open the throttle by hand slightly then disconnect the nipple, at the end of the inner part of the accelerator cable, from the throttle valve spindle plate (see illustration).
3 If required, refer to Chapter 11 and remove the facia trim panels from underneath the steering column, to gain extra clearance.
4 Working under the facia, lift the accelerator pedal to the top of its travel. Extract the plastic retainer from the end of the accelerator pedal lever, to free the accelerator cable from the pedal lever. On models with automatic transmission, slacken the locknut and extract the retainer from the pedal lever.
5 At the point where the cable passes through the bulkhead, press out the plastic grommet so that the cable can move freely.
6 Release the cable from its securing clips and guide it out through the bulkhead grommet into the engine bay (see illustration).

Refitting

7 Refit the accelerator cable by following the removal procedure in reverse. Note that the cable is fitted with guide rings at various points along its length. These indicate the locations at which the cable should be pressed into its securing clips.
8 Place the threaded section of the cable into the cable support bracket at the front of the inet manifold. Turn the adjusting nut until it is 3 mm away from the support bracket, then tighten the locknut to the specified torque (see illustration).

9 Check the adjustment of the accelerator cable as described in following sub-Section.

Adjustment

10 Ensure that the engine has reached normal operating temperature, before attempting to adjust the accelerator cable. This will ensure that the fast idle thermo valve has deactivated. In addition, ensure that all electrical and mechanical loads are switched off. Turn off the air conditioning, where fitted, and on models with automatic transmission, select Park.
11 Grip the inner part of the accelerator cable, at a point mid-way between the cable support bracket and the throttle spindle plate. Move the cable up and down and measure the amount by which deflects. Compare the measurement with the figure given in the Specifications, to determine whether adjustment is necessary.
12 To adjust the cable, slacken the locknut at the cable support bracket and turn the adjustment nut. Carry out the deflection measurement described in the previous paragraph. Repeat until the correct deflection is obtained. On completion tighten the locknut to the specified torque.
13 As a final check, carry out the following: press the accelerator pedal to the floor and check that the throttle opens to its end stop. Release the pedal and check that the throttle closes completely.

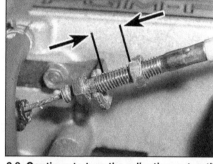

2.8 Continue to turn the adjusting nut until it is 3 mm away from the support bracket

3 Air cleaner - removal and refitting

Removal

1 Refer to Chapter 1 for details of the air cleaner filter element removal.
2 Pull the intake air ducting from the air cleaner assembly. The large diameter hose clip is spring-loaded and does not need to be slackened.
3 Release the hose clip and disconnect the breather hose from the side of the ducting (see illustration).
4 Slacken the large diameter clip, disconnect the air intake ducting from the throttle body and remove it from the engine bay (see illustrations).

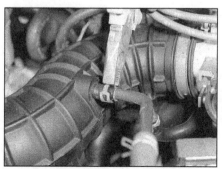

3.3 Release the hose clip and disconnect the breather hose from the side of the ducting

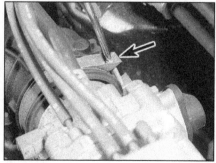

3.4a Slacken the large diameter clip, disconnect the air intake ducting from the throttle body . . .

3.4b ... and remove it from the engine bay

3.5 Remove the mounting bolts and detach the air scoop from the bodywork

5 Remove the mounting bolts and detach the air scoop from the bodywork **(see illustration)**.
6 Remove the air cleaner mounting bolts **(see illustration)**.
7 Detach the resonator stubs from the ports on the inner wing and lift the air cleaner out of the engine bay **(see illustration)**.

Refitting

8 Refit the air cleaner by following the removal procedure in reverse.

---

4 PGM FI system - fault diagnosis

General Information

1 Fault diagnosis of the PGM-FI engine management system can be carried out without the need for dedicated electronic test equipment. The engine management system wiring harness incorporates a diagnostic socket, which can be used to set the PGM-FI Engine Control Module (ECM) in a self-diagnostic mode. In this mode, the ECM will display any stored fault codes by flashing the CHECK ENGINE warning lamp. This is located on the instrument panel, above the temperature gauge, next to the hazard flasher warning lamp. **Note:** *This lamp may also light up briefly when the ignition switch is turned on. This is a normal bulb testing routine and is no cause for concern, providing the lamp extinguishes once the engine has started.*
2 It should be noted that the fault diagnosis procedure described in this section will only allow faults registered by the PGM-FI ECM to be displayed - there may be other fuel or ignition system related faults which the ECM cannot detect.
3 Testing the PGM-FI system components individually, with standard workshop equipment, in an attempt to locate a fault by elimination is a time consuming operation that is unlikely to be fruitful (particularly if the fault occurs intermittently). It also carries a high risk of damage to the ECM's internal components. Problems with the systems operation that cannot be pinpointed by reference to this Section should be referred to a Rover dealer or fuel injection system specialist for assessment. Once the fault has has been identified, the removal/refitting sequences detailed in the remainder of this Chapter should then allow the appropriate component(s) to renewed as required.

Displaying fault codes

4 Ensure that the ignition is switched off.
5 Locate the Service Check Connector. This is a blue, plastic two-pin connector, situated beneath the facia panel, to the left of the passenger's footwell (RHD vehicles) or to the right of the passenger's footwell (LHD vehicles). It may be necessary to fold back the carpet trim to gain access.

⚠ *Warning: Observe the notes in Section 1 and Chapters 10 and 12 regarding the dangers of disturbing the airbag (SRS) system wiring when working in this area.*

6 The connector has orange/red and green/white coloured cables running to it (depending on market) and will not be connected to anything. Using a short length of bare copper wire, connect the two connector pins together, by inserting the ends of the wire into the empty terminals.
7 Turn on the ignition and observe the CHECK ENGINE warning lamp on the instrument panel. If there are faults stored, a sequence of flashes will be seen - the number of flashes and the length of each flash represents a fault code. For example: three short flashes indicates fault code No 3, one short flash immediately followed by four long flashes indicates fault code No 14, etc. After a pause, the flash code will be displayed again - this process repeats continuously whilst the ignition is switched on.
8 Note that if more than one fault has been logged, these will displayed one after each other. For example, one short flash immediately followed by two long flashes (pause) four short flashes immediately followed by one long flash indicates fault codes No 12 and 41 respectively. The sequence will then repeat, as long as the ignition is switched on.
9 Use the table at the top of the following page to interpret the correct code. On completion, switch off the ignition.

3.6 Remove the air cleaner mounting bolts (arrowed)

3.7 Detach the resonator stubs from the ports (arrowed) on the inner wing and lift the air cleaner out of the engine bay

Fault Code	Source
0	Engine Control Module (ECM)
1	Heated Oxygen Sensor (HO2S)
3	Manifold Absolute Pressure (MAP) Sensor
4	Crankshaft Position (CKP) sensor
5	Manifold Absolute Pressure (MAP) Sensor
6	Engine Coolant Temperature (ECT) sensor
7	Throttle Position (TP) sensor
8	Top Dead Centre (TDC) sensor
9	No 1 Cylinder Position (CYP) sensor
10	Intake Air Temperature (IAT) sensor
12	Exhaust Gas Recirculation (EGR) system
13	Barometric Pressure (BARO) sensor
14	Idle Air Control (IAC) valve
15	Ignition output signal
17	Vehicle Speed sensor (VSS)
30	Auto Transmission gear selection signal #A
31	Auto Transmission gear selection signal #B
41	Heated Oxygen Sensor Heater
43	Fuel supply system

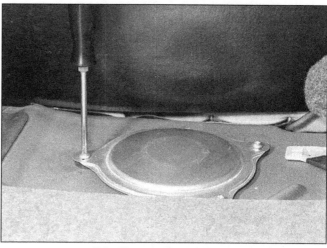

5.5a Remove the screws . . .

Resetting the Engine Control Module (ECM)

10 Once the fault has been identified and rectified, the ECM must be reset, to cancel any stored fault codes.

11 Ensure that the ignition is switched off. Make sure that you have a record of the security code for the radio/cassette player (if fitted). Note that this procedure will also erase the clock settings and radio station presets.

12 Remove the jumper wire from the Service Check Connector.

5.5b . . . and lift off the fuel gauge sender unit cover panel

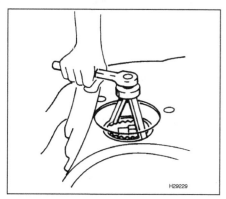

5.7 Using the specially-shaped service tool to remove the sender unit

13 Lift the lid from the engine bay fusebox and remove the BACK UP (RADIO) fuse from its socket for at least 10 seconds. This is a 7.5A rated fuse - its location is indicated by the diagram on the underside of the fusebox lid. Refit the fuse and close the fuse box lid.

14 All the original fault codes will now have been erased from the ECM memory. If the ENGINE CHECK lamp illuminates again during driving, then either the original fault has re-occurred or a new fault exists. Seek advice from a Rover dealer or fuel injection specialist.

5 Fuel gauge sender unit - removal and refitting

Removal

1 Ideally, the sender unit should be removed when the fuel in the tank is at its lowest level. Remove the fuel filler cap briefly, to depressurise the tank.

2 Disconnect the battery cable and position it away from the terminal.

3 Pivot the rear seat uprights forward and lay them flat against the seat bench. Cover the surrounding area with a dust sheet.

4 Peel the boot carpet trim away from the floor, to expose the metal access cover.

5 Remove the screws and lift off the cover panel, togther with the seal **(see illustrations)**.

6 Unplug the wiring from the top of the sender unit at the connector.

7 Ideally, the sender unit should be removed with the appropriate Rover service tool (which is a specially shaped spanner) **(see illustration)**. However if one of these cannot be hired or borrowed, the unit can be removed using a pair of slip-jointed (water pump) pliers, if care is exercised.

8 Unscrew the sender unit and withdraw it from the from the top of the fuel tank. Take

great care to avoid damaging the float arm. Allow it to drain for a few seconds before removing to completely.

9 Check the condition of the sealing ring. Renew it if it shows signs of deterioration.

10 The electrical resistance of the sender unit can be checked, using a multimeter, at all float arm positions. Connect the meter probes to the sender unit connector pins, as indicated in the illustration **(see illustration)**. Compare your measurements with the Specifications.

Refitting

11 Refit the sender unit by following the removal procedure in reverse. Ensure that the tab in the senser unit engages with the cut-out in the fuel tank. Note the FRONT marking on the access cover, which must face towards the front of the vehicle.

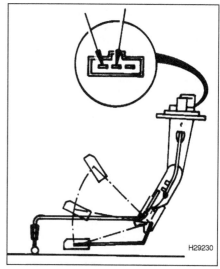

5.10 To check the electrical resistance of the sender unit, apply the multimeter probes to the sender unit connector pins (arrowed)

6 Fuel pump - removal and refitting

Removal

1 Disconnect the battery negative cable and position it away from the terminal. Depressurise the fuel system as described in Section 11.

2 Refer to Section 7 and remove the fuel tank from the underside of the vehicle.

3 Unbolt the evaporative loss valve from the fuel pump flange and position it to one side.

4 Slacken the banjo bolt and detach the fuel delivery line union from the top of the fuel pump. Remove the sealing washers, noting that new ones must be used on refitting.

5 Release the hose clip and detach the fuel return hose from the top of the fuel pump.

6 Remove the fuel pump mounting nuts and withdraw the pump assembly from the top of the fuel tank (**see illustration**).

7 Recover the flange seal if it is loose. Renew the seal it shows signs of deterioration.

Refitting

8 Refitting is a reversal of removal. Use new sealing washers when refitting the fuel delivery line banjo bolt. Ensure that the fuel pump mounting nuts are tightened to the specified torque.

9 Refit the fuel tank as described in Section 7.

7 Fuel tank - removal and refitting

Removal

Note: *This operation must be carried out when the fuel tank is practically empty.*

1 Park the vehicle on a level surface and chock the front wheels. Select first gear, or Park on models with automatic transmission.

2 Disconnect the battery negative cable and position it away from the terminal.

3 Jack up the rear of the vehicle and rest it securely on axle stands. Remove the left-hand rear roadwheel.

4 Position a suitable container under the fuel tank, then remove the drain bolt and drain the residual fuel from the tank.

5 Refer to Section 5 and disconnect the wiring from the top of the fuel gauge level sender.

6 Remove the screws and and press-studs, then lift off the protective covers to gain access to the fuel pipe connections, at the left-hand side of the fuel tank, and the evaporative loss two-way valve, at the rear upper rear edge of the fuel tank.

7 Slacken the nut and separate the fuel delivey line union.

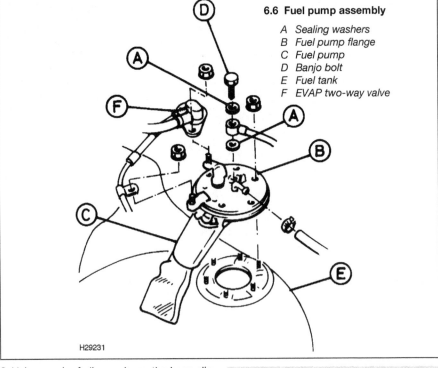

6.6 Fuel pump assembly

A Sealing washers
B Fuel pump flange
C Fuel pump
D Banjo bolt
E Fuel tank
F EVAP two-way valve

H29231

8 Using a pair of pliers, release the hose clip and detach the fuel return hose.

9 Slacken the large hose clip and detach the fuel filler neck from the fuel tank.

10 Use a pair of pliers to release the clip, then detach the breather hose from the port on the fuel tank.

11 Position a trolley jack under the tank with a block wood to prevent the jack head from damaging the surface of the tank. Raise the jack to support the tank.

12 Slacken and withdraw the mounting bolts then remove both tank mounting straps.

13 Slowly lower the tank away from the underside of the vehicle. The tank may stick to the underseal - if this is the case then carefully lever it free with a length of wood; do not use metallic tools which may damage the tank.

14 Disconnect the fuel pump wiring from the multiplug connector as it becomes accessible.

15 Release the evaporative loss hoses from their clips, then detach them from the two-way valve at the top of the tank.

16 If required, the level sender unit and fuel pump and may be removed as described in Sections 5 and 6 respectively.

Refitting

17 Refitting is a reversal of removal. Ensure that all fixings are tightened to the correct torque (where specified) and that all hoses are securely reconnected and routed.

18 On completion, refit the drain bolt, with a new sealing washer and tighten it to the specified torque.

8 Throttle body - removal and refitting

Removal

1 Disconnect the battery negative cable and position it away from the terminal.

2 Slacken the large clip and detach the air intake ducting from the throttle body.

3 Release the clip with a pair of pliers, then detach the charcoal canister hose from the port on the top of the throttle body.

4 With reference to Chapter 1, partially drain the cooling system. Disconnect both coolant hoses from the base of the throttle body.

5 Refer to Section 2 and detach the accelerator cable from the throttle spindle disc.

6 On models with automatic transission, disconnect the control cable from the throttle spindle disc. Unbolt the cable bracket from the side of the throttle body.

7 Unplug the remaining vacuum hoses from the throttle body, labelling them carefully to aid refitting later.

8 Unplug the wiring from the throttle position sensor, at the multiplug connector (**see illustration**).

9 Remove the nuts and lift the throttle body away from the inlet manifold. Recover the gasket.

Refitting

10 Refitting is a reversal of removal, noting the following points:

a) *Use a new throttle body to inlet manifold gasket.*

b) With reference to Section 2, check and if necessary adjust the operation of the accelerator cable.
c) Where applicable, refer to Chapter 7B and adjust the automatic transmission throttle control cable.
d) Refer to Section 12 and check the engine idle speed.
e) Refill the cooling system with reference to Chapter 1.

9 Inlet manifold - removal and refitting

Removal

1 Disconnect the battery negative cable and position it away from the terminal.
2 Refer to Chapter 1 and drain the cooling system.
3 Refer to Section 11 and depressurise the fuel system.
4 Slacken the hose clip and disconnect the air intake ducting from the throttle body.
5 Refer to Section 10 and remove the fuel rail and fuel injectors.
6 With reference to Section 8, remove the throttle body from the inlet manifold.
7 Refer to Chapter 4B and unbolt the EGR valve from the inlet manifold.
8 With reference to Chapter 3 carry out the following:
a) Disconnect the coolant hoses from the thermostat housing.
b) Unbolt the thermostat housing from side of the inlet manifold, then separate it from the metal connecting pipe. Recover the O-ring seal, if it works loose.
9 Disconnect the brake servo vacuum hose from the port on the side of the inlet manifold.
10 Unbolt the support bracket from the underside of the inlet manifold.
11 Disconect the hoses from the IAC valve and fast-idle thermo-valve. Label them to aid correct refitting later.
12 Unplug the engine electrical harness at the multiplug connector blocks.

8.8 Unplug the wiring from the throttle position sensor, at the multiplug connector

13 Slacken and withdraw the through-bolts and nuts, then separate the upper section of the manifold from the lower section. Check that nothing remains connected to the upper section, then lift it out of the engine bay (see illustration). Recover the gasket.
14 Progressively slacken and remove the inlet manifold-to-cylinder head bolts. Lift the manifold away from the head and recover the gasket.

Refitting

15 Refit the inlet manifold by following the removal procedure in reverse, noting the following points:
a) Use new manifold gaskets.
b) Tighten the manifold-to-cylinder head and upper-to-lower manifold nuts and bolts to the specified torque settings.
c) Check that all vacuum, electrical and coolant connections are remade corrrectly and securely.
d) On completion, check carefully for fuel and coolant leaks before bringing the vehicle back into service.

10 PGM-FI fuel injection system components - removal and refitting

1 Carry out the following, before disturbing any of the fuel injection system components:
a) Read through the Precautions in Section 1 of this Chapter.
b) Disconnect the battery negative cable and position it away from the terminal.

Throttle position (TP) sensor

3 The throttle position sensor is located on the throttle body, between the engine and the bulkhead. It is matched to the throttle body assembly and cannot be renewed separately. Refer to Section 8 for a description of the throttle body renewal procedure.

Idle air control (IAC) valve

Removal

4 The IAC valve is located between the upper section of the inlet manifold and the cylinder head.

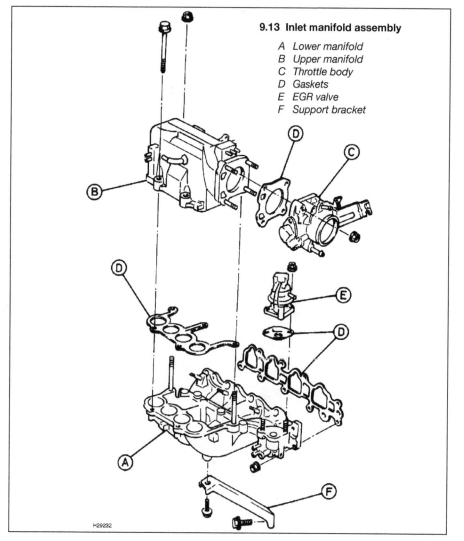

9.13 Inlet manifold assembly

A Lower manifold
B Upper manifold
C Throttle body
D Gaskets
E EGR valve
F Support bracket

10.7 Idle Air Control valve securing bolts (arrowed)

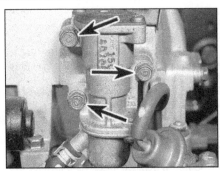

10.11 Fast Idle Thermo valve securing bolts (arrowed)

10.15 Inlet Air Temperature sensor securing screws (arrowed)

5 Release the hose clips with pliers and detach the hoses from the ports at the base of the valve.

6 Unplug the wiring from the valve at the connector.

7 Slacken and withdraw the securing bolts and remove the valve from the manifold (see illustration).

Refitting

8 Refitting is a reversal of removal. Use a new gasket and tighten the bolts to the specified torque.

Fast idle thermo valve

Removal

9 The IAC valve is located between the upper section of the inlet manifold and the cylinder head, adjacent to the fuel pressure regulator.

10 Release the hose clips with pliers and detach the hoses from the ports at the base of the valve. Label them carefully to ensure correct refitting.

11 Slacken and withdraw the securing bolts and remove the valve from the manifold (see illustration).

Refitting

12 Refitting is a reversal of removal. Use a new gasket and tighten the bolts to the specified torque.

Intake Air Temperature (IAT) sensor

Removal

13 The IAT sensor is located on the rear lower edge of the upper section of the inlet manifold.

14 Unplug the wiring from the sensor at the connector.

15 Remove the securing screws and lift out the sensor (see illustration).

Refitting

16 Refitting is a reversal of removal. Use a new gasket and tighten the screws to the specified torque.

Engine Coolant Temperature (ECT) sensor

Removal

17 The ECT sensor is located at the end of the cylinder head, beneath the ignition distributor. Do not confuse it with the temperature gauge sender nearby - the gauge sender is the one with a single connector terminal (see illustration).

18 Refer to Chapter 1 and partially drain the cooling system.

19 Unplug the wiring from the ECT sensor at the connector.

20 Carefully unscrew the sensor from the cylinder head and recover the O-ring seal.

Refitting

21 Refitting is reversal of removal. Use a new O-ring seal and tighten the sensor body to the specified torque.

Heated Oxygen Sensor (HO₂S)

Removal

22 The Lambda sensor is threaded into the exhaust downpipe, and is easily accessible from the front of the engine bay (see illustration).

23 Unplug the wiring harness from the oxygen sensor at the connector, which is mounted on the bracket to the right of the sensor itself.

24 Note: *As a flying lead remains connected to the sensor after is has been disconnected, if the appropriate size of open-ended spanner is not available, a slotted socket will be required to remove the sensor.* Working under the vehicle, slacken and withdraw the sensor, taking care to avoid damaging the sensor probe as it is removed.

Refitting

25 Apply a little anti-seize grease to the sensor threads - avoid contaminating the probe tip.

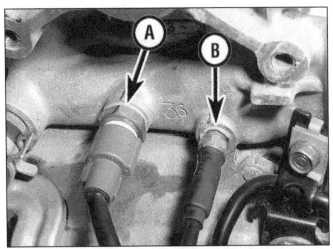

10.17 Engine coolant temperature sensor (A) and temperature gauge sender (B)

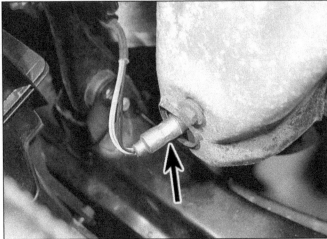

10.22 The Lambda sensor (arrowed) is threaded into the exhaust downpipe

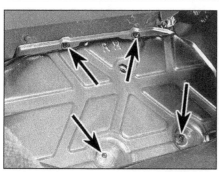

10.33 Peel back the carpet, then remove the nuts (arrowed) and lift off the ECM cover

10.34 Release the ECM from its mountings

10.39a Unplug the wiring connectors from the fuel injectors (arrowed)

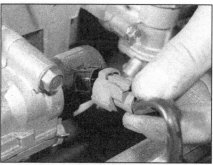

10.39b Unplug the wiring from the IAC valve

26 Refit the sensor to its housing, tightening it to the correct torque. Restore the harness connection.

Crankshaft position sensor/No 1 cylinder position/Top Dead Centre (CKP/CYP/TDC) sensor

27 The CKP/CYP/TDC sensors are all combined into one multi-function unit, which is integral with the ignition distributor housing. The sensor unit can only be renewed by overhauling the distributor; it is recommended that this operation is entrusted to a Rover dealer or and automotive electrical specialist.

PGM-FI main relay

Removal

28 The relay is mounted on a bracket behind the facia, adjacent to the steering column.
29 Slide the relay and the wiring connector from the bracket.
30 Unplug the wiring from the base of the relay, at the multiplug connector.

Refitting

31 Refitting is a reversal of removal.

Engine Control Module (ECM)

Caution: Electronic control units contain components that are sensitive to the levels of static electricity generated by a person during normal activity. Once the multiplug harness connector has been unplugged, the exposed ECU connector pins can freely

conduct stray static electricity to these components, damaging or even destroying them - the damage will be invisible and may not manifest itself immediately. Expensive repairs can be avoided by observing the following basic handling rules:

a) Handle a disconnected ECU by its case only; do not allow fingers or tools to come into contact with the connector pins.
b) When carrying an ECU around, earth yourself from time to time, by touching an earthed metal object such as an unpainted water pipe, this will discharge any potentially damaging static that may have built up.
c) Do not leave the ECU unplugged from its connector for any longer than is absolutely necessary.

Removal

32 The ECM is located beneath the carpet trim in the front passenger's footwell.
33 Release the carpet from its fixings, and peel it back to expose the ECM cover plate (see illustration).
34 Remove the nuts and lift off the cover. Release the ECM from its mounting studs (see illustration).
35 Unplug the wiring from the ECM at the multiplug connectors.

Refitting

36 Refitting is a reversal of removal.

Fuel rail and fuel injectors

Removal

37 Refer to Section 11 and depressurise the fuel system.
38 Refer to the relevant sub-Section and remove the fuel pressure regulator from the fuel rail.
39 Unplug the injector wiring connectors, labelling them to aid correct refitting later. In addition, unplug the wiring from the IAC valve (see illustrations)
40 Remove the screws and lift off the plastic wiring harness guide (see illustrations).
41 Slacken and remove the union nut, then disconnect the fuel supply pipe from the end of the fuel rail. Recover the sealing washers (see illustrations).

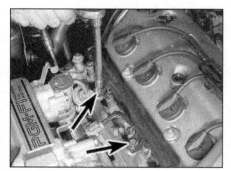

10.40a Remove the screws (arrowed) . . .

10.40b . . . and lift off the plastic wiring harness guide

10.41a Slacken and remove the union nut . . .

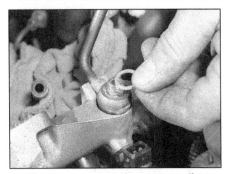

10.41b . . . recover the upper sealing washer . . .

10.41c . . . disconnect the fuel supply pipe . . .

10.41d . . . and recover the lower sealing washer

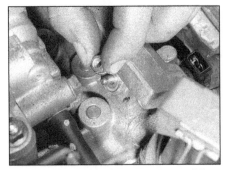

10.42a Slacken and remove the retaining nuts . . .

10.42b . . . then carefully lift off the fuel rail

42 Slacken and remove the retaining nuts, then carefully lift off the fuel rail. Note that the injectors may remain in the manifold. Recover the injector upper O-ring seals and the cushion rings from the fuel rail (see illustrations).

43 The injectors can be removed individually by easing them carefully from the fuel rail, together with the injector lower seal. Recover the insulating rings from the manifold, once the injectors have been removed (see illustrations).

44 If a faulty injector is suspected, before condemning it, it is worth trying the effect of one of the proprietary injector-cleaning

treatments. In addition, most fuel injection specialists offer a fuel injector cleaning service.

Refitting

45 Fit a new set of cushion rings onto inlet ports the fuel injectors.

46 Smear the new injector upper O-rings with clean engine oil and press them into the recesses at the top of each injector.

47 Fit a new set of insulating rings into the ports at the inlet manifold.

48 Smear the new injector lower seals with clean engine oil and press them into the inlet manifold, above the insulating rings.

49 Carefully press the injectors into the fuel rail, taking care not to damage the O-ring seals.

50 Ensure that the fuel rail spacers are correctly fitted to each mounting stud, then place the fuel rail and injectors in position over the inlet manifold. Guide the injector nozzles into their respective ports, taking care not to damage the lower seals.

51 At each injector, align the marking on the plastic connector moulding with the corresponding marking on the fuel rail.

52 Fit the fuel rail securing nuts and tighten them to the specified torque.

53 Connect the fuel delivery hose to the fuel rail, using new 6 mm washer and banjo bolt sealing washers. Tighen the bolt to the specified torque.

54 Reconnect the injector wiring, then refit the harness guide and tighten the securing screws. Reconnect the wiring for the IAC valve.

55 Refit the fuel pressure regulator, as desribed in the relevant sub-Section.

56 Check that all vacuum and electrical connections are remade corrrectly and securely.

57 On completion, check exhaustively for fuel leaks before bringing the vehicle back into service.

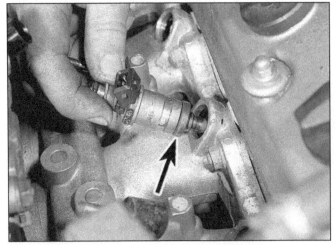

10.43a If the injectors remain in the manifold, ease them out carefully, together with the lower seals (arrowed)

10.43b Recover the insulating rings from the manifold, once the injectors have been removed

10.59 Disconnect the vacuum hose from the port on the top of the fuel pressure regulator

10.60 Slacken the clip and disconnect the fuel return hose from the bottom of the regulator

10.61a Remove the securing screws . . .

Fuel pressure regulator

Removal

58 Refer to Section 11 and depressurise the fuel system.
59 Disconnect the vacuum hose from the port on the top of the fuel pressure regulator **(see illustration)**.
60 Slacken the clip and disconnect the fuel return hose from the bottom of the regulator **(see illustration)**. Be prepared for an amount of fuel loss - position a small container and some old rags underneath the regulator housing.
61 Remove the securing screws and lift out the regulator body, recovering the O-ring seal if it is loose **(see illustrations)**.

Refitting

62 Renew the regulator O-ring seal if it appears worn or damaged.
63 Refit the fuel pressure regulator by following the removal procedure in reverse. On completion, tighten the securing screws to the specified torque.

Manifold absolute pressure (MAP) sensor

Removal

64 The MAP sensor mounted within the vacuum control unit, at the rear of the engine bay.
65 Unclip the plastic cover panel.
66 Unplug the wiring from the sensor at the multiway connector.

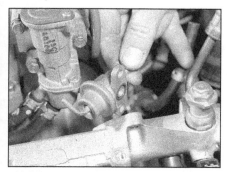

10.61b . . . and lift out the regulator body

67 Detach the vacuum hose from the port at the base of the valve.
68 Remove the screws and lift the valve from its mountings.

Refitting

69 Refitting is a reversal of removal.

Barometric Pressure (BARO) sensor

70 The BARO sensor is integral with the ECM and cannot be renewed separately.

11 Fuel injection system - depressurisation

> ⚠️ **Warning: Refer to the Precautions given in Section 1 of this Chapter.**

1 Disconnect the battery negative cable and position it away from the terminal.
2 The service port is located at the far left hand end of the fuel rail.
3 Pad the area surrounding the service port with plenty of absorbent rags, and position a small container under the port, to catch any fuel spills.
4 Hold the union nut still with a ring spanner, then slowly slacken the drain bolt, to release the fuel pressure **(see illustration)**. When the flow of fuel ceases, remove the bolt and renew the sealing washer.
5 Refit the drain bolt and tighten it to the specified torque.

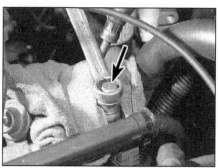

11.4 Hold the union nut still with a ring spanner, then slowly slacken the drain bolt (arrowed), to release the fuel pressure

12 Idle speed adjustment and exhaust CO content check

Exhaust CO content - checking

1 A description of this procedure is given in Chapter 1. Note that the engine idle speed must be checked and if necessary adjusted before an accurate CO check can be obtained.

Engine idle speed - checking and adjustment

2 Take the vehicle on a short run to allow it to warm up to normal operating temperature. Allow it to idle and wait until the auxiliary cooling fan has cut in and out again, at least twice, before proceeding.
3 Stop the engine and connect a tachometer to the engine, in accordance with the manufacturer's instructions. Failing this, the tachometer built into the vehicles own instrument panel will be accurate enough for the purposes of this test.
4 Refer to Section 10 and disconnect the wiring from the IAC valve, on the inlet manifold.
5 Check that all electrical and mechanicals loads are off. Ensure that the headlights, blower motor, rear window demister, direction indicators and air conditioning are switched off, and on vehicles with automatic transmission, ensure that Park or Neutral is selected.
6 Start the engine with the accelerator pedal slightly depressed. Hold the engine speed steady at 1000 rpm, then **slowly** release the pedal until the engine maintains a steady idle.
7 Check the engine idle speed reading on the tachometer.
8 If the idle speed requires adjustment, extract the plastic plug from the adjustment hole at the top of the throttle body and insert a flat-bladed screwdriver. Turn the adjustment screw until the idle speed is correct **(see illustration)**.
9 Switch off the engine and ignition. Reconnect the wiring to the IAC valve.

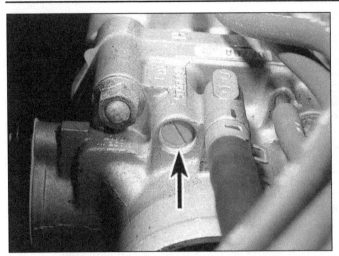

12.8 Idle speed adjustment screw (arrowed)

13.4 To reset the inertia switch, depress the centre of the round rubber cover (arrowed) - centre console removed for clarity

10 The disconnected IAC valve wiring will have been registered by the Engine Control Module (ECM) as a fault. The ECM must therefore be reset to cancel the fault - refer to Section 4 for a description of this procedure.

11 Restart the engine and recheck the engine idle speed.

12 Switch on the main beam headlights and the rear window demister, and check that the correct idle speed is maintained.

13 Where applicable, switch on the air conditioning, with the blower motor set to HI and allow the engine to idle for a few minutes. Check that the correct idle speed is maintained, as the air conditioning compressor cuts in and out.

14 On completion, fit a new plastic plug to adjustment hole at the top of the throttle body.

15 If the idle speed cannot be adjusted to the correct value, is unstable, or drops so low that the engine stalls during these tests, refer to Section 4 and obtain a readout of the ECM fault code log, in an attempt to locate the problem. Failing this, the vehicle should be referred to a Rover dealer or fuel injection system specialist for assessment.

13 Fuel cut-off inertia switch - resetting

1 The inertia switch (where fitted) is mounted on a bracket behind the lower part of the facia. Access can be gained by reaching behind the centre console, from the driver's side footwell.

2 The electrical supply to the PGM-FI fuel pump passes through the inertia switch. In the event of a collision, the mechanical shock causes the inertia switch to trip, cutting the electrical supply to the fuel pump, as a safety measure.

3 If the vehicle has been involved in an accident, make sure that there is no damage to the fuel system components before proceeding.

4 To reset the inertia switch, depress the centre of the round rubber cover, at the top of the switch body **(see illustration)**.

5 Check that the supply to the fuel pump is restored by switching on the ignition. A buzzing noise should be audible for a few seconds, in the area of the fuel tank, as the fuel pump primes the fuel delivery system.

Chapter 4 Part B
Emission control and exhaust systems

Contents

Degrees of difficulty

Easy, suitable for novice with little experience	Fairly easy, suitable for beginner with some experience	Fairly difficult, suitable for competent DIY mechanic	Difficult, suitable for experienced DIY mechanic	Very difficult, suitable for expert DIY or professional

Specifications

Torque wrench settings	Nm	lbft
EGR valve	22	16
Exhaust manifold-to-cylinder head nuts	32	24
Exhaust manifold-to-downpipe nuts	55	41
Exhaust manifold heat shield securing nuts	22	16
Exhaust manifold support bracket bolts	45	33
Oxygen sensor	45	33
Downpipe-to-hanger bracket nuts	18	13
Catalytic converter-to-downpipe nuts	34	25
Catalytic converter-to-intermediate pipe nuts	34	25
Intermediate pipe-to-tailpipe nuts	55	41
Exhaust pipe heat shield securing nuts	10	7

1 General information

Caution: If the radio/cassette in your vehicle is equipped with an anti-theft system, make sure you have the correct activation code before disconnecting the battery.

Emission control systems

1 All models use unleaded petrol and are controlled by engine management systems that are tuned to give the best compromise between driveability, fuel consumption and exhaust emission production.

2 A number of auxiliary systems are fitted, to help minimise the release of harmful emissions. A crankcase emission control system that reduces the release of pollutants from the engines lubrication system is fitted to all models. The production of harmful exhaust gas pollutants is reduced by a combination of an exhaust catalytic converter and an Exhaust Gas Recirculation (EGR) system. An evaporative loss emission control system, which reduces the release of gaseous hydrocarbons from fuel stored in the fuel tank to the atmosphere, is also fitted.

Crankcase emission control

3 The engine is sealed to allow the emission of combustion blow-by gases and oil vapour to be controlled. The gases are drawn from the cylinder head cover into the inlet tract, where they are recycled and burned by the engine during normal combustion.

4 Under conditions of high manifold depression (i.e. idling, deceleration) the gases will be sucked positively out of the crankcase. Under conditions of low manifold depression (i.e. acceleration, high engine speeds) the gases are forced out of the crankcase by the (relatively) higher crankcase pressure; if the engine is worn, the raised crankcase pressure (due to increased blow-by past the piston rings) will cause some of the flow to return under all manifold conditions. A Positve Crankcase Ventilation (PCV) valve, mounted on the camshaft cover, contols the flow of gases from the engine. See Chapter 1 for further details, as the renewal of the PCV valve is part of the routine maintenance schedule.

Exhaust emission control - petrol models

5 To minimise the amount of pollutants which escape into the atmosphere, all models have a catalytic converter fitted in line with the exhaust system.

6 The fuelling system is of the closed-loop type. An oxygen sensor, mounted upstream of the catalytic converter in the exhaust system informs the engine management system ECM of the amount of oxygen present in the exhaust gas and hence how efficiently the fuel mixture is being burnt. This allows the PGM-FI ECM to adjust the the the air/fuel mixture electronically, by altering the fuel injector pulse width, to optimise combustion. The chemically-correct ratio for the complete combustion of petrol is 14.7 parts (by weight) of air to 1 part of fuel; this is known as the Stoichiometric ratio.

7 The oxygen sensor only begins working properly when its oxygen-sensitive tip is heated above a particular temperature by the exhaust gases passing over it. After the engine is started from cold, when the exhaust gases are relatively cool, a heating element built into the oxygen sensor allows the sensor's tip to be rapidly heated to its optimum operating temperature. This allows the fuelling to be accurately controlled during warm-up, when exhaust emissions are at their highest. The oxygen sensor heater is controlled by the PGM-FI ECM via a relay.

8 An Exhaust Gas Recirculation (EGR) system is fitted to all models. This reduces the levels of hydrocarbons of nitrogen oxides produced during combustion by directing a variable proportion of the exhaust gas back into the inlet manifold, via a plunger valve. The system is controlled electronically by the PGM-FI engine management ECM.

Evaporative emission control

9 To minimise the escape of unburned hydrocarbons into the atmosphere, an evaporative loss emission control system is fitted to all models. The fuel tank filler cap is sealed and a charcoal-filled canister mounted in the engine collects the petrol vapours released from the fuel contained in the fuel tank. It stores them until they can be drawn from the canister (under the control of the PGM-FI ECM) via the purge valves into the inlet tract, where they are then burned by the engine during normal combustion.

10 To ensure that the engine runs correctly when it is cold and/or idling and to protect the catalytic converter from the effects of an over-rich mixture, the purge control valves are not opened by the ECM until the engine has warmed up, and the engine is under load; the valve is then pulsed to allow the stored vapour to pass into the inlet tract.

Exhaust system

11 The exhaust system comprises a cast exhaust manifold, a downpipe with an integral flexible coupling, a separate, 3-way catalytic converter, an intermediate pipe with an integral, in-line silencer, and a tailpipe incorporating the rear tailbox. The exhaust system is supported by number of mounting brackets and rubber couplings.

12 The individual sections of the exhaust system are connected by means of gasketed flange joints. Pressed metal shields are mounted above the exhaust pipe at certain points, to protect the floorpan and surrounding components from the heat produced by the exhaust system.

4.2 EGR valve location on the inlet manifold

2 Evaporative loss emission control system - information and component renewal

Information

1 The evaporative loss emission control system consists of a fuel tank-mounted two-way valve, a solenoid purge valve, the charcoal canister and a series of connecting vacuum hoses.

Component renewal

Solenoid purge valve

2 The purge valve is part of the Vacuum Control Unit - see Section 6 for details.

Charcoal canister

3 Locate the canister on the right-hand side of the engine bay. Compress the tabs to release the hose clips, then disconnect the vacuum hoses from the canister. Label the hoses for position, to aid correct refitting.

4 Slide the canister upwards away from its mounting bracket and remove it from the engine bay.

5 Refitting is a reversal of removal.

Two-way valve

6 The two-way valve is mounted on the top of the fuel tank and its removal is described as part of the fuel tank removal procedure. Refer to Chapter 4A for details.

3 Crankcase emission system - general information

1 The crankcase emission control system consists of a series of hoses that connect the the camshaft cover vent to the air intake, via a Positive Crankcase Ventilation (PCV) valve.

2 The only component requiring maintenace is the PCV valve; its renewal is part of the routine maintenance schedule, which is detailed in Chapter 1.

4 Exhaust Gas Recirculation (EGR) system - information and component renewal

Information

1 The EGR system consists of an EGR valve, an EGR vacuum control solenoid, an EGR modulator valve and a series of connecting vacuum hoses.

2 The EGR valve is mounted on a flange joint at the inlet manifold. Exhaust gas is directed to the valve by means of a port integral to the cylinder head **(see illustration)**.

3 Both the EGR vacuum control solenoid and the EGR modulator valve are integral with the Vacuum Control Unit - refer to Section 6 for details of their removal.

Component renewal

EGR valve

4 Disconnect the vacuum hose from the port at the side of the EGR valve.

5 Release the clip and unplug the wiring from the feedback potentiometer at the top of the EGR valve.

6 Remove the nuts and lift the EGR valve from the inlet manifold flange. Discard the gasket.

7 Refitting is a reversal of removal, noting the following points:
  a) *Use a new flange joint gasket.*
  b) *Fit new self-locking nuts (where applicable) and tighten them to the specified torque.*

EGR vacuum control solenoid/EGR modulator valve

8 Refer to the information given in Section 6.

5 Exhaust manifold - removal and refitting

Removal

1 Disconnect the battery negative cable and position it away from the terminal.

2 Refer to Chapter 4A and unplug the wiring from the oxygen sensor at the connector.

3 Remove the securing bolts and lift the pressed metal heat shield from the front of the exhaust manifold. On models with air conditioning, remove the heat shield from the side of the manifold.

4 Unbolt the oxygen sensor from the manifold, with reference to Chapter 4A. Take great care to avoid damaging the sensor tip.

5 Remove the nuts and separate the exhaust downpipe from the base of the manifold. Discard the gasket - a new item must be used on refiting.

6 Remove the bolts and detach the support bracket from the manifold, at the rear of the lower flange joint.

7 Progressively slacken and withdraw each of the exhaust manifold securing nuts.

8 Lift the manifold from its mounting studs and remove the gasket **(see illustration)**.

Refitting

9 Refitting is a reversal of removal, noting the following points:
  a) *Ensure that the mating surfaces of the cylinder head and the manifold are completely clean, free of corrosion. Avoid scoring the mating surfaces during the cleaning process, as this may cause the gasket to leak.*
  b) *Renew the gasket if it appears worn, or was damaged during removal.*
  c) *Use new manifold securing nuts and tighten them to the specified torque.*
  d) *When refitting the downpipe to the manifold, use new self-locking nuts and a new gasket. Tighten the nuts to the specified torque.*
  e) *Refit the oxygen sensor in accordance with the instruction in Chapter 4A.*

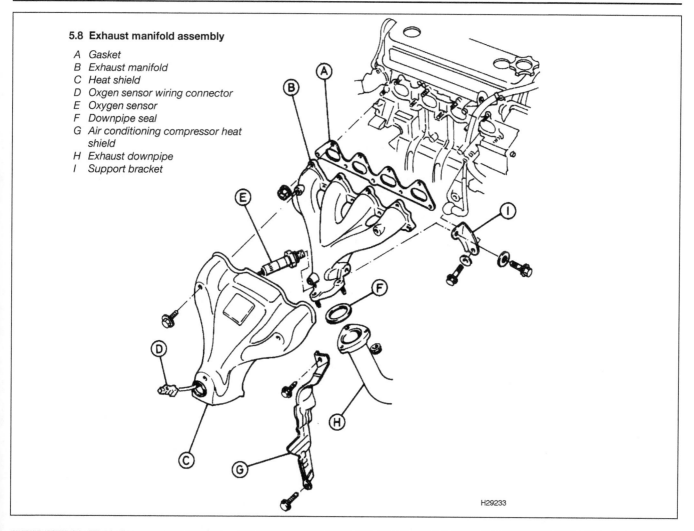

5.8 Exhaust manifold assembly

A *Gasket*
B *Exhaust manifold*
C *Heat shield*
D *Oxgen sensor wiring connector*
E *Oxygen sensor*
F *Downpipe seal*
G *Air conditioning compressor heat shield*
H *Exhaust downpipe*
I *Support bracket*

H29233

6 Vacuum Control Unit - general information

1 The vacuum control unit incorporates the EGR vacuum control solenoid, the EGR modulator valve, the evaporative loss purge solenoid and the Manifold Absolute Pressure (MAP) sensor **(see illustration)**. Each device is mounted on a common bracket and can be removed individually.

2 To remove one of the devices wihtin the vacuum control unit, first depress the locking tabs at either side of the control unit, then remove the plastic cover panel.

3 Ensure that the ignition is switched off, then unplug the wiring harness from the relevant device the appropriate connector.

4 Pull the vacuum hoses from the relevant ports, making a note of their orientation to aid refitting later. Note that each hose has a identification number marked on it.

5 Remove the screws and lift the relevant device from the common mounting bracket.

6 Refitting is a reversal of removal. Ensure that all vacuum hoses are correctly refitted.

6.1 Vacuum control unit assembly

A *EGR vacuum control solenoid*
B *EVAP purge solenoid*
C *EGR modulator valve*
D *MAP sensor*
E *Vacuum hose connections*

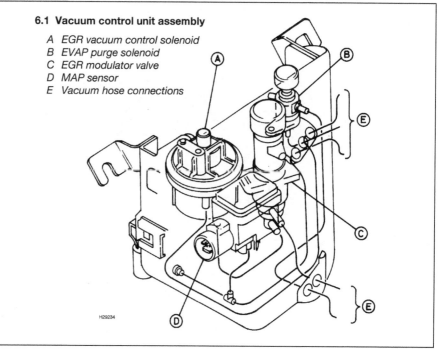

H29234

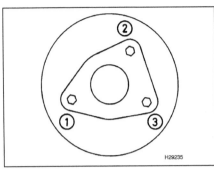

7.6 Tightening sequence for downpipe-to-catalytic converter nuts - viewed from engine side

7 Exhaust system - component renewal

General information

1 Each exhaust section can be removed individually or, alternatively, the complete system can be removed as a unit. To remove the system or part of the system, first jack up the front or rear of the car as applicable and support it on axle stands. Alternatively, position the vehicle on a set of ramps.

Component renewal

Downpipe

2 Place blocks of wood, or a trolley jack, under the front of the intermediate pipe, to act as a support.
3 Remove the nuts and separate the downpipe from the hanger bracket in front of the flexible coupling.
4 Slacken and remove the nuts securing the downpipe to the catalytic converter. Remove the nuts and bolts and recover the gasket from the joint.
5 Refer to Section 5 and unbolt the downpipe

from the exhaust manifold. Recover the gasket then withdraw the downpipe from underneath the vehicle.
6 Refitting is a reversal of removal, noting the following points:
a) Use new gaskets and self-locking nuts at all disturbed joints.
b) Tighten the downpipe-to-catalytic converter nuts in the sequence shown **(see illustration)**.

Catalytic converter

7 Place blocks of wood or a trolley jack under the downpipe and intermediate pipe to act as supports. Unbolt the heat shields from the underside of the catalytic converter casing.
8 Slacken and remove the nuts securing the downpipe to the catalytic converter, and the catalytic converter to the intermediate pipe. Withdraw the bolts and remove the gaskets from the joints.
9 Free the catalytic converter from the intermediate pipe then withdraw it from underneath the vehicle.
10 Refitting is a reversal of removal, noting the following points:
a) Use new gaskets and self-locking nuts at all disturbed joints.
b) Tighten the downpipe-to-catalytic converter nuts in the sequence shown **(refer to illustration 7.6)**.

Intermediate pipe

11 Place blocks of wood or a trolley jack under the downpipe and tailpipe to act as supports.
12 Slacken and remove the nuts securing the intermediate pipe to the catalytic converter, and the intermediate pipe to the tailpipe. Withdraw the bolts and remove the gaskets from the joints.
13 Disengage the intermediate pipe mountings from the rubber hangers and remove it from underneath the vehicle.
14 Refitting is a reversal of removal, noting the following:

a) Use new gaskets and self-locking nuts at all disturbed joints **(see illustration)**.
b) Inspect the rubber mountings for signs of damage or deterioration, and renew as necessary.

Tailpipe

15 Place blocks of wood or a trolley jack under the intermediate pipe to act as a support.
16 Slacken and remove the nuts securing the intermediate pipe to the tailpipe. Withdraw the bolts and remove the gasket from the joint.
17 Unhook the tailpipe from its mounting rubbers and remove it from the vehicle.
18 Refitting is a reversal of removal, noting the following:
a) Use new gaskets and self-locking nuts at all disturbed joints.
b) Inspect the rubber mountings for signs of damage or deterioration, and renew as necessary.

Complete system

19 Disconnect the downpipe from the manifold as described earlier in this Chapter.
20 With the aid of an assistant, free the system from all its mounting rubbers and manoeuvre it out from underneath the vehicle.
21 Prior to tightening the exhaust system fasteners, ensure all rubber mountings are correctly seated and that there is adequate clearance between the exhaust system and vehicle underbody **(see illustration)**.

Heatshields

22 The heatshields are secured to the underside of the body by a mixture of nuts, bolts and clips. Each shield can be removed once the relevant exhaust section has been removed. Note that if the shield is being removed to gain access to a component located behind it, in some cases it may prove sufficient to remove the retaining nuts and/or bolts and simply lower the shield, without the need to disturb the exhaust system.

7.14 Use new gaskets when reconnecting exhaust system joints

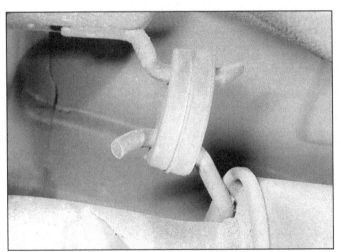

7.21 Ensure all rubber mountings are correctly seated

8 Catalytic converter - general information and precautions

1 The catalytic converter is a simple device with no moving parts, which needs no maintenance. There are, however, some facts of which an owner should be aware if the catalytic converter is to function properly for its full service life.

a) DO NOT use leaded petrol in a car equipped with a catalytic converter - the lead will coat the precious metals reagents, reducing their converting efficiency and will eventually destroy the converter.

b) Always keep the ignition and fuel systems well-maintained in accordance with the manufacturer's schedule.

c) If the engine develops a misfire, unburnt fuel will be supplied to the catalytic converter, which could cause it to overheat - avoid using the vehicle until the fault is cured.

d) DO NOT push- or tow-start the car - this could soak the catalytic converter in unburned fuel, causing it to overheat when the engine eventually starts.

e) DO NOT switch off the ignition at high engine speeds.

f) In some cases a sulphurous smell (like that of rotten eggs) may be noticed from the exhaust. This is common to many catalytic converter-equipped cars; the effect should fade after the car has covered a few thousand miles. Low quality fuel with a high sulphur content will exacerbate this effect.

g) The catalytic converter, used on a well-maintained and well-driven car, should last for between 50 000 and 100 000 miles - if the converter is no longer effective it must be renewed.

h) DO NOT use fuel or engine oil additives - they may cause the engine to emit substances which are harnful to the catalytic converter.

i) DO NOT continue to use the car if the engine burns oil to the extent of leaving a visible trail of blue smoke.

j) Remember that the catalytic converter operates at very high temperatures. Therefore after a long run, to prevent the risk of fire, avoid parking the car over dry undergrowth, long grass or piles of dead leaves.

k) The precious metal reagents inside the catalytic converter are applied to a ceramic block, which is very FRAGILE and can easily be broken by a hard impact. Do not strike the catalytic converter casing with tools during servicing work.

Chapter 5 Part A
Starting and charging systems

Contents

Degrees of difficulty

Easy, suitable for novice with little experience		**Fairly easy,** suitable for beginner with some experience		**Fairly difficult,** suitable for competent DIY mechanic		**Difficult,** suitable for experienced DIY mechanic		**Very difficult,** suitable for expert DIY or professional	

Specifications

General
System type . . . . 12 volt, negative earth

Starter motor
Rating:
    Models with manual transmission . . . . 1.4 kW
    Models with automatic transmission . . . . 1.6 kW

Alternator
Output . . . . 70/80 A, at 13.5 V
Brush length:
    New . . . . 10.5 mm
    Service limit . . . . 5.5 mm
Drivebelt deflection, with test force applied (see text):
    Used belt . . . . 10 to 12 mm
    New belt:
        Models with air conditioning . . . . 4.5 to 7.0 mm
        Models without air conditioning . . . . 8.5 to 11.0 mm

Torque wrench settings

	Nm	lbf ft
Alternator upper mounting bolt	45	33
Alternator lower mounting bolt locknut	22	16
Starter motor lower mounting bolt:		
Models with automatic transmission	45	33
Models with manual transmission	75	55
Starter motor upper mounting bolt	45	33

1 General information and precautions

General information

1 The engine electrical system consists mainly of the charging and starting systems. Because of their engine-related functions, these components are covered separately from the body electrical devices such as the lights, instruments, etc (which are covered in Chapter 12). On petrol engine models, refer to Part B of this Chapter for information regarding the ignition system.

2 The electrical system is of the 12-volt negative earth type.

3 The battery may of the low maintenance or maintenance-free (sealed for life) type and is charged by the alternator, which is belt-driven from the crankshaft pulley.

4 The starter motor is of the pre-engaged type incorporating an integral solenoid. On starting, the solenoid moves the drive pinion into engagement with the flywheel ring gear before the starter motor is energised. Once the engine has started, a one-way clutch prevents the motor armature being driven by the engine until the pinion disengages from the flywheel.

Precautions

5 Further details of the various systems are given in the relevant Sections of this Chapter. While some repair procedures are given, the usual course of action is to renew the component concerned. The owner whose interest extends beyond mere component renewal should obtain a copy of the *Automobile Electrical & Electronic Systems Manual*, available from the publishers of this manual.

6 It is necessary to take extra care when working on the electrical system to avoid damage to semi-conductor devices (diodes and transistors), and to avoid the risk of personal injury. In addition to the precautions given in *Safety first!* at the beginning of this manual, observe the following when working on the system:

7 *Always remove rings, watches, etc before working on the electrical system.* Even with the battery disconnected, capacitive discharge could occur if a components live terminal is earthed through a metal object. This could cause a shock or nasty burn.

8 *Do not reverse the battery connections.* Components such as the alternator, electronic control units, or any other components having semi-conductor circuitry could be irreparably damaged.

9 If the engine is being started using jump leads and a slave battery, connect the batteries *positive-to-positive* and *negative-to-negative* (see *Jump starting*). This also applies when connecting a battery charger.

10 Never disconnect the battery terminals, the alternator, any electrical wiring or any test instruments when the engine is running.

11 Do not allow the engine to turn the alternator when the alternator is not connected.

12 Never test for alternator output by touching the output lead to earth.

13 Never use an ohmmeter or continuity tester of the type incorporating a hand-cranked or high-voltage generator for circuit testing.

14 Always ensure that the battery negative lead is disconnected when working on the electrical system.

15 Before using electric-arc welding equipment on the car, disconnect the battery, alternator and components such as the fuel injection/ignition electronic control unit to protect them from damage caused by large earth currents.

Caution: If the radio/cassette in your vehicle is equipped with an anti-theft system, make sure you have the correct activation code before disconnecting the battery.

16 Certain radio/cassette units fitted as standard equipment by Rover are equipped with a built-in security code to deter thieves. If the power source to the unit is cut, the anti-theft system will activate. Even if the power source is immediately reconnected, the radio/cassette unit will not function until the correct security code has been entered. Therefore, if you do not know the correct security code for the radio/cassette unit **do not** disconnect the battery negative terminal of the battery or remove the radio/cassette unit from the vehicle. Refer to vehicles in-car entertainment manual for further information.

2 Battery - testing and charging

Standard and low maintenance battery - testing

1 If the vehicle covers a small annual mileage it is worthwhile checking the specific gravity of the electrolyte every three months to determine the state of charge of the battery. Use a hydrometer to make the check and compare the results with the following table

	Ambient temperature	
	Above 25ºC	Below 25ºC
Fully charged	1.210 to 1.230	1.270 to 1.290
70 % charged	1.170 to 1.190	1.230 to 1.250
Discharged	1.050 to 1.070	1.110 to 1.130

Note that the specific gravity readings assume an electrolyte tempera-ture of 15ºC (60ºF); for every 10ºC (48ºF) below 15ºC (60ºF) subtract 0.007. For every 10ºC (48ºF) above 15ºC (60ºF) add 0.007.

2 If the battery condition is suspect, first check the specific gravity of electrolyte in each cell. A variation of 0.040 or more between any cells indicates loss of electrolyte or deterioration of the internal plates.

3 If the specific gravity variation is 0.040 or more, the battery should be renewed. If the cell variation is satisfactory but the battery is discharged, it should be charged as described later in this Section.

Maintenance-free battery - testing

4 In cases where a sealed for life maintenance-free battery is fitted, topping-up and testing of the electrolyte in each cell is not possible. The condition of the battery can therefore only be tested using a battery condition indicator or a voltmeter.

5 Certain models may be fitted with a maintenance-free battery, with a built-in charge condition indicator. The indicator is located in the top of the battery casing, and indicates the condition of the battery from its colour. If the indicator shows green, then the battery is in a good state of charge. If the indicator turns darker, eventually to black, then the battery requires charging, as described later in this Section. If the indicator shows clear/yellow, then the electrolyte level in the battery is too low to allow further use, and the battery should be renewed. **Do not** attempt to charge, load or jump start a battery when the indicator shows clear/yellow.

6 If testing the battery using a voltmeter, the test is only accurate if the battery has not been subjected to any kind of charge for the previous six hours. If this is not the case, switch on the headlights for 30 seconds, then wait four to five minutes before testing the battery after switching off the headlights. All other electrical circuits must be switched off, so check that the doors and tailgate are fully shut when making the test.

7 If the voltage reading is less than 12.2 volts, then the battery is discharged, whilst a reading of 12.2 to 12.4 volts indicates a partially discharged condition.

8 If the battery is to be charged, remove it from the vehicle and charge it as described later in this Section.

Standard and low maintenance battery - charging

Note: *The following is intended as a guide only. Always refer to the manufacturers recommendations (often printed on a label attached to the battery) before charging a battery.*

9 Charge the battery at a rate equivalent to 10% of the battery capacity (eg for a 45 Ah battery charge at 4.5 A) and continue to charge the battery at this rate until no further rise in specific gravity is noted over a four hour period.

10 Alternatively, a trickle charger charging at the rate of 1.5 amps can safely be used overnight.

11 Specially rapid boost charges which are claimed to restore the power of the battery in 1 to 2 hours are not recommended, as they can cause serious damage to the battery plates through overheating.

12 While charging the battery, note that the temperature of the electrolyte should never exceed 37.8ºC (100ºF).

Maintenance-free battery - charging

Note: *The following is intended as a guide only. Always refer to the manufacturers recommendations (often printed on a label attached to the battery) before charging a battery.*

13 This battery type takes considerably longer to fully recharge than the standard type, the time taken being dependent on the extent of discharge, but it can take anything up to three days.

14 A constant voltage type charger is required, to be set, when connected, to 13.9 to 14.9 volts with a charger current below 25 amps. Using this method, the battery should be usable within three hours, giving a voltage reading of 12.5 volts, but this is for a partially discharged battery and, as mentioned, full charging can take considerably longer.

15 If the battery is to be charged from a fully discharged state (condition reading less than 12.2 volts), have it recharged by your Rover dealer or local automotive electrician, as the charge rate is higher and constant supervision during charging is necessary.

3 Battery - removal and refitting

Removal

Note: *If the vehicle has a security coded radio, check that you have a copy of the code number before disconnecting the battery cable; refer to Chapter 12 for details.*

1 Slacken the clamp screw and disconnect the battery negative cable from the terminal.

2 Peel back the cover and disconnect the battery positive cable in the same manner.
3 Slacken and remove the nuts, then lift off the battery clamping plate.
4 Remove the battery from the engine bay.

Refitting

5 Refit the battery by following the removal procedure in reverse. Tighten the battery clamping plate nuts securely.

4 Alternator/charging system - testing in vehicle

Note: *Refer to the warnings given in Safety first! and in Section 1 of this Chapter before starting work.*

1 If the ignition warning light fails to illuminate when the ignition is switched on, first check the alternator wiring connections for security. If satisfactory, check that the warning light bulb has not blown, and that the bulbholder is secure in its location in the instrument panel. If the light still fails to illuminate, check the continuity of the warning light feed wire from the alternator to the bulbholder. If all is satisfactory, the alternator is at fault and should be renewed or taken to an auto-electrician for testing and repair.
2 If the ignition warning light illuminates when the engine is running, stop the engine and check that the drivebelt is correctly tensioned (see Section 9) and that the alternator connections are secure. If all is satisfactory so far, check the alternator brushes for wear, as

5.6 Slacken and remove the nut, then disconnect the wiring from the B-terminal

5.8 Slacken and withdraw the alternator upper mounting bolt

described in Section 6. If the fault persists, the alternator should be renewed, or taken to an auto-electrician for testing and repair.
3 If the alternator output is suspect even though the warning light functions correctly, the regulated voltage may be checked as follows.
4 Connect a voltmeter across the battery terminals and start the engine.
5 Increase the engine speed until the voltmeter reading remains steady; the reading should be approximately 12 to 13 volts, and no more than 14 volts.
6 Switch on as many electrical accessories (eg, the headlights, heated rear window and heater blower) as possible, and check that the alternator maintains the regulated voltage at around 13 to 14 volts.
7 If the regulated voltage is not as stated, the fault may be due to worn brushes, weak brush springs, a faulty voltage regulator, a faulty diode, a severed phase winding or worn or damaged slip rings. The brushes and slip rings may be checked (see Section 6), but if the fault persists, the alternator should be renewed or taken to an auto-electrician for testing and repair.

5 Alternator - removal and refitting

Removal

1 Disconnect the battery negative cable and position it away from the terminal.

5.7 Prise the wiring retaining clip from the top of the alternator

5.9 Remove the locknut and alternator lower mounting bolt

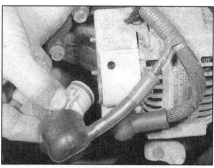
5.5 Prise open the rubber cap, then unplug the 4-way connector from the rear of the alternator

2 With reference to Chapter 10, relieve the tension from the power steering drive belt and slip the belt from the pump pulley.
3 The power steering pump must now be removed from its mounting bracket to allow the alternator to be removed - refer to Chapter 10 for details.
4 With reference to Section 9, relieve the tension from the alternator drive belt and slip the belt from the alternator pulley.
5 Prise open the rubber cap, then unplug the 4-way connector from the rear of the alternator **(see illustration)**.
6 Lift off the rubber cap to expose the B-terminal post. Slacken and remove the nut, then disconnect the wiring from the terminal post **(see illustration)**.
7 Prise the wiring retaining clip from the top of the alternator **(see illustration)**.
8 Slacken and withdraw the alternator upper mounting bolt **(see illustration)**.
9 Remove the locknut, then unscrew the alternator lower mounting bolt and withdraw it from the adjuster bolt bracket **(see illustration)**.
10 Slacken and withdraw the securing bolt, then remove the power steering pump adjustment bolt bracket **(see illustrations)**.
11 Pivot the base of alternator upwards, then lift the alternator from its mounting bracket and out of the engine bay **(see illustration)**.

Refitting

12 Refitting is a reversal of removal. On completion, refer to Section 9 and refit the alternator drivebelt.

5.10a Slacken and withdraw the securing bolt . . .

5.10b . . . then remove the power steering pump adjustment bolt bracket

5.11 Pivot the base of alternator upwards, then lift it from its mounting bracket

6 Alternator brush holder module - renewal

1 With the alternator on the bench, remove the nuts that secure the metal rear cover in position **(see illustration)**.
2 Remove the locknut from the threaded B-terminal post. Recover the washer and lift off the insulating collar **(see illustration)**.
3 Lift off the metal rear cover **(see illustration)**.
4 Remove the securing screws and detach the brush holder module from the casing **(see illustration)**. Take care to avoid snapping the brush conductors, as they pass over the slip rings.
5 The amount of useful wear left in the brush conductors can be ascertained by measuring their visible free length **(see illustration)**.

Compare the measurement with the limit quoted in the Specifications. Renew the brush holder module if the conductors are worn beyond this limit.
6 Refit the brush holder module by following the removal procedure in reverse. To enable the brushes to be fitted over the slip rings at the end of the alternator shaft, hold the ends of the brushes inside the holder with the blade of a screwdriver until the holder is in position **(see illustration)**.

7 Starting system - testing

Note: *Refer to the precautions given in Safety first! and in Section 1 of this Chapter before starting work.*

1 If the starter motor fails to operate when the ignition key is turned to the appropriate position, the following possible causes may be to blame.
(a) The battery is faulty.
(b) The electrical connections between the switch, solenoid, battery and starter motor are somewhere failing to pass the necessary current from the battery through the starter to earth.
(c) The solenoid is faulty.
(d) The starter motor is mechanically or electrically defective.
2 To check the battery, switch on the headlights. If they dim after a few seconds, this indicates that the battery is discharged - recharge or renew the battery. If the headlights glow brightly, operate the ignition switch and observe the lights. If they dim, then this indicates that current is reaching the starter motor, therefore the fault must lie in the starter motor. If the lights continue to glow brightly (and no clicking sound can be heard from the starter motor solenoid), this indicates that there is a fault in the circuit or solenoid - see following paragraphs. If the starter motor turns slowly when operated, but the battery is in good condition, then this indicates that either the starter motor is faulty, or there is considerable resistance somewhere in the circuit.
3 If a fault in the circuit is suspected, disconnect the battery leads (including the earth connection to the body), the starter/solenoid wiring and the engine/transmission earth strap. Thoroughly clean

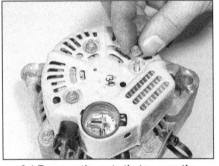

6.1 Remove the nuts that secure the alternator rear cover

6.2 Remove the locknut from the threaded B-terminal post. Recover the washer and lift off the insulating collar

6.3 Lift off the metal rear cover

6.4 Remove the securing screws and detach the brush holder module

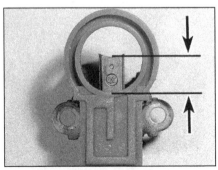

6.5 The amount of wear left in the brush conductors can be ascertained by measuring their visible free length (arrowed)

6.6 Hold the brushes inside the holder with the blade of a screwdriver until they are in position over the slip rings

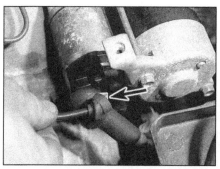

8.3 Unplug the spade connector (arrowed) from the S-terminal at the rear of the alternator

8.4 Prise off the rubber cap, then slacken the locknut and detach the wiring from the B-terminal

8.6a Slacken and remove the upper . . .

the connections, and reconnect the leads and wiring, then use a voltmeter or test lamp to check that full battery voltage is available at the battery positive lead connection to the solenoid, and that the earth is sound.

Smear petroleum jelly around the battery terminals to prevent corrosion - corroded connections are amongst the most frequent causes of electrical system faults.

4 If the battery and all connections are in good condition, check the circuit by disconnecting the wire from the solenoid blade terminal. Connect a voltmeter or test lamp between the wire end and a good earth (such as the battery negative terminal), and check that the wire is live when the ignition switch is turned to the start position. If it is, then the circuit is sound - if not the circuit wiring can be checked as described in Chapter 12.
5 The solenoid contacts can be checked by connecting a voltmeter or test lamp between the battery positive feed connection on the starter side of the solenoid, and earth. When the ignition switch is turned to the start position, there should be a reading or lighted bulb, as applicable. If there is no reading or lighted bulb, the solenoid is faulty and should be renewed.
6 If the circuit and solenoid are proved sound, the fault must lie in the starter motor.

Begin checking the starter motor by removing it (see Section 8), and having the brushes checked by an automotive specialist. If the fault does not lie in the brushes, the motor windings must be faulty. In this event, it may be possible to have the starter motor overhauled by a specialist, but check the availability and cost of spares before proceeding, as it may prove more economical to obtain a new or exchange motor.

8 Starter motor - removal and refitting

Removal

1 Disconnect the battery negative cable and position it away from the terminal.
2 Detach the engine wiring harness from the bracket on the top of the starter motor. Remove the screws and detach the bracket from the starter motor.
3 Unplug the spade connector from the S-terminal at the rear of the alternator **(see illustration)**.
4 Prise off the rubber cap, then slacken the locknut and detach the wiring from the B-terminal **(see illustration)**.
5 On models with automatic transmisison, release the starter motor wiring from the bracket at the transmission housing.
6 Slacken and remove the upper and lower mounting bolts, then withdraw the starter motor from the bellhousing **(see illustrations)**.

Refitting

7 Refit the starter motor by following the removal procedure in reverse, noting the following points:
(a) As the starter is being inserted in to the bellhousing, rotate it slightly, to allow the pinion teeth to engage with the flywheel/torque converter ring gear.
(b) When reconnecting the B-terminal wiring, ensure that the crimped side of the ring terminal faces away from the plastic insulator, so that it lies flat.
(c) On completion, tighten the starter motor securing bolts to the specified torque.

9 Alternator auxiliary drivebelt - removal, refitting and adjustment

Removal

1 Disconnect the battery negative cable and position it away from the terminal.
2 Refer to Chapter 10 and remove the power steering pump drivebelt.
3 Slacken (but do not remove) the alternator upper mounting bolt.
4 Underneath the alternator, slacken the locknut and lower mounting bolt **(see illustration)**.
5 Turn the adjustment bolt anti-clockwise, to relieve the tension on the drivebelt **(see illustration)**.

8.6b . . . and lower mounting bolts . . .

8.6c . . . then withdraw the starter motor from the bellhousing

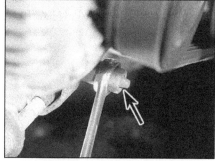

9.4 Underneath the alternator, slacken the locknut . . .

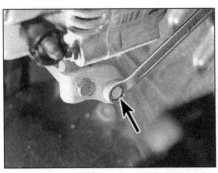

9.5 . . . and turn the adjustment bolt anti-clockwise, to relieve the tension on the drivebelt

6 When enough slack has been generated, slip the belt off the alternator pulley.

7 Mark the belt to indicate its direction of rotation, if it is to be re-used.

8 Pass the belt under the crankshaft pulley (and where applicable, the air conditioning compressor pulley) and remove it from the engine bay.

Refitting

9 Refit the belt by following the removal procedure in reverse. Observe the direction of rotation markings, where applicable; if the belt is fitted the wrong way around, accelerated wear will result.

Adjustment

10 With the belt correctly seated on the alternator, crankshaft (and where applicable, the air conditioning compressor) pulleys, turn the adjustment bolt at the base of the alternator clockwise, to take up the slack in the belt.

11 At a point mid-way between the top of the crankshaft pulley and the alternator pulley, apply a force of approximately 10 kg at right-angles to the belts direction of movement, and measure the amount by which it deflects. This is best achieved by hooking the end of a spring balance under the belt and pulling until 10kg is registered. Pad the belt with a short piece of wood, to prevent the spring balance hook from damaging it **(see illustrations)**.

12 Compare the measurement with the Specifications. Tighten or slacken the adjustment bolt, to achieve the correct deflection.

13 Tighten the upper mounting bolt and the lower mounting bolt locknut to the specified torque.

14 Start and run the engine for a few minutes, then stop the engine and re-check the belt tension. Adjust it if necessary.

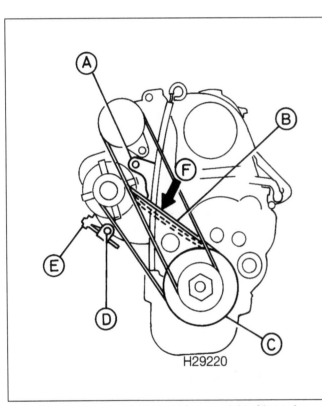

9.11a Alternator drivebelt routing - models without air conditioning (viewed from timing belt end)

A Alternator upper mounting bolt
B Drivebelt
C Crankshaft pulley
D Alternator lower mounting bolt locknut
E Adjustment bolt
F Deflection measurement point

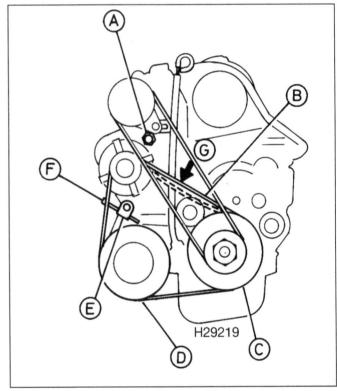

9.11b Alternator drivebelt routing - models with air conditioning (viewed from timing belt end)

A Alternator upper mounting bolt
B Drivebelt
C Crankshaft pulley
D Air conditioning compressor pulley
E Alternator lower mounting bolt locknut
F Adjustment bolt
G Deflection measurement point

Chapter 5 Part B
Ignition system

Contents

Degrees of difficulty

Easy, suitable for novice with little experience 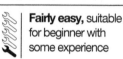	Fairly easy, suitable for beginner with some experience	Fairly difficult, suitable for competent DIY mechanic	Difficult, suitable for experienced DIY mechanic	Very difficult, suitable for expert DIY or professional 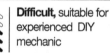

Specifications

General
Type . . . . PGM-FI
Firing order . . . . 1-3-4-2, No 1 cylinder at timing belt end of engine

Ignition coil
Primary winding resistance . . . . 0.6 - 0.8 Ω
Secondary resistance . . . . 13 - 19 kΩ

Distributor
Type . . . . Breakerless
Dwoll angle . . . . Controlled by PGM-FI engine management system
Ignition timing basic setting . . . . 15 ± 2° at 770 ± 50 rpm
Advance and retard . . . . Controlled by PGM-FI engine management system

Spark plugs
Manufacturer's recommendation:
    Type . . . . NGK ZFR6F-11
    Electrode gap . . . . 1.0 - 1.1 mm
Champion recommendation:
    Type RC9MCC
    Electrode gap . . . . 0.9 mm

Torque wrench settings

	Nm	lbf ft
Distributor clamp bolts	18	13
Spark plugs	18	13

1 General information

1 PGM-FI is an integrated engine management systems, which control both the fuel injection and ignition. This Chapter deals with the ignition system components only - refer to Chapter 4A for details of the fuel injection system components.

2 The igniton system comprises four spark plugs, four HT leads, the distributor, an electronic ignition coil, and an electronic Engine Control Module (ECM) together with its associated sensors, actuators and wiring.

3 The basic operation is as follows: the Ignition Control Module (ICM) supplies a voltage to the input stage of the ignition coil which causes the primary windings in the coil to be energised. The supply voltage is periodically interrupted by the PGM-FI Engine Control Module (ECM) and this results in the collapse of primary magnetic field, which then induces a much larger voltage - called the HT voltage - in the secondary windings of the coil. This voltage is directed, by the distributor via the HT leads, to the spark plug in the cylinder currently on its ignition stroke. The spark plug electrodes form a gap small enough for the HT voltage to arc across, and the resulting spark ignites the fuel/air mixture in the cylinder. The timing of this sequence of events is critical and is regulated solely by the ECM. There are no conventional mechanical or vacuum advance mechanisms. The basic ignition timing setting can be adjusted by altering the position of the alternator - refer to Section 5 for details.

4 The ECM calculates and controls the ignition timing and dwell angle primarily according to engine speed, crankshaft position, intake manifold depression and coolant temperature information received from sensors mounted on and around the engine.

5 It should be noted that fault diagnosis of the PGM-FI engine management system can be carried out without the need for dedicated electronic test equipment. The engine management system wiring harness incorporates a diagnostic socket, which can be used to set the PGM-FI ECM in a self-diagnostic mode. In this mode, the ECM will display any stored fault codes by flashing a warning lamp mounted on the instrument panel. Refer to Chapter 4A for details.

6 Testing the PGM-FI system components individually, with standard workshop equipment, in an attempt to locate a fault by elimination is a time consuming operation that is unlikely to be fruitful (particularly if the fault occurs dynamically). It also carries a high risk of damage to the ECM's internal components. Problems with the systems operation that cannot be pinpointed by reference to Chapter 4A should be referred to a Rover dealer or automotive electrical specialist for assessment. Once the fault has has been identified, the removal/refitting sequences detailed in the following Sections will then allow the appropriate component(s) to renewed as required.

Caution: If the radio/cassette in your vehicle is equipped with an anti-theft system, make sure you have the correct activation code before disconnecting the battery.

2 Ignition system - testing

 Warning: Extreme care must be taken when working on the system with the ignition switched on; it is possible to get a substantial electric shock from a vehicles ignition system. Persons with cardiac pacemaker devices should keep well clear of the ignition circuits, components and test equipment. Always switch off the ignition before disconnecting or connecting any component and when using a multi-meter to check resistances.

General

1 Most ignition system faults are likely to be due to loose or dirty connections or to tracking (unintentional earthing) of HT voltage due to dirt, dampness or damaged insulation, rather than by the failure of any of the systems components. **Always** check all wiring thoroughly before condemning an electrical component and work methodically to eliminate all other possibilities before deciding that a particular component is faulty.

2 The old practice of checking for a spark by holding the live end of an HT lead a short distance away from the engine is not recommended; not only is there a high risk of an electric shock, but the HT coil could be damaged. Similarly, **never** try to diagnose misfires by pulling off one HT lead at a time.

Engine will not start

3 If the engine either will not turn over at all, or only turns very slowly, check the battery and starter motor. Connect a voltmeter across the battery terminals (meter positive probe to battery positive terminal), disconnect the ignition coil HT lead from the distributor cap and earth it, then note the voltage reading obtained while turning over the engine on the starter for (no more than) ten seconds. If the reading obtained is less than approximately 9.5 volts, first check the battery, starter motor and charging systems (see Chapter 5A).

4 If the engine turns over at normal speed but will not start, check the HT circuit by connecting a timing light (following the manufacturer's instructions) and turning the engine over on the starter motor; if the light flashes, voltage is reaching the spark plugs, so these should be checked first. If the light does not flash, check the HT leads themselves followed by the distributor cap, carbon brush and rotor arm using the information given in Chapter 1.

5 If there is a spark, check the fuel system for faults referring to Chapter 4A for further information.

6 If there is still no spark, then the problem must lie within the engine managment system. Under these circumstances, the vehicle should be referred to a Rover dealer or an automotive electronics specialist for assessment.

Engine misfires

7 An irregular misfire suggests either a loose connection or intermittent fault on the primary circuit, or an HT fault on the coil side of the rotor arm.

8 With the ignition switched off, check carefully through the system ensuring that all connections are clean and securely fastened. If the equipment is available, check the LT circuit as described above.

9 Check that the HT coil, the distributor cap and the HT leads are clean and dry. Check the leads themselves and the spark plugs (by substitution, if necessary), then check the distributor cap, carbon brush and rotor arm as described in Chapter 1.

10 Regular misfiring is almost certainly due to a fault in the distributor cap, HT leads or spark plugs. Use a timing light (see *Engine will not start*) to check whether HT voltage is present at all leads.

11 If HT voltage is not present on one particular lead, the fault will be in that lead or in the distributor cap. If HT is present on all leads, the fault will be in the spark plugs; check and renew them if there is any doubt about their condition.

12 If no HT voltage is present, check the HT coil; its secondary windings may be breaking down under load.

All models

13 Problems with the systems operation that cannot be pinpointed using the guidelines in the preceeding paragraphs should be referred to a Rover dealer or an automotive electronics specialist for assessment.

3 HT coil - removal and refitting

Removal

Note: *The ignition coil is integrated into the distributor body; a design which eliminates the need for a conventional king lead.*

1 Disconnect the battery negative cable and position it away from the terminal.

2 With reference to Section 7, remove the rotor arm and distributor cap.

3.3 Detach the moisture barrier from the distributor body

3 Detach the moisture barrier from the distributor body **(see illustration)**.
4 Remove the screws and disconnect the wiring from the base of the ignition coil. Label each cable carefully to aid refitting later **(see illustration)**
5 Slacken and withdraw the securing screws, then remove the coil from the distributor **(see illustrations)**.

Refitting

6 Refitting is a reversal of removal. Ensure that the wiring is reconnected in the correct order, as follows (terminals viewed from the front of the coil) :

(a) Left terminal - black/yellow cable.
(b) Right terminal - white/blue cable.

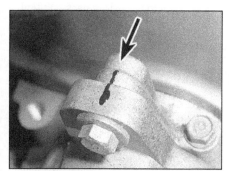

4.3 Mark the relationship between the distributor flange and the cylinder head, with a dab of paint (arrowed)

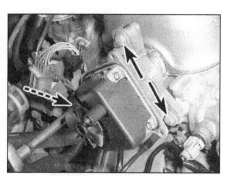

4.6 Slacken and withdraw the three distributor clamp bolts (arrowed)

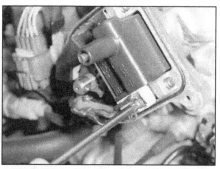

3.4 Remove the screws and disconnect the wiring from the base of the igntion coil

4 Distributor - removal and refitting

Removal

1 Disconnect the battery negative cable and position it away from the terminal.
2 Refer to Chapter 2A and position the engine at TDC on cylinder No 1.
3 Mark the relationship between the distributor flange and the cylinder head, to preserve the ignition timing basic setting **(see illustration)**.
4 Disconnect the HT leads from the distributor cap. Original equipment HT leads and distributor caps have markings to indicate

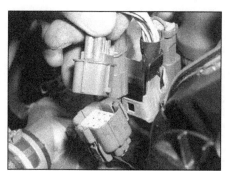

4.5 Disconnect the LT wiring from the distributor at the multiplug connectors

4.7 Withdraw the distributor from the cylinder head

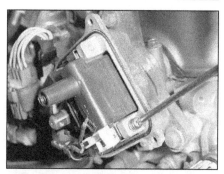

3.5a Slacken and withdraw the securing screws . . .

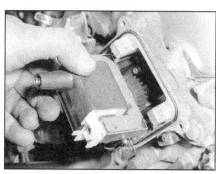

3.5b . . . then remove the coil from the distributor

their respective cylinder numbers - if these are not visible, make a careful note of the fitted position of each lead to aid correct refitting later.
5 Disconnect the LT wiring from the distributor at the multiplug connectors **(see illustration)**. Label the connectors to ensure correct refitting.
6 Slacken and withdraw the three distributor clamp bolts **(see illustration)**.
7 Withdraw the distributor from the cylinder head **(see illustration)**. Be prepared for a small amount of oil leakage from the cylinder head as you do this; pad the surrounding area with absorbent rags.
8 Remove the O-ring seal from the base of the distributor shaft **(see illustration)**.

Refitting

8 Coat a new O-ring seal with clean engine oil and fit it to the base of the distributor shaft.

4.8 Remove the O-ring seal (arrowed) from the base of the distributor shaft

4.9 Ensure that the distributor rotor arm contact is pointing towards the No 1 cylinder terminal on the distributor cap

4.10 Note that the distributor drive gear dogs are offset from the centre of the shaft

9 Ensure that the engine is still set to TDC on cylinder No 1, as described in Chapter 2A. Also ensure that the distributor rotor arm contact is pointing to the No 1 cylinder terminal on the distributor cap - remove the cap to verify this, if required **(see illustration)**.
10 Insert the distributor into the cylinder head, ensuring that the drive gear engages with the recesses at the end of the camshaft. Note that the drive gear dogs are offset; this ensures that the drive gear cannot be accidentally engaged the wrong way around **(see illustration)**.
11 Insert the distributor clamp bolts and hand tighten them. Rotate the distributor body, to line up the alignment markings made on the cylinder head and distributor flange, during removal. If these marks have been lost, or if a new distributor is being fitted, temporarily position the distributor body such that the clamp bolts are at the centre of the elongated mounting holes in the disitributor flange.
12 Reconnect the wiring to the distributor at the multiplug connectors.
13 Plug the HT leads into the distributor cap, ensuring that the correct firing order is preserved - refer to the Specifications.
14 Check, and if necessary adjust, the ignition timing with reference to Section 5.

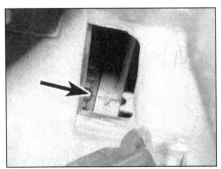

5.8 Pull the rubber bung from the timing inspection window, at the transmission bellhousing

15 On completion, tighten the distributor clamp bolts to the specified torque.

5 Ignition timing - checking and adjusting

Ignition timing - checking

1 Take the vehicle on a short run to allow it to warm up to normal operating temperature. Allow it to idle and wait until the auxiliary cooling fan has cut in and out again, at least twice, before proceeding.
2 Stop the engine, switch off the ignition and connect a tachometer to the engine, in accordance with the manufacturer's instructions. Failing this, the tachometer built into the vehicle's own instrument panel will be accurate enough for the purposes of this test.
3 Connect a strobe timing light to the engine, in accordance with the manufacturer's instructions, such that it triggers from No 1 cylinder HT lead.
4 With reference to Chapter 4A, check that the engine idle speed is correct. Adjust it, if necessary.
5 Ensure that the ignition is switched off and check that all electrical and mechanicals loads are off.
6 Locate the Service Check Connector. This is a blue, plastic two-pin connector, situated beneath the facia panel, to the left of the passenger's footwell (RHD vehicles) or to the right of the passenger's footwell (LHD vehicles). It may be necessary to fold back the carpet trim to gain access. The connector has orange/red and green/white coloured cables running to it (depending on market) and will not be connected to anything.

Warning: Observe the notes in Chapters 10 and 12 regarding the dangers of disturbing the airbag (SRS) system wiring when working in this area.

7 Using a short length of bare copper wire, connect the two connector pins together, by inserting the ends of the wire into the empty terminals.
8 Pull the rubber bung from the timing inspection window, at the transmisison bellhousing **(see illustration)**.
9 Turn on the ignition, start the engine and allow it to idle.
10 Direct the beam from timing light at the pointer visible through the inspection window. The flashing strobe should freeze the motion of the rotating flywheel/driveplate, allowing the timing marks on its surface to be viewed. If the mark appears to be moving back and forth, this may be due erratic idling - check that all of the car's electrical accessories are switched off and that the auxiliary cooling fan is not running. The engine should be at normal operating temperature, but the idle speed may be become unstable if it is particularly hot day and the engine has been idling for some time.
11 Read off the ignition timing by observing the position of the **RED** marking on the flywheel/driveplate in relation to the pointer at the side of the inspection window. Observe from directly above the window, to obtain an accurate reading. Do not confuse the white TDC marking with the red timing marking.
12 If the marking and pointer are not aligned, then the ignition timing is incorrect and in need of adjustment. If the pointer is between the red and white marks, the ignition timing is retarded. If the pointer is below the red mark, the ignition timing is advanced.

Ignition timing - adjusting

13 To adjust the basic ignition timing setting, first switch off the engine, to avoid the risk of a getting a shock from the HT voltage. Refer to Section 4 and slacken the distributor clamp bolts slightly.

It is good idea to mark the relationship between the distributor body and the

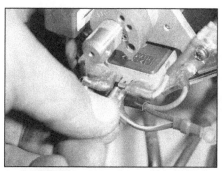

6.4 Unplug the wiring from the base of the module, at the insulated spade connectors

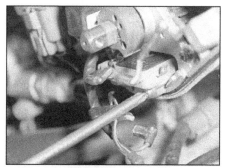

6.5a Slacken the securing screws at the base of the module

6.5b Withdraw the screws . . .

cylinder head with a dab of touch-up paint, before adjustment is attempted. This gives a reference point that can be reverted to if the timing setting is inadvertently lost during adjustment.

14 Turn the distributor *by a small amount* anti-clockwise to advance (or clockwise to retard) the ignition timing. Tighten the bolts lightly and re-check the timing using the stroboscopic light, as described in the previous sub-section. Repeat this process, until the timing setting is correct, then tighten the distributor clamp bolts securely and disconnect the stroboscopic light.
15 On completion, switch off the engine and ignition. Disconnect the jumper wire from the Service Check Connector and refit the inspection window rubber bung.

6 PGM-FI ignition system components - removal and refitting

1 The following ignition components are shared with the fuel injection side of the PGM-FI system - refer to Chapter 4A for details:
 (a) Engine Coolant Temperature (ECT) sensor
 (b) Crankshaft position/No 1 cylinder position/Top Dead Centre (CKP/CYP/TDC) sensor
 (c) PGM-FI main relay
 (d) Engine Control Module (ECM)
 (e) Manifold absolute pressure (MAP) sensor

Ignition Control Module

Removal

2 With reference to Section 7, remove the distributor cap and rotor arm.
3 Lift off the moisture barrier (refer to Section 3).
4 Unplug the wiring from the base of the module, at the insulated spade connectors **(see illustration)**. Label each cable carefully, to aid correct refitting later.
5 Slacken and withdraw the two screws from the base of the ICM, then slide the module from the distributor **(see illustrations)**.

Refitting

6 Refitting is a reversal of removal. Ensure that the wiring is reconnected in the correct order, as follows (terminals viewed from the front of the module):
 (a) Front left terminal - yellow/green cable
 (b) Front center terminal - black/yellow cable
 (c) Front right terminal - white/blue cable
 (d) Right side terminal - blue cable

7 Distributor cap and rotor arm - renewal

Removal

1 Disconnect the battery negative cable and position it away from the terminal.
2 If required, the HT leads may be unplugged from the distributor cap terminals. Original

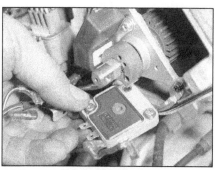

6.5c . . . then slide the module from the distributor (shown with HT coil removed for clarity)

equipment HT leads and distributor caps have markings to indicate their respective cylinder numbers - if these are not visible, make a careful note of the fitted position of each lead to aid correct refitting later. Note that No 1 cylinder is the one nearest the timing belt end of the engine. The firing order is given in the Specifications.
3 Remove the screws and lift off the distributor cap **(see illustrations)**.
4 Slacken and remove the screw, at the side of the rotor arm shaft **(see illustration)**. It may be necessary to rotate the crankshaft to gain access to the screw head. Do this by turning the engine in its normal direction of rotation (anti-clockwise), using a wrench and socket on the crankshaft sprocket - see Chapter 2A for greater detail.

7.3a Remove the screws . . .

7.3b . . . and lift off the distributor cap

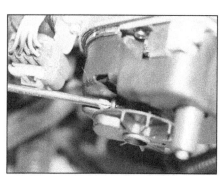

7.4 Slacken and remove the screw, at the side of the rotor arm shaft

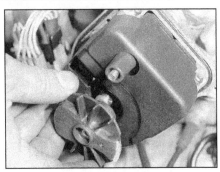
7.5 Remove the rotor arm

5 Slide the rotor arm from the end of the distributor shaft **(see illustration).**

6 Wipe the inside of the distributor cap clean, then carefully inspect it inside and out for signs of cracks, black carbon tracks (tracking) and worn, burned or loose contacts.

7 Check that the cap centre carbon brush is in good condition and is free to move against spring pressure, allowing it to make good contact with the top of the rotor arm.

8 Inspect the metal terminals on the inside the cap. Surface corrosion and light deposits can be removed with fine-grade emery paper, but more serious wear will mean the renewal of the distributor cap.

9 Inspect the moisture barrier for signs of damage or deterioration.

10 Examine the rotor arm contacts closely. Light deposits can be removed with fine-grade emery paper, but if the contacts are badly pitted, the rotor arm should be renewed.

Refitting

11 Refit the rotor arm and distributor cap by following the removal procedure in reverse.

Chapter 6
Clutch

Contents

Degrees of difficulty

Easy, suitable for novice with little experience	Fairly easy, suitable for beginner with some experience	Fairly difficult, suitable for competent DIY mechanic	Difficult, suitable for experienced DIY mechanic	Very difficult, suitable for expert DIY or professional 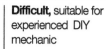

Specifications

General
Type . . . .   Single dry plate with diaphragm spring, hydraulically operated

Clutch pedal adjustment data
Pedal height . . . .   210 mm
Pedal pushrod linkage freeplay . . . .   1 to 7 mm
Pedal free play . . . .   9 to 15 mm
Pedal stroke . . . .   142 mm

Clutch mechanism
Friction plate:
  Friction material thickness:
    Standard . . . .   8.5 to 9.2 mm
    Service limit . . . .   6.5 mm
  Friction material-to-rivet head depth:
    Standard . . . .   1.4 mm
    Service limit . . . .   0.2 mm
  Maximum runout . . . .   1.0 mm
Pressure plate:
  Maximum warpage of machined surface . . . .   0.15 mm
  Maximum diaphragm spring finger height difference . . . .   1.0 mm

Torque wrench settings

	Nm	lbf ft
Hydraulic hose union nut:		
Master cylinder union	19	14
All other unions	15	11
Hydraulic pipe union bolt	30	22
Master cylinder:		
Pushrod clevis locknut	15	11
Retaining nuts	13	10
Reservoir mounting bolts	10	7
Pedal stop bolt locknut	10	7
Pressure plate retaining bolts	26	19
Release fork pivot stud	30	22
Slave cylinder:		
Retaining bolts	22	16
Bleed screw	8	6

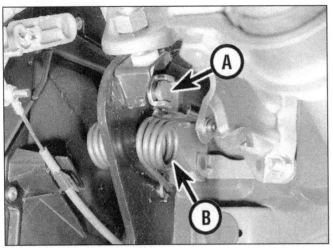

2.2 Clutch pedal pushrod clevis pin (A) and return spring (B)

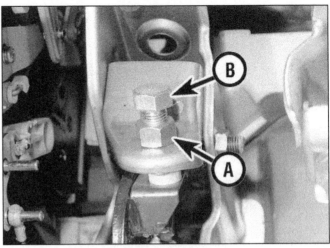

2.12a Adjust the clutch pedal height by slackening the lock nut (A) and rotating the stop bolt (B)

1 General information

Caution: If the radio/cassette in your vehicle is equipped with an anti-theft system, make sure you have the correct activation code before disconnecting the battery.

1 The clutch consists of a friction plate, a pressure plate assembly, a release bearing and the release mechanism; all of these components are contained in the large cast-aluminium alloy bellhousing, sandwiched between the engine and the transmission. The clutch release mechanism is hydraulically-operated.

2 The friction plate is fitted between the engine flywheel and the clutch pressure plate, and is allowed to slide on the transmission input shaft splines.

3 The pressure plate assembly is bolted to the engine flywheel. When the engine is running, drive is transmitted from the crankshaft, via the flywheel, to the friction plate (these components being clamped securely together by the pressure plate assembly) and from the friction plate to the transmission input shaft.

4 To interrupt the drive, the spring pressure must be relaxed. Depressing the pedal pushes on the master cylinder pushrod. This hydraulically forces the slave cylinder piston which is connected to the end of the clutch release fork lever. The release fork acts on its pivot and presses the release bearing against the pressure plate spring fingers. This causes the springs to deform and releases the clamping force on the pressure plate. The hydraulic clutch is self-adjusting and requires no manual adjustment.

2 Clutch pedal - removal, refitting and adjustment

Removal

1 To improve access to the pedal, undo the retaining screw then unclip the driver's side lower facia panel and remove it from the vehicle (see Chapter 11).

2 Remove the split pin and withdraw the clevis pin securing the clutch pedal to the master cylinder pushrod (see illustration). Discard the split pin, a new one should be used on refitting.

3 Slacken and remove the nut from the pivot bolt then withdraw the bolt and carefully remove the pedal from the vehicle, releasing the pedal return spring pressure.

4 Carefully unhook the return spring ends from its pivot bushes and remove the spring from the pedal mounting bracket.

5 Withdraw the spacer from the pedal pivot and inspect the pivot bushes, including the return spring bushes, for signs of wear of damage and renew as necessary.

Refitting

6 Prior to refitting, apply a smear of multi-purpose grease to the pedal pivot bushes, the spacer and the pushrod clevis and pin.

7 Manoeuvre the return spring into position ensuring its ends are correctly located in the mounting bracket bushes.

8 Insert the spacer into the pedal pivot and manoeuvre the pedal into position. Ensure the clutch pedal is correctly engaged with the pushrod clevis and the return spring then insert the pivot bolt and securely tighten its retaining nut.

9 Insert the clevis pin and secure it in position with a new split pin.

10 Check the operation of the clutch pedal and, if necessary, adjust as described below then refit the facia panel.

Adjustment

11 The clutch hydraulic system is self-adjusting and therefore requires no checking or manual adjustment other than ensuring the fluid level remains correct. The following is a check of the pedal action which should only be necessary should the pedal/master cylinder be disturbed or a fault be suspected.

12 Peel back the carpet from underneath the clutch pedal, and ensure that there are no obstructions between the pedal and floor panel. Measure the distance from the centre of the clutch pedal pad to the floor. Note: This measurement can be taken with the carpet in position, so long as the thickness of the carpet is added onto the pedal height measurement. The pedal height should be as given in the Specifications at the start of this Chapter. If adjustment is necessary, slacken the locknut and adjust the height using the pedal stop bolt (see illustrations). Once the pedal height is correctly set, tighten the stop bolt locknut to the specified torque.

13 Once the pedal height is correctly set, with the clutch pedal in the at-rest position, check the freeplay in the pedal pushrod linkage by gently rocking the pedal whilst measuring the distance that the clutch pedal pad travels. Note: This check is measuring the slack in the pushrod/clevis pin only and should not be confused with the pedal freeplay check (paragraph 14) which also measures the initial movement of the master cylinder piston. If the freeplay is not within the specified limits, slacken the pushrod clevis locknut and adjust the pushrod freeplay by rotating the pushrod with a pair of pliers. Once the freeplay is correctly set, tighten the locknut to the specified torque.

14 Slowly depress the clutch pedal, and measure the distance that the clutch pedal pad travels from the at-rest position to the point where resistance in the hydraulic circuit is felt. This is the pedal free play, and should be within the range given in this Chapters

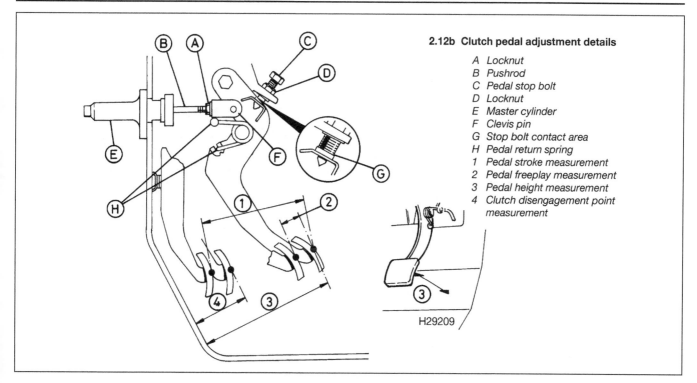

2.12b Clutch pedal adjustment details

A Locknut
B Pushrod
C Pedal stop bolt
D Locknut
E Master cylinder
F Clevis pin
G Stop bolt contact area
H Pedal return spring
1 Pedal stroke measurement
2 Pedal freeplay measurement
3 Pedal height measurement
4 Clutch disengagement point measurement

H29209

Specifications, if not then it is likely that there is air in the hydraulic system and the system should be bled as described in Section 5.

15 With all adjustments correctly set, depress the pedal and check that the pedal stroke is as specified. With the engine idling, fully depress the clutch pedal and select 1st gear. Slowly release the pedal until the point is found where the is just starting to bite. Hold the pedal in this position and measure the distance between the pedal pad and the floor. This distance should be at least 90 mm. If the pedal pad-to-floor clearance is less than this, it is likely that there is air present in the hydraulic system. Bleed the system as described in Section 5 and repeat the check. If the clearance is still less than specified then it is likely that the clutch or master/slave cylinder are faulty. Seek the advice of your Rover dealer on the best course of action.

3 Clutch master cylinder - removal, overhaul and refitting

Removal

1 Remove all traces or dirt from the fluid reservoir and the master cylinder body. If necessary, to improve access, slacken the retaining clips and remove the intake duct connecting the air cleaner housing the manifold.

2 Position a suitable container beneath the master cylinder then slacken the retaining clip and disconnect the fluid supply hose from the top of the master cylinder **(see illustration)**.

3.2 Exploded view of the clutch master cylinder

A Fluid hose
B Cap
C Fluid reservoir
D Fluid union
E Sealing washer
F Master cylinder body
G Split pin
H Pushrod
I Piston assembly
J Clevis
K Clevis pin
L Dust cover
M Circlip
N Retaining washer
O Piston seals
P Locknut

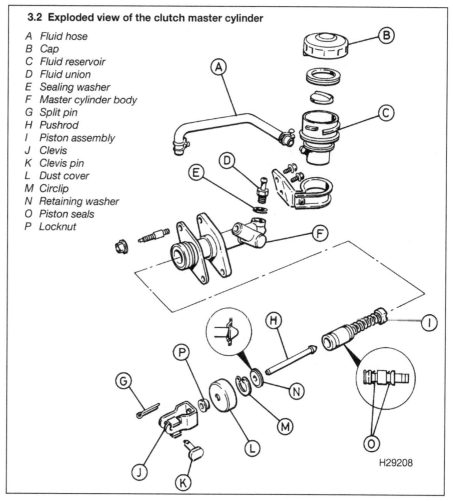

H29208

Allow the fluid drain fully then undo the bolts securing the fluid reservoir mounting bracket to the bulkhead and remove the assembly from the engine compartment.

3 Slacken the union nut and free the hydraulic hose from the master cylinder. Plug the hose end and master cylinder port to minimise fluid loss and prevent dirt entry. Wash off any spilt fluid.

4 Working inside the vehicle, carry out the operations described in paragraphs 1 and 2 of Section 2.

5 Slacken and remove the retaining nuts, located on either side of the pedal mounting bracket, then return to the engine compartment and remove the master cylinder. Recover the gasket which is fitted between the cylinder and bulkhead and discard it; a new one should be used on refitting.

Overhaul

6 Remove all traces of dirt from the outside of the cylinder and carefully clamp the cylinder in a vice equipped with soft jaws.

7 Release the dust cover from the rear of the master cylinder to gain access to the piston retaining clip.

8 Compress the retaining clip and withdraw the pushrod and piston assemblies from the body.

9 Examine the surfaces of the piston and cylinder. If they are scored or corroded, renew the master cylinder complete.

> **HAYNES HiNT** *If the piston assembly is stuck in the master cylinder body, apply compressed air (only low pressure should be needed, such as that generated by a foot pump) to the fluid port to push the piston out of position. Take great care to ensure the piston is not forcibly ejected.*

10 If the cylinder is in good condition, obtain a new piston assembly and renew any other components which show signs of damage or deterioration.

11 Ensure all components are clean and dry and lubricate the piston assembly with fresh hydraulic fluid.

12 Carefully enter the piston assembly into the cylinder with a twisting motion, taking great care not to trap the seal lips.

13 Fit the pushrod assembly to the end of the piston and install the circlip, making sure it is correctly located in the cylinder groove. Check the operation of the piston and pushrod assembly, then seat the pushrod dust cover on the master cylinder body.

Refitting

14 Ensure the cylinder and bulkhead mating surfaces are clean and dry then fit the new gasket and manoeuvre the master cylinder into position.

15 From inside the vehicle, ensure that the pushrod clevis is correctly engaged with the pedal then refit the master cylinder retaining nuts and tighten them to the specified torque.

16 Apply a smear of multi-purpose grease to the clevis pin then insert the pin and secure it in position with a new split pin.

17 Reconnect the hydraulic pipe to the master cylinder and tighten the union nut to the specified torque.

18 Refit the fluid reservoir to the bulkhead and tighten its retaining bolts to the specified torque. Reconnect the fluid hose to the master cylinder and securely tighten its retaining clip.

19 Refill the master cylinder reservoir with the correct type of fluid and bleed the hydraulic system as described in Section 5.

20 On completion check the clutch pedal adjustment as described in Section 2.

4 Clutch slave cylinder - removal, overhaul and refitting

Removal

1 Minimise fluid loss by first removing the master cylinder reservoir cap, and then tightening it down onto a piece of polythene to obtain an airtight seal.

2 Wipe away all traces of dirt around the hydraulic pipe union on the slave cylinder and unscrew the union nut. Carefully ease the pipe out of the cylinder, and plug or tape over its end to prevent dirt entry. Wipe off any spilt fluid immediately.

3 Unscrew the retaining bolts and remove the cylinder assembly from the front of the transmission housing **(see illustration)**. Whilst the cylinder is removed, take precautions to ensure the slave cylinder piston is not ejected by the spring.

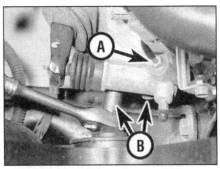

4.3 Unscrew the union nut (A) then undo the retaining bolts (B) and remove the slave cylinder

Overhaul

4 Remove all traces of dirt from the outside of the cylinder.

5 Withdraw the pushrod and remove the dust cover from the cylinder then remove the piston assembly and spring **(see illustration)**.

6 Examine the surfaces of the piston and cylinder. If they are scored or corroded, renew the slave cylinder complete.

7 If the cylinder is in good condition, obtain a piston repair kit which will contain the piston seals and dust cover along with a sachet of brake grease.

8 Carefully remove the seals from the piston whilst noting each ones correct fitted location and orientation. Lubricate the new seals with the grease supplied in the repair kit and ease them onto the piston, ensuring each is fitted in the correct location and is the correct way around.

9 Fit the spring to the piston and carefully enter the assembly into the cylinder. Ease the

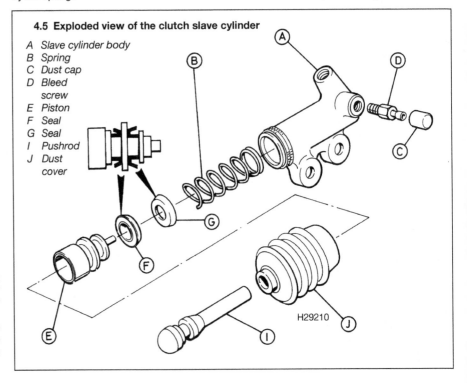

4.5 Exploded view of the clutch slave cylinder

A Slave cylinder body
B Spring
C Dust cap
D Bleed screw
E Piston
F Seal
G Seal
I Pushrod
J Dust cover

H29210

piston into position with a twisting motion, taking great care not to trap the seal lips.

10 Depress the piston and fit the dust cover, making sure it is correctly located on the cylinder body. Lubricate the pushrod ends with the grease supplied and insert it into the dust cover. If the cylinder is not to fitted straight away, take precautions to ensure the piston is not expelled by spring pressure.

Refitting

11 Apply a smear of grease to the release fork and pushrod contact areas. Refit the slave cylinder to the transmission unit, tightening its retaining bolts to the specified torque.

12 Reconnect the hydraulic pipe to the slave cylinder and tighten its union nut to the specified torque. Remove the polythene from the master cylinder.

13 Bleed the hydraulic system as described in Section 5.

14 On completion check the clutch pedal adjustment as described in Section 2.

5 Clutch hydraulic system - bleeding

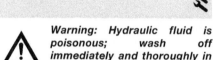

⚠ **Warning: Hydraulic fluid is poisonous; wash off immediately and thoroughly in the case of skin contact, and seek immediate medical advice if any fluid is swallowed or gets into the eyes. Certain types of hydraulic fluid are flammable, and may ignite when allowed into contact with hot components; when servicing any hydraulic system, it is safest to assume that the fluid is flammable, and to take precautions against the risk of fire as though it is petrol that is being handled. Hydraulic fluid is also an effective paint stripper, and will attack plastics; if any is spilt, it should be washed off immediately, using copious quantities of fresh water. Finally, it is hygroscopic (it absorbs moisture from the air) - old fluid may be contaminated and unfit for further use. When topping-up or renewing the fluid, always use the recommended type, and ensure that it comes from a freshly opened sealed container.**

1 The correct operation of any hydraulic system is only possible after removing all air from the components and circuit; this is achieved by bleeding the system.

2 During the bleeding procedure, add only clean, unused hydraulic fluid of the recommended type; never re-use fluid that has already been bled from the system. Ensure that sufficient fluid is available before starting work.

3 If there is any possibility of incorrect fluid being already in the system, the hydraulic circuit must be flushed completely with uncontaminated, correct fluid.

5.5 Slave cylinder bleed screw (arrowed)

4 If hydraulic fluid has been lost from the system, or air has entered because of a leak, ensure that the fault is cured before continuing further.

5 The bleed screw is screwed directly into the top of the slave cylinder body, which is on the front of transmission housing **(see illustration)**.

6 Check that all pipes and hoses are secure, unions tight and the bleed screw is closed. Clean any dirt from around the bleed screw.

7 Unscrew the master cylinder fluid reservoir cap, and top the master cylinder reservoir (see 'Weekly checks'); refit the cap loosely, and remember to maintain the fluid level at least above the MIN level line throughout the procedure, or there is a risk of further air entering the system.

8 There are a number of one-man, do-it-yourself bleeding kits currently available from motor accessory shops. It is recommended that one of these kits is used whenever possible, as they greatly simplify the bleeding operation, and reduce the risk of expelled air and fluid being drawn back into the system. If such a kit is not available, the basic (two-man) method must be used, which is described in detail below.

9 If a kit is to be used, prepare the vehicle as described previously, and follow the kit manufacturer's instructions, as the procedure may vary slightly according to the type being used; generally, they are as outlined below in the relevant sub-section.

Bleeding - basic (two-man) method

10 Collect a clean glass jar, a suitable length of plastic or rubber tubing which is a tight fit over the bleed screw, and a ring spanner to fit the screw. The help of an assistant will also be required.

11 Remove the dust cap from the slave cylinder bleed screw. Fit the spanner and tube to the screw, place the other end of the tube in the jar, and pour in sufficient fluid to cover the end of the tube.

12 Ensure that the fluid level is maintained at least above the MIN line in the reservoir throughout the procedure.

13 Have the assistant fully depress the clutch pedal several times to build up pressure, then maintain it on the final downstroke.

14 While pedal pressure is maintained, unscrew the bleed screw (approximately one turn) and allow the compressed fluid and air to flow into the jar. The assistant should maintain pedal pressure and should not release it until instructed to do so. When the flow stops, tighten the bleed screw again, have the assistant release the pedal slowly, and recheck the reservoir fluid level.

15 Repeat the steps given in paragraphs 13 and 14 until the fluid emerging from the bleed screw is free from air bubbles. If the master cylinder has been drained and refilled allow approximately five seconds between cycles for the master cylinder passages to refill.

16 When no more air bubbles appear, tighten the bleed screw securely, remove the tube and spanner, and refit the dust cap. Do not overtighten the bleed screw.

Bleeding - using a one-way valve kit

17 As their name implies, these kits consist of a length of tubing with a one-way valve fitted, to prevent expelled air and fluid being drawn back into the system; some kits include a translucent container, which can be positioned so that the air bubbles can be more easily seen flowing from the end of the tube.

18 The kit is connected to the bleed screw, which is then opened. The user returns to the driver's seat, depresses the clutch pedal with a smooth, steady stroke, and slowly releases it; this is repeated until the expelled fluid is clear of air bubbles.

19 Note that these kits simplify work so much that it is easy to forget the clutch fluid reservoir level; ensure that this is maintained at least above the MIN level line at all times.

Bleeding - using a pressure-bleeding kit

20 These kits are usually operated by the reservoir of pressurised air contained in the spare tyre. However, note that it will probably be necessary to reduce the pressure to a lower level than normal; refer to the instructions supplied with the kit.

21 By connecting a pressurised, fluid-filled container to the clutch fluid reservoir, bleeding can be carried out simply by opening the bleed screw and allowing the fluid to flow out until no more air bubbles can be seen in the expelled fluid.

22 This method has the advantage that the large reservoir of fluid provides an additional safeguard against air being drawn into the system during bleeding.

All methods

23 When bleeding is complete, and correct pedal feel is restored, tighten the bleed screw to the specified torque and wash off any spilt fluid. Refit the dust cap to the bleed screw.

24 Check the hydraulic fluid level in the master cylinder reservoir, and top-up if necessary (see 'Weekly checks' and Chapter 1).

6.4 Removing the clutch pressure plate and friction plate

6.7a Using vernier calipers, measure clutch friction plate thickness . . .

6.7b . . . and check the depth of the rivets below the friction material surface

25 Discard any hydraulic fluid that has been bled from the system; it will not be fit for re-use.

26 Check the operation of the clutch pedal as described in Section 2. If the clutch is still not operating correctly, air must still be present in the system, and further bleeding is required. Failure to bleed satisfactorily after a reasonable repetition of the bleeding procedure may be due to worn master cylinder/slave cylinder seals.

6 Clutch assembly - removal, inspection and refitting

⚠️ **Warning: Dust created by clutch wear and deposited on the clutch components may contain asbestos, which is a health hazard. DO NOT blow it out with compressed air, or inhale any of it. DO NOT use petrol or petroleum-based solvents to clean off the dust. Brake system cleaner or methylated spirit should be used to flush the dust into a suitable receptacle. After the clutch components are wiped clean with rags, dispose of the contaminated rags and cleaner in a sealed, marked container.**

Note: *Although some friction materials may no longer contain asbestos, it is safest to assume that they do, and to take precautions accordingly.*

Removal

1 Unless the complete engine/transmission unit is to be removed from the car and separated for major overhaul (see Chapter 2), the clutch can be reached by removing the transmission as described in Chapter 7A.

2 Before disturbing the clutch, use chalk or a marker pen to mark the relationship of the pressure plate assembly to the flywheel.

3 Working in a diagonal sequence, slacken the pressure plate bolts by half a turn at a time, until spring pressure is released and the bolts can be unscrewed by hand.

4 Prise the pressure plate assembly off its locating dowels, and collect the friction plate, noting which way round the friction plate is fitted **(see illustration)**.

Inspection

Note: *Due to the amount of work necessary to remove and refit clutch components, it is usually considered good practice to renew the clutch friction plate, pressure plate assembly and release bearing as a matched set, even if only one of these is actually worn enough to require renewal. It is also worth considering the renewal of the clutch components on a preventive basis if the engine and/or transmission have been removed for some other reason.*

5 Remove the clutch assembly.

6 When cleaning clutch components, read first the warning at the beginning of this Section; remove dust using a clean, dry cloth, and working in a well-ventilated atmosphere.

7 Check the friction plate facings for signs of wear, damage or oil contamination. If the friction material is cracked, burnt, scored or damaged, or if it is contaminated with oil or grease (shown by shiny black patches), the friction plate must be renewed. Measure the friction plate thickness and check the depth of the rivets below the friction material surface **(see illustrations)**. If the friction plate thickness or the depth of any rivet is equal to, or less than, the service limit given in the Specifications, then the friction plate must be renewed.

8 If the friction material is still serviceable, check that the centre boss splines are unworn, that the torsion springs are in good condition and securely fastened, and that all the rivets are tight. If any wear or damage is found, the friction plate must be renewed.

9 If the friction material is fouled with oil, this must be due to an oil leak from the crankshaft left-hand oil seal, from the sump-to-cylinder block joint, or from the transmission input shaft. Renew the seal or repair the joint, as appropriate, as described in Chapter 2 or 7, before installing the new friction plate.

10 Check the pressure plate assembly for obvious signs of wear or damage; shake it to check for loose rivets or worn or damaged fulcrum rings, and check that the drive straps securing the pressure plate to the cover do not show signs (such as a deep yellow or blue discoloration) of overheating. If the diaphragm spring is worn or damaged, or if its pressure is in any way suspect, the pressure plate assembly should be renewed.

11 Examine the machined bearing surfaces of the pressure plate and of the flywheel; they should be clean, completely flat, and free from scratches or scoring. If either is discoloured from excessive heat, or shows signs of cracks, it should be renewed - although minor damage of this nature can sometimes be polished away using emery paper. Using a straight-edge and feeler blades check the pressure plate surface for warpage at several points around its diameter, if the warpage exceeds the specified limit the plate must be renewed.

12 Check that the release bearing contact surface rotates smoothly and easily, with no sign of noise or roughness. Also check that the surface itself is smooth and unworn, with no signs of cracks, pitting or scoring. If there is any doubt about its condition, the bearing must be renewed.

Refitting

13 On reassembly, ensure that the bearing surfaces of the flywheel and pressure plate are completely clean, smooth, and free from oil or grease. Use solvent to remove any protective grease from new components.

14 Fit the friction plate so that its spring hub assembly faces away from the flywheel; there may also be a marking showing which way round the plate is to be refitted.

15 Refit the pressure plate assembly, aligning the marks made on dismantling (if the original pressure plate is re-used), and locating the pressure plate on its locating dowels. Fit the pressure plate bolts, but tighten them only finger-tight, so that the friction plate can still be moved.

16 The friction plate must now be centralised, so that when the transmission is refitted, its input shaft will pass through the splines at the centre of the friction plate.

17 Centralisation can be achieved by passing a screwdriver or other long bar through the friction plate and into the hole in the crankshaft; the friction plate can then be moved around until it is centred on the crankshaft hole. Alternatively, a clutch-aligning-tool can be used to eliminate the guesswork; these can be obtained from most accessory shops **(see illustration)**. A home-made aligning tool can be fabricated from a

6.17 Using a clutch aligning tool to centralise the friction plate

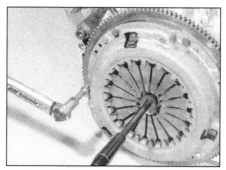

6.18 Ensure the friction plate is centralised then tighten the pressure plate retaining bolts to the specified torque

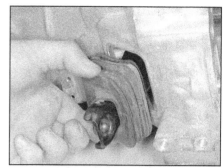

7.2 Remove the rubber gaiter from the end of the clutch release fork

length of metal rod or wooden dowel which fits closely inside the crankshaft hole, and has insulating tape wound around it to match the diameter of the friction plate splined hole.

18 When the friction plate is centralised, tighten the pressure plate bolts evenly and in a diagonal sequence to the specified torque setting **(see illustration)**.

19 Refit the transmission as described in Chapter 7A.

7 Clutch release mechanism - removal, inspection and refitting

Note: *Refer to the warning concerning the dangers of asbestos dust at the beginning of Section 6.*

Removal

1 Unless the complete engine/transmission unit is to be removed from the car and separated for major overhaul (see Chapter 2), the clutch release mechanism can be reached by removing the transmission only, as described in Chapter 7A.

2 Disengage the release fork gaiter from the transmission housing and slide it off of the fork **(see illustration)**.

3 Using pliers, compress the outer ends release fork retaining spring then disengage

the spring from the fork. Remove the fork and release bearing assembly from the bellhousing. If necessary, the release fork pivot stud can be unscrewed and removed from the transmission.

Inspection

4 Check the release mechanism, renewing any component which is worn or damaged. Carefully check all bearing surfaces and points of contact.

5 When checking the release bearing itself, note that it is often considered worthwhile to renew it as a matter of course. Check that the contact surface rotates smoothly and easily, with no sign of noise or roughness, and that the surface itself is smooth and unworn, with no signs of cracks, pitting or scoring. If there is any doubt about its condition, the bearing must be renewed.

Refitting

6 Where necessary, refit the release fork pivot stud to the transmission housing and tighten it to the specified torque.

7 Apply a smear of high-melting point grease (Rover recommend the use of Urea Grease UM264 - available from your Rover dealer) to the release fork pivot and the contact surfaces of the release fork, bearing and transmission housing **(see illustration)**.

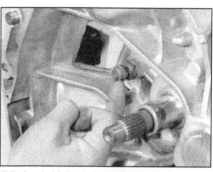

7.7 Apply high-melting point grease to the contact surfaces of the pivot stud, release fork and bearing

8 Pass the inner end of the retaining spring through the slot in the release fork and locate the spring ends in the fork slots **(see illustration)**.

9 Engage the release bearing with the end of the fork and manoeuvre the assembly into position. Slide the release bearing onto the transmission housing and clip the release fork onto its pivot stud **(see illustrations)**.

10 Ensure the release fork is clipped securely onto its pivot then slide the gaiter into position, making sure it is correctly engaged in the bellhousing.

11 Check the operation of the release mechanism then refit the transmission as described in Chapter 7A.

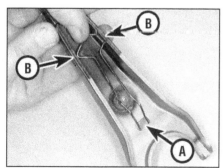

7.8 Locate the inner end of the spring in the slot (A) and clip the spring ends into the side slots (B)

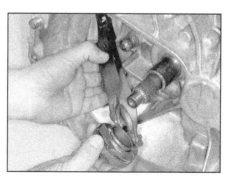

7.9a Engage the release bearing with the fork then manoeuvre the assembly into position . . .

7.9b . . . and clip the fork securely onto its pivot stud

Notes

Chapter 7 Part A
Manual transmission

Contents

Degrees of difficulty

Easy, suitable for novice with little experience	Fairly easy, suitable for beginner with some experience	Fairly difficult, suitable for competent DIY mechanic 	Difficult, suitable for experienced DIY mechanic	Very difficult, suitable for expert DIY or professional

Specifications

General

Type . . . . Manual, five forward speeds and reverse. Synchromesh on all forward speeds

Torque wrench settings	Nm	lbf ft
Engine-to-transmission unit bolts	65	47
Engine/transmission right-hand mounting:		
Mounting through-bolt	65	47
Mounting-to-transmission nuts	39	29
Engine/transmission rear mounting bracket bolts	55	41
Flywheel lower cover plate bolts	12	9
Front crossmember mounting bolts	60	44
Gearchange mechanism:		
Lever mounting bolts	22	16
Cable mounting bracket-to-transmission bolts	22	16
Cable mounting plate-to-body bolts	10	7
Shift cable-to-lever retaining nut	3	2
Manual transmission:		
Drain plug	40	29
Filler/level plug	45	33
Reversing light switch	25	18
Roadwheel nuts	110	81
Speedometer drive bolt	18	12

1 General information

Caution: If the radio/cassette in your vehicle is equipped with an anti-theft system, make sure you have the correct activation code before disconnecting the battery.

1 The transmission is contained in a cast-aluminium alloy casing bolted to the engine's right-hand end, and consists of the gearbox and final drive differential - often called a transaxle.

2 Drive is transmitted from the crankshaft via the clutch to the input shaft, which has a splined extension to accept the clutch friction plate, and rotates in sealed ball-bearings. From the input shaft, drive is transmitted to the output shaft, which rotates in a roller bearing at its right-hand end, and a sealed ball-bearing at its left-hand end. From the output shaft, the drive is transmitted to the differential crownwheel, which rotates with the differential case and planetary gears, thus driving the sun gears and driveshafts. The rotation of the planetary gears on their shaft allows the inner roadwheel to rotate at a slower speed than the outer roadwheel when the car is cornering.

3 The input and output shafts are arranged side by side, parallel to the crankshaft and driveshafts, so that their gear pinion teeth are in constant mesh. In the neutral position, the output shaft gear pinions rotate freely, so that drive cannot be transmitted to the crownwheel.

4 Gear selection is via a floor-mounted lever and selector cable mechanism. The selector cables cause the appropriate selector fork to move its respective synchro-sleeve along the shaft, to lock the gear pinion to the synchro-hub. Since the synchro-hubs are splined to the output shaft, this locks the pinion to the shaft, so that drive can be transmitted. To ensure that gear-changing can be made quickly and quietly, a synchro-mesh system is fitted to all forward gears, consisting of baulk rings and spring-loaded fingers, as well as the gear pinions and synchro-hubs. The synchro-mesh cones are formed on the mating faces of the baulk rings and gear pinions.

2.3a Remove the split pin and washer (arrowed) . . .

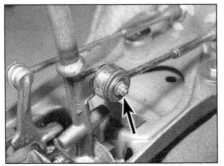

2.3b . . . then undo the retaining nut and washer (arrowed) and detach the gearchange cables

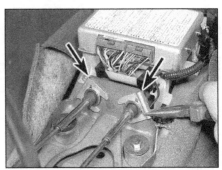

2.4 Slide out the retaining clips (arrowed) and free the cables from the lever mounting plate

2 Gearchange cables - removal and refitting

Removal

1 Remove the centre console assembly as described in Chapter 11. To improve access to the transmission end of the cables, remove the air cleaner housing duct (see Chapter 4).

2 Prior to removal make alignment marks between the cables and gearchange/ transmission levers to avoid confusion on refitting.

3 Position the gearchange lever in the neutral position then remove the split pin and washers and detach the select cable from the base of the lever. Slacken and remove the retaining nut and washer and free the shift cable from the lever (see illustrations). Take care not to disturb the position of the transmission shift and select levers whilst the cables are disconnected.

4 Slide out the retaining clips and free the cables from the gearchange lever mounting bracket (see illustration).

5 From inside the engine compartment, remove the split pin, metal washer and plastic washer securing each cable to the transmission levers and free the cables (see illustrations).

6 Slide out the retaining clips securing the cables to the transmission bracket (see

illustration). Work back along the cables, freeing them from any relevant retaining clips and brackets whilst noting the correct routing.

7 Firmly apply the handbrake then jack up the front of the vehicle and support it on axle stands. Slacken and remove the bolts securing the cable mounting plate to the floor then manoeuvre the cable assembly away from the vehicle.

8 Examine each cable, looking for worn end fittings or a damaged outer casing, and for signs of fraying of the inner wire. Check the cable's operation; the inner wire should move smoothly and easily through the outer casing. Remember that a cable that appears serviceable when tested off the car may well be much heavier in operation when in its working position. Renew the cable if it shows signs of excessive wear or any damage. The cable split pins and retaining nut should be renewed whenever they are disturbed.

Refitting

9 Refitting is a reversal of the removal procedure, noting the following.
   a) Apply a smear of multi-purpose grease to the cable end fittings and the lever pivots. If new cables are being fitted, transfer the marks made prior to removal to aid refitting.
   b) Ensure the cables are correctly routed and tighten the mounting plate bolts to the specified torque. Reconnect the cables and secure them in position with new split pins and a retaining nut.

c) Check the operation of the gearchange mechanism before refitting the centre console (see Chapter 11).

3 Gearchange lever - removal and refitting

Removal

1 Remove the centre console as described in Chapter 11.

2 Disconnect the gearchange cables from the lever as described in paragraphs 3 and 4 of Section 2.

3 Slacken and remove the bolts securing the lever assembly to the body and remove it from the vehicle, along with its mounting rubbers and spacers. Renew the mounting rubbers if they show signs of damage or deterioration.

Refitting

4 Prior to refitting apply multi-purpose grease to all the lever assembly pivot points and to the cable end fittings.

5 Ensure the mounting rubbers are correctly positioned on either side of the lever mounting plate and insert the spacers. Refit the gearchange lever assembly to the vehicle and tighten its retaining bolts to the specified torque.

6 Ensure the cables are correctly routed then engage the cables with their respective locations in the lever base and secure then in position with the retaining clips.

2.5a Withdraw the split pin . . .

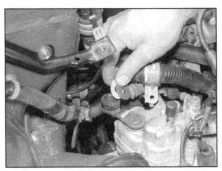

2.5b . . . then lift off the metal and plastic washers and detach the gearchange cable from the selector lever

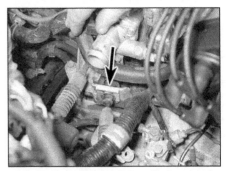

2.6 Slide out the retaining clip (arrowed) and free the cable from its mounting bracket

7 Reconnect the select cable to the lever then refit the washers and secure them in position with a new split pin. Locate the shift cable on the lever then refit the washer and secure it in position with a new retaining nut.
8 Check the operation of the gearchange mechanism then refit the centre console as described in Chapter 11.

4 Oil seals - renewal

Driveshaft oil seals

Right-hand oil seal

1 Chock the rear wheels, apply the handbrake, then jack up the front of the car and support it on axle stands. Remove the appropriate front roadwheel.
2 Drain the transmission oil as described in Chapter 1.
3 Working as described in Chapter 8, free the inner end of the driveshaft from the transmission, and place it clear of the seal, noting that there is no need to unscrew the driveshaft retaining nut; the driveshaft can be left secured to the hub. Support the driveshaft, to avoid placing any strain on the driveshaft joints or gaiters.
4 Carefully prise the oil seal out of the transmission using a large flat-bladed screwdriver.
5 Remove all traces of dirt from the area around the oil seal aperture, then apply a smear of grease to the outer lip of the new oil seal. Ensure the seal is correctly positioned, with its sealing lip facing inwards, and drive it squarely into position, using a suitable tubular drift (such as a socket) which bears only on the hard outer edge of the seal. Ensure the seal is fitted so that its outer surface is flush with the transmission housing.
6 Refit the driveshaft as described in Chapter 8.
7 Refill the transmission with the specified type and amount of oil, (see Chapter 1).

Left-hand oil seal

8 Remove the intermediate shaft as described in Chapter 8.

9 Renew the oil seal as described in paragraphs 4 and 5.
10 Refit the intermediate shaft as described in Chapter 8 and refill the transmission with the specified type and amount of oil as described in Chapter 1.

Input shaft and gearchange lever shaft oil seals

11 To renew these oil seals, the transmission must be dismantled. This task should therefore be entrusted to a Rover dealer or transmission specialist.

5 Reversing light switch - testing, removal and refitting

Testing

1 The reversing light circuit is controlled by a plunger-type switch that is screwed into the top of the transmission casing. If a fault develops in the circuit, first ensure that the circuit fuse has not blown.
2 To test the switch, trace the wiring back from the switch and disconnect the wiring connector **(see illustration)**. Use a multimeter (set to the resistance function) or a battery-and-bulb test circuit to check that there is continuity between the switch terminals only when reverse gear is selected. If this is not the case, and there are no obvious breaks or other damage to the wires, the switch is faulty, and must be renewed.

Removal

3 To improve access to the switch, remove the air cleaner housing duct (see Chapter 4).
4 Disconnect the wiring connectors, then unscrew the switch and remove it from the transmission casing along with its sealing washer.

Refitting

5 Fit a new sealing washer to the switch, then screw it back into position in the top of the transmission housing and tighten it to the specified torque. Reconnect the wiring connectors, and test the operation of the circuit. Refit any components removed for access.

5.4 Disconnecting the reversing light switch wiring connectors

6 Speedometer drive - removal and refitting

1 All models are fitted with an electrically-operated speedometer which is operated by the vehicle speed sensor which is mounted onto the top of the speedometer drive. On early models the speedometer drive assembly also acts as a speed sensor for the power steering system; the speedometer drive is connected into the power steering hydraulic circuit and contains two valves which affect the pressure in the power steering hydraulic system, depending on the vehicle speed.

Removal

2 The speedometer drive is situated on the top of the transmission housing, next to the inner end of the left-hand driveshaft. To improve access remove the air cleaner housing duct (see Chapter 4); on some models it may also be necessary to unbolt the support bracket from the side of the rear engine/transmission mounting.
3 Disconnect the wiring connector from the vehicle speed sensor which is fitted to the top of the speedometer drive. If necessary, undo the retaining bolts then carefully lift the sensor away from the transmission housing, along with its drive pin **(see illustrations)**. Discard the sensor sealing ring, this should be renewed whenever it is disturbed **(see illustration)**.

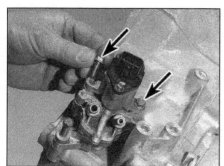

6.3a Slacken and remove the retaining bolts (arrowed) . . .

6.3b . . . then lift off the speed sensor . . .

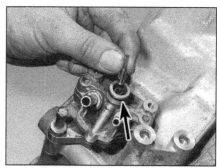

6.3c . . . and withdraw the drive pin (sensor sealing ring arrowed)

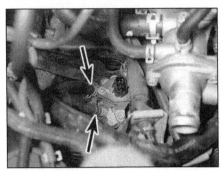

6.4 On early models release the retaining clips and disconnect the power steering hoses (arrowed) from the speedometer drive

6.5a Slacken and remove the retaining bolt . . .

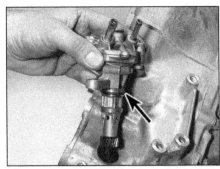

6.5b . . . and lift out the speedometer drive housing assembly noting the correct fitted location of the sealing ring (arrowed)

4 On early models where the speedometer drive is connected into the power steering hydraulic circuit, release the retaining clips and disconnect the fluid hoses from the drive **(see illustration)**. Plug the hose ends and drive unions to minimise fluid loss and prevent the entry of dirt into the system.

5 Slacken and remove the retaining bolt(s) and withdraw the speedometer drive and driven pinion assembly from the transmission housing, along with its sealing ring **(see illustrations)**.

6 On early models where the drive assembly is connected into the power steering hydraulic system, the speedometer assembly must not be dismantled. If it is faulty, it must be renewed. On later models, the driven pinion can be renewed separately; to remove the pinion, slide out the retaining clip then withdraw the pinion from the housing.

Refitting

7 On later models, where necessary, lubricate the driven pinion with clean transmission oil and insert it into the housing. Refit the pinion retaining clip making sure it is correctly located in the pinion groove.

8 On all models, fit a new sealing ring to the speedometer housing and lubricate it with a smear of oil of oil to ease installation.

9 Ease the speedometer drive into position in the transmission, ensuring that the drive and driven pinions are correctly engaged, and tighten the retaining bolt to the specified torque.

10 Where necessary, fit a new sealing ring to the top of the speedometer housing and insert the vehicle speed sensor drive pin. Manoeuvre the sensor into position, ensuring it is correctly engaged with the drive pin, and securely tighten its retaining bolts.

11 Reconnect the wiring connector to the speed sensor.

12 Refit the mounting support bracket (where removed) and refit the air cleaner duct. On early models where the drive assembly is connected into the power steering hydraulic circuit, on completion, bleed the hydraulic system as described in Chapter 10.

7 Transmission - removal and refitting

Removal

1 Chock the rear wheels, then firmly apply the handbrake. Jack up the front of the vehicle, and securely support it on axle stands. Remove both front roadwheels then undo the retaining screws and fasteners and remove the undercover from beneath the engine/transmission unit.

2 Drain the transmission oil as described in Chapter 1, then refit the drain and filler plugs, and tighten them to their specified torque settings.

3 Remove the battery and mounting plate, and the starter motor (see Chapter 5).

4 Remove the air cleaner housing as described in Chapter 4.

5 Disconnect the wiring connector from the reversing light switch. Undo the retaining bolts and disconnect the earth straps and wiring retaining clips from the transmission housing **(see illustrations)**.

6 Remove the split pins and washers securing the gearchange cables to the transmission levers (see Section 2) then undo the retaining bolts and free the cable mounting bracket from the top of the transmission.

7 Disconnect the wiring connector from the vehicle speed sensor which is fitted to the top of the speedometer drive (see Section 6). On early models where the speedometer drive is connected into the power steering hydraulic circuit, release the retaining clips and disconnect the hoses from the drive. Plug the hose ends and drive unions to minimise fluid loss and prevent the entry of dirt.

8 Starting at the master cylinder, work along the clutch hydraulic hose/pipe unscrewing all the mounting bracket bolts and free the pipe/hose from all the relevant clips. Slacken and remove the slave cylinder retaining bolts and position the pipe/hose and cylinder assembly clear of the transmission unit **(see illustrations)**. Fully retract the pushrod into the slave cylinder and secure it in position with a stout elastic band or cable tie (to prevent the piston being accidentally expelled by spring pressure).

Caution: Whilst the cylinder is removed from the transmission, do not depress the clutch pedal.

7.5a Undo the retaining bolts and disconnect the earth lead and wiring clips from the front . . .

7.5b . . . and top of the transmission housing

7.8a Undo the retaining screws and free the clutch hydraulic hose/pipe from the top of the transmission housing

7.8b Undo the retaining bolts (arrowed) and free the clutch slave cylinder from the transmission

7.11 Crossmember front mounting bolts (arrowed)

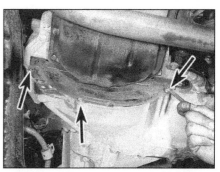

7.12 Undo the retaining bolts (arrowed) and remove the flywheel lower cover plate

9 Working as described in Chapter 10, remove the front suspension right-hand radius rod to gain the clearance necessary to remove the transmission unit.

10 Referring to Chapter 8, remove the intermediate shaft and disconnect the right-hand driveshaft from the transmission unit. Note that it is not necessary to remove the right-hand driveshaft completely, it can be left attached to the hub assembly and released from the transmission as the hub is pulled outwards. **Note:** *Do not allow the shaft to hang down under its own weight as this could damage the constant velocity joints/gaiters.*

11 Unscrew the mounting bolts and remove the crossmember from underneath the engine/transmission unit, freeing it from the exhaust system mounting rubber **(see illustration)**.

12 Undo the retaining bolts and remove the flywheel lower cover plate from the transmission **(see illustration)**.

7.16a Slacken and remove the through-bolt . . .

13 To improve access, unscrew the bolts and remove support bracket from the underside of the manifold.

14 Place a jack with a block of wood beneath the engine, to take the weight of the engine. Alternatively, attach a couple of lifting eyes to the engine, and fit a hoist or support bar to take the engine weight. Also place a jack and block of wood beneath the transmission, and raise the jack to take the weight of the transmission.

15 Slacken and remove the three bolts securing the engine/transmission rear mounting bracket to the transmission housing.

16 Slacken and remove the through-bolt and nut from the right-hand engine/transmission mounting, then undo the nuts and remove the mounting from the top of the transmission unit **(see illustrations)**.

17 With the jack positioned beneath the transmission taking the weight, slacken and remove the remaining bolts securing the transmission housing to the engine. Note the correct fitted positions of each bolt, and the necessary brackets, as they are removed, to use as a reference on refitting. Make a final check that all components have been disconnected, and are positioned clear of the transmission so that they will not hinder the removal procedure.

18 With the bolts removed, move the trolley jack and transmission to the right, to free it from its locating dowels. Once the transmission is free, lower the jack and manoeuvre the unit out from under the car.

Remove the locating dowels from the transmission or engine if they are loose, and keep them in a safe place.

Refitting

19 The transmission is refitted by a reversal of the removal procedure, bearing in mind the following points:

a) Apply a smear of high-melting point grease (Rover recommend the use of Urea Grease UM264 - available from your Rover dealer) to the release fork pivot and the contact surfaces of the release fork, bearing and transmission housing.
b) Ensure the locating dowels are correctly positioned prior to installation **(see illustration)**.
c) Tighten all nuts and bolts to the specified torque (where given).
d) Renew the driveshaft oil seals (see Section 4) then refit the intermediate shaft and driveshafts as described in Chapter 8.
e) Reconnect the gearchange cables to the transmission and secure them in position with new split pins (see Section 2).
f) Refit the slave cylinder and ensure the hydraulic pipe/hose is securely retained by all the necessary clips. On completion, check the operation of the clutch as described in Chapter 6.
g) On completion, refill the transmission with the specified type and quantity of lubricant, as described in Chapter 1.
h) On early models where the speedometer drive is connected into the power steering system, on completion bleed the hydraulic system as described in Chapter 10.

7.16b . . . then undo the mounting nuts (arrowed) . . .

7.16c . . . and remove the right-hand engine/transmission mounting

7.19 Ensure the locating dowels (arrowed) are in position prior to refitting the transmission

8 Transmission overhaul - general information

1 Overhauling a manual transmission unit is a difficult and involved job for the DIY home mechanic. In addition to dismantling and reassembling many small parts, clearances must be precisely measured and, if necessary, changed by selecting shims and spacers. Internal transmission components are also often difficult to obtain, and in many instances, extremely expensive. Because of this, if the transmission develops a fault or becomes noisy, the best course of action is to have the unit overhauled by a specialist repairer, or to obtain an exchange reconditioned unit.

2 Nevertheless, it is not impossible for the more experienced mechanic to overhaul the transmission, provided the special tools are available, and the job is done in a deliberate step-by-step manner, so that nothing is overlooked.

3 The tools necessary for an overhaul include internal and external circlip pliers, bearing pullers, a slide hammer, a set of pin punches, a dial test indicator, and possibly a hydraulic press. In addition, a large, sturdy workbench and a vice will be required.

4 During dismantling of the transmission, make careful notes of how each component is fitted, to make reassembly easier and more accurate.

5 Before dismantling the transmission, it will help if you have some idea what area is malfunctioning. Certain problems can be closely related to specific areas in the transmission, which can make component examination and replacement easier. Refer to the Fault finding Section of this manual for more information.

Chapter 7 Part B
Automatic transmission

Contents

Degrees of difficulty

| Easy, suitable for novice with little experience | | Fairly easy, suitable for beginner with some experience | | Fairly difficult, suitable for competent DIY mechanic | | Difficult, suitable for experienced DIY mechanic | | Very difficult, suitable for expert DIY or professional | |

Specifications

General

Type . . . . Electronically-controlled dual-mode automatic with four forward speeds and reverse

Torque wrench settings	Nm	lbf ft
Driveplate lower cover plate bolts	12	9
Engine/transmission right-hand mounting:		
Mounting through-bolt	65	48
Mounting-to-transmission nuts	39	29
Engine/transmission rear mounting bracket bolts	55	41
Engine-to-transmission unit bolts	65	48
Front crossmember mounting bolts	60	44
Roadwheel nuts	110	81
Selector cable:		
Adjuster locknut	7	5
Cable-to-selector lever bolts	10	7
Grommet and retaining clip bolts	12	9
Transmission lever retaining bolt	14	10
Transmission retaining plate bolts	18	13
Speedometer drive bolt	18	13
Torque converter-to-driveplate bolts	12	9
Transmission control electrical components:		
Speed sensor bolt	12	9
Solenoid valve assembly bolts	12	9

1 General information

Caution: If the radio/cassette in your vehicle is equipped with an anti-theft system, make sure you have the correct activation code before disconnecting the battery.

1 Most models covered in this manual were offered with the option of a four-speed, electronically-controlled automatic transmission, consisting of a torque converter, an epicyclic geartrain, and hydraulically-operated clutches and brakes. The unit is controlled by the electronic control unit (ECU) via four electrically-operated solenoid valves. The transmission unit has two driving modes; normal and sport mode. The normal mode is the standard mode for driving in which the transmission shifts up at relatively low engine speeds to combine reasonable performance with economy. If the transmission unit is switched into sport mode, using the button on the selector lever, the transmission shifts up only at high engine speeds, giving improved acceleration and overtaking performance. When the transmission is in sport mode, the indicator light in the instrument panel is illuminated.

2 The torque converter provides a fluid coupling between engine and transmission, which acts as an automatic clutch, and also provides a degree of torque multiplication when accelerating.

3 The epicyclic geartrain provides either of the four forward or one reverse gear ratios, according to which of its component parts are held stationary or allowed to turn. The components of the geartrain are held or released by brakes and clutches which are activated by the control unit. A fluid pump within the transmission provides the necessary hydraulic pressure to operate the brakes and clutches.

4 Driver control of the transmission is by a seven-position selector lever. The transmission has two drive positions, D4 which allows automatic changing throughout the range of all four gear ratios and D3 which allows automatic changing only through the first three ratios. An automatic kickdown facility shifts the transmission down a gear if the accelerator pedal is fully depressed. The transmission also has two hold positions, 1 means only the first gear ratio is used and 2 locks the transmission so that first and second gear ratios are used. The hold positions are useful for providing engine braking when travelling down steep gradients. Note, however, that the transmission should *never* be shifted down a position at high engine speeds.

5 Due to the complexity of the automatic transmission, any repair or overhaul work must be left to a Rover dealer with the necessary special equipment for fault diagnosis and repair. The contents of the following Sections are therefore confined to supplying general information, and any service information and instructions that can be used by the owner.

2 Selector cable - adjustment

1 Start the engine and allow it to idle. Move the selector lever into the Reverse position, check that the transmission engages reverse gear then switch off the engine.

2 Remove the centre console as described in Chapter 11 and move the selector lever back to the Neutral position.

3 Withdraw the retaining clip securing the selector cable to the adjuster on the base of the selector lever. Check that the cable end fitting hole is perfectly aligned with the adjuster hole. If adjustment is necessary, slacken the locknut and rotate the adjuster. Once the cable and adjuster holes are correctly aligned, tighten the adjuster locknut to the specified torque. Refit the cable retaining clip ensuring that it slides easily into position **(see illustration)**.

4 Start the engine and move the selector lever through its complete operating range, checking that each gear engages correctly. If necessary, readjust the cable by repeating the operations described in paragraphs 1 to 3.

5 Once the cable is correctly adjusted, check the operation of the selector lever position switch (see Section 10) before refitting the centre console as described in Chapter 11.

3 Selector cable - removal and refitting

Removal

1 Remove the centre console as described in Chapter 11.

2 Position the selector lever in the Neutral position then remove the retaining clip securing the end of the selector cable to the adjuster on the base of the selector lever **(see illustration)**.

3 Slacken and remove the bolts securing the end of the selector outer cable in position and free the cable from its bracket.

4 Firmly apply the handbrake then jack up the front of the vehicle and support it on axle stands.

5 Undo the retaining screws and remove the selector cable retaining plate from the base of the transmission unit.

6 Bend back the locking plate tabs then unscrew the retaining bolt and free the selector lever from the transmission shaft. Discard the locking plate; a new one should be used on refitting.

7 Remove the exhaust system heatshield to gain access to the complete length of the selector cable. Note that on some models it maybe necessary to remove the intermediate section of the exhaust system to enable the heatshield to be removed (see Chapter 4).

8 Work back along the cable, noting its correct routing, and free it from all the relevant retaining clips. Undo the bolts securing the cable retaining clip and grommet to the vehicle body and remove the cable from underneath the vehicle.

9 If necessary, with the cable removed, make alignment marks between the cable and transmission selector lever. Pull out the split pin then withdraw the retaining plate and separate the selector lever from the transmission end of the cable, taking care not to lose the bush from the cable end fitting **(see illustration)**.

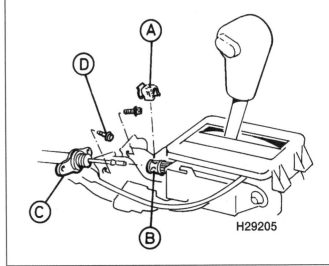

3.2 Selector cable-to-lever attachment details

A Cable retaining clip
B Adjuster
C Cable end fitting
D Retaining bolts

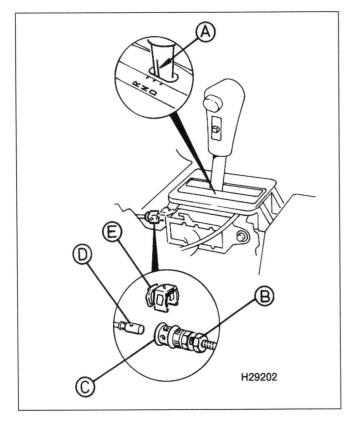

2.3 Selector cable adjustment details

A Selector lever position mark
B Adjuster locknut
C Adjuster
D Cable end fitting
E Retaining clip

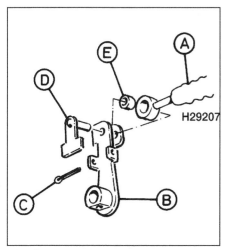

3.9 Selector cable-to-transmission lever attachment details

A Cable end fitting D Retaining plate
B Selector lever E Bush
C Split pin

10 Examine the cable, looking for worn end fittings or a damaged outer casing, and for signs of fraying of the inner cable. Check the cable's operation: the inner cable should move smoothly and easily through the outer casing. Remember that a cable that appears serviceable when tested off the car may well be much heavier in operation when compressed into its working position. Renew the cable if it shows any signs of excessive wear or any damage.

Refitting

11 Where necessary, apply a smear of grease to the selector cable transmission end fitting and insert the bush. Engage the selector lever with the cable, aligning the marks made prior to removal, then insert the retaining plate and secure it in position with a new split pin.
12 Manoeuvre the cable into position from underneath the vehicle, ensuring it is correctly routed. Pass the cable up through the floor and tighten the cable grommet and retaining clip bolts to the specified torque.
13 Engage the selector lever with the transmission shaft. Fit the new locking plate to the lever retaining bolt then refit the bolt, tightening it to the specified torque setting. Secure the bolt in position by bending the retaining plate tabs down against the flats of the bolt head.
14 Refit the retaining plate to the transmission unit, making sure it is correctly engaged with the selector cable, and tighten its retaining bolts to the specified torque. Lower the vehicle to the ground.
15 From inside the vehicle, engage the selector cable with the selector lever adjuster then refit outer cable retaining bolts and tighten them to the specified torque. Align the inner cable with the adjuster and secure it in position with the retaining clip.

16 Adjust the selector cable as described in Section 2 then refit the centre console as described in Chapter 11.

4 Selector lever assembly - removal and refitting

Removal

1 Disconnect the selector cable from the base of the lever as described in paragraphs 1 to 3 of Section 3.
2 Disconnect the wiring connectors from the selector lever position switch, the sport mode switch and the illumination bulb.
3 Slacken and remove the selector lever mounting bolts and remove the assembly from the vehicle.

Refitting

4 Refitting is the reverse of removal. Prior to refitting the centre console, adjust the selector cable as described in Section 2.

5 Kickdown cable - adjustment

1 Prior to checking the kickdown cable adjustment, ensure the accelerator cable is correctly adjusted (see Chapter 4) then warm the engine up to normal operating temperature and check that the engine idles at the specified speed.
2 Locate the kickdown lever which is situated on the front of the transmission housing, next to the fluid level dipstick.
3 Slacken the kickdown cable locknut and adjuster nut to obtain some slack in the kickdown cable. Ensure both the throttle linkage and the transmission kickdown lever are in the fully closed positions then remove all free play from the kickdown cable using the adjuster nut. Hold the adjuster nut stationary and securely tighten the locknut.
4 Operate the throttle linkage and check that the kickdown lever moves easily and returns smoothly to its stop. If necessary, readjust the cable as described above.

6 Kickdown cable - removal and refitting

Removal

1 Working at the transmission end of the cable, detach the inner cable from the kickdown lever then slacken the locknut and adjuster nut and free the cable from its mounting bracket.
2 Work back along the cable, freeing it from all the necessary clips and ties, whilst noting its correct routing.

3 Unscrew the bolt securing the upper end of the cable to its mounting bracket then free the inner cable from the throttle cam and remove the cable from the engine compartment.
4 Examine the cable, looking for worn end fittings or a damaged outer casing, and for signs of fraying of the inner cable. Check the cable's operation; the inner cable should move smoothly and easily through the outer casing. Remember that a cable that appears serviceable when tested off the car may well be much heavier in operation when compressed into its working position. Renew the cable if it shows any signs of excessive wear or any damage. Whilst the cable is removed, manually move the transmission kickdown lever, checking that it moves easily and returns smoothly to its stop; if not consult your Rover dealer on the best course of action.

Refitting

5 Manoeuvre the cable into position, ensuring it is correctly routed, and connect the inner cable to the throttle cam. Refit the outer cable retaining bolt and tighten it securely.
6 Secure the cable in position with all the relevant clips and ties and pass the lower end of the cable through its mounting bracket.
7 Engage the inner cable with the kickdown lever and adjust the cable as described in Section 5.

7 Speedometer drive - removal and refitting

Refer to Chapter 7A.

8 Oil seals - renewal

Driveshaft oil seals

1 Refer to Chapter 7A.

Torque converter oil seal

2 Remove the transmission as described in Section 11.
3 Carefully slide the torque converter off of the transmission shaft whilst being prepared for fluid spillage.
4 Remove the sealing ring from its recess on the outside of the torque converter flange.
5 Remove all traces of dirt from the area around the oil seal aperture then fit the new sealing ring, ensuring its is correctly located in its recess.
6 Lubricate the sealing ring with clean transmission fluid then carefully ease the torque converter into position.
7 Refit the transmission as described in Section 11.

9 Fluid cooler - general information

1 The transmission fluid cooler is an integral part of the radiator assembly. Refer to Chapter 3 for removal and refitting details, if the cooler is damaged the complete radiator assembly must be renewed.

10 Transmission control system electrical components - removal and refitting

Selector lever position switch

1 The selector lever position switch controls the gear position indicator in the instrument panel. In addition to this, it is also performs the reversing light and starter inhibitor switch functions, preventing the engine being started when the transmission is in gear. If at any time the gear position indicator display or the reversing light operation becomes faulty, or it is noted that the engine can be started with the selector lever in any position other than Park or Neutral, then it is likely that the switch is faulty. If adjustment fails to correct the fault then the complete switch must be renewed as a unit.

Removal

2 Remove the centre console as described in

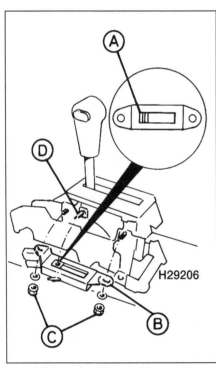

10.4 Selector lever position switch refitting details

A Switch slide
B Switch
C Retaining nuts
D Selector lever pin

Chapter 11 and position the selector lever in the Park position.

3 Disconnect the wiring connector(s) then undo the retaining nuts and washers and remove the switch from the side of the selector lever assembly.

Refitting and adjustment

4 Position the switch slide fully forwards and manoeuvre the switch into position. Ensure that the switch slide is correctly engaged with the selector lever pin then locate the switch on its studs and refit the washers and mounting nuts, tightening them securely **(see illustration)**.

5 Reconnect the wiring connectors then check the operation of switch with the selector lever in the Park and Neutral positions; the position display indicator should function correctly and the engine should start in both positions. Move the selector lever to the Reverse position and check the operation of the reversing lights. If necessary slight adjustments can be made by slackening the switch mounting nuts and repositioning the switch.

6 Once the switch is operating correctly, refit the centre console as described in Chapter 11.

Sport mode switch

Removal

7 Remove the centre console as described in Chapter 11.

8 Undo the retaining screws and remove the selector lever trim cover from around the lever.

9 Trace the wiring connector back from the switch and disconnect it from the main wiring harness. Release the wiring from any necessary clips.

10 Carefully prise out the sport mode switch cover from the selector lever handle to gain access to the switch retaining screws.

11 Undo the retaining screws and withdraw the switch from the selector lever handle.

Refitting

12 Refitting is the reverse of removal. Check the operation of the switch prior to refitting the centre console.

Electronic control unit (ECU)

Removal

13 The ECU is located in the front passenger footwell.

14 Disconnect the battery negative terminal and peel back the passenger compartment carpet to reveal the ECU cover.

15 Slacken and remove the retaining nuts and carefully lift off the cover; the transmission ECU is the smaller of the two control unit, the larger unit is the engine management ECU.

16 Disconnect the wiring connector(s) then undo the retaining bolts and remove the ECU from the vehicle.

Refitting

17 Refitting is the reverse of removal ensuring that the wiring is securely reconnected.

Mainshaft and countershaft speed sensors

18 The speed sensors are located on the right-hand end of the transmission assembly; the mainshaft sensor is at the front of the transmission unit and the countershaft sensor at the rear **(see illustration)**. Both sensors are removed and refitted as follows.

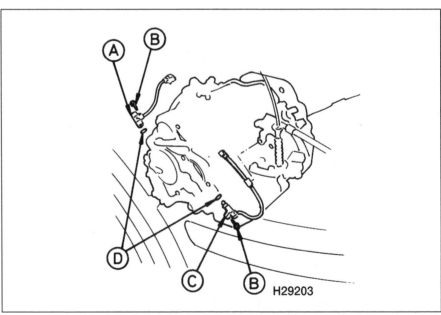

10.18 Mainshaft and countershaft speed sensors

A Countershaft speed sensor
B Retaining bolt
C Mainshaft speed sensor
D Sealing ring

Removal

19 Disconnect the battery negative terminal. To improve access to the sensor, firmly apply the handbrake then jack up the front of the vehicle and support it on axle stands.

20 Trace the wiring back from the sensor and disconnect it from the main wiring harness.

21 Remove all traces of dirt from around the sensor then slacken and remove the retaining bolt. Carefully withdraw the sensor from the transmission unit and plug the sensor aperture to prevent the entry of dirt. Remove the sensor sealing ring and discard it; a new one should be used on refitting.

Refitting

22 Fit the new sealing ring to the sensor recess and lubricate it with clean transmission fluid to ease installation.

23 Ease the sensor into position then refit the retaining bolt, tightening it to the specified torque setting.

24 Reconnect the wiring connector then lower the vehicle to the ground and reconnect the battery.

Lock-up and shift control solenoid valve assemblies

25 The solenoid valve assemblies are mounted on the front, left-hand end of the transmission unit; the lock-up solenoid valve assembly is the upper pair of valves and the shift control valve assembly is the lower pair of valves. Each valve assembly can be removed and refitted as follows.

Removal

26 Disconnect the battery negative terminal. If necessary, to improve access to the lower assembly, firmly apply the handbrake then jack up the front of the vehicle and support it on axle stands.

27 Trace the wiring back from the valve assembly and disconnect it from the main wiring harness.

28 Remove all traces of dirt from around the solenoid valve assembly then slacken and remove the retaining bolts and lift the assembly away from the transmission unit (note the correct fitted location of the wiring bracket when removing the upper valve assembly) **(see illustration)**. Recover the filter which is fitted between the assembly and the transmission unit and discard; this should be renewed whenever the valve assembly is removed. If the valve is to be removed for some time, plug the transmission fluid passages to prevent the entry of dirt.

Refitting

29 Ensure the mating surfaces are clean and dry and position the new filter on the transmission unit.

30 Fit the valve assembly and wiring bracket (where fitted) and tighten the retaining bolts to the specified torque setting.

31 Reconnect the wiring connector then lower the vehicle to the ground and reconnect the battery.

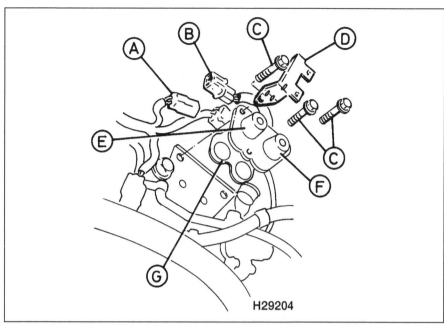

10.28 Lock-up solenoid valve assembly details

A Wiring connector
B Wiring connector
C Retaining bolts
D Wiring bracket
E Valve assembly A
F Valve assembly B
G Filter

11 Automatic transmission - removal and refitting

Removal

1 Chock the rear wheels, apply the handbrake, and place the selector lever in the Neutral position. Jack up the front of the vehicle, and securely support it on axle stands. Remove both front roadwheels then undo the retaining bolts and remove the undercover from beneath the engine/transmission unit.

2 Drain the transmission fluid as described in Chapter 1, then refit the drain plug and tighten it to the specified torque.

3 Remove the battery and mounting plate and the starter motor (see Chapter 5).

4 Remove the air cleaner housing as described in Chapter 4.

5 Disconnect the wiring connectors from the mainshaft and countershaft speed sensors and the lock-up and shift solenoid valve assemblies on the transmission unit. Undo the retaining bolt(s) and disconnect the earth strap(s) from the transmission housing. Release all wiring from any necessary clips and position it clear of the transmission unit.

6 Make identification marks between the oil cooler hoses and their unions on the front of the transmission housing. Clamp the hoses to minimise fluid loss then slacken the hose clamps and disconnect the hoses from the transmission. Plug the hose and transmission union ends to prevent the entry of dirt into the hydraulic system.

7 Undo the retaining screws and remove the selector cable retaining plate from the base of the transmission unit. Bend back the locking plate tabs then unscrew the retaining bolt and free the selector lever from the transmission shaft. Discard the locking plate, a new one should be used on refitting (see Section 3), and position the cable clear of the transmission unit.

8 Slacken the locknut and adjuster nut then detach the kickdown cable and position it clear of the transmission unit (see Section 6).

9 Disconnect the wiring connector from the vehicle speed sensor which is fitted to the top of the speedometer drive. On early models where the speedometer drive is connected into the power steering hydraulic circuit, release the retaining clips and disconnect the hoses from the drive. Plug the hose ends and drive unions to minimise fluid loss and prevent the entry of dirt.

10 Working as described in Chapter 10, remove the front suspension right-hand radius rod to gain the clearance necessary to remove the transmission unit.

11 Referring to Chapter 8, remove the intermediate shaft and disconnect the right-hand driveshaft from the transmission unit. Note that it is not necessary to remove the right-hand driveshaft completely, it can be left attached to the hub assembly and released from the transmission as the hub is pulled outwards. **Note:** *Do not allow the shaft to hang down under its own weight as this could damage the constant velocity joints/gaiters.*

12 Unscrew the mounting bolts and remove the crossmember from underneath the engine/transmission unit, detaching it from the exhaust system mounting.

13 Undo the retaining bolts and remove the driveplate lower cover plate from the transmission, to gain access to the torque converter retaining bolts. Slacken and remove the visible bolt(s) then, using a socket and extension bar to rotate the crankshaft pulley, undo the remaining bolts securing the torque converter to the driveplate as they become accessible. There are eight bolts in total.

14 To ensure that the torque converter does not fall out as the transmission is removed, slide the converter along the shaft and fully into the transmission housing. If necessary, secure it in position using a length of metal strip bolted to one of the starter motor bolt holes.

15 To improve access, unscrew the bolts and remove support bracket from the underside of the manifold.

16 Place a jack with a block of wood beneath the engine, to take the weight of the engine. Alternatively, attach a couple of lifting eyes to the engine, and fit a hoist or support bar to take the engine weight. Also place a jack and block of wood beneath the transmission, and raise the jack to take the weight of the transmission.

17 Slacken and remove the three bolts securing the engine/transmission rear mounting bracket to the transmission housing.

18 Slacken and remove the through-bolt and nut from the right-hand engine/transmission mounting then undo the nuts and remove the mounting from the top of the transmission unit.

19 Loosen the engine/transmission mounting through-bolt, but do not remove it.

20 With the jack positioned beneath the transmission taking the weight, slacken and remove the remaining bolts securing the transmission housing to the engine. Note the correct fitted positions of each bolt, and the necessary brackets, as they are removed, to use as a reference on refitting. Make a final check that all components have been disconnected, and are positioned clear of the transmission so that they will not hinder the removal procedure.

21 With the bolts removed, move the trolley jack and transmission to the right, to free it from its locating dowels. Once the transmission is free, lower the jack and manoeuvre the unit out from under the car. Remove the locating dowels from the transmission or engine if they are loose, and keep them in a safe place.

Refitting

22 The transmission is refitted by a reversal of the removal procedure, bearing in mind the following points.
a) Ensure the engine/transmission locating dowels are correctly positioned prior to installation.
b) Once the transmission and engine are correctly joined, refit the securing bolts.
c) Tighten all nuts and bolts to the specified torque (where given).
d) Refit the torque converter-to-driveplate bolts and tighten them lightly only to start

then go around and tighten them to the specified torque setting in a diagonal sequence.
e) Renew the driveshaft oil seals (see Chapter 7A) and refit the driveshafts to the transmission as described in Chapter 8.
f) Adjust the selector cable and kickdown cables as described in Sections 2 and 5.
g) On completion, refill the transmission with the specified type and quantity of fluid as described in Chapter 1.
h) On early models where the speedometer drive is connected into the power steering system, on completion bleed the hydraulic system as described in Chapter 10.

12 Automatic transmission overhaul - general information

1 In the event of a fault occurring with the transmission, it is first necessary to determine whether it is of a mechanical or hydraulic nature, and to do this, special test equipment is required. It is therefore essential to have the work carried out by a Rover dealer if a transmission fault is suspected.

2 Do not remove the transmission from the car for possible repair before professional fault diagnosis has been carried out, since most tests require the transmission to be in the vehicle.

Chapter 8
Driveshafts

Contents

Degrees of difficulty

Easy, suitable for novice with little experience	Fairly easy, suitable for beginner with some experience	Fairly difficult, suitable for competent DIY mechanic 	Difficult, suitable for experienced DIY mechanic	Very difficult, suitable for expert DIY or professional

Specifications

General

Lubrication (overhaul or repair only) . . . . Use only special grease supplied in sachets with gaiter/overhaul kits

Torque wrench settings

	Nm	lbf ft
Suspension lower arm-to-hub carrier nut (castellated with split pin) . . .	55	41
Driveshaft flange nut (staked)	250	185
Intermediate shaft bracket-to-engine		
Flange bolts	35	26
Dowel bolts	35	26

1 General information

Caution: If the radio/cassette in your vehicle is equipped with an anti-theft system, make sure you have the correct activation code before disconnecting the battery.

1 Power is transmitted from the gearbox to the road wheels by the driveshafts, via plunge-type, inboard constant velocity (CV) joints and Rzeppa-type, outboard CV joints.

2 An intermediate driveshaft, with its own support bearing is fitted between the gearbox and left-hand driveshaft. This layout equalises driveshaft angles at all suspension positions and reduces driveshaft flexing, improving directional stability under acceleration.

3 The outboard CV joints allow smooth transmission of drive to the wheels at all steering and suspension angles. Drive is transmitted by means of a number of radially static steel balls that run in grooves between the two halves of the joint. The joints are protected by rubber gaiters and are packed with grease, to provide permanent lubrication. In the event of wear being detected, the joint can be removed from the driveshaft and renewed. Normally, the CV joints do not require additional lubrication, unless they have been overhauled or the rubber gaiters have been damaged, allowing the grease to become contaminated. Refer to Chapter 1 for guidance in checking the condition of the driveshaft gaiters.

4 The inboard CV joints are of the plunge-cup type; drive is transmitted across the joint by means of three roller bearings, mounted on the driveshaft in a tripod arrangement, that are radially static but are free to slide in the grooves. This arrangement permits lateral movement of the driveshaft, which in turn allows the effective length of the driveshaft to alter with suspension travel, without the need for spline joints. As with the CV joints, the universal joints are lubricated by grease, packed into the gaiters, which only requires replenishment in the event of joint overhaul or rubber gaiter damage.

5 To check for driveshaft wear, road test the vehicle, driving it slowly in a circle first on full steering lock to one side, then to the other and listen for a metallic clicking sound coming from the area behind the front wheels. If such a sound is heard, this indicates wear in the outer constant velocity joint. If vibration proportional to road speed is felt through the car when accelerating or on over-run, or when drive is taken up from a standstill, there is a possibility of wear in the inner CV joints.

6 To check the joints for wear, remove the driveshafts as described in Section 2, then dismantle them as described in Section 3. Refer to a Rover dealer for information on the availability of driveshaft components.

2.3 Use a mallet and punch to relieve the staking, before slackening the driveshaft nut

2.7 Grasp the driveshaft with one hand pull the splined section of the driveshaft out of the hub

2 Driveshafts - removal and refitting

Removal

1 Park the vehicle on a level surface, apply the handbrake and chock the rear wheels. Disconnect the battery negative cable and position it away from the terminal.

2 At the applicable roadwheel, remove the wheel trim, or wheel centre cap on vehicles fitted with alloy wheels.

3 Use a mallet and punch to relieve the staking (see illustration), then slacken the driveshaft nut by one turn. Bear in mind the torque to which this nut is tightened when selecting a wrench and socket to remove it. If the roadwheel slips as you try to slacken the nut, have an assitant apply the footbrake to brace the wheel.

4 Slacken the road wheel bolts by half a turn, then raise the front of the vehicle, rest it securely on axle stands and remove the roadwheel.

5 Referring to Chapter 10 for guidance, unbolt the suspension lower arm from the base of the hub carrier.

6 Remove the driveshaft nut. Note that a **new** nut must be used on reassembly. Turn the steering to full lock, to give greater clearance.

7 Grasp the driveshaft with one hand pull the splined section of the driveshaft out of the hub **(see illustration)**. The driveshaft may be difficult to extract - if this is the case, refit the old nut to protect the driveshaft threads, then tap the end of the driveshaft with a soft-faced mallet, to loosen it from the hub. Alternatively, a suitable three-legged puller may be used.

8 To remove the left-hand driveshaft, use a stout flat-bladed screwdriver or a prybar to prise the plunge-cup section of the inboard CV joint away from the end of the intermediate shaft. Use just enough force to overcome the circlip, located at the end of the intermediate shaft **(see illustration)**.

9 To remove the right-hand driveshaft, insert a stout flat-bladed screwdriver or a prybar between the transmission housing and inboard CV joint, then prise the plunge-cup section of the joint of the out of the differential **(see illustration)**. Use just enough force to overcome the circlip, located at the inboard end of the CV joint. Take great care to avoid levering against the transmission oil seal, as this may damage it.

10 Withdraw the driveshaft out through the wheelarch.

11 Loosely refit the suspension lower arm to the base of the hub carrier, to preven the bushes from being strained.

Refitting

12 Before refitting, renew the cirlip at the inboard end of the driveshaft, or intermediate shaft, as applicable **(see illustration)**. Ensure that the splines at the outboard end of the driveshaft are clean, then apply a smear of anti-seize grease to the splines.

2.8 To remove the left-hand driveshaft, prise the inboard CV joint away from the end of the intermediate shaft

2.9 To remove the right-hand driveshaft, prise the inboard CV joint out of the differential casing

2.12 Before refitting the driveshaft, renew the cirlip (arrowed) at the inboard end

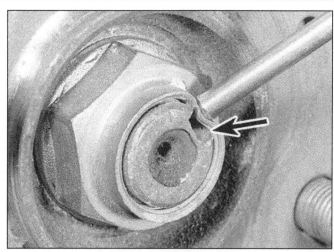

2.18 Stake the driveshaft nut flange into the groove in the end of the driveshaft, using a punch

13 After separating the suspension lower arm from the hub carrier again, pivot the hub carrier away from the vehicle and push the splined end of the driveshaft into the hub.

14 Fit and partially tighten the new driveshaft nut; do not tighten it to the final torque at this stage.

15 Support the driveshaft with one hand and push the steering swivel member back towards the vehicle, re-engaging the inboard joint with the end of the intermediate shaft/differential, as applicable. Tap on the end of the driveshaft with a soft-faced mallet, until the circlip at the inboard end of the driveshaft snaps into position. Pull on the driveshaft, to ensure that it is held securely.

16 Refer to Chapter 10 and refit the suspension lower arm to the base of the hub carrier.

17 Refit the roadwheel and nuts, then lower the vehicle to the ground.

18 Tighten the driveshaft nut to the specified torque, then stake the nut flange into the groove in the end of the driveshaft **(see illustration)**.

19 Tighten the wheel nuts to the specified torque. Refit the wheel trim/centre cap, as applicable.

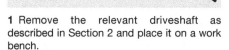

3 Driveshaft - overhaul

1 Remove the relevant driveshaft as described in Section 2 and place it on a work bench.

2 At both CV joints, release the clips from the rubber gaiters by folding back the locking tabs. If the clips are of the welded type, snip through them using a stout pair of cutters, or cut them off with a hacksaw **(see illustration)**. Note that the clips cannot be refitted once they have been removed; new items must be used.

3 Fold the rubber gaiter away from the inboard joint. Be prepared for the loss of some lubricant as you do this - the viscosity of driveshaft joint grease reduces after it has been in use for some time. Position a small container and/or some rags underneath the joint to catch any spillage.

4 Mark the relationship between the driveshaft and the plunge cup **(see illustration)**, then separate the inboard CV joint by withdrawing the driveshaft. **Note:** The

tripod part of the joint will remain on the driveshaft, but note that the three roller bearings are not held on the tripod by circlips and will fall off as the driveshaft is withdrawn, if they are not held in position. It is important that the roller bearings are marked as they are removed from the tripod, to preserve their order, if the joint is to be re-used. Bear this in mind when carrying out the steps in the following paragraph.

5 Remove the three roller bearings from the legs of the tripod joint one by one, making a careful note of their fitted positions, to ensure that they are fitted to the same leg on reassembly.

6 Using a hammer and centre punch, or a dab of paint, to mark the relationship between the shaft and tripod joint. Remove the outer circlip with a pair of circlip pliers, then using a three-legged puller, draw the tripod joint off the end of the driveshaft. Ensure that the legs of the puller bear upon the cast centre section of the joint, not the legs **(see illustration)**. Remove and discard the inner circlip.

7 Fold the rubber gaiter away from the outboard joint. Again, be prepared for the loss of some lubricant as you do this

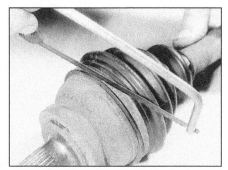

3.2 If the clips are of the welded type, or are badly corroded, cut them off with a hacksaw (outboard joint shown)

3.4 Mark the relationship between the driveshaft and the plunge cup, then withdraw the driveshaft

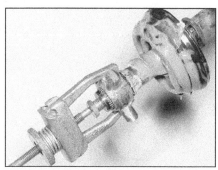

3.6 After removing the outer circlip, draw the tripod joint off the end of the driveshaft using a puller if necessary

3.10 Using a soft metal punch and a mallet, drive the outboard joint from the end of the driveshaft

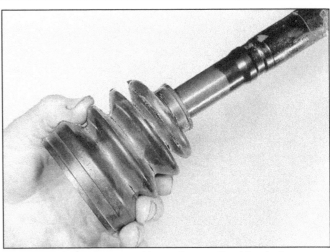

3.16 Fit the new rubber gaiters to the driveshaft

8 At the outboard CV joint, use a scribe or a dab of paint to mark the relationship between the joint and the driveshaft.

9 Mount the driveshaft vertically in a jaws of a vice, with the outboard CV joint facing down. Protect the surface of the driveshaft from the vice jaws with strips of wood or aluminium.

10 Using a soft metal punch and a mallet, drive the outboard joint from the end of the driveshaft **(see illustration)**. If it proves difficult to remove, rotate the shaft through half a turn and strike the joint on the opposite side.

11 With the joint removed, extract the circlip from the end of the driveshaft and discard it - a new item must be used on reassembly.

12 Remove the remainder of the clips that secure the rubber gaiters to the driveshaft. If the clips are difficult to remove due to corrosion, cut them off carefully with a hacksaw or side cutters.

13 Slide both rubber gaiters off the driveshaft and discard them; it is recommended that new ones are fitted on reassembly as a matter

of course. Thoroughly clean the driveshaft splines, CV joint and tripod joint components with paraffin or a suitable solvent, taking care not to obliterate the alignment marks made during removal.

14 Examine the outboard CV joint components for wear and damage; in particular, check the balls and corresponding grooves for pitting and corrosion. If evidence of wear is visible, then the joint must be renewed.

15 Examine the tripod joint components for wear. Check that the three rollers are free to rotate without resistance or roughness and are not worn, damaged or corroded. If any such deterioration is discovered, the tripod joint must be renewed.

16 Commence reassembly as follows. Wrap PVC insulating tape around the splined ends of the driveshaft, to protect the inner surfaces of the new rubber gaiters. Fit the new rubber gaiters to the driveshaft, but do not secure them in position yet **(see illustration)**

17 Pack the outboard CV joint with grease

from the service kit, pushing it into the ball grooves and expelling any air that may be trapped underneath.

18 Fit a new circlip to the outboard end of the driveshaft. Ensure the inner stopper ring is properly seated in its groove **(see illustration)**.

19 Lubricate the splines of the driveshaft with a smear of grease, then insert the end of the shaft into CV joint, observing the alignment marks made during removal. Ensure that the circlip snaps into the groove inside the joint; pull on the shaft to check that it is held securely in position.

20 Slide the inboard gaiter up to the newly-fitted joint, then secure it to the driveshaft with a new clip. Pack the gaiter with grease from the service kit.

21 Fit the gaiter in position over the joint, briefly lifting the lip to expel any trapped air, and secure it with a new clip. To do this, engage the inner tab with its corresponding slot, then fold back the tail and secure it by bending the locking tabs over it (refer to the illustrations in paragraph 27 for guidance).

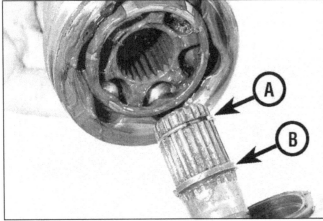

3.18 Fit a new circlip to the outboard end of the driveshaft and ensure the inner stopper ring is properly seated in its groove

A Circlip　　　　　　　　*B Stopper ring*

3.22 Fit a new inner circlip into the groove (arrowed) at the inboard end of the driveshaft

3.23a Using the alignment marks made during removal, drive the tripod joint onto the splines of the driveshaft . . .

22 Fit a new inner circlip into the groove at the inboard end of the driveshaft **(see illustration)**.
23 Using the alignment marks made during removal, fit the tripod joint onto the splines of the driveshaft. Tap it into position using a soft-faced mallet, and an old socket as a drift. Refit the circlip **(see illustrations)**.

24 Fit the roller bearings to the legs of the tripod joint, with the square flanges facing inwards. Observe the alignment marks made during dismantling **(see illustration)**. Lubricate them with grease from the service kit.
25 Slide the rubber gaiter over the tripod joint and secure it to the driveshaft with a new clip. Pack the gaiter with grease from the service kit **(see illustration)**. Pack additional grease into the plunge cup section of the joint.
Caution: Do not allow grease to come into contact with vehicles paintwork, as discolouring may result.
26 Fit the tripod joint and driveshaft into the plunge cup section of the inboard joint, observing the alignment markings made during dismantling.
27 Slide the rubber gaiter over the joint. Briefly lift the lip of the gaiter to expel all the air from the joint, then secure it in place with a clip **(see illustrations)**.
28 Refit the driveshaft as desrcribed in Section 2.

4 Intermediate driveshaft and support bearing assembly - removal and refitting

Removal

1 Disconnect the battery negative cable and position it away from the terminal.
2 With the vehicle parked on a level surface, apply the handbrake and chock the rear wheels. Slacken the left-hand road wheel bolts, then raise the front of the vehicle, rest it securely on axle stands and remove the road wheel; refer to *Jacking, Towing and Wheel Changing* at the end of this manual for guidance.
3 Referring to Chapter 10 for guidance, unbolt the suspension lower arm from the base of the hub carrier.
4 With reference to Section 2, lever between the inboard CV joint and the end of the

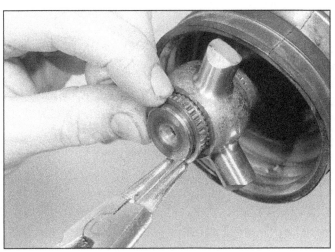

3.23b . . . and refit the circlip

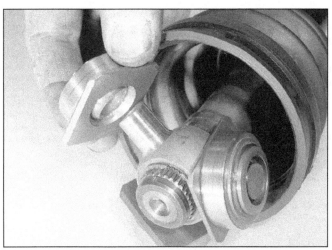

3.24 Fit the roller bearings to the tripod joint, with the square flanges facing inwards. Observe the alignment marks made during dismantling, to preserve their order

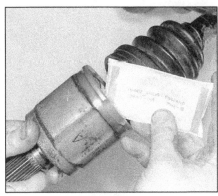

3.25 Pack the plunge cup section of the inboard joint with grease from the service kit

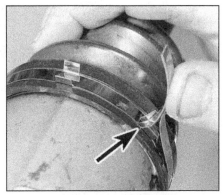

3.27a To fit a new driveshaft gaiter clip, engage the inner tab with its corresponding slot (arrowed) . . .

3.27b . . . then fold back the tail and secure it in position, by bending the locking tabs over it

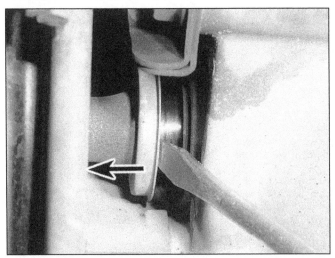

4.4 Prise the intermediate shaft out of the differential casing. Take great care to avoid levering against the oil seal

4.7 Slacken and remove the bolts (arrowed), then free the intermediate shaft bearing bracket from the engine block

intermediate shaft. Use just enough force to overcome the tension of the securing circlip at the end of the intemediate shaft (see illustration).

5 Pivot the hub carrier away from the vehicle and separate the driveshaft from the end of the intermediate shaft. Note that the outboard end of the driveshaft need not be unbolted from the hub.

6 Use a length of wire or cable ties to support the inboard end of the driveshaft - this will keep it away from the working area and prevent the outboard CV joint from being strained.

7 Slacken and remove the bolts, then free the intermediate shaft bearing bracket from the engine block. Note that two are dowel bolts -

make a note of their fitted positions to avoid confusion during refitting (see illustration).

8 Support the free end of intermediate shaft to prevent damage to the oil seal at the transmission.

9 At the tranmission housing, Withdraw the shaft squarely, to avoid damaging the oil seal.

Refitting

10 Apply a light smear of molybdenum-based grease to the splines at both ends of the intermediate shaft (see illustration).

11 Offer the intermediate shaft and bearing assembly up to the transmission and cylinder block.

12 Insert the inboard end of the shaft squarely into the transmission (see illustration). Tap on the end of the shaft with

a soft-faced mallet, until the circlip at the inboard end snaps into position in the differential.

13 Align the bearing bracket with its mounting holes on the the engine block. Insert the securing bolts, noting that two of them are dowel bolts with different diameter shanks. Tighten the bolts to the specified torque.

14 Refit the left hand driveshaft to the end of the intermediate shaft, as described in Section 2.

15 Referring to Chapter 10 for guidance, refit the suspension lower arm to the base of the hub carrier.

16 Refit the roadwheel and lower the vehicle to the ground. On completion tighten the roadwheel bolts to the specified torque.

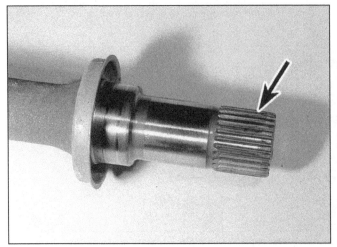

4.10 Apply a smear of molybdenum-based grease to the splines at the ends of the intermediate shaft

4.12 Insert the inboard end of the shaft squarely into the differential casing

Chapter 9
Braking system

Contents

Degrees of difficulty

Easy, suitable for novice with little experience	**Fairly easy,** suitable for beginner with some experience	**Fairly difficult,** suitable for competent DIY mechanic	**Difficult,** suitable for experienced DIY mechanic	**Very difficult,** suitable for expert DIY or professional

Specifications

General

System type . . . . Dual hydraulic circuit, split diagonally. Disc brakes front and rear. Anti-lock braking (ALB) system fited to certain models. Vacuum servo assistance on all models; cable-operated handbrake on rear brakes

Front brakes

Type . . . . Vented disc, with single-piston sliding caliper
Disc thickness:
  New . . . . 23.0 mm
  Minimum thickness after machining . . . . 21.0 mm
  Maximum disc run-out . . . . 0.1 mm
Brake pad friction material minimum thickness . . . . 1.6 mm

Rear brakes

Type . . . . Solid disc, with single-piston sliding caliper
Disc thickness:
  New . . . . 10.0 mm
  Minimum thickness after machining . . . . 8.0 mm
  Maximum disc run-out . . . . 0.1 mm
Brake pad friction material minimum thickness . . . . 1.6 mm

Torque wrench settings	Nm	lbf ft
Bleed screws	10	7
Brake hose union bolt	35	26
Brake pipe union nuts	20	15
Brake servo-to-bulkhead nuts	13	10
Front brake caliper bracket-to-hub bolts	110	81
Front brake caliper guide pin bolt	50	37
Front brake disc-to-hub bolts	55	41
Front hub-to-hub carrier bolts	45	33
Master cylinder-to-servo unit nuts	15	11
Rear brake caliper bracket-to-suspension bolts	39	29
Rear brake caliper guide pin bolt	27	20
Roadwheel nuts	100	74

1 General information

1 The braking system is of the vacuum servo-assisted, dual-circuit hydraulic type. The arrangement of the hydraulic system is such that each circuit operates one front and one rear brake from a tandem master cylinder. Under normal circumstances, both circuits operate in unison; however, in the event of hydraulic failure in one circuit, full braking force will still be available at two wheels. On models not equipped with anti-lock brakes (ALB), a pressure-regulating valve is also incorporated in the hydraulic circuit, to regulate the pressure applied to the rear brakes, and thus reduce the possibility of the rear wheels locking under heavy braking. Section 16 describes the ALB system in greater detail.

2 All models are fitted with front and rear disc brakes. The disc brakes are actuated by single-piston sliding type calipers, which ensures that equal pressure is applied to each disc pad. The rear brake caliper incorporates a mechanical handbrake mechanism.

Note: *When servicing any part of the system, work carefully and methodically; also observe scrupulous cleanliness when overhauling any part of the hydraulic system. Always renew components (in axle sets, where applicable) if in doubt about their condition, and use only genuine Rover replacement parts, or at least those of known good quality. Note the warnings given in Safety first! and at the relevant points in this Chapter, concerning the dangers of asbestos dust and hydraulic fluid.*

2 Brake pedal – removal and refitting

Removal

1 Working from inside the car, undo the five screws, and remove the right-hand lower facia panel.

2 At the point where the servo unit pushrod is secured to the brake pedal, extract the split pin then withdraw the clevis pin.

3 Using pliers, carefully unhook the brake pedal return spring from the pedal, to release all the spring tension.

4 Slacken and remove the nut and washers (as applicable) from the end brake pedal pivot bolt, then withdraw the pivot bolt.

5 Remove the brake pedal, together with the return spring, and pivot bolt bushes.

6 Examine all brake pedal components for signs of wear, paying particular attention to the pedal bushes, the pivot bolt and the return spring; renew worn components as necessary.

Refitting

7 Refitting is a reverse of the removal, but lubricate the bushes, pivot bolt and clevis pin with a multi-purpose grease. On completion, check the operation of the pedal, and ensure it returns smoothly to the at-rest position under the pressure of the return spring.

3 Vacuum servo unit – testing, removal and refitting

Testing

1 To test the operation of the servo unit, depress the footbrake several times to exhaust the vacuum, then start the engine, keeping the pedal firmly depressed. As the engine starts, there should be a noticeable give in the brake pedal as the vacuum builds up. Allow the engine to run for at least two minutes, then switch it off. If the brake pedal is now depressed it should feel normal, but further applications should result in the pedal feeling firmer, with the pedal stroke decreasing with each application.

2 If the servo does not operate as described, inspect the servo unit check valve, as described in Section 4.

3 If the servo unit still fails to operate satisfactorily, the fault lies within the unit itself. Repairs to the unit are possible, but special tools are required, and the work should be entrusted to a suitably-equipped Rover dealer.

Removal

4 Remove the brake master cylinder, as described in Section 7.

5 On right hand-drive vehicles, remove the engine bay fusebox from the bodywork.

6 On vehicles with manual transmission, refer to Chapter 6 and remove the clutch fluid reservoir together with its support bracket.

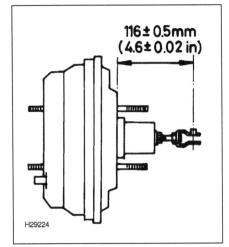

116 ± 0.5mm
(4.6 ± 0.02 in)

H29224

3.13 Before refitting the servo, check and if neccessary adjust the length of the input pushrod as shown

7 Using a suitable pair of pliers, release the retaining clip, and disconnect the vacuum hose from the servo unit.

8 Where applicable on right-hand drive vehicles, refer to Chapter 4A and remove the accelerator cable grommet from the bulkhead.

9 With reference to Chapter 11, remove the retaining screws, and remove the driver's side lower facia panel.

10 Refer to Section 2 and detach the vacuum unit pushrod from the brake pedal. Loosen the locknut and unscrew the clevis from the end of the pushrod.

11 Remove the four servo unit mounting nuts.

12 Working in the engine compartment, lift the servo from its mountings then manoeuvre it out of position, noting the gasket which is fitted to its rear surface.

Refitting

13 Before refitting the servo, check and if neccessary adjust the length of the input pushrod as shown **(see illustration)**.

14 Fit a new gasket to the rear of the servo unit, and reposition the unit in the engine compartment.

15 From inside the car, ensure the servo unit pushrod is correctly engaged with the brake pedal, then refit the servo unit mounting nuts, and tighten them to the specified torque.

16 Refit the servo unit pushrod-to-brake pedal clevis pin, and secure it in position with a new split pin.

17 Refit the right-hand lower facia panel, tightening its retaining screws securely.

18 From inside the engine compartment, connect the vacuum hose to the servo unit, and secure it in position with its retaining clip. Refit the fuel filter mounting bolts, and tighten them securely.

19 Refit the brake master cylinder, clutch fluid reservoir and engine bay fusebox. Press the accelerator cable grommet back into position.

20 On completion, start the engine and thoroughly check the operation of the braking system, before bringing the vehicle back into service on the public highway.

4 Vacuum servo unit check valve – removal, testing and refitting

Removal

1 Using a suitable pair of pliers, release the retaining clips, then disconnect the check valve from the vacuum hoses **(see illustration)**.

Testing

2 Examine the vacuum pipe and hoses for damage, splits, cracks or general deterioration, and renew as necessary. Make sure that the check valve is working correctly

4.1 Brake servo vacuum check valve (arrowed)

by blowing through the hose from the servo unit end. Air should flow in this direction, but not when blown through from the inlet manifold hose end. Renew the check valve if its operation is not satisfactory.

Refitting

3 Refitting is a reversal of the removal procedure, noting the following points.
  a) *Observe the orientation arrow when refitting the valve to vacuum hoses (see illustration).*
  b) *Ensure that all vacuum hoses are securely held in position by their retaining clips.*
  c) *On completion, start the engine and check the operation of the servo unit as described in Section 3.*

5 Hydraulic system – bleeding

Note: *Hydraulic fluid is poisonous; wash off immediately and thoroughly in the case of skin contact, and seek immediate medical advice if any fluid is swallowed or gets into the eyes. Certain types of hydraulic fluid are inflammable, and may ignite when allowed into contact with hot components; when servicing any hydraulic system it is safest to assume that the fluid is inflammable, and to take the same precautions against the risk of fire as you would with petrol. Finally, it is hygroscopic (it absorbs moisture from the air) – old fluid stored for several months may be*

4.3 Observe the orientation arrow (arrowed) when refitting the valve to vacuum hoses

contaminated and unfit for further use. When topping-up or renewing the fluid, always use the recommended type, and ensure that it comes from a freshly-opened sealed container.

 Warning: Hydraulic fluid is an effective paint stripper, and will attack plastics; if any is spilt, it should be washed off immediately, using copious quantities of fresh water.

General

1 The correct operation of any hydraulic system is only possible after removing all air from the components and circuit; this is achieved by bleeding the system.
2 During the bleeding procedure, add only clean, unused hydraulic fluid of the recommended type; never re-use fluid that has already been bled from the system. Ensure that sufficient fluid is available before starting work.
3 If there is any possibility of incorrect fluid being in the system already, the brake components and circuit must be flushed completely with uncontaminated, correct fluid, and new seals should be fitted to the various components.
4 If hydraulic fluid has been lost from the system, or air has entered because of a leak, ensure that the fault is cured before proceeding further.
5 Park the car on level ground, switch off the engine and select first or reverse gear, then chock the wheels and release the handbrake.
6 Check that all pipes and hoses are secure, that fluid unions are tight and bleed screws closed. Clean any dirt from around the bleed screws.
7 Unscrew the master cylinder reservoir cap and top the master cylinder reservoir up to the MAX level line; refit the cap loosely. Remember to maintain the fluid level at least above the MIN level line throughout the following procedure, or there is a risk of further air entering the system.
8 There are a number of one-man, do-it-yourself brake bleeding kits currently available from motor accessory shops. It is recommended that one of these kits is used whenever possible, as they greatly simplify the bleeding operation, and also reduce the risk of expelled air and fluid being drawn back into the system. If such a kit is not available, the basic (two-man) method must be used, which is described in detail below.
9 If a one-man kit is to be used, prepare the car as described previously, and follow the kit manufacturer's instructions in the first instance (the procedure may vary slightly according to the type being used; generally, they are as outlined below in the relevant sub-section).
10 Whichever method is used, the same sequence must be followed (paragraphs 11 and 12) to ensure the removal of all air from the system.

Bleeding sequence

11 If the system has been only partially disconnected, and suitable precautions were taken to minimise fluid loss, it should be necessary only to bleed that part of the system (ie the primary or secondary circuit).
12 If the complete system is to be bled, then it should be done working in the following sequence.
  a) *Right-hand rear brake.*
  b) *Left-hand front brake.*
  c) *Left-hand rear brake.*
  d) *Right-hand front brake.*

Bleeding – basic (two-man) method

13 Collect a clean glass jar, a suitable length of plastic or rubber tubing which is a tight fit over the bleed screw, and a ring spanner to fit the screw. The help of an assistant will also be required.
14 Remove the dust cap from the first screw in the sequence. Fit the spanner and tube to the screw, place the other end of the tube in the jar and pour sufficient fluid into the jar to cover the open end of the tube.
15 Ensure that the master cylinder reservoir fluid level is maintained at least above the MIN level line throughout the procedure.
16 Have the assistant fully depress the brake pedal several times to build up pressure, then hold the pedal depressed on the final stroke.
17 While pedal pressure is maintained, unscrew the bleed screw (approximately one turn) and allow the compressed fluid and air to flow into the jar. The assistant should maintain pedal pressure, following it down to the floor if necessary, and should not release the pedal until instructed to do so. When the flow stops, tighten the bleed screw again, **then** the pedal should be released slowly, recheck the reservoir fluid level, and top-up if necessary.
18 Repeat the steps given in paragraphs 16 and 17 until the fluid emerging from the bleed screw is free from air bubbles. If the master cylinder has been drained and refilled, and air is being bled from the first screw in the sequence, allow approximately five seconds between cycles for the master cylinder passages to refill.
19 When no more air bubbles appear, tighten the bleed screw securely, remove the tube and spanner, and refit the dust cap. Do not overtighten the bleed screw.
20 Repeat the procedure on the remaining screws in the sequence, until all air is removed from the system and the brake pedal feels firm again.

Bleeding – using a one-way valve kit

21 As their name implies, these kits consist of a length of tubing with a one-way valve fitted, to prevent expelled air and fluid being drawn back into the system; some kits include a translucent container, which can be positioned so that the air bubbles can be more easily seen flowing from the end of the tube.

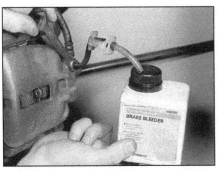

5.22 Brake bleeding kit and ring spanner connected to the caliper bleed screw

22 The kit is connected to the bleed screw, which is then opened **(see illustration)**. The user returns to the driver's seat, and depresses the brake pedal with a smooth, steady stroke and slowly releases it; this is repeated until the expelled fluid is clear of air bubbles.

23 Note that these kits simplify work so much that it is easy to forget to top-up the master cylinder reservoir fluid level; ensure that this is maintained at least above the MIN level line at all times.

Bleeding – using a pressure-bleeding kit

24 These kits are usually operated by the reservoir of pressurised air contained in the spare tyre – although note that it will probably be necessary to reduce the pressure to lower than normal; refer to the instructions supplied with the kit.

25 By connecting a pressurised, fluid-filled container to the master cylinder reservoir, bleeding can be carried out simply by opening each screw in turn (in the specified sequence) and allowing the fluid to flow out, until no more air bubbles can be seen in the expelled fluid.

26 This method has the advantage that the large reservoir of fluid provides an additional safeguard against air being drawn into the system during bleeding.

27 Pressure-bleeding is particularly effective when bleeding difficult systems, or when bleeding the complete system at the time of routine fluid renewal.

6.1 Seal the brake hose with a proprietary hose clamp before disconnection

All methods

28 When bleeding is complete and firm pedal feel is restored, wash off any spilt fluid, tighten the bleed screws securely and refit their dust caps.

29 Check the hydraulic fluid level, and top-up if necessary (refer to Chapter 1).

30 Discard any hydraulic fluid that has been bled from the system; it will definitely not be fit for re-use.

31 Check the feel of the brake pedal. If it feels at all spongy, air must still be present in the system, and further bleeding is required. Failure to bleed satisfactorily after a reasonable repetition of the bleeding procedure may be due to worn master cylinder seals.

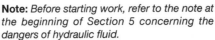

6 Hydraulic pipes and hoses – renewal

Note: *Before starting work, refer to the note at the beginning of Section 5 concerning the dangers of hydraulic fluid.*

1 If any pipe or hose in the main braking system is to be renewed, minimise fluid loss by first removing the master cylinder reservoir cap, and then tightening it down onto a piece of polythene (taking care not to damage the sender unit) to obtain an airtight seal. Alternatively, the flexible hoses can be sealed, if required, using a proprietary brake hose clamp **(see illustration)**. Metal brake pipe unions can be plugged (care must be taken not to allow dirt into the system) or capped, immediately they are disconnected. Place a wad of rag under any union that is to be disconnected, to catch any spilt fluid.

2 If a flexible hose is to be disconnected, unscrew the brake pipe union nut before removing the spring clip which secures the hose to its mounting bracket.

3 To unscrew the union nuts, it is preferable to obtain a brake pipe spanner of the correct size; these are available from most large motor accessory shops. Failing this, a close-fitting open-ended spanner will be required – though if the nuts are tight or corroded, their flats may be rounded-off if the spanner slips. In such a case, a self-locking wrench is often the only way to unscrew a stubborn union, but it follows that the pipe and the damaged nuts must be renewed on reassembly. Always clean a union and the surrounding area before disconnecting it. If disconnecting a component with more than one union, make a careful note of the connections before disturbing any of them.

4 If a brake pipe is to be renewed, it can be obtained, cut to length and with the union nuts and end flares in place, from Rover dealers. All that is then necessary is to bend it to shape, following the line of the original, before fitting it to the car. Alternatively, most motor accessory shops can make up brake

pipes from kits, but this requires very careful measurement of the original to ensure that the replacement is of the correct length. The safest answer is usually to take the original to the shop as a pattern.

5 On refitting, do not overtighten the union nuts. The specified torque wrench settings (where given) are not high, and it is not necessary to exercise brute force to obtain a sound joint. When refitting flexible hoses, always renew any sealing washers used; again, note the torque settings specified.

6 Ensure that the pipes and hoses are correctly routed, with no kinks, and that they are secured in the clips or brackets provided. After fitting, remove the polythene from the reservoir, and bleed the hydraulic system as described in Section 5. Wash off any spilt fluid, and check carefully for fluid leaks.

7 Master cylinder – removal and refitting

Note: *Before starting work, refer to the note at the beginning of Section 5 concerning the dangers of hydraulic fluid.*

Removal

1 Remove the master cylinder reservoir cap, having disconnected the sender unit wiring connector(s). Remove the reservoir filter (where fitted), and syphon the hydraulic fluid from the reservoir. **Note:** *Do not syphon the fluid by mouth, as it is poisonous; use a syringe or an old poultry baster.* Alternatively, open any convenient bleed screw in the system, and gently pump the brake pedal to expel the fluid through a plastic tube connected to the screw (see Section 5, and use a one-man bleed tube or bottle if possible).

2 Wipe clean the area around the brake pipe unions on the side of the master cylinder, and place absorbent rags beneath the pipe unions to catch any surplus fluid. Unscrew the union nuts, and carefully withdraw the pipes. Plug or tape over the pipe ends and master cylinder orifices, to minimise the loss of brake fluid and to prevent the entry of dirt into the system. Wash off any spilt fluid immediately with cold water.

3 Slacken and remove the nuts and washers securing the master cylinder to the vacuum servo unit, then withdraw the unit from the engine compartment. Remove the O-ring from the rear of master cylinder, and discard it.

Refitting

Note: *If the master cylinder has been overhauled or renewed, the clearance between the secondary piston and the servo unit pushrod must be adjusted. This operation can only be completed using specially shaped service tools and with a specified vacuum depression applied to the servo unit. For this reason, it is recommended that the adjustment be carried out by a Rover dealer.*

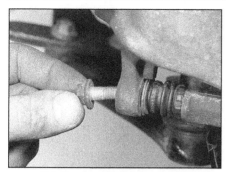

8.2 Remove the lower caliper guide pin bolt . . .

8.3 . . . and pivot the caliper up away from the disc to gain access to the brake pads

8.4a Remove the outboard pad and shim . . .

4 Remove all traces of dirt from the master cylinder and servo unit mating surfaces, and fit a new O-ring to the groove on the master cylinder body.
5 Fit the master cylinder to the servo unit, ensuring that the servo unit pushrod enters the master cylinder bore centrally. Refit the master cylinder washers and mounting nuts, and tighten them to the specified torque.
6 Wipe clean the brake pipe unions, then refit them to the master cylinder ports and tighten them to the specified torque setting.
7 Refill the master cylinder reservoir with new fluid, and bleed the hydraulic system as described in Section 5.

8 Front brake pads – renewal

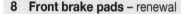

⚠️ *Warning: Renew both sets of front brake pads at the same time – never renew the pads on only one wheel, as uneven braking may result. Note that the dust created by wear of the pads may contain asbestos, which is a health hazard. Never blow it out with compressed air, and don't inhale any of it. An approved filtering mask should be worn when working on the brakes. DO NOT use petroleum-based solvents to clean brake parts – use brake cleaner or methylated spirit only.*

1 Chock the rear wheels, firmly apply the handbrake, then jack up the front of the car and support it on axle stands. Remove both front roadwheels.

2 Remove the lower caliper guide pin bolt, if necessary using a slim open-ended spanner to prevent the guide pin itself from rotating **(see illustration)**.
3 Pivot the caliper up away from the disc to gain access to the brake pads, and tie it to the suspension strut using a piece of wire **(see illustration)**.
4 Remove the brake pads from the caliper mounting bracket, noting the correct fitted position of the pad retainer springs and pad shims **(see illustrations)**.
5 First measure the thickness of friction material remaining on each brake pad. If either pad is worn at any point to the specified minimum thickness or less, all four pads must be renewed. The pads should also be renewed if any are fouled with oil or grease; there is no satisfactory way of degreasing friction material once contaminated. If any of the brake pads is worn unevenly, or fouled with oil or grease, trace and rectify the cause before reassembly. New brake pad kits are available from Rover dealers, and include new shims and pad retainer springs.
6 If the brake pads are still serviceable, carefully clean them using a clean, fine wire brush or similar, paying particular attention to the sides and back of the metal backing. Clean out the grooves in the friction material (where applicable), and pick out any large embedded particles of dirt or debris. Carefully clean the pad retainer springs, and the pad locations in the caliper body and mounting bracket.

7 Prior to fitting the pads, check that the guide pins are free to slide easily in the caliper bracket, and check that the rubber guide pin gaiters are undamaged . Brush the dust and dirt from the caliper and piston, but do not inhale it as it is injurious to health. Inspect the dust seal around the piston for damage, and the piston for evidence of fluid leaks, corrosion or damage. If attention to any of these components is necessary, refer to Section 9.
8 On refitting, first fit the pad retainer springs to the caliper mounting bracket.
9 Apply a thin smear of high-temperature brake grease or anti-seize compound to the sides and back of each pads metal backing, and to those surfaces of the caliper body and mounting bracket which bear on the pads.
10 Install the brake pads in the caliper mounting bracket, ensuring that the friction material is against the disc. If fitting original equipment pads, note that the inboard pad has a wear indicator tab, which must face towards the vehicle **(see illustration)**.
11 Fit the shims to the back of both pads, and apply a thin smear of lubricant to the back of each shim. Do not allow the lubricant to foul the friction material. Note that there are two shims fitted to the back of the inboard pad, but only one on the outboard pad.
12 If new brake pads have been fitted, the caliper piston must be pushed back into the cylinder to make room for them. Either use a G-clamp or similar tool, or use suitable pieces of wood as levers. Provided that the master cylinder reservoir has not been overfilled with hydraulic fluid, there should be no spillage,

8.4b . . .and the inboard pad and shims from the carrier bracket

8.4c Remove the pad retainer springs

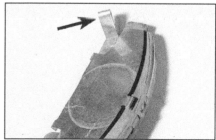

8.10 Fit the shims to the back of the pads - the inboard pad has a wear indicator tab (arrowed) which must face towards the vehicle

8.13 Tighten the lower guide pin bolt to the specified torque

but keep a careful watch on the fluid level while retracting the piston. If the fluid level rises above the MAX level line at any time, the surplus should be syphoned off or ejected via a plastic tube connected to the bleed screw (see Section 7, paragraph 1).

13 Pivot the caliper body down over the brake pads, then refit the bottom guide pin bolt, and tighten it to the specified torque wrench setting **(see illustration)**.

14 Check that the caliper body slides smoothly in the mounting bracket, then depress the brake pedal repeatedly until the pads are pressed into firm contact with the brake disc, and normal (non-assisted) pedal pressure is restored.

15 Repeat the above procedure on the remaining front brake caliper.

16 Refit the roadwheels, then lower the car to the ground, and tighten the roadwheel nuts to the specified torque setting.

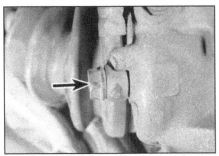

9.3 Undo the brake hose union bolt (arrowed) and disconnect the hose from the caliper

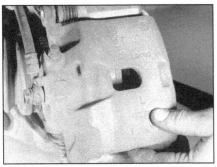

9.5a Carefully lift the caliper assembly off the brake pads

17 Check and if necessary top-up the hydraulic fluid level as described in Chapter 1.

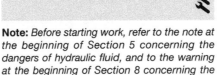

9 Front brake caliper – removal, overhaul and refitting

Note: *Before starting work, refer to the note at the beginning of Section 5 concerning the dangers of hydraulic fluid, and to the warning at the beginning of Section 8 concerning the dangers of asbestos dust.*

Removal

1 Chock the rear wheels, firmly apply the handbrake, then jack up the front of the car and support on axle stands. Remove the appropriate front roadwheel.

2 Minimise fluid loss by first removing the master cylinder reservoir cap, and then tightening it down onto a piece of polythene sheet to obtain an airtight seal (taking care not to damage the sender unit). Alternatively, use a brake hose clamp, a G-clamp or a similar tool to clamp the flexible hose.

3 Clean the area around the union, then undo the brake hose union bolt and disconnect the hose from the caliper **(see illustration)**. Plug the end of the hose and the caliper orifice to prevent dirt entering the hydraulic system. Discard the sealing washers; they must be renewed whenever disturbed.

4 Unscrew the two caliper guide pin bolts, if necessary using a slim open-ended spanner to prevent the guide pins themselves from rotating **(see illustration)**.

9.4 Removing the caliper upper guide pin bolt

9.5b If required, remove the bolts . . .

5 Carefully lift the caliper assembly off the brake pads **(see illustration)**. Note that the brake pads need not be disturbed, and can be left in position in the caliper mounting bracket. Alternatively, the whole carrier bracket may be unbolted from the hub carrier **(see illustrations)**.

Overhaul

6 With the caliper on the bench, wipe away all traces of dust and dirt, but *avoid inhaling the dust, as it is injurious to health*. On models with automatic transmission, remove the pad centre spring from the caliper body.

7 Withdraw the partially-ejected piston from the caliper body, and remove the dust seal. The piston can be withdrawn by hand, or if necessary pushed out by applying compressed air to the union bolt hole. Only low pressure should be required, such as that generated by a bicycle pump or car footpump. Pad the end of the piston with a block of wood, as it will leave the caliper bore with some force. Take care to avoid pinching your fingers when this happens.

8 Using a small wooden or plastic implement (ie not a screwdriver), extract the piston hydraulic seal, taking great care not to damage the caliper bore.

9 Withdraw the guide pins from the caliper mounting bracket, and remove the guide pin gaiters. Label each guide pin, to ensure that they are refitted to the same bores. On models with manual transmission, remove the bushing from the upper guide pin.

10 Thoroughly clean all components using only methylated spirit, isopropyl alcohol or new hydraulic fluid. Never use mineral-based solvents such as petrol or paraffin, which will attack the hydraulic systems rubber components. Dry the components immediately, using compressed air or a clean, lint-free cloth. Use compressed air to blow clear the fluid passages.

11 Check all components, and renew any that are worn or damaged. Check particularly the cylinder bore and piston; these should be renewed if they are scratched, worn or corroded in any way (note that this means the renewal of the complete body assembly). Similarly check the condition of the guide pins and their bores in the mounting bracket; both guide pins should be undamaged and (when

9.5c . . . and unbolt the carrier bracket from the hub carrier

cleaned) should be a reasonably tight sliding fit in the mounting bracket bores. If there is any doubt about the condition of any component, renew it.

12 If the assembly is fit for further use, obtain the appropriate repair kit; the components are available from Rover dealers in various combinations.

13 Renew all rubber seals, dust covers and caps, and also the sealing washers disturbed on dismantling, as a matter of course; these should never be re-used.

14 On reassembly, ensure that all components are absolutely clean and dry.

15 Soak the piston and the new piston fluid seal in clean hydraulic fluid, and smear clean fluid on the cylinder bore surface.

16 Fit the new piston fluid seal, using only your fingers (no tools) to manipulate it into the cylinder bore groove. Fit the new dust seal to the piston, refit it to the cylinder bore using a twisting motion, and ensure that the piston enters squarely into the bore. Press the piston fully into the bore, then secure the dust seal to the caliper body.

17 Apply the grease supplied in the repair kit, or a good quality high-temperature brake grease (silicone- or PBC/Poly Butyl Cuprysil-based) or anti-seize compound to the guide pins, and fit the new gaiters. Fit the guide pins to the caliper mounting bracket, ensuring that the gaiters are correctly located in the grooves on both the guide pin and mounting bracket.

Refitting

18 On models with atomatic transmission, refit the pad centre spring to the caliper body.

19 Carefully slide the caliper into position over the brake pads. Refit the caliper guide pin bolts to their original bores, then tighten them to the specified torque setting. **Note:** *On models with manual transmission, fit the bushing to the upper guide pin.*

20 Position new sealing washers on each side of the hose union, and refit the brake hose union bolt. Ensure that the brake hose union is correctly positioned between the lugs on the caliper, then tighten the union bolt to the specified torque setting.

21 Remove the brake hose clamp, where fitted, and bleed the hydraulic system as described in Section 5. Note that, providing the precautions described were taken to

minimise brake fluid loss, it should only be necessary to bleed the relevant front brake.

22 Refit the roadwheel, then lower the car to the ground and tighten the roadwheel nuts to the specified torque.

10 Front brake disc – inspection, removal and refitting

Note: *Before starting work, refer to the warning at the beginning of Section 8 concerning the dangers of asbestos dust.*

Inspection

Note: *If either disc requires renewal, both should be renewed at the same time, to ensure even and consistent braking.*

1 Chock the rear wheels, firmly apply the handbrake, then jack up the front of the car and support on axle stands. Remove the appropriate front roadwheel.

2 Slowly rotate the brake disc so that the full area of both sides is checked; remove the brake pads, as described in Section 8, if better access is required to the inboard surface. Light scoring is normal in the area swept by the brake pads, but if heavy scoring is found, the disc must be renewed. The only alternative to this is to have the disc surface-ground until it is flat again, but this must not reduce the disc to less than the minimum thickness specified. Note that larger Rover service dealers have the facilities to re-finish discs without removing them from the vehicle.

3 It is normal to find a lip of rust and brake dust around the discs perimeter; this can be scraped off if wished. If, however, a solid lip has formed due to excessive wear of the brake pad swept area, then the discs thickness must be measured using a micrometer . Take measurements at four places around the disc, at the inside and outside of the pad swept area; if the disc has worn at any point to the specified minimum thickness or less, or if any measurement differs from the others by more than the maximum specified variation, the disc must be renewed **(see illustration)**.

4 If the disc is thought to be warped, it can be checked for run-out (6 mm in from the disc's outer edge) either using a dial gauge mounted on any convenient fixed point, while the disc is

10.3 Measuring the thickness of the brake disc using a micrometer

slowly rotated **(see illustration)**. Alternatively, use feeler gauges (at several points all around the disc) to measure the clearance between the disc and a fixed point, such as the caliper mounting bracket. If the measurements obtained are at the specified maximum or beyond, the disc is excessively warped, and must be renewed; however it is worth checking first that the hub bearing is in good condition (see Chapter 10). Also try the effect of removing the disc and turning it through 180° to reposition it on the hub; if run-out is still excessive, the disc must be renewed.

5 Check the disc for cracks (especially around the stud holes), and for any other wear or damage. Renew it if any of these are found.

Removal

6 Unscrew the two bolts securing the caliper mounting bracket to the hub carrier, then lift off the whole caliper assembly. Note that there is no need to separate the hydraulic hose from the caliper.

7 Using a length of wire or a cable tie, secure the caliper to the front suspension coil spring, to keep it away from the work area. Ensure that the hydraulic brake hose is not strained or kinked.

8 With reference to Chapter 8, remove the relevant driveshaft nut and separate the driveshaft from the hub carrier. Note that this will involve unbolting the suspenion lower arm from the base of the hub carrier.

9 Turn the steering to full lock to improve access, then working behind the hub carrier, remove the four bolts and lift the hub and disc assembly from the hub carrier **(see illustrations)**.

10.4 Measuring the brake disc runout using a dial gauge

10.9a Remove the four bolts . . .

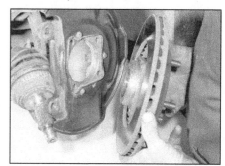

10.9b . . . and lift the hub and disc assembly from the hub carrier

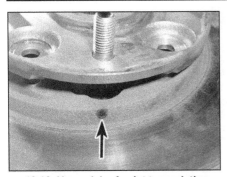

10.10 Use a dab of paint to mark the relationship between the disc and hub

10 Place the assembly on a workbench, then mark the relationship between the brake disc and hub with a small dab of paint **(see illustration)**

11 Brace the disc by holding a stout bar between two of the roadwheel studs, then slacken and remove all four disc securing bolts **(see illustration)**.

12 Rotate the brake disc, so that the star-shaped lugs of the hub line up with the similarly shaped recesses in the brake disc, then lift the disc from the hub **(see illustrations)**.

Refitting

13 If a new disc has been fitted, use a suitable solvent to wipe any preservative coating from the disc before fitting it.

10.11 Slacken and remove the disc securing bolts

14 Ensure that the mating surfaces of the disc and hub are clean and flat.

15 Line up the star-shaped lugs on the hub mating flange with the similar recesses in the brake disc, then fit the disc to the hub.

16 Turn the disc so that the bolt holes line up. Where applicable, check that the markings made during removal are also aligned.

17 Brace the disc by holding a stout bar between two of the roadwheel studs, then insert and tighten all four disc securing bolts to the specified torque **(see illustration)**.

18 Offer up the hub and disc assembly to the hub carrier. Note that the mating surfaces hub and hub carrier are both asymmetrically shaped; this ensures that they can only be fitted together the correct way around **(see illustrations)**.

19 Insert the hub-to-hub carrier securing bolts and tighten them to specified torque **(see illustration)**.

20 Refit the driveshaft to the hub, with reference to Chapter 8, then reconnect the suspension lower arm to the base of the hub carrier with reference to Chapter 10.

21 Refit the brake caliper with reference to Section 9.

22 Refer to the *Inspection* sub-section and check the brake disc run-out.

23 Refit the roadwheel(s) and lower the vehicle to the ground. Check the operation of the braking system exhaustively before bringing the vehicle back into service on the public highway.

11 Rear brake pads – renewal

![warning] Warning: Renew both sets of rear brake pads at the same time – never renew the pads on only one wheel, as uneven braking may result. Note that the dust created by wear of the pads may contain asbestos, which is a health hazard. Never blow it out with compressed air, and don't inhale any of it. An approved filtering mask should be worn when working on the brakes. DO NOT use petroleum-based

10.12a Rotate the brake disc, so that the star-shaped lugs of the hub line up with the recesses in the brake disc . . .

10.18a The mating surfaces hub . . .

10.12b . . . then lift the disc from the hub

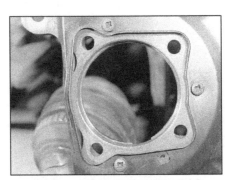

10.18b . . . and hub carrier are both asymmetrically shaped to ensure correct orientation

10.17 Brace the disc by holding a stout bar between the roadwheel studs, then insert and tighten all four disc securing bolts to the specified torque

10.19 Insert the hub-to-hub carrier securing bolts and tighten them the to specified torque

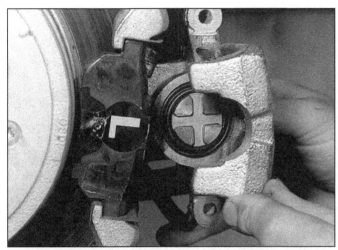

11.3 Lift the caliper away from the disc, noting the upper pad spring which is fitted to the roof of the caliper

11.4 Remove the brake pads from the caliper mounting bracket

solvents to clean brake parts – use brake cleaner or methylated spirit only.

1 Park the vehicle on a level surface, then chock the front wheels, and select first gear (manual transmission) or Park (automatic transmission). Jack up the rear of the car, support it securely on axle stands and remove the rear roadwheels. Release the handbrake.

2 Undo the two bolts securing the caliper shield in position, and remove the shield from the rear of the caliper.

3 Remove both the caliper guide pin bolts, if necessary using a slim open-ended spanner to prevent the guide pins from rotating. Lift the caliper away from the disc, noting the upper pad spring which is fitted to the roof of the caliper **(see illustration)**. Tie the caliper to the suspension strut using a piece of wire, to avoid straining the hydraulic hose.

4 Remove the brake pads from the caliper mounting bracket, noting the correct fitted positions of the brake pads, pad retainer springs and pad shims **(see illustration)**.

5 Inspect the pads (and brake caliper) as described in Section 8 and if necessary, renew the pads as a complete axle set.

6 Commence refitting, by clipping the pad retainer springs onto the caliper mounting bracket.

7 Apply a thin smear of Molykote M77 compound to the sides and back of each pads metal backplate, and to those surfaces of the caliper body and mounting bracket which bear on the pads. In the absence of this compound, a good quality high-temperature brake grease (silicone-or PBC/Poly Butyl Cuprysil-based) or anti-seize compound may be used. Fit the shims to the back of both pads, noting that the smaller shim must be fitted to the piston-side pad, and apply a thin smear of lubricant to the back of each shim **(see illustration)**. Do not allow the lubricant to foul the friction material.

8 Install the brake pads in the caliper mounting bracket, ensuring that the friction

material is against the disc, and that the pad with the smaller shim attached is fitted on the inside.

9 If new pads have been fitted, it will be necessary to retract the piston fully into the caliper bore, by rotating it in a clockwise direction **(see illustration)**. This can be achieved using a suitable pair of circlip pliers as a peg spanner, or by fabricating a peg spanner for the task. Provided that the master cylinder reservoir has not been overfilled with hydraulic fluid, there should be no spillage, but keep a careful watch on the fluid level while retracting the piston. If the fluid level rises above the MAX level line at any time, the surplus should be syphoned off or ejected via a plastic tube connected to the bleed screw (see Section 7 and use a one-man bleed tube or bottle if possible).

10 Ensure the upper pad spring is still in position in the caliper, then slide the caliper into position in its mounting bracket. When fitting the caliper, ensure that the lug on the rear of the piston side pad is located in one of the piston slots. Refit the caliper guide pin bolts, and tighten them to the specified torque setting.

11 Depress the footbrake, several times if necessary, to bring the piston into contact with the pads, then check that the lug on the

piston-side pad is located in one of the piston slots. If necessary, remove the caliper and adjust the piston position as described above. Refit the shield to the rear of the caliper, and tighten its bolts securely.

12 Repeat the above procedure on the remaining rear brake caliper.

13 Once both sets of pads have been renewed, repeatedly depress the brake pedal until normal (non-assisted) pedal operation returns, then repeatedly apply the handbrake to set the handbrake adjustment. Check the operation of the handbrake and, if necessary, adjust the cable as described in Chapter 1.

14 Refit the roadwheels, then lower the car to the ground and tighten the roadwheel nuts to the specified torque.

15 Check the hydraulic fluid level, as described in Chapter 1.

12 Rear brake caliper – removal, overhaul and refitting

Note: *Before starting work, refer to the note at the beginning of Section 5 concerning the dangers of hydraulic fluid, and to the warning at the beginning of Section 8 concerning the dangers of asbestos dust.*

11.7 Refitting the smaller piston-side pad shim

11.9 Using a pair of circlip pliers to retract the piston

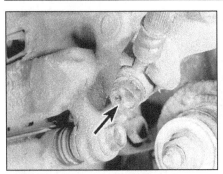

12.5 Undo the brake hose union bolt and disconnect the hose from the caliper

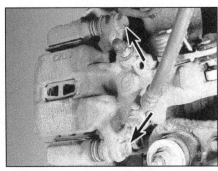

12.6 Remove both the caliper guide pin bolts (arrowed)

Removal

1 Chock the front wheels, then jack up the rear of the car and support on axle stands. Remove the rear wheel.

2 Undo the two bolts securing the caliper shield in position, and remove the shield from the rear of the caliper.

3 Extract the spring clip and clevis pin securing the handbrake cable to the caliper handbrake lever, then remove the clip securing the outer cable to its mounting bracket, and detach the handbrake cable from the caliper (see Section 14).

4 Minimise fluid loss by first removing the master cylinder reservoir cap, and then tightening it down onto a piece of polythene to obtain an airtight seal (taking care not to damage the sender unit). Alternatively, use a brake hose clamp, a G-clamp or a similar tool to clamp the flexible hose.

5 Clean the area around the hose union, then undo the brake hose union bolt and disconnect the hose from the caliper **(see illustration)**. Plug the end of the hose and the caliper orifice to prevent dirt entering the hydraulic system. Discard the sealing washers; they must be renewed whenever disturbed.

6 Remove both the caliper guide pin bolts, if necessary using a slim open-ended spanner to prevent the guide pins from rotating **(see illustration)**. Lift the caliper away from the disc, noting the upper pad spring which is fitted to the roof of the caliper. Note that the brake pads need not be disturbed, and can be left in position in the caliper mounting bracket.

Overhaul

7 With the caliper on the bench, wipe away all traces of dust and dirt, but *avoid inhaling the dust, as it is injurious to health.*

8 Using a small screwdriver, carefully prise out the dust seal from the caliper bore.

9 Remove the piston from the caliper bore by rotating it in an anti-clockwise direction. This can be achieved using a suitable pair of circlip pliers as a peg spanner, or by fabricating a peg spanner for the task. Once the piston turns freely but does not come out any further, the piston can be withdrawn by hand, or if necessary pushed out by applying compressed air to the union bolt hole. Only low pressure should be required, such as that generated by a bicycle pump or car footpump.

10 Remove the piston (fluid) seal, taking great care not to scratch the caliper bore.

11 With the piston removed, depress the spring cover and extract the circlip from the caliper bore. Release the tension on the spring cover, then withdraw it from the caliper bore, together with the spring, spacer, bearing, adjusting bolt and cup **(see illustration)**.

12 Remove the adjusting bolt piston, noting the O-ring fitted to the rear of the piston, and withdraw the small pushrod **(see illustration)**.

13 Unclip the return spring, then withdraw the handbrake mechanism cam, lever and dust seal from the caliper as a complete assembly **(see illustration)**.

14 Withdraw the guide pins from the caliper mounting bracket, and remove the guide pin gaiters.

15 Inspect all the caliper components as described in Section 9, and renew as necessary.

16 On reassembly, ensure that all components are absolutely clean and dry.

17 Apply a good quality high-temperature brake grease (silicone- or PBC/Poly Butyl Cuprysil-based) or anti-seize compound to the handbrake mechanism cam and lever assembly. Press a new handbrake lever dust seal into place on the caliper, then fit the cam mechanism and lever assembly to the caliper.

18 Fit a new O-ring to the adjusting bolt piston, then insert the small pushrod into the rear of the piston, and install the adjusting bolt piston assembly in the caliper bore. Ensure that the pins on the rear surface of the piston engage with the holes at the end of the caliper bore, and that the small pushrod engages with the recess in the handbrake cam. Operate the handbrake lever and check that the piston is free to move smoothly.

19 Fit a new cup to the head of the adjusting bolt, then refit the adjusting bolt, followed by the bearing, spacer, spring and spring seat.

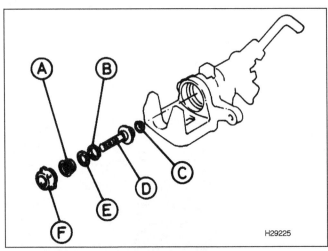

H29225

12.11 Rear caliper adjusting bolt and spring assembly

A Spring
B Bearing
C Cup
D Adjusting bolt
E Spacer
F Spring cover

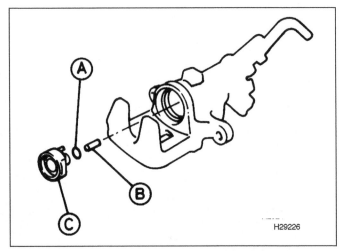

H29226

12.12 Rear caliper adjusting bolt piston assembly

A O-ring
B Pushrod
C Adjusting bolt piston

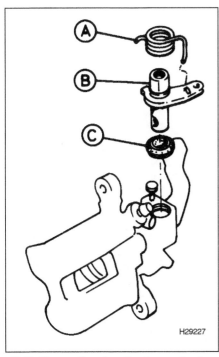

12.13 Rear caliper handbrake mechanism

A Return spring
B Handbrake lever/cam assembly
C Dust seal

Ensure that the spring is fitted with the smallest tapered coils innermost.

20 Depress the spring seat slightly, the secure the spring seat and its associated components in the caliper bore with the circlip. Ensure that the circlip is correctly seated in its groove before releasing te spring seat.

21 Soak the piston and the new piston (fluid) seal in clean hydraulic fluid, and smear clean fluid in the cylinder bore.

22 Fit the new piston (fluid) seal, using only your fingers (no tools) to manipulate it into the cylinder bore groove, and refit the piston assembly. Turn the piston clockwise, using the method employed on dismantling, until it is fully retracted into the caliper bore.

23 Fit the dust seal to the caliper, ensuring that it is correctly located in the caliper and also in the groove on the piston.

24 Apply the grease supplied in the repair kit, or a good quality high-temperature brake grease (silicone- or PBC/Poly Butyl Cuprysil-based) or anti-seize compound to the guide pins, and fit the new gaiters. Fit the guide pins to the caliper mounting bracket, ensuring that the gaiters are correctly located in the grooves on both the guide pin and mounting bracket.

25 Where applicable, refit the pad centre spring to the caliper body.

Refitting

26 Ensure the upper pad spring is still in position in the caliper, then slide the caliper into position in the mounting bracket. When fitting the caliper, ensure that the lug on the rear of the piston-side pad is located in the

centre of the caliper piston, at the point where the two piston slots cross. Refit the caliper guide pin bolts, and tighten them to the specified torque setting.

27 Position a new sealing washer on each side of the hose union, and refit the brake hose union bolt. Ensure that the brake hose union is correctly positioned between the lugs on the caliper, then tighten the union bolt to the specified torque setting.

28 Remove the brake hose clamp, where fitted, and bleed the hydraulic system as described in Section 5. Note that, providing the precautions described were taken to minimise brake fluid loss, it should only be necessary to bleed the relevant rear brake.

29 Refit the handbrake outer cable to its mounting bracket, and secure it in position with the retaining clip. Ensure the return spring is located in the groove in the operating lever, then refit the handbrake cable-to-lever clevis pin, and secure it in position with the spring clip.

30 Depress the brake pedal several times until normal (non-assisted) operation returns, then check and if necessary adjust the handbrake cable, as described in Chapter 1.

31 Refit the shield to the rear of the caliper, and tighten its retaining bolts securely.

32 Refit the roadwheel, then lower the vehicle to the ground and tighten the roadwheel nuts to the specified torque.

33 Check the hydraulic fluid level (Chapter 1).

34 Test the operation of the braking system thoroughly, before bringing the vehicle back into service on the public highway.

13 Rear brake disc – inspection, removal and refitting

Note: *Before starting work, refer to the warning at the beginning of Section 8 concerning the dangers of asbestos dust.*

Inspection

Note: *If either disc requires renewal, both should be renewed at the same time, to ensure even and consistent braking.*

1 Chock the front wheels, then jack up the rear of the car and support on axle stands. Remove the appropriate rear roadwheel.

13.5a Remove the two screws securing the brake disc to the hub, and remove the disc

2 Inspect the disc as described in Section 10, paragraphs 2 to 5.

Removal

3 Undo the two caliper shield retaining bolts, and remove the shield from the rear of the caliper.

4 Undo the two bolts securing the caliper mounting bracket to the suspension assembly, and slide the caliper assembly off the disc. Using a piece of wire or string, tie the caliper to the rear suspension coil spring, to avoid placing any strain on the hydraulic brake hose.

5 Use chalk or paint to mark the relationship of the disc to the hub, then remove the two screws securing the brake disc to the hub, and remove the disc. If the disc is a tight fit on the hub, it can be drawn off by screwing two bolts into the jacking holes provided **(see illustrations)**.

Refitting

6 Refitting is the reverse of the removal procedure, noting the following points.

(a) Ensure that the mating surfaces of the disc and hub are clean and flat.
(b) Align the marks made on removal (if applicable).
(c) If a new disc has been fitted, use a suitable solvent to wipe any preservative coating from the disc before refitting the caliper.
(d) Tighten the disc retaining screws, caliper bracket bolts and roadwheel nuts to their specified torque wrench settings.

14 Handbrake cables – removal and refitting

Removal

1 Firmly chock the front wheels, then jack up the rear of the vehicle and support it on axle stands. The handbrake cable consists of two sections, a right- and left-hand section, which are linked to the lever assembly by an equalizer plate; each section can be removed individually.

13.5b If the disc is a tight fit on the hub, it can be drawn off by screwing two bolts into the jacking holes provided

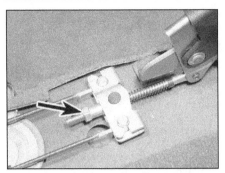

14.3 Slacken off the handbrake cable adjusting nut (arrowed), at the rear of the threaded rod

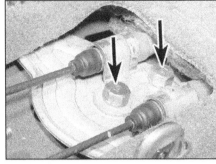

14.4 Undo the bolts (arrowed) securing the outer cable retaining plate to the floorpan

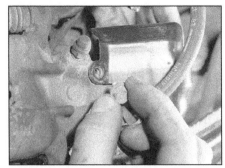

14.5a Working underneath the car, remove the brake caliper shield retaining bolts . . .

2 With reference to Chapter 11, remove the rear section of the centre console to expose the handbrake cables.

3 Slacken off the handbrake cable adjusting nut, at the rear of the threaded rod (see illustration). Disconnect the relevant handbrake cable from the equalizer plate.

4 Undo the bolts securing the outer cable retaining plate to the floorpan (see illustration). Remove the retaining plate, then detach the relevant inner cable from the equalizer plate and release the cable grommet from the floorpan.

5 Working underneath the car, remove the brake caliper shield retaining bolts, and remove the shield from the caliper (see illustrations).

6 Extract the spring clip and pin securing the handbrake cable to the caliper handbrake lever (see illustration).

7 Remove the clip securing the outer cable to its mounting bracket, and detach the handbrake cable from the caliper (see illustration).

8 Release the main silencer from its three rubber mountings, and carefully lower the tailpipe section to gain access to the heat shield. Undo the three heat shield retaining

bolts, and remove the shield from the vehicle underbody.

9 Work along the length of the cable section, and remove all the bolts securing the outer cable to the vehicle underbody and suspension arms. Once free, withdraw the cable from underneath the vehicle, and if necessary repeat the procedure for the remaining cable section.

Refitting

10 Refitting is a reversal of the removal sequence, noting the following points.

(a) Lubricate all exposed linkages and cable pivots with a good quality multi-purpose grease.

(b) Ensure the outer cable grommets are correctly located in the floorpan, and that all retaining clip fixings are tightened securely.

(c) Prior to refitting the rear centre console section, adjust the handbrake cable as described in Chapter 1.

(d) Thoroughly check the operation of the handbrake system, before bringing the vehicle back into service on the public highway.

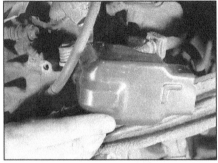

14.5b . . . and remove the shield from the caliper

15 Stop-lamp switch – removal, refitting and adjustment

Removal

1 Ensure that the ignition is switched off. Working from inside the car, undo the screws and remove the driver's side lower facia panel.

2 Unplug the wiring connector from the stop-lamp switch (see illustration).

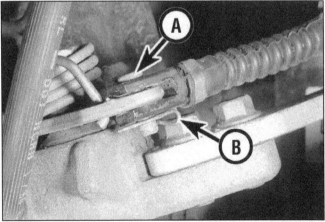

14.6 Extract the spring clip and pin securing the handbrake cable to the caliper handbrake lever

A Pin   B Spring clip

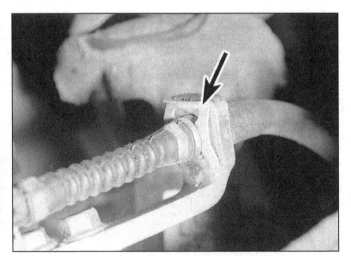

14.7 Remove the clip (arrowed) securing the handbrake outer cable to its mounting bracket

15.2 Unplug the wiring connector (arrowed) from the stop-lamp switch

switch terminals as soon as the pedal is depressed. If necessary, reposition the switch until it operates as specified.

6 Once the stop-lamp switch is correctly adjusted, hold the switch stationary and tighten the locknut securely.

7 Connect the wiring connector to the switch, and refit the lower facia panel.

3 Slacken the stop-lamp switch locknut, and unscrew the switch from its mounting bracket.

Refitting and adjustment

4 Screw the switch back into position in the mounting bracket.

5 Connect an ohmmeter across the stop-lamp switch terminals, and screw the switch in until an open-circuit is present between the switch terminals. Gently depress the pedal, and check that continuity exists between the

16 Anti-lock braking system (ALB) – general information

1 ALB is available as an option on all models covered in this manual. The purpose of the system is to prevent wheel(s) locking during heavy braking, and this is achieved by controlling the pressure applied to the brakes when they are on the point of locking. When a wheel is about to lock, hydraulic pressure to that brake is momentarily reduced, so that the wheel keeps turning, and pressure is then re-applied – this cycle can take place several times a second under heavy braking.

2 The system is comprised of an Electronic Control Unit (ECU), four roadwheel sensors

(one fitted to each wheel), the modulator block which contains the modulator valves and solenoid control valves, the ALB pump and motor unit, and the accumulator unit **(see illustration)**. The latter components are all linked via a high-pressure hydraulic circuit. The master cylinder is connected to the modulator valves; the valves then distribute the main braking hydraulic system to the brake caliper. **Note:** *The ALB high-pressure hydraulic control circuit is a sealed circuit, and is completely separate from the main hydraulic braking system; the two hydraulic circuits are not linked in any way.*

3 The ALB system is controlled by the ECU which itself receives signals from the four wheel sensors (one fitted on each hub), which monitor the speed of rotation of each wheel. By comparing these speed signals from the four wheels, the ECU can determine the speed at which the vehicle is travelling. It can then use this information to determine when a wheel is decelerating at an abnormal rate compared to the speed of the vehicle, and can therefore predict when a wheel is about to lock.

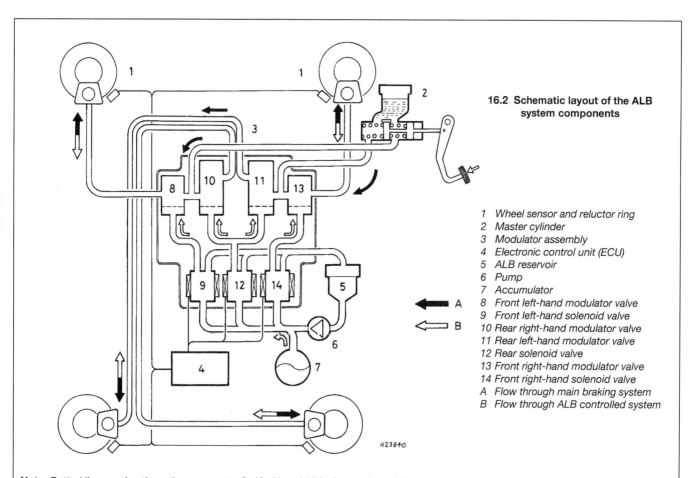

16.2 Schematic layout of the ALB system components

1 Wheel sensor and reluctor ring
2 Master cylinder
3 Modulator assembly
4 Electronic control unit (ECU)
5 ALB reservoir
6 Pump
7 Accumulator
8 Front left-hand modulator valve
9 Front left-hand solenoid valve
10 Rear right-hand modulator valve
11 Rear left-hand modulator valve
12 Rear solenoid valve
13 Front right-hand modulator valve
14 Front right-hand solenoid valve
A Flow through main braking system
B Flow through ALB controlled system

H23840

Note: *Dotted line passing through components 8, 10, 11 and 13 indicates the dividing line between the ALB high-pressure hydraulic system (below the line) and the main braking hydraulic system (above the line)*

4 During normal operation, the system functions in the same way as a normal braking system does, with the modulator valves having no effect on the braking system. At this stage, the modulator valves are fully open, and are isolated by the solenoid control valves from the ALB pump pressure which is present in the accumulator unit.

5 If the ECU senses that a wheel is about to lock, the ECU will gradually open the relevant solenoid valve in the modulator block. This then allows the hydraulic pressure present in the accumulator unit through to the relevant modulator valve. The cut-off valve within the modulator valve then closes, which isolates the relevant brake caliper from the master cylinder, effectively sealing-in the hydraulic pressure.

6 If the speed of rotation of the wheel continues to decrease at an abnormal rate, the ECU then opens the solenoid valve further. This increases the pressure present in chamber C of the modulator valve, and causes the valve to rise further **(see illustrations)**. As it rises, the pressure in chamber A of the valve decreases, which draws the fluid back from the relevant brake caliper, effectively reducing the pressure in the main braking system and releasing the relevant brake. At the same time, the pressure in chamber B of the modulator valve is increased, and fluid is forced back into the master cylinder reservoir, causing pulses in the main braking hydraulic system. This pulsing can be felt through the brake pedal.

7 Once the speed of rotation of the wheel returns to an acceptable rate, the ECU operates the solenoid valve to fully exhaust the hydraulic pressure present in chamber C of the modulator valve. The modulator valve then falls again, the cut-off valve opens, and normal operation of the braking system returns.

8 The ECU completes a self-checking sequence each time the engine is started, and will illuminate the ALB warning lamp on the instrument panel. If the system is functioning correctly and no fault is found, the warning lamp will go out after a few seconds. Should a fault be present in the system, the ALB warning lamp will remain lit. If this is the case, the car must immediately be taken to a Rover dealer for inspection.

9 If the ABS develops a fault, the vehicle must be examined by a Rover dealer, who will have the dedicated test equipment required for fault diagnosis. For safety reasons, owners are strongly advised against attempting to diagnose complex problems with the ABS using standard workshop equipment.

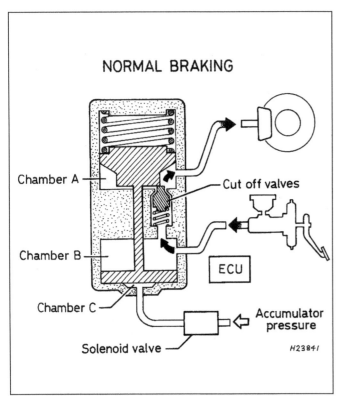

16.6a Modulator valve operation during normal braking

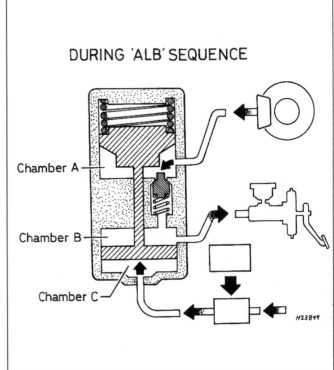

16.6b Modulator valve operation during ALB sequence

Chapter 10
Suspension and steering

Contents

Degrees of difficulty

Easy, suitable for novice with little experience		Fairly easy, suitable for beginner with some experience		Fairly difficult, suitable for competent DIY mechanic		Difficult, suitable for experienced DIY mechanic		Very difficult, suitable for expert DIY or professional	

Specifications

Front suspension

Type .... Independent double wishbone with upper and lower control arms. Gas-filled shock absorber and coil spring assembly. Anti-roll bar fitted to all models

Rear suspension

Type .... Independent double wishbone with upper and lower control arms, and trailing arm. Gas-filled shock absorber and coil spring assembly. Anti-roll bar fitted to all models

Wheel bearings

Endfloat at hub (front and rear) .... 0.0 to 0.05 mm

Steering

Type .... Power-assisted steering on all models. Speed-sensitive on later models
Turns lock-to-lock 3.14
Power steering pump drivebelt tension:
    Used drivebelt .... 13.0 to 16.0 mm deflection midway between the pump and crankshaft pulleys with force of 98 N
    New drivebelt .... 11.0 to 12.5 mm deflection midway between the pump and crankshaft pulleys with force of 98 N

Wheel alignment and steering angles

Front wheel:
    Camber angle .... 0° 00 ± 1°
    Caster angle .... 3° 00 ± 1°
    Toe setting (total) .... 0 ± 3.0 mm toe-out
Rear wheel:
    Camber angle .... - 0° 30 ± 30
    Toe setting (total) .... 2.0 ± 2.0 mm toe-in

Roadwheels

Type	Pressed-steel or aluminium alloy (depending on model)

Size:

Steel	5J x 14 and 5.5J x 15
Alloy	5.5J x 15

Tyres

Pressures - see 'Weekly checks'.

Size:

620i and Si	185/70 R14 88H
620Si with ABS	185/65 R15 88H
620Li and GSi	195/60 R15 87V

Torque wrench settings

	Nm	lbf ft
Front suspension		
Anti-roll bar to lower arm	19	14
Front suspension lower balljoint nut	55	41
Front suspension upper balljoint nut	44	32
Hub carrier to lower arm balljoint	55	41
Hub carrier-to-shock absorber/coil spring assembly pinch-bolt	44	32
Hub to hub carrier	45	33
Lower arm inner mounting bolt	55	41
Radius arm front mounting nut	68	50
Radius arm to lower arm	105	77
Shock absorber/coil spring assembly fork to lower arm	65	48
Shock absorber/coil spring assembly self-locking piston nut	30	22
Shock absorber/coil spring assembly upper mounting nut	39	29
Upper arm to body	65	48
Upper balljoint cover	10	7
Rear suspension		
Anti-roll bar link to trailing arm	36	27
Anti-roll bar mounting	22	16
Anti-roll bar to link	13	10
Lower arms inner mounting bolts	65	48
Lower arms-to-hub carrier bolt	65	48
Rear hub nut	185	137
Rear suspension lower balljoint nut	44	32
Rear suspension upper balljoint nut	44	32
Shock absorber/coil spring assembly self-locking piston nut	30	22
Shock absorber/coil spring assembly to hub carrier	55	41
Shock absorber/coil spring upper mounting nut	39	29
Splash guard to hub carrier	10	7
Trailing arm front mounting and pivot bolts	65	48
Trailing arm-to-hub carrier nuts	36	27
Upper arm to body	39	29
Steering		
Airbag module side Torx bolts	10	7
Column universal joint clamp bolt	28	21
Hydraulic lines to power steering gear:		
From pump	38	28
To oil cooler	13	10
To reservoir	29	21
To speed sensor	13	10
Power steering pump mounting and adjustment lock bolts	45	33
Power steering pump pressure union bolt	11	8
Speed sensor to transmission	18	13
Steering gear mounting:		
Mounting bolt	50	37
Mounting clamp bolt	39	29
Steering column:		
Upper mounting nuts	13	10
Lower mounting clamp bolts	22	16
Steering wheel	50	37
Track rod end to steering arm	44	32
Track rod end-to-track rod locknut	45	33
Roadwheels		
Roadwheel nuts	110	81

2.2 Loosening the driveshaft nut

2.3 Brake hose bracket on the front hub carrier

2.6a Extract the split pin

1 General information

Caution: If the radio/cassette in your vehicle is equipped with an anti-theft system, make sure you have the correct activation code before disconnecting the battery.

The front suspension is of fully independent design with upper and lower control arms, shock absorber/coil spring assemblies and an anti-roll bar.

The rear suspension is of fully independent design with trailing arms, two unequal length lower control arms, an upper control arm, shock absorber/coil spring assemblies and an anti-roll bar.

All models are fitted with a power-assisted rack-and-pinion steering gear. The hydraulic system is powered by a belt-driven pump, which is driven from the crankshaft pulley. The hydraulic fluid is cooled by passing it through a single bore cooling tube located in front of the radiator. On later models the power steering is speed-sensitive with more assistance at low speeds, and reduced assistance at higher speeds to give a positive feel for cruising. This system uses a hydraulic control valve incorporated in the vehicle speed sensor on the transmission.

The steering column has a universal joint fitted at its lower end. The joint is clamped to the inner column and steering gear pinion shaft.

The steering gear is mounted on the engine compartment bulkhead, and incorporates track rods with outer balljoints attached to the steering arms on the hub carriers.

2 Front hub carrier - removal, overhaul and refitting

Removal

1 Apply the handbrake, then loosen the wheel nuts on the relevant wheel and jack up the front of the vehicle. Support the vehicle on axle stands (see *Jacking and Vehicle Support*). Remove the roadwheel.
2 Have an assistant apply the footbrake. Using a socket and extension bar, loosen the driveshaft nut **(see illustration)**. Unscrew and remove the nut. If the nut is damaged, obtain a new one for refitting.
Caution: The nut is very tight!
3 Unbolt the brake hose bracket from the hub carrier, then unbolt the brake caliper and suspend it to one side with a length of wire attached to the coil spring. Unbolt and remove the caliper bracket **(see illustration)**.
4 Remove the ABS wheel sensor wiring support, then unbolt the wheel sensor from the hub carrier leaving the wiring attached to the sensor.
5 Disconnect the track-rod end from the hub carrier with reference to Section 21.
6 Extract the split pin, then unscrew the nut securing the lower control arm to the hub

carrier until it is flush with the end of the balljoint stud **(see illustration)**.
7 Using a balljoint removal tool, separate the lower control arm from the bottom of the hub carrier. Unscrew and remove the nut **(see illustrations)**.
8 Unbolt and remove the protector cover from the hub carrier upper balljoint.
9 Extract the split pin, then unscrew the nut securing the upper control arm to the hub carrier until it is flush with the end of the balljoint stud **(see illustration)**.
10 Using a balljoint removal tool, separate the upper control arm from the top of the hub carrier. Support the hub carrier, then unscrew and remove the nut.
11 Carefully pull the hub carrier, together with the hub and disc, from the end of the driveshaft, while tapping the end of the driveshaft with a soft-faced mallet. Support the driveshaft with a length of wire to prevent damage to the inner CV joint.
12 With the hub carrier assembly on the bench, unbolt and remove the hub and disc.
13 Remove the screws and withdraw the splash guard from the hub carrier.

Overhaul

14 Check the lower balljoint for excessive wear. If evident, it can be renewed however special tools are required and the work should be carried out by a Rover dealer or suitably-equipped garage.
15 Check the balljoint rubber dust cover for damage and splits. If evident the cover can be renewed separately. Prise off the circlips and

2.7a Using a balljoint removal tool to separate the lower arm from the hub carrier . . .

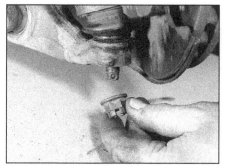

2.7b . . . and remove the nut from the lower balljoint

2.9 Front suspension upper balljoint

2.27 Staking the driveshaft nut

remove the old dust cover, then clean the seating and fit the new cover. Secure with the new circlips.

Refitting

16 Before reassembly, clean all the components and examine them for damage.
17 Locate the splash guard on the hub carrier making sure that the location peg engages with the hole, then tighten the screws securely.
18 Refit the hub and disc and tighten the bolts to the specified torque.
19 Apply a little grease to the splines on the driveshaft, then locate the hub carrier together with the hub and disc on the driveshaft splines. Remove the support wire.
20 Locate the upper end of the hub carrier on the balljoint stud on the upper arm and screw on the nut loosely.
21 Locate the lower end of the hub carrier on the balljoint stud on the lower arm and screw on the nut. Tighten the nut to the specified torque then align the split pin holes and fit a new split pin. If necessary the nut may be tightened to align the holes.
22 Tighten the upper balljoint nut to the specified torque and fit a new split pin. If necessary the nut may be tightened to align the holes.
23 Refit the protector cover to the upper balljoint and tighten the bolt.
24 Reconnect the track-rod end to the hub carrier with reference to Section 21.
25 Refit the ALB sensor and wiring and tighten the bolts. Make sure the wiring is not twisted.

26 Refit the caliper bracket, followed by the caliper and brake hose bracket and tighten the bolts to the specified torque (refer to Chapter 9).
27 While an assistant depresses the footbrake, fit and tighten the driveshaft nut to the specified torque (refer to Chapter 8). Stake the nut collar into the groove in the driveshaft **(see illustration)**.
28 Refit the roadwheel and tighten the nuts to the specified torque, then lower the vehicle to the ground.

3 Front hub bearings - checking and renewal

Checking

1 Apply the handbrake, then loosen the wheel nuts on the relevant wheel and jack up the front of the vehicle. Support the vehicle on axle stands (see *Jacking and Vehicle Support*). Remove the roadwheel.
2 Unbolt the brake hose bracket from the hub carrier, then unbolt the brake caliper and suspend it to one side with a length of wire attached to the coil spring. Unbolt and remove the caliper bracket.
3 Wear in the front hub bearings can be checked by measuring the amount of side play present. To do this, a dial gauge should be fixed so that its probe is in contact with the wheel contact face of the hub. Attempt to move the hub in and out, and check that the play is within the limits given in the Specifications. Excessive play indicates wear in the bearings, and in this case they must be renewed.

Renewal

Note: *Removal of the bearing renders it unserviceable for further use.*

4 Remove the front hub carrier as described in Section 2 but do not remove the splash guard.
5 With the hub and disc on the bench, unscrew the bolts and separate the disc from the hub.
6 The hub must now be pressed from the wheel bearing housing. To successfully carry

out this work it will also be necessary to support the bearing housing while the hub is being removed. If the necessary equipment is not available, have the work carried out by a Rover dealer or engineering works. Note also that the outer bearing race will have to be removed from the hub before fitting the hub to the new bearings.
7 Before installing the new bearing housing, thoroughly clean the hub and wipe dry.
8 Support the hub with the wheel studs facing downwards, then locate the new bearing housing on the hub making sure it is the correct way round.
9 Using a suitable metal tube located only on the inner race, press the bearing housing fully onto the hub.
10 Clean the contact surfaces of the disc and hub, then reassemble the disc to the hub and tighten the bolts to the specified torque (refer to Chapter 9).
11 Refit the front hub carrier with reference to Section 2.

4 Front shock absorber/coil spring assembly - removal, overhaul and refitting

Removal

1 Apply the handbrake, then loosen the wheel nuts on the relevant wheel and jack up the front of the vehicle. Support the vehicle on axle stands (see *Jacking and Vehicle Support*). Remove the roadwheel.
2 Unbolt the brake hose bracket from the hub carrier.
3 Disconnect the front anti-roll bar from the lower control arm with reference to Section 7.
4 Position a trolley jack under the lower control arm to support it when the shock absorber assembly is removed.
5 Unscrew and remove the pinch-bolt securing the fork to the bottom of the shock absorber assembly **(see illustration)**.
6 Unscrew and remove the bolt securing the fork to the lower control arm, then withdraw the fork. If the fork is tight on the shock absorber, tap it free with a hammer **(see illustrations)**.

4.5 Removing the fork-to-shock absorber pinch-bolt

4.6a Unscrew the nut . . .

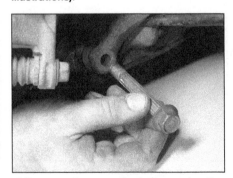

4.6b . . . and remove the bolt securing the fork to the lower control arm . . .

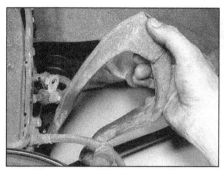

4.6c ... then withdraw the fork

4.7a Unscrew the upper mounting nuts ...

4.7b ... and withdraw the shock absorber/coil spring assembly from under the wheel arch

7 Open the bonnet. Support the shock absorber assembly from under the front wheel arch, then unscrew the upper mounting nuts from inside the engine compartment and withdraw the unit from under the wheel arch **(see illustrations)**.

Warning: Do not unscrew the centre nut from the top of the shock absorber.

Overhaul

Note: *Suitable coil spring compressor tools will be required for this operation.*

8 With the assembly on the bench, check the shock absorber for leaking fluid, dents, cracks or other obvious damage. Check the coil spring for chips or cracks which could cause premature failure and inspect the spring seats for hardness or general deterioration.

9 Clamp the lower end of the shock absorber assembly in a vice fitted with jaw protectors.

10 Fit spring compressors to the spring, and compress the spring until there is no pressure on the upper mounting and the central nut is raised from the washer.

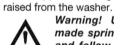
Warning! Use only purpose-made spring compressor tools and follow the manufacturer's instructions.

11 Mark the relationship of the shock absorber assembly components to ensure correct reassembly **(see illustration)**. As the components are removed, lay them out in order to ensure correct refitting.

12 Unscrew the self-locking central nut from the top of the shock absorber assembly while holding the shaft stationary with an Allen key **(see illustrations)**.

13 Remove the washer, upper mounting, collar, mounting plate, lower mounting rubber, and upper spring seat **(see illustrations)**.

14 Remove the coil spring (with compressors fitted), followed by the dust cover, stop plate and bump stop (note which way round it is fitted) **(see illustrations)**. If the compressors are to be left in position on the coil spring, put the spring in a safe place away from the work area as a precaution.

15 With the shock absorber assembly now dismantled, examine all the components for wear and damage. Check the rubber components for deterioration. Examine the shock absorber for damage and signs of fluid leakage, and check the piston rod for pitting along its entire length. While holding it in an upright position, test the operation of the shock absorber by moving the rod through a

4.11 Mark the spring and mounting in relation to each other

4.12a Unscrewing the central nut while holding the shaft stationary with an Allen key

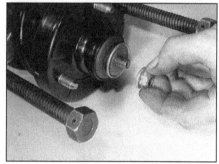

4.12b Removing the central nut

4.13a Remove the washer ...

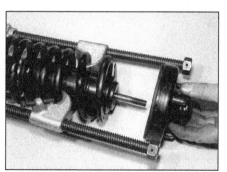

4.13b ... and upper mounting

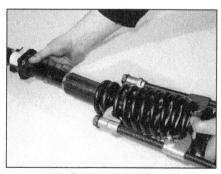

4.14a Remove the coil spring (with compressors fitted) ...

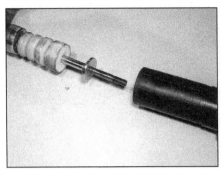

4.14b ... followed by the dust cover ...

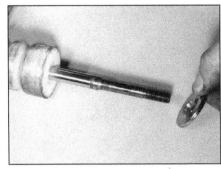

4.14c ... stop plate ...

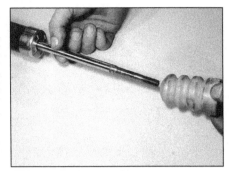

4.14d ... and bump stop

full stroke, and then through short strokes of 50 to 100 mm. In both cases, the resistance felt should be smooth and continuous. If the resistance is jerky, or uneven, or if there is any visible sign of wear or damage to the shock absorber, renewal is necessary.

 Warning: The shock absorber is filled with nitrogen gas and oil at high pressure. To ensure safe disposal, the pressure should be released by drilling a 2.0 mm diameter hole in the shock absorber body near its base.

16 Renew the coil spring if it is damaged or distorted.

17 To reassemble the shock absorber, first extend the piston rod as far as it will go.

18 Fit the bump stop, stop plate and dust cover onto the piston rod, making sure that the bump stop is the correct way round (ie largest diameter uppermost).

19 Ensure that the coil spring is compressed sufficiently to enable the upper mounting components to be fitted, then fit the spring over the piston rod, ensuring that the lower end of the spring is correctly located on the lower spring seat **(see illustration)**.

20 Locate the upper spring seat on the coil spring, followed by the lower mounting rubber, mounting plate, collar, upper mounting rubber, washer and nut. Before tightening the nut, position the components with the previously made marks aligned. Where new components are being fitted, transfer the marks from the old components.

21 Tighten the self-locking nut to the specified torque while holding the piston rod with an Allen key.

22 Release the compressors while guiding the spring ends onto the seats.

23 Remove the assembly from the vice.

Refitting

24 Manoeuvre the shock absorber assembly into position under the wheel arch, passing the mounting studs through the holes in the body turret. Refit the upper mounting nuts loosely, but do not fully tighten them at this stage.

25 Fit the fork to the bottom of the shock absorber, making sure that the alignment tab enters the slot in the fork. Insert the pinch-bolt and screw on the nut loosely. **Note:** *The left- and right-hand forks are different and must not be interchanged. The left-hand fork is marked ML and the right-hand fork is marked MR.*

26 Locate the fork on the lower control arm, and insert the bolt with its head facing forwards. Screw on the nut loosely.

27 Using a trolley jack under the lower control arm, raise the front suspension until the weight of the vehicle is just supported.

28 Tighten the fork-to-shock absorber pinch-bolt, upper mounting nuts and fork-to-lower control arm bolt to the specified torques.

29 Reconnect the front anti-roll bar to the lower control arm with reference to Section 7.

30 Refit the brake hose bracket to the shock absorber assembly and tighten the bolts.

31 Refit the roadwheel and lower the vehicle to the ground.

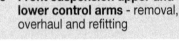

5 Front suspension upper and lower control arms - removal, overhaul and refitting

Upper control arm

Removal

1 Apply the handbrake, then loosen the wheel nuts on the relevant wheel and jack up the front of the vehicle. Support the vehicle on axle stands (see *Jacking and Vehicle Support*). Remove the roadwheel.

2 Position a trolley jack under the lower control arm to support the hub carrier when it is disconnected from the upper control arm.

3 Unbolt and remove the protector cover from the upper balljoint.

4 Extract the split pin, then unscrew the nut securing the upper control arm to the hub carrier until it is flush with the end of the balljoint stud.

5 Using a balljoint removal tool, separate the upper control arm from the top of the hub carrier. Support the hub carrier, then unscrew and remove the nut.

6 Unscrew the nuts and remove the inner pivot bolts from the upper control arm. Note that the bolt heads face each other. If necessary, unscrew the support mounting nuts in the engine compartment, Withdraw the upper control arm from under the wheel arch **(see illustration)**.

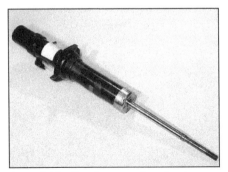

4.14e Front suspension shock absorber/coil spring assembly removed from the vehicle

4.19 Ensure that the lower end of the spring is correctly located on the lower spring seat

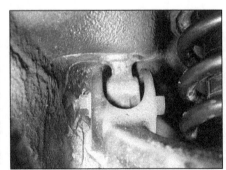

5.6 Upper control arm inner pivot bolt

5.17 Lower control arm inner pivot bolt

Overhaul

7 If the inner pivot bushes are worn, remove the anchor bolts from the body by unscrewing the nuts located in the engine compartment. It may be possible to obtain new bushes or anchors, but check with your Rover dealer first.

8 Check the upper balljoint for excessive wear. If evident the complete upper control arm must be renewed.

9 Check the rubber dust cover for damage and splits. If evident the cover can be renewed separately. Prise off the circlip and remove the old dust cover, then clean the seating and fit the new cover. Secure with the new circlip.

Refitting

10 Refitting is a reversal of removal, but tighten the nuts and bolts to the specified torque. Make sure that the pivot bolts are located with their heads facing each other. Fit a new split pin to the balljoint nut. Where necessary, tighten the nut further until the split pin hole is aligned with the serrations on the nut. **Note:** *The left- and right-hand upper control arms are different and must not be interchanged. The left-hand arm is marked ML or MLG, and the right-hand arm is marked MR or MRG.* Have the front wheel alignment checked and adjusted at the earliest opportunity.

Lower control arm

Removal

11 Apply the handbrake, then loosen the wheel nuts on the relevant wheel and jack up the front of the vehicle. Support the vehicle on axle stands (see *Jacking and Vehicle Support*). Remove the roadwheel.

12 Disconnect the front anti-roll bar from the lower control arm with reference to Section 7.

13 Unscrew and remove the bolt securing the shock absorber lower fork to the lower control arm, noting that its head is facing the front of the vehicle.

14 Unscrew the bolts securing the radius arm to the lower control arm.

15 Extract the split pin, then unscrew the nut securing the lower control arm to the hub carrier until it is flush with the end of the balljoint stud.

16 Using a balljoint removal tool, separate the lower control arm from the bottom of the hub carrier. Unscrew and remove the nut.

17 Unscrew and remove the pivot bolt from the inner end of the lower control arm, noting that its head is facing the front of the vehicle **(see illustration)** . Withdraw the lower control arm.

Overhaul

18 Check the inner pivot and shock absorber fork rubber bushes for excessive wear. The bushes may be renewed separately, however a press is required and the work should be carried out by a Rover dealer or suitably-equipped garage. After installation the edges of the bush outer casing must be flush with the lower control arm.

Refitting

19 Refitting is a reversal of the removal procedure, but tighten the nuts and bolts to the specified torque. **Note:** *The left- and right-hand lower control arms are different due to the position of the anti-roll bar mounting on the rear of the arm.* Have the front wheel alignment checked and adjusted at the earliest opportunity.

---

6 Front suspension radius rod - removal and refitting

Removal

1 Apply the handbrake, then loosen the wheel nuts on the relevant wheel and jack up the front of the vehicle. Support the vehicle on axle stands (see *Jacking and Vehicle Support*). Remove the roadwheel.

2 Remove the plug from the undershield for access to the front of the radius rod.

3 Unscrew and remove the nut from the front end of the radius rod, and recover the washer and rubber bush. Note which way round the washer and bush are fitted, and keep the bush identified for position.

4 Unbolt the radius rod from the lower control arm, then withdraw it rearwards and recover the sleeve, rubber bush and washer noting which way round they are fitted. Check carefully if a shim is fitted behind the rear washer as the caster angle is determined by this shim. It is permitted to fit a maximum of two shims.

5 Examine the radius rod for damage. Check the rubber bushes for excessive wear and deterioration and obtain new ones if necessary.

Refitting

6 Refitting is a reversal of removal, but tighten the mounting bolts and nut to the specified torque. Make sure that any shims removed are refitted in the same positions. Note that the two rubber bushes are different but they should be marked to indicate their correct fitment. The front bush is thicker than the rear

bush. The smaller diameter ends of the bushes must face the convex sides of the washers. Have the front wheel alignment checked and adjusted at the earliest opportunity.

---

7 Front suspension anti-roll bar - removal and refitting

Removal

1 Apply the handbrake, then loosen the wheel nuts on both front wheels and jack up the front of the vehicle. Support the vehicle on axle stands (see *Jacking and Vehicle Support*). Remove both front roadwheels.

2 Check if the anti-roll bar is marked with a dab paint to indicate the rear-facing side. If necessary, make a mark since the bar is symmetrical and can easily be refitted the wrong way round.

3 Unscrew the bolts securing the anti-roll bar to the subframe. Recover the clamps **(see illustration)**.

4 Working on one side at a time, unscrew the nut from the top of the bolt securing the anti-roll bar to the lower control arm. Remove the washer and rubber then withdraw the bolt downwards and recover the remaining components noting the location of the rubbers, spacers and washers.

5 Remove the anti-roll bar from under the vehicle.

6 Note the positions of the rubbers then pull them from the anti-roll bar.

7 Check the anti-roll bar and mounting components for damage and wear and renew as necessary.

Refitting

8 Refitting is a reversal of removal, but make sure that the paint mark on the anti-roll bar is facing rearwards, and that the rubbers, spacers and washers are fitted in their correct positions as noted during removal. The washers must be fitted with the convex sides contacting the rubbers, and the end mounting bolts must be fitted with their heads facing downwards. Tighten the nuts and bolts to the specified torque.

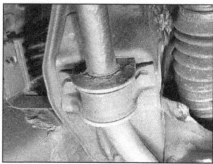

7.3 Front anti-roll bar clamp and bolts

8.5 Removing the cap from the rear hub

8 Rear hub and bearings - checking and renewal

Checking

1 Chock the front wheels then jack up the rear of the vehicle and support on axle stands (see *Jacking and Vehicle Support*). Remove the relevant rear wheel. Release the handbrake.

2 Wear in the rear hub bearings can be checked by measuring the amount of side play present. To do this, a dial gauge should be fixed so that its probe is in contact with the outer face of the hub. Attempt to move the hub in and out, and check that the amount of play is within the tolerances given in the Specifications. Excessive play indicates wear in the bearings, and in this case the complete hub must be renewed. It is not possible to renew the bearings separately as the outer races are formed on the hub itself.

Removal

3 Remove the rear brake caliper and mounting bracket with reference to Chapter 9, however do not disconnect the flexible hydraulic hose. Unbolt the hose mounting bracket and support the caliper to one side.

4 Remove the rear brake disc as described in Chapter 9.

5 Using a screwdriver or small chisel, remove the cap from the rear hub **(see illustration)**.

6 Unstake the hub retaining nut, then unscrew the nut and remove the thrust washer.

Caution: Take care, the nut is very tight!

7 Withdraw the rear hub from the stub axle.

8 Examine the hub nut and renew it if the staking has rendered it unsuitable for further use.

Refitting

9 Thoroughly clean the stub axle, then slide the hub assembly into position.

10 Fit the thrust washer, then refit the nut and tighten to the specified torque.

11 Check that the hub spins freely, then stake the edge of the nut into the groove in the stub axle.

12 Refit the hub cap by lightly tapping it around the edge until it is seated.

13 Refit the brake disc and brake caliper with reference to Chapter 9. Refit the hose mounting bracket and tighten the bolts.

14 Refit the wheel, apply the handbrake and lower the vehicle to the ground.

9 Rear hub carrier - removal, overhaul and refitting

Removal

1 Chock the front wheels then jack up the rear of the vehicle and support on axle stands (see *Jacking and Vehicle Support*). Remove both rear wheels. Release the handbrake.

2 Remove the rear hub (see Section 8).

3 Unbolt the splash guard from the rear hub carrier.

4 Support the weight of the rear hub carrier using a trolley jack.

5 Unscrew and remove the rear shock absorber/coil spring assembly lower mounting bolt, noting that its head is facing the rear of the vehicle.

6 Unscrew and remove the through-bolt securing the outer ends of the lower arms to the bottom of the hub carrier. Note that the bolt head faces the front of the vehicle.

7 Unscrew and remove the bolts securing the trailing arm to the hub carrier.

8 Unbolt the protector cover from the rear suspension upper balljoint **(see illustration)**.

9 Extract the split pin and unscrew the nut from the balljoint stud.

10 Using a balljoint separator tool, disconnect the balljoint from the top of the hub carrier. Withdraw the hub carrier from under the vehicle.

Overhaul

11 Check the shock absorber/coil spring assembly lower rubber mounting bush for wear and damage. The bush may be renewed separately, however a press is required. If necessary, have the work carried out by a Rover dealer or suitably-equipped garage. It will be necessary to press out the studs at the bottom of the hub carrier before pressing out the bush.

10.4 Rear shock absorber/coil spring assembly upper mounting nuts viewed from inside the luggage compartment

9.8 Removing the protector cover from the rear suspension upper balljoint

Refitting

12 Refitting is a reversal or removal, but tighten the mounting nuts and bolts to the specified torque. Before tightening the lower arm outer through-bolt, raise the rear suspension using a trolley jack until the weight of the vehicle is supported.

10 Rear shock absorber/coil spring assembly - removal, overhaul and refitting

Removal

1 Chock the front wheels then jack up the rear of the vehicle and support on axle stands (see *Jacking and Vehicle Support*). Remove the relevant rear wheel. Release the handbrake.

2 Support the rear hub carrier with a trolley jack positioned beneath the rear of the trailing arm. Do not raise the vehicle off the axle stands.

3 Remove the rear seat as described in Chapter 11.

4 Unscrew and remove the shock absorber/coil spring assembly upper mounting nuts **(see illustration)**.

5 Unscrew and remove the shock absorber/coil spring assembly lower mounting bolt, noting that its head is facing the rear of the vehicle **(see illustration)**.

6 Lower the rear shock absorber/coil spring assembly from the body turret and withdraw from the vehicle.

10.5 The rear shock absorber/coil spring assembly lower mounting bolt

Overhaul

Note: *Suitable coil spring compressor tools will be required for this operation.*

7 With the assembly on the bench, check the shock absorber for leaking fluid, dents, cracks or other obvious damage. Check the coil spring for chips or cracks which could cause premature failure and inspect the spring seats for hardness or general deterioration.

8 Clamp the lower end of the shock absorber assembly in a vice fitted with jaw protectors.

9 Fit spring compressors to the spring, and compress the spring until there is no pressure on the upper mounting and the central nut is raised from the washer.

 Warning! Use only purpose-made spring compressor tools and follow the manufacturer's instructions.

10 Mark the relationship of the shock absorber assembly components to ensure correct reassembly. As the components are removed, lay them out in order to ensure correct refitting.

11 Unscrew the self-locking central nut from the top of the shock absorber assembly while holding the shaft stationary with an Allen key.

12 Remove the washer, upper mounting rubber, collar, mounting plate and seal, lower mounting rubber, and upper spring seat.

13 Remove the coil spring (with compressors fitted), followed by the dust cover, stop plate, bump stop (note which way round it is fitted) and lower spring seat. If the compressors are to be left in position on the coil spring, put the spring in a safe place away from the work area as a precaution.

14 With the shock absorber assembly now dismantled, examine all the components for wear and damage. Check the rubber components for deterioration. Examine the shock absorber for damage and signs of fluid leakage, and check the piston rod for pitting along its entire length. While holding it in an upright position, test the operation of the shock absorber by moving the rod through a full stroke, and then through short strokes of 50 to 100 mm. In both cases, the resistance felt should be smooth and continuous. If the resistance is jerky, or uneven, or if there is any visible sign of wear or damage to the shock absorber, renewal is necessary.

 Warning: The shock absorber is filled with nitrogen gas and oil at high pressure. To ensure safe disposal, the pressure should be released by drilling a 2.0 mm diameter hole in the shock absorber body near its base.

15 Renew the coil spring if it is damaged or distorted.

16 To reassemble the shock absorber, first extend the piston rod as far as it will go and locate the lower spring seat.

17 Fit the bump stop, stop plate and dust cover onto the piston rod, making sure that the bump stop is the correct way round (ie largest diameter uppermost).

18 Ensure that the coil spring is compressed sufficiently to enable the upper mounting components to be fitted, then fit the spring over the piston rod, ensuring that the lower end of the spring is correctly located on the lower spring seat.

19 Locate the upper spring seat on the coil spring, followed by the lower mounting rubber, mounting plate, collar, upper mounting rubber and seal, washer and nut. Before tightening the nut position the components with the previously made marks aligned. Where new components are being fitted, transfer the marks from the old components.

20 Tighten the self-locking nut to the specified torque while holding the piston rod with an Allen key.

21 Release the compressors while guiding the spring ends onto the seats.

22 Remove the assembly from the vice.

Refitting

23 Manoeuvre the shock absorber assembly into position under the wheel arch, passing the mounting studs through the holes in the body turret and locating the lower end over the bottom of the hub carrier. Refit the upper mounting nuts loosely, but do not fully tighten them at this stage. The welded nut on the lower end of the assembly must face the front of the vehicle.

24 Insert the lower mounting bolt loosely.

25 Raise the trolley jack to take the weight of the rear of the vehicle, then tighten the upper mounting nuts and lower mounting bolt to the specified torque. Lower the vehicle onto the axle stands.

26 Refit the rear seat (see Chapter 11).

27 Refit the rear wheel, then apply the handbrake and lower the vehicle to the ground.

---

11 Rear suspension upper and lower control arms - removal, overhaul and refitting

Upper arm

Removal

1 Chock the front wheels then jack up the rear of the vehicle and support on axle stands (see *Jacking and Vehicle Support*). Remove the relevant rear wheel.

2 Unbolt the protector cover from the upper balljoint.

3 Extract the split pin and unscrew the nut from the balljoint stud.

4 Using a balljoint separator tool, disconnect the balljoint from the top of the hub carrier.

5 Unscrew and remove the inner mounting bolts and withdraw the upper arm from the body **(see illustration)**.

Overhaul

6 If the inner pivot bush is worn, have the old bush pressed out and a new one fitted by a Rover dealer or suitably-equipped garage.

7 Check the outer balljoint for excessive wear. If evident, renew the complete upper arm.

8 Check the rubber dust cover for damage and splits. If evident, the cover can be renewed separately. Prise off the circlip and remove the old dust cover, then clean the seating and fit the new cover. Secure with the new circlip.

Refitting

9 Refitting is a reversal of removal, but tighten the balljoint nut and inner mounting bolts to the specified torque. Fit a new split pin to the balljoint nut. Where necessary, tighten the nut further until the split pin hole is aligned with the serrations on the nut. **Note:** *The left- and right-hand upper control arms are different and must not be interchanged. The left-hand arm is marked L, and the right-hand arm is marked R.* Have the rear wheel alignment checked and adjusted at the earliest opportunity.

Lower arms

Removal

10 Chock the front wheels then jack up the rear of the vehicle and support on axle stands (see *Jacking and Vehicle Support*). Remove the relevant rear wheel.

11 Unscrew and remove the through-bolt securing the outer ends of the lower arms to the bottom of the hub carrier. Note that the bolt head faces the front of the vehicle.

12 Detach the handbrake cable from the lower arm with reference to Chapter 9.

13 If removing the rear lower arm, mark the position of the bolt head in relation to the bracket in order to retain the rear wheel toe setting.

14 Unscrew and remove the inner pivot bolts and withdraw the lower arms.

Overhaul

15 Check the bushes in the lower arms for damage and excessive wear. If evident, renew the arm complete since it is not possible to renew the bushes separately.

Refitting

16 Refitting is a reversal of removal, but use a trolley jack to raise the rear suspension so that the weight of the vehicle is supported

11.5 Rear suspension upper control arm inner mounting bolts

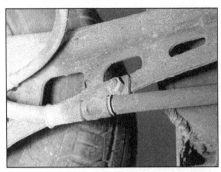

12.2 Handbrake cable support bracket on the rear suspension trailing arm

before tightening the lower arm mounting bolts to the specified torque. Make sure that the rear lower arm inner pivot bolt is refitted with the previously made marks aligned in order to retain the rear wheel toe setting. The position of the cam on the bolt should be the same on each side of the vehicle. Have the rear wheel alignment checked and adjusted at the earliest opportunity.

12 Rear suspension trailing arm - removal, overhaul and refitting

Removal

1 Chock the front wheels then jack up the rear of the vehicle and support on axle stands (see *Jacking and Vehicle Support*). Remove the relevant rear wheel.
2 Unbolt the brake flexible hydraulic hose bracket and handbrake cable support bracket from the rear suspension trailing arm **(see illustration)**.
3 Unbolt the anti-roll bar link from the trailing arm.
4 Unscrew and remove the bolts securing the trailing arm to the hub carrier.
5 Unbolt the front mounting bracket from the underbody, and withdraw the trailing arm from under the vehicle **(see illustration)**.
6 Unscrew and remove the front pivot bolt and remove the trailing arm from the front bracket. Note that the bolt head faces the outside of the vehicle.

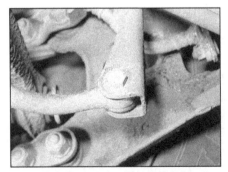

13.6 Rear anti-roll bar link joint

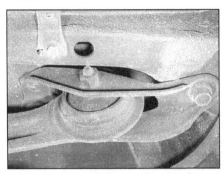

12.5 Rear suspension trailing arm front mounting on the underbody

Overhaul

7 Check the bushes in the trailing arm for damage and excessive wear. If evident, renew the arm complete since it is not possible to renew the bushes separately.

Refitting

8 Refitting is a reversal of removal but tighten the bolts to the specified torque. The front pivot bolt should be inserted loose initially, then fully tightened with the weight of the vehicle supported on the rear suspension.

13 Rear suspension anti-roll bar - removal and refitting

Removal

1 Chock the front wheels then jack up the rear of the vehicle and support on axle stands (see *Jacking and Vehicle Support*). Remove both rear wheels.
2 Unscrew and remove the bolts securing the tops of the anti-roll bar links to the rear trailing arms. Note the location of the washers, rubbers and sleeve.
3 Mark the top of the anti-roll bar with a dab of paint as an aid to refitting.
4 Unscrew the bolts securing the anti-roll bar to the mounting brackets. Recover the clamps.
5 Remove the anti-roll bar from under the vehicle.
6 Unscrew and remove the bolts and remove the links from the anti-roll bar **(see illustration)**.
7 Note the positions of the rubbers then pull them from the anti-roll bar.
8 Check the anti-roll bar and mounting components for damage and wear and renew as necessary.

Refitting

9 Refitting is a reversal of removal, but make sure that the rubbers and washers are fitted in their correct positions as noted during removal. Delay fully tightening the mounting bolts until the full weight of the vehicle is on the rear suspension. Tighten the nuts and bolts to the specified torque.

14 Steering wheel - removal and refitting

Models without airbag

Removal

1 Disconnect the battery negative lead.
2 Position the steering wheel with the front wheels pointing straight-ahead.
3 Insert the ignition key and turn it to the accessories position to release the steering lock.
4 Using a screwdriver, prise the badge from the centre of the steering wheel.
5 Mark the steering wheel hub in relation to the inner column.
6 Using a socket unscrew and remove the steering wheel retaining nut.
7 Ease the steering wheel off the column splines by rocking it back and forth.

Refitting

8 Refitting is a reversal of removal, but note the following:
 a) Ensure that the direction indicator switch is in the central (cancelled/off) position, and make sure that the slots in the steering wheel engage with the tabs on the switch sleeve as the wheel is refitted.
 b) Align the marks made on the wheel and the steering column shaft before removal.
 c) Tighten the securing nut to the specified torque.
 d) If necessary, the position of the steering wheel on the column shaft splines can be altered in order to centralise it (ensure that the front roadwheels are pointing in the straight-ahead position).

Models with airbag

⚠ **Warning: Refer to the precautions given in Chapter 12 before proceeding, noting that several modifications have been made to the SRS system. Before commencing work, disconnect the negative and positive cables from the battery, and wait ten minutes. Take great care not to drop the steering wheel centre pad, or to allow objects to impact the steering wheel centre pad, during this procedure.**

Removal

9 Ensure that the ignition is switched off and the front wheel in the straight-ahead position, then disconnect the battery negative lead. *Wait for ten minutes before carrying out any further work.*
10 On later models only (from VIN 144845) carry out the procedure in this paragraph. Remove the screws and withdraw the access panel from the rear of the steering wheel. Remove the short connector from the inside of the access panel. Unplug the airbag module-to-cable reel connector and plug the short connector into the airbag module side of this connector to disable the airbag module.

14.11 Removing the access panels from each side of the steering wheel rear cover

11 Prise out the access panels from each side of the steering wheel rear cover **(see illustration)**.

12 Using a special Torx bit, unscrew and remove the left-hand side Torx bolt retaining the airbag module to the steering wheel. The removal of this bolt will automatically disable the airbag **(see illustration)**.

13 Unscrew and remove the right-hand side Torx bolt.

14 Withdraw the module from the steering wheel, then pull out the red connector locks and disconnect the wiring from the slip ring and airbag assembly **(see illustrations)**. The slip ring connector locates through a hole in the steering wheel. Where necessary, also disconnect the cruise control wiring. **Take care not to drop the airbag module, and do not attempt to dismantle it - place the module in a safe area away from children.**

14.12 Removing the air bag Torx bolts from the steering wheel

Check the condition of the connector locks and renew them if necessary.

15 Mark the steering wheel hub in relation to the inner column.

16 Using a socket unscrew and remove the steering wheel retaining nut **(see illustration)**.

17 Ease the steering wheel off the column splines by rocking it back and forth.

Caution: While the steering wheel is removed, DO NOT turn the inner steering column, otherwise the airbag reel may be damaged!

Refitting

18 Refitting is a reversal of removal, but note the following:

a) *Ensure that the direction indicator switch is in the central (cancelled/off) position, and make sure that the slots in the steering wheel engage with the tabs on*

the switch sleeve as the wheel is refitted. Align the pins on the airbag reel/slip ring with the holes in the steering wheel.

b) *Align the marks made on the wheel and the inner steering column before removal.*

c) *Tighten the securing nut to the specified torque* **(see illustration)**.

d) *If the steering wheel is not centralised with the front wheels straight-ahead, adjust the position of the track rod ends with reference to Section 21.*

e) *After refitting the steering wheel, check the SRS system by switching on the ignition. The SRS indicator light should illuminate for approximately 6 seconds then go out, and the LED self-diagnosis light should blink once.*

---

15 Steering column - removal, inspection and refitting

 Warning: On models equipped with an airbag system, follow the safety recommendations given in Chapter 12 to prevent personal injury.

Removal

1 Disconnect the battery negative lead.

2 Remove the steering wheel as described in Section 14.

3 Remove the facia lower trim panel with reference to Chapter 11.

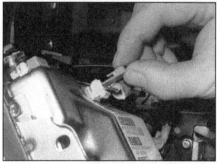

14.14a Pull out the red connector lock . . .

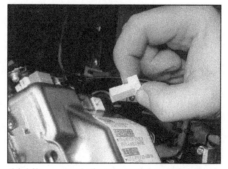

14.14b . . . and disconnect the wiring from the airbag assembly

14.14c Pull out the red connector lock . . .

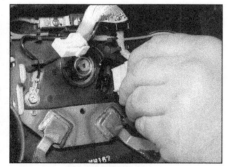

14.14d . . . and disconnect the wiring from the slip ring

14.16 The steering wheel retaining nut

14.18 Tightening the steering wheel nut with a torque wrench

15.4a Removing the lower shroud from the steering column

15.4b Removing the upper shroud from the steering column

4 Remove the screws, and withdraw the upper and lower shrouds from the steering column **(see illustrations)**.
5 Extract the connector locks, and disconnect the wiring from the rear of the slip ring or airbag reel. Check the condition of the connector locks and renew them if necessary.
6 Remove the screws and withdraw the slip ring or airbag reel from the top of the steering column. Also remove the cancelling sleeve.
7 Disconnect the wiring, then remove the screws and withdraw the combination switch from the top of the column.
8 Remove the screws and clips and withdraw the steering column lower joint cover from the bulkhead **(see illustrations)**.
9 Unscrew and remove the clamp bolts from the universal joint, then slide the joint upwards onto the inner column **(see illustration)**. Note that the inner column and steering gear pinion

shaft are designed so that the clamp bolts can only be inserted with the universal joint correctly positioned on the splines.
10 Unscrew the bolts and remove the lower mounting clamp **(see illustration)**.
11 Unscrew the upper mounting nuts and withdraw the steering column from inside the vehicle **(see illustration)**.
12 Slide the universal joint from the bottom of the inner column.

Inspection

13 Examine the column and mountings for signs of damage and deformation, and renew as necessary.
14 Check the steering shaft for free play in the column bearings, and check the universal joint for wear. If any damage or excessive wear is evident, the column must be renewed as an assembly.

15 Check the lower mounting collar on the column and renew it if necessary.
16 Check the tilt mechanism for wear and damage and renew if necessary.

Refitting

17 Slide the universal joint onto the bottom of the inner column, making sure that the bolt hole is aligned with the flat on the column. Insert the clamp bolt loosely.
18 Inside the vehicle, locate the bottom of the universal joint on the steering gear pinion shaft making sure that the bolt hole is aligned with the flat on the shaft. Insert the clamp bolt loosely.
19 Locate the steering column on the upper mounting studs, and loosely fit the mounting nuts.
20 Refit the lower mounting clamp, and insert the bolts loosely.
21 Tighten the upper and lower mounting nuts/bolts to the specified torque.
22 Tighten the universal joint clamp bolts to the specified torque.
23 Refit the lower joint cover and tighten the screws.
24 Refit the combination switch and tighten the screws. Reconnect the wiring.
25 Refit the cancelling sleeve and airbag reel/slip ring and tighten the screws.
26 Reconnect the wiring to the slip ring or airbag reel and fit new connector locks.
27 Refit the steering column shrouds.
28 Refit the facia lower trim panel with reference to Chapter 11.
29 Refit the steering wheel with reference to Section 14.
30 Reconnect the battery negative lead.

16 Ignition switch/steering column lock - removal and refitting

Removal

Note: *New shear-bolts must be used when refitting the lock assembly.*
1 Remove the steering column as described in Section 15.
2 Remove the screws and withdraw the cover and switch from the steering lock **(see illustration)**.

15.8a Remove the clips . . .

15.8b . . . and remove the steering column lower joint cover from the bulkhead

15.9 Steering inner column universal joint

15.10 Steering column lower mounting clamp bolts

15.11 Steering column upper mounting nuts

16.2 Ignition switch and cover retaining screws

3 To remove the lock assembly, drill out and remove the two shear-bolts and withdraw the lock and clamp from the steering column.

Refitting

4 Refitting is a reversal of removal, but use new shear-bolts and tighten the screws until the heads break off **(see illustration)**.

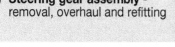

17 Steering gear assembly - removal, overhaul and refitting

Warning: On models equipped with an airbag system, follow the safety recommendations given in Chapter 12 to prevent personal injury.
Note: *A balljoint separator tool will be required for this operation.*

Removal

1 Apply the handbrake, then jack up the front of the vehicle and support securely on axle stands (see *Jacking and Vehicle Support*).
2 Move the steering wheel so that the front wheels are pointing in the straight-ahead position, then remove both front roadwheels. On models fitted with an airbag, lock the steering wheel in the straight-ahead position otherwise the airbag slip ring may be damaged on refitting.
3 Working beneath the facia, remove the screws and clips and withdraw the steering column lower joint cover from the bulkhead.
4 Mark the universal joint and steering gear pinion shaft in relation to each other, then unscrew and remove the both clamp bolts securing the universal joint to the pinion shaft and column. Slide the joint upwards as far as possible.
5 In the engine compartment, position a suitable container beneath the fluid feed hose on the power steering pump then loosen the clip and disconnect the hose. Allow the fluid to drain into the container. On later models, remove the evaporative emission carbon canister (see Chapter 4B) and disconnect the fluid lines at the steering gear.
6 Unbolt the cover from under the steering gear, then clean the area around the pressure and return lines.

16.4 Fitting new shear-bolts to the ignition/steering lock

7 Move the container beneath the steering gear, then identify the position of each hydraulic fluid line. Unscrew the union nuts and disconnect the pressure and return lines. Tape over or plug the ends of the lines to prevent entry of dust and dirt.
8 Disconnect the track rod ends from the hub carriers with reference to Section 21. Also remove the track rod ends from the track rods.
9 Remove the exhaust front pipe with reference to Chapter 4. On automatic transmission models, remove the selector cable from the side of the transmission.
10 Unscrew the steering gear mounting bolts and air transfer hose clamp.
11 Manoeuvre the steering gear out from under the vehicle, taking care not to damage the surrounding components.

Overhaul

12 Examine the assembly for obvious signs of wear or damage.
13 Check the rack for smooth operation through its full stroke of movement, and check that there is no binding or free play.
14 Check the track-rods for deformation and cracks.
15 Check the condition of the steering gear rubber gaiters, and renew if necessary with reference to Section 18.
16 Examine the track-rod ends for wear or damage, and renew if necessary with reference to Section 21.
17 No overhaul of the power steering gear is possible by the home mechanic, and if worn or damaged, the complete assembly (including track-rods) must be renewed.

17.19 The arrow on the steering gear mounting clamp must face forwards

Refitting

18 Before refitting the steering gear, make sure that it is centralised by turning the pinion shaft fully anti-clockwise then counting the number of turns necessary to the opposite lock. Finally turn the shaft back half way.
19 Manoeuvre the steering gear into position and insert the pinion shaft through the hole in the bulkhead. Refit the mounting bolts and air transfer hose clamp making sure that the arrow on the clamp faces forwards **(see illustration)**. Tighten the bolts to the specified torque.
20 Refit the exhaust front pipe together with a new gasket with reference to Chapter 4A. On automatic transmission models, refit the selector cable.
21 Refit and reconnect the track rod ends to the hub carriers with reference to Section 21.
22 Reconnect the hydraulic pressure and return lines to the steering gear and tighten the union nuts to the specified torques.
23 Refit the cover beneath the steering gear hydraulic lines. Where removed, refit the evaporative emission carbon canister with reference to Chapter 4B.
24 Reconnect the hose to the power steering pump and refit the clip.
25 Inside the vehicle, slide the universal joint onto the pinion shaft making sure that the bolt holes are aligned with the flats on the inner column and pinion shaft. Insert the bolts and tighten to the specified torque.
26 Refit the steering column lower joint cover.
27 Lower the vehicle to the ground, then fill the hydraulic system with the specified fluid and bleed as described in Section 19.

18 Steering gear rubber gaiters - renewal

Note: *New gaiter retaining clips should be used on refitting.*

1 Remove the relevant track-rod end as described in Section 21.
2 If not already done, unscrew the track-rod end locknut from the end of the track-rod.
3 Note the fitted position of the gaiter on the track-rod, then release the gaiter securing clips. Slide the gaiter from the steering gear, and off the end of the track-rod.
4 Thoroughly clean the track-rod and the steering gear housing, then scrape off all the grease from the old gaiter, and apply it to the track rod inner balljoint. If grease has been lost, apply new grease to the balljoint. Smear a little silicone grease onto the gaiter contact surfaces on the steering gear and track rod.
5 Slide the new gaiter onto the track-rod, and locate it on the steering gear housing. Locate the outer end of the gaiter in the special indentation on the track rod. Secure the gaiter in position with new retaining clips.
6 Screw the track-rod end locknut onto the track-rod.
7 Refit the track rod end with reference to Section 21.

19.5 Topping up the power steering pump fluid reservoir

19 Power steering hydraulic system - bleeding

General

1 The following symptoms indicate that there is air present in the power steering hydraulic system:

a) Generation of air bubbles in fluid reservoir.
b) Clicking noises from power steering pump.
c) Excessive buzzing from power steering pump.

2 Before bleeding the hydraulic system check that there are no fluid leaks from the pressure and return hoses. Also check the cooling tube located at the front of the radiator and the interconnecting hoses for possible leaks.

3 Note that when the vehicle is stationary, or while moving the steering wheel slowly, a hissing noise may be produced in the steering gear or the fluid pump. This noise is inherent in the system, and does not indicate any cause for concern.

Bleeding

4 Following any operation in which the power steering fluid lines have been disconnected, the power steering system must be bled to remove all air and obtain proper steering performance.

5 With the front wheels in the straight-ahead position, check the fluid level in the reservoir located on the left-hand side of the engine compartment, and if necessary top-up to the relevant level mark **(see illustration)**

6 Disconnect the ignition coil HT lead from the distributor and connect it to earth with a bridging wire. Crank the engine for 5 seconds in order to prime the power steering pump, then top up the fluid level.

7 Turn the steering to full right-hand lock, then crank the engine again for 5 seconds. Top up the fluid level.

8 Turn the steering to full left-hand lock, and crank the engine again for 5 seconds. Top up the fluid level.

9 Reconnect the ignition coil HT lead, then start the engine and allow it to run at idle speed. Have an assistant turn the steering from lock-to-lock, and observe the fluid level. If the fluid level drops, add more fluid, and repeat the operation until the fluid level no longer drops and there are no air bubbles in the fluid.

10 Once the fluid level has stabilised and all air has been bled from the system, switch off the engine. Make sure the filler cap is securely fitted to the reservoir.

20 Power steering pump and speed sensor - removal, refitting and drivebelt adjustment

Power steering pump

Removal

Note: New copper washers must be fitted when reconnecting the high-pressure fluid hose union to the pump.

1 In the engine compartment, position a suitable container beneath the fluid feed hose on the power steering pump then loosen the clip and disconnect the hose. Allow the fluid to drain into the container. Plug the end of the hose to prevent entry of dust and dirt.

2 Unscrew and remove the union bolt securing the pressure hose to the top of the power steering pump. Recover the sealing washers (note some models have a single O-ring with a union bolted to the top of the pump) **(see illustration)**. Tape over the end of the hose to prevent entry of dust and dirt.

3 Loosen the pump upper mounting bolt and lower mounting nut.

20.2 Unbolting the union from the top of the power steering pump

4 Back off the adjustment bolt to release the tension on the drivebelt, then slip the drivebelt from the pump pulley.

5 Remove the upper mounting bolt then remove the lower mounting nut. Slide the pump from the lower adjustment bolt, and withdraw it from the engine compartment **(see illustrations)**. To prevent fluid spilling onto the paintwork, wrap the pump is cloth rag before removing it from the engine.

6 Tape over or plug the fluid apertures in the pump to prevent entry of dust and dirt. If necessary, unbolt the adjustment bolt from the bracket **(see illustration)**.

Refitting and drivebelt adjustment

7 Refitting is a reversal of removal but use new copper washers (or O-ring if fitted) when reconnecting the high-pressure fluid hose union, tighten the union bolt(s) to the specified torque, tension the drivebelt as described in the following paragraph, and bleed the hydraulic system as described in Section 19 of this Chapter.

8 To adjust the tension of the power steering pump drivebelt, slightly loosen the pump upper and lower mounting bolts then tighten the adjustment bolt until the deflection midway between the pulleys under firm thumb pressure is as given in the Specifications. Tighten the mounting bolts after making the adjustment **(see illustration)**.

Speed sensor

Removal

9 The power steering speed sensor is mounted on top of the transmission and consists of a bi-

20.5a Removing the power steering pump upper mounting bolt

20.5b Removing the power steering pump from the lower adjustment bolt

20.6 Power steering pump adjustment bolt located on the bracket

20.8 Adjusting the tension of the power steering pump drivebelt

rotor pump fitted in the power steering hydraulic circuit. The pump effectively regulates the assistance provided to the steering according to the speed of the vehicle. The speedometer speed sensor is mounted on top of the power steering speed sensor.

10 To remove the sensor first unscrew the nut and bolt and remove the mounting stay from the transmission.
11 Disconnect the vehicle speed sensor wiring from the sensor.
12 Unscrew the mounting bolt and withdraw the sensor from the transmission.
13 Identify the hoses for position, then clamp them using hose clamps.
14 Loosen the clips and disconnect the hoses. Be prepared for some loss of fluid.

Refitting

15 Refitting is a reversal of removal, but bleed the hydraulic system as described in Section 19.

21 Track-rod end - removal and refitting

Note: *A balljoint separator tool will be required for this operation.*

Removal

1 Apply the handbrake, then jack up the front of the vehicle and support on axle stands (see *Jacking and Vehicle Support*). Remove the relevant front roadwheel.

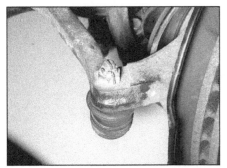

21.2 Track rod end-to-steering arm balljoint

2 Remove the split pin, then partially unscrew the castellated nut securing the track-rod end to the steering arm on the hub carrier **(see illustration)**. Using a balljoint separator tool, separate the track-rod end from the hub carrier. Remove the nut. Discard the split pin - a new one must be used on refitting.
3 Counterhold the track-rod end using the flats provided, then loosen the track-rod end locknut **(see illustration)**.
4 Counting the exact number of turns required to do so, unscrew the track-rod end from the track-rod.

Refitting

5 Carefully clean the track-rod end and the track-rod threads. If the balljoint boot is damaged it can be renewed separately by removing the circlip.
6 Renew the track-rod end if the movement of the balljoint is either sloppy or too stiff. Also check for other signs of damage such as worn threads.
7 Screw the track-rod end onto the track-rod by the number of turns noted before removal, then tighten the track-rod end locknut.
8 Ensure that the balljoint taper is clean, then engage the taper with the steering arm on the hub carrier.
9 Refit the castellated nut, and tighten to the specified torque.
10 If necessary, tighten the nut further until the nearest serrations in the nut are aligned with the split pin hole in the balljoint stud, then fit a new split pin.
11 Refit the roadwheel, and lower the vehicle to the ground.
12 Have the front wheel alignment checked and adjusted at the earliest opportunity.

22 Wheel alignment and steering angles - general information

Wheel alignment - definitions

1 A vehicle's steering and suspension geometry is defined in four basic settings - all angles are expressed in degrees (toe settings are also expressed as a measurement); the

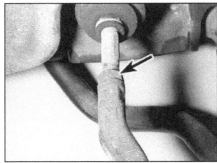

21.3 Track rod end locknut

steering axis is defined as an imaginary line drawn through the axis of the front suspension balljoints, extended where necessary to contact the ground.
2 Camber is the angle between each roadwheel and a vertical line drawn through its centre and tyre contact patch, when viewed from the front or rear of the car. Positive camber is when the roadwheels are tilted outwards from the vertical at the top; negative camber is when they are tilted inwards.
3 Camber is not adjustable, and is given for reference only; while it can be checked using a camber checking gauge, if the figure obtained is significantly different from that specified, the vehicle must be taken for careful checking by a professional, as the fault can only be caused by wear or damage to the body or suspension components.
4 Castor is the angle between the steering axis and a vertical line drawn through each roadwheel centre and tyre contact patch, when viewed from the side of the car. Positive castor is when the steering axis is tilted so that it contacts the ground ahead of the vertical; negative castor is when it contacts the ground behind the vertical.
5 Castor is adjustable by inserting or removing shims to reposition the radius rod at its front mounting. It can be checked using a castor checking gauge.
6 Steering axis inclination/SAI - also known as **kingpin inclination/KPI** - is the angle between the steering axis and a vertical line drawn through each roadwheel centre and tyre contact patch, when viewed from the front or rear of the car. SAI/KPI is not adjustable.
7 Toe is the difference, viewed from above, between lines drawn through the roadwheel centres and the cars centre-line. Toe-in is when the roadwheels point inwards, towards each other at the front, while toe-out is when they splay outwards from each other at the front.
8 The front wheel toe setting is adjusted by screwing the track-rod ends onto or off of the track-rods, to alter the effective length of the track-rod assemblies. Rear wheel toe is adjusted on the lower arm inner mounting bolts. Note that when checking the rear wheel toe setting, the handbrake must be released.

Wheel alignment - checking

9 Due to the special measuring equipment necessary to check the wheel alignment, and the skill required to use it properly, the checking and adjustment of these settings is best left to a Rover dealer or similar expert. Note that most tyre-fitting shops now possess sophisticated checking equipment.

Chapter 11
Bodywork and fittings

Contents

Degrees of difficulty

Easy, suitable for novice with little experience		Fairly easy, suitable for beginner with some experience		Fairly difficult, suitable for competent DIY mechanic		Difficult, suitable for experienced DIY mechanic		Very difficult, suitable for expert DIY or professional

Specifications

Torque wrench settings	Nm	lbf ft
Bonnet hinges	10	7
Bumper beams	22	16
Bumper mounting nuts	22	16
Door lock	5	4
Door mounting bolts	30	22
Door striker	18	13
Exterior door handle	5	4
Passenger air bag:		
Module mounting bracket and joint bracket nuts	10	7
Air bag mounting nuts	6	4
Seat belts:		
Front inertia reel lower bolt (large)	33	24
Front inertia reel upper bolt (small)	10	7
Front adjustment and pillar mounting bolt	33	24
Stalk to front seat	35	26
Rear stalks	33	24
Rear belt front mounting	33	24
Rear inertia reel large bolt	33	24
Rear inertia reel small bolt	10	7
Seats:		
Front	35	26
Rear (fixed)	10	7
Rear (folding)	22	16
Rear seat side cushions	10	7
Window channel	8	6
Window glass to regulator	6	4
Window regulator	8	6

1 General information

Caution: If the radio/cassette in your vehicle is equipped with an anti-theft system, make sure you have the correct activation code before disconnecting the battery.

The bodyshell is made of pressed-steel sections, and is available only as a four-door Saloon. Most components are welded together, but some use is made of structural adhesives. The front wings are bolted to the main body.

The front and rear body sections incorporate crumple zones and the doors are fitted with side bars. The lower areas of the body and doors are coated with an anti-stone chipping protective material.

Extensive use is made of plastic materials, mainly in the interior, but also in exterior components. The outer sections of the front and rear bumpers are injection-moulded from a synthetic material which is very strong, yet light. Plastic components such as wheel arch liners are fitted to the underside of the vehicle, to improve the body's resistance to corrosion.

2 Maintenance - bodywork and underframe

The general condition of a vehicles bodywork is the one thing that significantly affects its value. Maintenance is easy, but needs to be regular. Neglect, particularly after minor damage, can lead quickly to further deterioration and costly repair bills. It is important also to keep watch on those parts of the vehicle not immediately visible, for instance the underside, inside all the wheelarches, and the lower part of the engine compartment.

The basic maintenance routine for the bodywork is washing - preferably with a lot of water, from a hose. This will remove all the loose solids which may have stuck to the vehicle. It is important to flush these off in such a way as to prevent grit from scratching the finish. The wheel arches and underframe need washing in the same way, to remove any accumulated mud, which will retain moisture and tend to encourage rust. Paradoxically enough, the best time to clean the underframe and wheel arches is in wet weather, when the mud is thoroughly wet and soft. In very wet weather, the underframe is usually cleaned of large accumulations automatically, and this is a good time for inspection.

Periodically, except on vehicles with a wax-based underbody protective coating, it is a good idea to have the whole of the underframe of the vehicle steam-cleaned, engine compartment included, so that a thorough inspection can be carried out to see what minor repairs and renovations are necessary. Steam-cleaning is available at many garages, and is necessary for the removal of the accumulation of oily grime, which sometimes is allowed to become thick in certain areas. If steam-cleaning facilities are not available, there are some excellent grease solvents available which can be brush-applied; the dirt can then be simply hosed off. Note that these methods should not be used on vehicles with wax-based underbody protective coating, or the coating will be removed. Such vehicles should be inspected annually, preferably just prior to Winter, when the underbody should be washed down, and any damage to the wax coating repaired. Ideally, a completely fresh coat should be applied. It would also be worth considering the use of such wax-based protection for injection into door panels, sills, box sections, etc, as an additional safeguard against rust damage, where such protection is not provided by the vehicle manufacturer.

After washing paintwork, wipe off with a chamois leather to give an unspotted clear finish. A coat of clear protective wax polish will give added protection against chemical pollutants in the air. If the paintwork sheen has dulled or oxidised, use a cleaner/polisher combination to restore the brilliance of the shine. This requires a little effort, but such dulling is usually caused because regular washing has been neglected. Care needs to be taken with metallic paintwork, as special non-abrasive cleaner/polisher is required to avoid damage to the finish. Always check that the door and ventilator opening drain holes and pipes are completely clear, so that water can be drained out. Brightwork should be treated in the same way as paintwork. Windscreens and windows can be kept clear of the smeary film which often appears, by the use of proprietary glass cleaner. Never use any form of wax or other body or chromium polish on glass.

3 Maintenance - upholstery and carpets

Mats and carpets should be brushed or vacuum-cleaned regularly, to keep them free of grit. If they are badly stained, remove them from the vehicle for scrubbing or sponging, and make quite sure they are dry before refitting. Seats and interior trim panels can be kept clean by wiping with a damp cloth. If they do become stained (which can be more apparent on light-coloured upholstery), use a little liquid detergent and a soft nail brush to scour the grime out of the grain of the material. Do not forget to keep the headlining clean in the same way as the upholstery. When using liquid cleaners inside the vehicle, do not over-wet the surfaces being cleaned. Excessive damp could get into the seams and padded interior, causing stains, offensive odours or even rot.

 If the inside of the vehicle gets wet accidentally, it is worthwhile taking some trouble to dry it out properly, particularly where carpets are involved. Do not leave oil or electric heaters inside the vehicle for this purpose.

4 Minor body damage - repair

Note: *For more detailed information about bodywork repair, Haynes Publishing produce a book by Lindsay Porter called The Car Bodywork Repair Manual. This incorporates information on such aspects as rust treatment, painting and glass-fibre repairs, as well as details on more ambitious repairs involving welding and panel beating.*

Repairs of minor scratches in bodywork

If the scratch is very superficial, and does not penetrate to the metal of the bodywork, repair is very simple. Lightly rub the area of the scratch with a paintwork renovator, or a very fine cutting paste, to remove loose paint from the scratch, and to clear the surrounding bodywork of wax polish. Rinse the area with clean water.

Apply touch-up paint to the scratch using a fine paint brush; continue to apply fine layers of paint until the surface of the paint in the scratch is level with the surrounding paintwork. Allow the new paint at least two weeks to harden, then blend it into the surrounding paintwork by rubbing the scratch area with a paintwork renovator or a very fine cutting paste. Finally, apply wax polish.

Where the scratch has penetrated right through to the metal of the bodywork, causing the metal to rust, a different repair technique is required. Remove any loose rust from the bottom of the scratch with a penknife, then apply rust-inhibiting paint to prevent the formation of rust in the future. Using a rubber or nylon applicator, fill the scratch with bodystopper paste. If required, this paste can be mixed with cellulose thinners to provide a very thin paste which is ideal for filling narrow scratches. Before the stopper-paste in the scratch hardens, wrap a piece of smooth cotton rag around the top of a finger. Dip the finger in cellulose thinners, and quickly sweep it across the surface of the stopper-paste in the scratch; this will ensure that the surface of the stopper-paste is slightly hollowed. The scratch can now be painted over as described earlier in this Section.

Repairs of dents in bodywork

When deep denting of the vehicles bodywork has taken place, the first task is to pull the dent out, until the affected bodywork almost attains its original shape. There is little point in trying to restore the original shape completely, as the metal in the damaged area will have stretched on impact, and cannot be reshaped fully to its original contour. It is better to bring the level of the dent up to a point which is about 3 mm below the level of the surrounding bodywork. In cases where the dent is very shallow anyway, it is not worth trying to pull it out at all. If the underside of the dent is accessible, it can be hammered out gently from behind, using a mallet with a wooden or plastic head. Whilst doing this, hold a suitable block of wood firmly against the outside of the panel, to absorb the impact from the hammer blows and thus prevent a large area of the bodywork from being belled-out.

Should the dent be in a section of the bodywork which has a double skin, or some other factor making it inaccessible from behind, a different technique is called for. Drill several small holes through the metal inside the area - particularly in the deeper section. Then screw long self-tapping screws into the holes, just sufficiently for them to gain a good purchase in the metal. Now the dent can be pulled out by pulling on the protruding heads of the screws with a pair of pliers.

The next stage of the repair is the removal of the paint from the damaged area, and from an inch or so of the surrounding sound bodywork. This is accomplished most easily by using a wire brush or abrasive pad on a power drill, although it can be done just as effectively by hand, using sheets of abrasive paper. To complete the preparation for filling, score the surface of the bare metal with a screwdriver or the tang of a file, or alternatively, drill small holes in the affected area. This will provide a really good key for the filler paste.

To complete the repair, see the Section on filling and respraying.

Repairs of rust holes or gashes in bodywork

Remove all paint from the affected area, and from an inch or so of the surrounding sound bodywork, using an abrasive pad or a wire brush on a power drill. If these are not available, a few sheets of abrasive paper will do the job most effectively. With the paint removed, you will be able to judge the severity of the corrosion, and therefore decide whether to renew the whole panel (if this is possible) or to repair the affected area. New body panels are not as expensive as most people think, and it is often quicker and more satisfactory to fit a new panel than to attempt to repair large areas of corrosion.

Remove all fittings from the affected area, except those which will act as a guide to the original shape of the damaged bodywork (eg headlight shells etc). Then, using tin snips or a hacksaw blade, remove all loose metal and any other metal badly affected by corrosion. Hammer the edges of the hole inwards, in order to create a slight depression for the filler paste.

Wire-brush the affected area to remove the powdery rust from the surface of the remaining metal. Paint the affected area with rust-inhibiting paint, if the back of the rusted area is accessible, treat this also.

Before filling can take place, it will be necessary to block the hole in some way. This can be achieved by the use of aluminium or plastic mesh, or aluminium tape.

Aluminium or plastic mesh, or glass-fibre matting, is probably the best material to use for a large hole. Cut a piece to the approximate size and shape of the hole to be filled, then position it in the hole so that its edges are below the level of the surrounding bodywork. It can be retained in position by several blobs of filler paste around its periphery.

Aluminium tape should be used for small or very narrow holes. Pull a piece off the roll, trim it to the approximate size and shape required, then pull off the backing paper (if used) and stick the tape over the hole; it can be overlapped if the thickness of one piece is insufficient. Burnish down the edges of the tape with the handle of a screwdriver or similar, to ensure that the tape is securely attached to the metal underneath.

Bodywork repairs - filling and respraying

Before using this Section, see the Sections on dent, deep scratch, rust holes and gash repairs.

Many types of bodyfiller are available, but generally speaking, those proprietary kits which contain a tin of filler paste and a tube of resin hardener are best for this type of repair. A wide, flexible plastic or nylon applicator will be found invaluable for imparting a smooth and well-contoured finish to the surface of the filler.

Mix up a little filler on a clean piece of card or board - measure the hardener carefully (follow the makers instructions on the pack), otherwise the filler will set too rapidly or too slowly. Using the applicator, apply the filler paste to the prepared area; draw the applicator across the surface of the filler to achieve the correct contour and to level the surface. As soon as a contour that approximates to the correct one is achieved, stop working the paste - if you carry on too long, the paste will become sticky and begin to pick-up on the applicator. Continue to add thin layers of filler paste at 20-minute intervals, until the level of the filler is just proud of the surrounding bodywork.

Once the filler has hardened, the excess can be removed using a metal plane or file. From then on, progressively-finer grades of abrasive paper should be used, starting with a 40-grade production paper, and finishing with a 400-grade wet-and-dry paper. Always wrap the abrasive paper around a flat rubber, cork, or wooden block - otherwise the surface of the filler will not be completely flat. During the smoothing of the filler surface, the wet-and-

dry paper should be periodically rinsed in water. This will ensure that a very smooth finish is imparted to the filler at the final stage.

At this stage, the dent should be surrounded by a ring of bare metal, which in turn should be encircled by the finely feathered edge of the good paintwork. Rinse the repair area with clean water, until all of the dust produced by the rubbing-down operation has gone.

Spray the whole area with a light coat of primer - this will show up any imperfections in the surface of the filler. Repair these imperfections with fresh filler paste or bodystopper, and once more smooth the surface with abrasive paper. Repeat this spray-and-repair procedure until you are satisfied that the surface of the filler, and the feathered edge of the paintwork, are perfect. Clean the repair area with clean water, and allow to dry fully.

 HAYNES HINT *If bodystopper is used, it can be mixed with cellulose thinners to form a really thin paste which is ideal for filling small holes.*

The repair area is now ready for final spraying. Paint spraying must be carried out in a warm, dry, windless and dust-free atmosphere. This condition can be created artificially if you have access to a large indoor working area, but if you are forced to work in the open, you will have to pick your day very carefully. If you are working indoors, dousing the floor in the work area with water will help to settle the dust which would otherwise be in the atmosphere. If the repair area is confined to one body panel, mask off the surrounding panels; this will help to minimise the effects of a slight mis-match in paint colours. Bodywork fittings (eg chrome strips, door handles etc) will also need to be masked off. Use genuine masking tape, and several thicknesses of newspaper, for the masking operations.

Before commencing to spray, agitate the aerosol can thoroughly, then spray a test area (an old tin, or similar) until the technique is mastered. Cover the repair area with a thick coat of primer; the thickness should be built up using several thin layers of paint, rather than one thick one. Using 400-grade wet-and-dry paper, rub down the surface of the primer until it is really smooth. While doing this, the work area should be thoroughly doused with water, and the wet-and-dry paper periodically rinsed in water. Allow to dry before spraying on more paint.

Spray on the top coat, again building up the thickness by using several thin layers of paint. Start spraying at one edge of the repair area, and then, using a side-to-side motion, work until the whole repair area and about 2 inches of the surrounding original paintwork is covered. Remove all masking material 10 to 15 minutes after spraying on the final coat of paint.

6.3a Unscrew the centre screw . . .

6.3b . . . and remove the clips from under the front of the front bumper

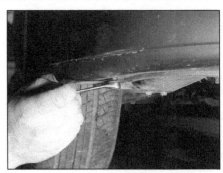

6.4 Removing the shouldered bolts from the front corners of the front bumper

Allow the new paint at least two weeks to harden, then, using a paintwork renovator, or a very fine cutting paste, blend the edges of the paint into the existing paintwork. Finally, apply wax polish.

Plastic components

With the use of more and more plastic body components by the vehicle manufacturers (eg bumpers, spoilers, and in some cases major body panels), rectification of more serious damage to such items has become a matter of either entrusting repair work to a specialist in this field, or renewing complete components. Repair of such damage by the DIY owner is not really feasible, owing to the cost of the equipment and materials required for effecting such repairs. The basic technique involves making a groove along the line of the crack in the plastic, using a rotary burr in a power drill. The damaged part is then welded back together, using a hot-air gun to heat up and fuse a plastic filler rod into the groove. Any excess plastic is then removed, and the area rubbed down to a smooth finish. It is important that a filler rod of the correct plastic is used, as body components can be made of a variety of different types (eg polycarbonate, ABS, polypropylene).

Damage of a less serious nature (abrasions, minor cracks etc) can be repaired by the DIY owner using a two-part epoxy filler repair material. Once mixed in equal proportions, this is used in similar fashion to the bodywork filler used on metal panels. The filler is usually cured in twenty to thirty minutes, ready for sanding and painting.

If the owner is renewing a complete component himself, or if he has repaired it with epoxy filler, he will be left with the problem of finding a suitable paint for finishing which is compatible with the type of plastic used. At one time, the use of a universal paint was not possible, owing to the complex range of plastics encountered in body component applications. Standard paints, generally speaking, will not bond to plastic or rubber satisfactorily. However, it is now possible to obtain a plastic body parts finishing kit which consists of a pre-primer treatment, a primer and coloured top coat. Full instructions are normally supplied with a kit, but basically, the method of use is to first apply the pre-primer to the component concerned, and allow it to dry for up to 30 minutes. Then the primer is applied, and left to dry for about an hour before finally applying the special-coloured top coat. The result is a correctly-coloured component, where the paint will flex with the plastic or rubber, a property that standard paint does not normally possess.

5 Major body damage - repair

Where serious damage has occurred, or large areas need renewal due to neglect, it means that complete new panels will need welding-in, and this is best left to professionals. If the damage is due to impact, it will also be necessary to check completely the alignment of the bodyshell, and this can only be carried

out accurately by a Rover dealer using special jigs. If the body is left misaligned, it is primarily dangerous, as the car will not handle properly, and secondly, as uneven stresses will be imposed on the steering, suspension and possibly transmission, causing abnormal wear, or complete failure, particularly to such items as the tyres.

6 Bumpers - removal and refitting

Front bumper

Removal

1 To improve access, apply the handbrake, then jack up the front of the vehicle and support on axle stands (see *Jacking and Vehicle Support*).
2 Open and support the bonnet.
3 Remove the two clips from under the centre front section of the front bumper. The clips are removed by removing the centre screw and prising out the clip with a screwdriver **(see illustrations)**.
4 Unscrew the shouldered bolts from the lower front corners of the bumper **(see illustration)**.
5 Under the front wings prise out the wheelarch liner as necessary, then remove the mounting screws from the upper rear extensions of the bumper **(see illustration)**.
6 Prise out the vents using a screwdriver, then unscrew the bolts securing the bumper to the front valance **(see illustrations)**.

6.5 Removing the rear mounting bolts from the front bumper

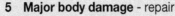

6.6a Prise out the vents . . .

6.6b . . . and unscrew the front bumper mounting bolts

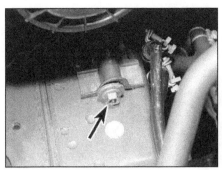

6.7a Nuts securing the front bumper studs

6.7b Remove the expansion tank bracket for access to the front bumper stud mounting nut on the right-hand side

6.8a Removing the front bumper

7 Working in the engine compartment beneath each headlight, unscrew the nuts from the bumper mounting studs. For access to the right-hand side, pull the coolant expansion tank from its mounting and place to one side, then unbolt and remove the bracket. There is no need to drain the cooling system **(see illustrations)**.
8 Withdraw the front bumper from the body taking care not to damage the paintwork. If necessary, the bumper beams may be removed by extracting the clips and bolts as necessary **(see illustration)**.

Refitting

9 Refitting is a reversal of removal.

Rear bumper

Removal

10 Chock the front wheels, then jack up the rear of the vehicle and support on axle stands (see *Jacking and Vehicle Support*).

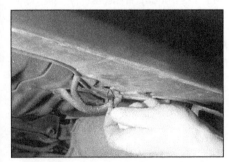

6.12 Removing the clip from under the rear bumper

11 Open the boot lid.
12 Remove the single clip from under the centre of the rear bumper **(see illustration)**. The clip is removed by removing the centre screw and prising it out with a screwdriver.
13 Using a screwdriver through the access hole in the rear wheelarch liners, unscrew and remove the screws securing the front upper extensions of the bumper to the body **(see illustration)**.
14 Remove the front lower mounting screws and the nuts securing the lower studs to the rear valance.
15 Working in the rear luggage compartment, prise out the covers then unscrew the nuts securing the bumper mounting upper studs to the rear valance **(see illustration)**.
16 Withdraw the rear bumper from the body taking care not to damage the paintwork **(see illustration)**. If necessary the bumper beams may be removed by extracting the clips and bolts as necessary.

Refitting

17 Refitting is a reversal of removal.

7 Radiator grille - removal and refitting

Removal

1 The radiator grille is incorporated in the front of the bonnet. Open and support the bonnet.

6.8b Showing the front bumper mounting studs

2 Unscrew the plastic nuts and withdraw the grille from the bonnet.

Refitting

3 Refitting is a reversal of removal, but position the grille with the location pins before fitting and tightening the nuts.

8 Bonnet - removal, refitting and adjustment

Removal

1 Open the bonnet and have an assistant support it. Using a pencil or felt tip pen, mark the outline of each bonnet hinge relative to the bonnet, to use as a guide on refitting.
2 Disconnect the windscreen washer fluid hose from the connector under the bonnet.

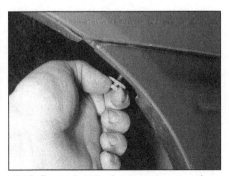

6.13 Removing the front upper mounting screws from the rear bumper

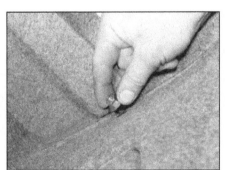

6.15 Removing the upper nuts securing the rear bumper to the rear valance

6.16 Withdrawing the rear bumper from the body

3 Unscrew the bolts securing the bonnet to the hinges and, with the help of an assistant, carefully lift the bonnet clear. Store the bonnet out of the way in a safe place.

4 Inspect the bonnet hinges for signs of wear and free play at the pivots, and if necessary renew.

Refitting

5 With the aid of an assistant, offer up the bonnet, and loosely fit the retaining bolts. Align the hinges with the marks made on removal, then tighten the retaining bolts securely.

6 Reconnect the windscreen washer fluid supply hose.

7 Adjust the alignment of the bonnet as follows.

Adjustment

8 Close the bonnet, and check for alignment with the adjacent panels. If necessary, slacken the hinge bolts and re-align the bonnet to suit. Once the bonnet is correctly aligned, tighten the hinge bolts securely.

9 Once the bonnet is correctly aligned, check that the bonnet fastens and releases in a satisfactory manner. If adjustment is necessary, slacken the bonnet lock retaining bolts, and adjust the position of the lock to suit. Once the lock is operating correctly, securely tighten its retaining bolts. Make sure that the bonnet striker enters the lock centrally.

10 If necessary, align the front edge of the bonnet with the wing panels by turning the support rubbers screwed into the body front panel, to raise or lower the front edge as required.

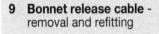

9 Bonnet release cable - removal and refitting

Removal

1 Open and support the bonnet.

2 Apply the handbrake, then jack up the front of the vehicle and support on axle stands (see *Jacking and Vehicle Support*). Remove the right-hand front wheel and remove the wheelarch liner.

3 Unbolt the lock then disconnect the release cable.

4 Working inside the vehicle, remove the trim panel for access to the bonnet release handle beneath the right-hand side of the drivers footwell **(see illustration)**.

5 Unscrew the mounting bolts and remove the release handle, then disconnect the cable.

6 Note the routing of the cable on the bulkhead, engine compartment and wheelarch, then free the cable from the retaining clips and withdraw it from the vehicle. As an aid to refitting, tie a length of string to the cable before removal. Pull the

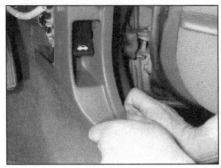

9.4 Removing the trim panel from the bonnet release handle

cable through into the engine compartment, then untie the string and leave it in place until the cable is to be refitted.

Refitting

7 Refitting is a reversal of removal, but use the string to pull the cable into position, and ensure that the bulkhead grommet is securely located. Make sure that the cable is routed as noted before removal without any sharp bends in it, and reposition the cable in its securing clips. Check the bonnet release mechanism for correct operation on completion.

10 Bonnet lock - removal and refitting

Removal

1 Open and support the bonnet.

2 Unscrew the three securing bolts, and remove the lock assembly from the cross-panel **(see illustration)**.

3 Unhook the end of the bonnet release cable from the lock lever, and withdraw the assembly from the vehicle.

Refitting

4 Refitting is a reversal of removal. If necessary, adjust the position of the lock, as described in Section 8.

10.2 Bonnet lock on the front cross-panel

11 Door - removal, refitting and adjustment

Removal

1 Disconnect the battery negative lead.

2 The wiring must be disonnected from the door before removing it. Remove the door inner trim panel as described in Section 12, then disconnect the wiring where it enters the front edge of the door.

3 Drive out the roll pin securing the door check arm to its body bracket **(see illustration)**.

4 Use a marker pen to mark around the door hinge positions as an aid to correct refitting.

5 With the aid of an assistant to support the door, remove the bolts and detach the door **(see illustration)**. If necessary, the door hinges can be unbolted from the body after marking their positions to aid refitting.

Refitting

6 Refitting is the reverse of the removal procedure, but make sure that the door fits correctly in its aperture with equal gaps at all points between it and the surrounding bodywork. The door must also be flush with the surrounding bodywork. If necessary, position the vehicle on a firm level surface and adjust the door as follows.

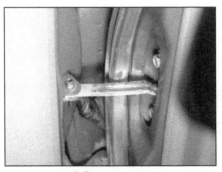

11.3 Door check arm

11.5 Door hinge

11.9 Door striker

12.3a Remove the front door interior handle retaining screw . . .

12.3b . . . and disconnect the handle from the operating rod

Adjustment

7 To adjust the front edge of the door so that it is flush with the surrounding bodywork, loosen the hinge bolts on the door itself. Move the door in or out, then tighten the bolts. Check that the bottom edge of the door is parallel with the sill, and that the waistline is aligned with the wing and other door. If necessary, a shim may be located between one of the hinges and the door.

8 To adjust the door backwards or forwards, or up and down within the body aperture, loosen the hinge bolts on the body. Move the door as necessary then tighten the bolts.

9 The striker alignment should be checked after either the door or the lock has been disturbed. To adjust a striker, slacken its screws, reposition it and securely tighten the screws **(see illustration)**.

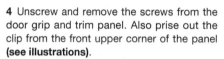

12 Door inner trim panel -
removal and refitting

Front door

Removal

1 Ensure the ignition and all accessories are switched off.

2 Using a small screwdriver, prise the screw cover from the interior door handle then unscrew and remove the screw.

3 Slide the interior door handle forwards and pull it outwards until the operating rod can be disconnected by prising up the plastic clip. Remove the interior door handle **(see illustrations)**.

4 Unscrew and remove the screws from the door grip and trim panel. Also prise out the clip from the front upper corner of the panel **(see illustrations)**.

5 Using a wide-bladed screwdriver, carefully prise out the trim panel clips and lift the panel from the upper shoulder and locking knob. As the panel is being removed, disconnect the wiring for the exterior mirror and security indicator (as applicable). Withdraw the trim panel from the door **(see illustration)**.

6 To remove the plastic membrane, first prise out the plastic inserts then disconnect the power door lock wiring. Peel away the membrane taking care not to tear it. Try to keep the sealant intact as far as possible, to ease refitting.

Refitting

7 Refitting is a reversal of removal, but make sure that the wiring is not trapped when refitting the trim panel.

Rear door

Removal

8 On models fitted with a manual window regulator, fully close the rear window and note the position of the regulator handle. It should be angled forwards and upwards 45° from the horizontal. Using a length of bent welding rod or similar, release the retaining spring from the window regulator handle and withdraw the handle from the splines. Recover the escutcheon.

12.4a Remove the front door grip screw . . .

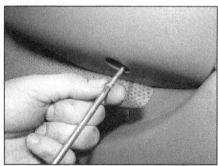

12.4b . . . the lower screw . . .

12.4c . . . the trim panel rear screw . . .

12.4d . . . then prise out the front clip

12.5 Door inner trim panel retaining clip

12.9a Prise out the screw cover . . .

12.9b . . . then unscrew the rear door interior handle retaining screw

13 Door handles and lock components - removal and refitting

Interior door handle (front and rear doors)

Removal

9 Using a small screwdriver, prise the screw cover from the interior door handle then unscrew and remove the screw **(see illustrations)**.
10 Slide the interior door handle forwards and pull it outwards until the operating rod can be disconnected by prising up the plastic clip. Remove the interior door handle **(see illustration)**.
11 Unscrew and remove the screws from the door grip. One screw is located at the front, and the other screw is located beneath the grip **(see illustrations)**.
12 Using a wide-bladed screwdriver, carefully prise out the trim panel clips and lift the panel from the upper shoulder. Where applicable on models with power windows,

disconnect the wiring from the power window switch. Withdraw the trim panel from the door **(see illustrations)**.
13 To remove the plastic membrane, prise out the plastic inserts then carefully peel away the membrane taking care not to tear it. Try to keep the sealant intact as far as possible, to ease refitting.

Refitting

14 Refitting is a reversal of removal, but on manual window models make sure that the regulator handle is positioned as noted during removal. Where applicable, make sure that the wiring is not trapped when refitting the trim panel.

1 Using a small screwdriver, prise the screw cover from the interior door handle then unscrew and remove the screw.
2 Slide the interior door handle forwards and pull it outwards until the operating rod can be disconnected by prising up the plastic clip. Remove the interior door handle.

Refitting

3 Refitting is a reversal of removal.

Exterior handle (front door)

Removal

4 Remove the door inner trim panel, interior door handle and membrane as described in Section 12.
5 Remove the window glass as described in Section 14.
6 Protect the paintwork around the exterior handle using adhesive tape.
7 Working through the hole in the inner door panel, pull out the retaining clip from the lock

12.10 Disconnecting the rear door interior handle from the operating rod

12.11a Removing the rear door grip front screw . . .

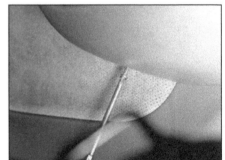

12.11b . . . and lower screw

12.12a Use a wide-bladed screwdriver to release the clips . . .

12.12b . . . then withdraw the inner trim panel from the rear door . . .

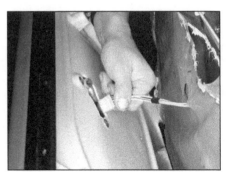

12.12c . . . and disconnect the wiring

13.7a Lock cylinder assembly on the front door exterior handle

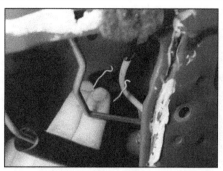

13.7b Removing the retaining clip from the front door lock cylinder

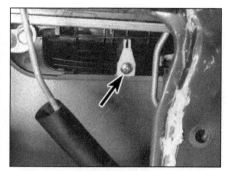

13.8a Screw and plastic clip on the front door exterior handle

cylinder taking care not to damage the cylinder switch then withdraw the lock cylinder from the rear of the exterior handle. The clip is not readily visible but can be removed by inserting a small screwdriver under the lock cylinder **(see illustrations)**.

8 Remove the screw and plastic clip from the inside of the handle, then unscrew the two mounting bolts (the rear one is accessed through the small hole in the door inner panel) **(see illustrations)**.

9 Carefully withdraw the exterior handle from the door, then use a screwdriver to prise out the operating rod joint **(see illustration)**. Note the position of the joint on the threads to ensure correct operation on refitting. The joint

can be separated from inside the door if necessary.

10 Release the clips and disconnect the wiring, then remove the lock cylinder from inside the door.

Refitting

11 Refitting is a reversal of removal, but check the operation of the exterior handle before refitting the door inner trim panel. Remove the protective tape on completion.

Exterior handle (rear door)

Removal

12 Fully raise the window glass.
13 Remove the door inner trim panel, interior

door handle and membrane as described in Section 12.

14 Protect the paintwork around the exterior handle using adhesive tape.

15 On the rear edge of the door, unscrew and remove the door lock mounting screws **(see illustration)**.

16 Unscrew the window rear channel lower mounting bolt. Also unbolt and remove the security plate **(see illustration)**.

17 Move the rear window channel and lock to one side, then unscrew the exterior handle mounting bolts. The rear bolt is accessed through the special hole, and the front bolt can be unscrewed using a spanner inserted behind the rear window **(see illustrations)**.

13.8b Front door exterior handle mounting bolts

13.9 Removing the front door exterior handle

13.15 Removing the rear door lock mounting screws

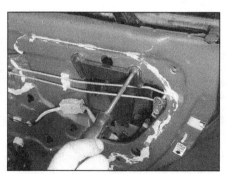

13.16 Removing the security plate from the rear door

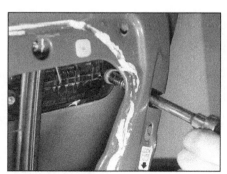

13.17a Removing the rear door exterior handle rear bolt

13.17b Removing the rear door exterior handle front bolt using a spanner behind the door glass

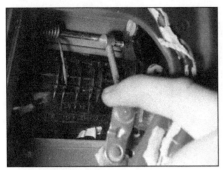

13.18a Disconnect the operating rod joint . . .

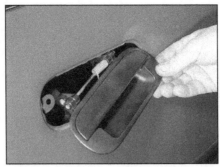

13.18b . . . and remove the exterior handle from the rear door

13.21 Unscrew the lock mounting screws . . .

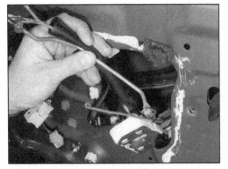

13.23 . . . and remove the front door lock through the aperture

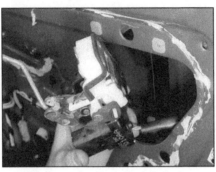

13.28 Removing the rear door lock . . .

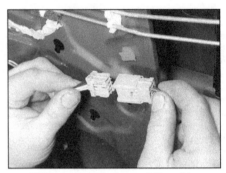

13.29 . . . and disconnect the wiring

18 Prise out the operating rod joint, then carefully withdraw the exterior handle from the door **(see illustrations)**. Note the position of the joint on the threads to ensure correct operation on refitting. The joint can be separated from inside the door if necessary.

Refitting

19 Refitting is a reversal of removal, but check the operation of the exterior handle before refitting the door inner trim panel. Remove the protective tape on completion.

Front door lock

Removal

20 Remove the exterior door handle as described previously in this Section.
21 On the rear edge of the door, unscrew and remove the door lock mounting screws **(see illustration)**.

22 Disconnect the central locking wiring at the connector.
23 Unscrew the bolt and move the door window rear channel to the rear, then withdraw the front door lock through the aperture in the inner door panel **(see illustration)**.

Refitting

24 Refitting is a reversal of removal, but check the operation of the door lock before refitting the door inner trim panel.

Rear door lock

Removal

25 Remove the exterior door handle as described previously in this Section.
26 Prise off the clip then pull the interior door handle operating rod from the top of the lock.

27 Prise off the clip then pull the locking knob operating rod from the lock.
28 Tilt the lock and remove it through the aperture in the door inner panel **(see illustration)**.
29 Disconnect the wiring **(see illustration)**.

Refitting

30 Refitting is a reversal of removal, but check the operation of the door lock before refitting the door inner trim panel.

---

14 Door window regulator and glass - removal and refitting

Front door window glass and regulator

Removal

1 Remove the door inner trim panel and membrane as described in Section 12.
2 Turn the ignition key to position II and lower the window until the bottom edge of the window is visible through the aperture in the door inner panel, and the front window and the glass front mounting bolt is visible through the small hole. Switch off the ignition.
3 Loosen the bolts securing the window glass to the guide, then support the glass and move the guide rearwards until it can be released from the window. Carefully tilt and lift the glass, and withdraw it from the outside of the door, manipulating the glass past the outer weather-strip as it is withdrawn **(see illustrations)**.

14.3a Move the regulator guide rearwards to release it from the window

14.3b Removing the window glass from the front door

14.6 Removing the rubber glass guides

14.8 Disconnecting the wiring for the front door window regulator

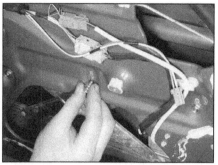

14.10 Remove the mounting bolts . . .

4 Remove the screws and withdraw the speaker from the door. Disconnect the wiring.
5 Prise the triangular cover from the front of the window aperture.
6 Pull the glass guides out of the front and rear channels, noting how they are fitted **(see illustration)**.
7 Unbolt and remove the front and rear window channels. Note that the upper end of the rear channel locates in a special hole.
8 Disconnect the wiring from the regulator motor **(see illustration)**.
9 Mark the position of the regulator mounting bolts using a marker pen or pencil.
10 Loosen the upper mounting bolts and remove the lower bolts **(see illustration)**. **Note:** *The upper mounting bolts holes are slotted to allow the regulator to be removed without removing the bolts.*

11 Release the regulator from the inner panel, and withdraw from the aperture in the door **(see illustration)**.
12 To remove the motor from the regulator, first mark the position of the sector gear with a marker pen. Unscrew the bolts and remove the motor.

Refitting

13 Refitting is a reversal of removal, but if necessary apply a little grease to the sliding surfaces of the regulator. Tighten the mounting bolts to the specified torque. Check the operation of the window before refitting the door inner trim panel. When fully raised, the upper edge of the glass must be aligned with the upper channel in the door. If necessary, adjust the window regulator position then tighten the bolts.

Rear door window glass and regulator

Removal

14 Remove the door inner trim panel and membrane as described in Section 12.
15 Lower the glass until the bolts securing the glass to the regulator are visible through the holes in the door inner panel **(see illustration)**. Where a manual regulator is fitted, temporarily refit the window regulator handle and lower the window. Where power windows are fitted, temporarily switch on the ignition and lower the window as necessary.
16 Support the glass then unscrew and remove the bolts securing it to the regulator **(see illustration)**. Lower the glass as far as possible and support on a block of wood.
17 Unscrew the window rear channel mounting screws noting that the two upper screws are located under the weatherstrip on top of the window frame. Access to the lower screw can be improved by unbolting and removing the security plate **(see illustrations)**.
18 Pull the window guide from the rear channel, then withdraw the channel upwards from the door **(see illustrations)**.
19 Ease the quarter light glass and rubber forwards, and withdraw from the door **(see illustration)**.
20 Raise the glass and withdraw it from the inside of the door, taking care not to scratch it on the inner door panel **(see illustration)**.

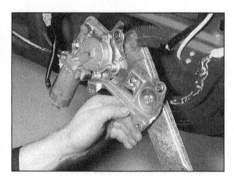

14.11 . . . and withdraw the regulator from the front door

14.15 Rear door window regulator-to-glass mounting bolts

14.16 Removing the window glass mounting bolts

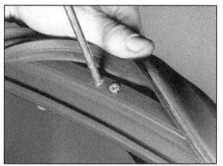

14.17a Removing the rear door rear window channel upper screws . . .

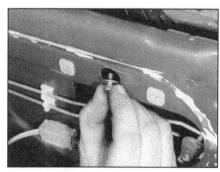

14.17b . . . and lower screw

14.18a Pull the rubber guide from the rear channel . . .

14.18b . . . then release the guide from the quarter window . . .

14.18c . . . and withdraw the channel upwards from the door

21 Mark the position of the regulator mounting bolts using a marker pen or pencil.
22 Unscrew and remove the regulator upper front and lower centre mounting bolts **(see illustration)**. Loosen the remaining regulator mounting bolts. **Note:** *These bolt holes are slotted to allow the regulator to be removed without removing the bolts.*
23 Release the regulator from the inner panel, and withdraw from the aperture in the door and disconnect the wiring **(see illustrations)**.
24 If required, pull the window guide from the front channel, then remove the nut and washer and withdraw the front channel from

the door. Note that the upper end of the channel locates in a special hole.

Refitting

25 Refitting is a reversal of removal, but if necessary apply a little grease to the sliding surfaces of the regulator. Tighten the mounting bolts to the specified torque. Check the operation of the window before refitting the door inner trim panel. When fully raised, the upper edge of the glass must be aligned with the upper channel in the door. If necessary, adjust the window regulator position then tighten the bolts.

15 Boot lid - removal, refitting and adjustment

Removal

1 Ensure that all lighting is switched off.
2 Open the boot lid and disconnect the wiring for the number plate lights and boot lid lock switch.
3 Cover the surrounding bodywork with cloth rags or similar material to protect it.
4 Mark the position of the hinges on the boot lid as an aid to refitting.

14.19 Removing the quarter light glass

14.20 Removing the rear door window glass

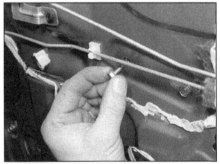

14.22 Remove the mounting bolts . . .

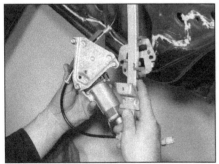

14.23a . . . withdraw the regulator . . .

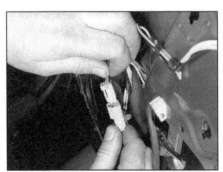

14.23b . . . and disconnect the wiring

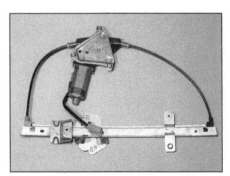

14.23c Rear door window regulator removed from the door

15.5 Boot lid mounting bolts on the hinge arms

15.11 Boot lid lock striker

15.12 Boot lid adjustable support rubber

5 With the help of an assistant support the boot lid, then unscrew the mounting bolts and withdraw the boot lid from the vehicle **(see illustration)**.

6 If necessary, the wiring loom can be removed from the boot lid. Tie a length of string to the loom before removing it and leave the string in place to aid refitting.

7 Removal of the torsion bars is best left to a Rover dealer who will have the specialised tool to release the bars from the side brackets.

Refitting

8 Refitting is a reversal of removal, but if necessary adjust the position of the boot lid as follows.

Adjustment

9 Close the boot lid and ensure that it sits flush with the surrounding panels and that there is an equal gap between the boot lid and each rear wing. The lid should close smoothly and positively, with no excessive force being applied. If this is not the case, adjustment is required.

10 If fore and aft adjustment is required, remove the trim from the rear shelf and loosen the hinge bolts. Move the boot lid within the elongated bolt holes, then tighten the bolts.

11 Check that the striker enters the lock centrally, and if necessary loosen the striker bolts and reposition it. Tighten the bolts after making the adjustment **(see illustration)**.

12 With the boot lid closed, press down on it and check that there is no excess movement in the lock. If necessary, turn the support rubbers screwed into the rear edge of the boot lid until it is supported correctly **(see illustration)**.

13 The position of the torsion bars may be adjusted if necessary to improve the boot lid opening, however this work should be entrusted to a Rover dealer.

16 Boot lid lock and lock cylinder - removal and refitting

Boot lid lock

Removal

1 Open the boot lid., then pull the plastic cover from the lock **(see illustration)**.

2 Release the clip and disconnect the operating rod from the lock cylinder. This will make the refitting procedure easier.

3 Disconnect the wiring for the central locking switch and courtesy light **(see illustration)**.

4 Unscrew the mounting bolts, then withdraw the lock and disconnect the lock cylinder operating rod **(see illustrations)**.

5 Disconnect the remote cable and withdraw the lock from the boot lid **(see illustration)**.

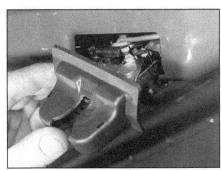

16.1 Removing the plastic cover from the boot lid lock

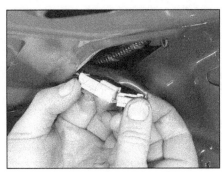

16.3 Disconnecting the wiring

16.4a Unscrew the mounting bolts . . .

16.4b . . . and withdraw the boot lid lock

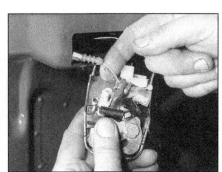

16.5 Disconnecting the remote cable from the boot lid lock

16.8 Disconnecting the operating rod from the boot lid lock

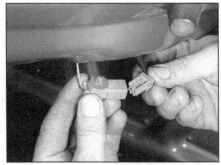

16.9 Disconnecting the wiring from the boot lid lock

16.10 Removing the lock cylinder and seal

Refitting

6 Refitting is a reversal of removal.

Lock cylinder

Removal

7 Open the boot lid.
8 Release the clip and disconnect the operating rod from the lock cylinder **(see illustration)**.
9 Disconnect the wiring **(see illustration)**.
10 Unscrew the mounting bolt and withdraw the lock cylinder from the boot lid. Recover the seal **(see illustration)**.

Refitting

11 Refitting is a reversal of removal.

17.2a Prise out the cover . . .

17 Boot lid and fuel filler flap release mechanism - removal and refitting

Removal

1 The mechanism is cable-operated, with levers mounted on the floor next to the driver's seat and release catches on the boot lid and the fuel filler flap. A lock cylinder is fitted inside the vehicle so that the levers may be locked with the ignition key.
2 To remove the lever unit, prise up the central cover and remove the screw. Lift the cover from the floor **(see illustrations)**.
3 Unscrew the mounting bolts and lift the lever assembly, then disconnect the cables. Identify the cables for position.
4 On RHD models the cables are routed across to the left-hand side of the vehicle then rearwards to the boot lid and fuel filler lid. On LHD models the cables are located on the left-hand side of the vehicle.
5 Remove the trim components as necessary for access to the cables, then release them from the clips.
6 Remove the boot lid lock as described in Section 16 to disconnect the cable from the lock, then release the cable from the boot lid arm **(see illustration)**. The fuel filler flap release cable is attached to the lock, and the lock may be removed from the body by twisting it clockwise.

Refitting

7 Refitting is a reversal of the removal procedure.

18 Exterior mirror and glass - removal and refitting

Mirror assembly (manual type)

Removal

1 Prise the cap from the control knob, then remove the screw and withdraw the knob.
2 Using a screwdriver, carefully prise the triangular cover from the front of the window glass aperture.
3 Support the exterior mirror, then remove the mounting screws and withdraw the mirror from the outside of the door.

Refitting

4 Refitting is a reversal of the removal procedure.

Mirror assembly (power type)

Removal

5 Remove the door inner trim panel and membrane as described in Section 12.
6 Disconnect the wiring plugs for the mirror, and release the cable from the clip **(see illustration)**.

17.2b . . . remove the screw . . .

17.2c . . . and lift the cover from the floor

17.6 Cable clip on the boot lid arm

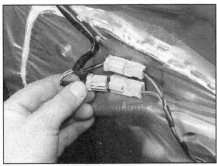

18.6 Disconnecting the mirror wiring

7 Using a screwdriver, carefully prise the triangular cover from the front of the window glass aperture **(see illustration)**.
8 Support the exterior mirror, then remove the mounting screws and withdraw the mirror from the outside of the door **(see illustrations)**.

Refitting

9 Refitting is a reversal of the removal procedure. Check the operation of the mirror before refitting the door inner trim panel.

Mirror glass (manual type)

Removal

10 Insert a crosshead screwdriver through the hole in the bottom of the mirror body, and loosen the mirror retaining screw.
11 Insert a small flat-bladed screwdriver between the mirror glass and the mirror body, and lever out the glass to release it from the

18.8a Remove the mounting screws . . .

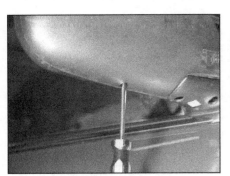

18.13 Loosening the exterior mirror retaining screw

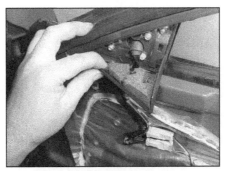

18.7 Removing the triangular cover from the front of the window aperture

securing clips. To prevent damage to the mirror body, locate the screwdriver on a cloth pad. If the clips are very tight it may be easier to remove the mirror first then remove the glass on the bench

Refitting

12 Refitting is a reversal of the removal procedure.

> **HAYNES HiNT** *To aid refitting, lightly grease the securing clips on the rear of the mirror glass.*

Mirror glass (power type)

Removal

13 Insert a crosshead screwdriver through the hole in the bottom of the mirror body, and loosen the retaining screw **(see illustration)**.

18.8b . . . and withdraw the mirror from the outside of the door

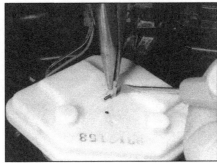

18.15a Pull up the stopper and extract the stopper pin . . .

14 Carefully lever out the mirror and actuator.
15 Pull the lock cap stopper and extract the stopper pin. Withdraw the mirror and stopper from the actuator **(see illustrations)**.

Refitting

16 Refitting is a reversal of the removal procedure, but apply a little grease to the two actuator points on the rear of the mirror.

19 Windscreen and rear window glass - general information

The windscreen and rear window are bonded in position with special adhesive. Renewal of these windows is a difficult, messy and time-consuming task, which is beyond the scope of the home mechanic. It is difficult, unless one has plenty of practice, to obtain a secure, waterproof fit. Furthermore, the task carries a high risk of breakage. In view of this, owners are strongly advised to have this work carried out by one of the many specialist windscreen fitters.

20 Sunroof components - general information

1 Removal, refitting and adjustment of the sunroof frame and drive components is best left to a Rover dealer who will have the necessary equipment and expertise to carry out the work. However removal of the glass and sunshade is possible, as described in the following paragraphs.
2 Open the sunshade and tilt the glass.
3 Mark the position of the side mounting screws on the glass brackets, then unscrew the screws and lift the glass from the brackets.
4 With the glass removed move the sunshade forwards, then extract the stoppers and withdraw the sunshade from the guide rails.
5 When refitting the sunshade and glass, apply locking fluid to the threads of the mounting screws before refitting and tightening them. The edges of the glass must be flush with the roof panel. If necessary, loosen the mounting screws and reposition the glass to adjust.

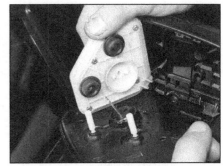

18.15b . . . then withdraw the mirror and stopper from the actuator

21 Body exterior fittings - removal and refitting

Rear number plate trim

Removal

1 Extract the clip from the upper lip of the trim.
2 Open the boot lid and remove the mounting nuts and washers. Withdraw the trim from the boot lid.

Refitting

3 Refitting is a reversal of removal.

Roof top mouldings

Removal

4 Apply tape to the roof along the edges of the moulding as a precaution against damaging the paintwork.
5 Using a small flat-bladed screwdriver, carefully prise up the moulding from the roof panel.

Refitting

6 Wipe clean the roof channel and check for rust and damaged paintwork. Renovate the paintwork as necessary.
7 Dip the moulding in warm soapy water, then align it with the channel and press it firmly into position. Remove the tape.

Roof side mouldings

Removal

8 Open the front door and remove the screw securing the moulding to the bottom of the windscreen pillar.
9 Carefully pull off the moulding and release it from the rear quarter moulding. The design of the clips is such that they are likely to be damaged as the moulding is pulled off and it will be necessary to obtain new clips.
10 Open the rear door and remove the screws securing the rear quarter moulding to the body.
11 Release the lower clip and withdraw the quarter moulding.

Refitting

12 Refitting is a reversal of removal, but renew the broken clips and locate them in the moulding before refitting. Press the moulding firmly into position to ensure the clips engage with the holes.

Sill mouldings

Removal

13 Remove the screws at the front of the moulding under the wheelarch.
14 Prise out the centre screws from the lower securing clips.
15 Slide the sill moulding forwards and remove it from the vehicle.
16 To remove the side mounting clips, turn them anticlockwise 45°.

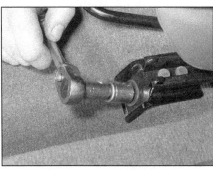

22.1 Removing the front seat front mounting bolts

Refitting

17 Before refitting locate all of the side clips in the moulding, then press the moulding into position until the clips engage with the sill. Insert the lower clips and finally refit the front screws.

Door and front wing mouldings

Removal

18 The mouldings are retained in position with clips and double-sided adhesive tape. Note that the metal core of the mouldings cannot be restored to its original shape after being bent.
19 Remove the door inner trim panel and membrane as described in Section 12 for access to the door moulding clips. When removing the front wing moulding, remove the wheelarch liner for access to the clips.
20 Apply tape along the edges of the mouldings to prevent damage to the paintwork.
21 On the front door unscrew the plastic nut from the rear of the moulding. On the rear door release the front clip by turning it through 90°.
22 Using pliers from the inside of the door or front wing, release the clips and push out the moulding. Using a screwdriver, prise the moulding away from the tape.
23 Remove all old adhesive tape from the door/wing by carefully heating it with a hot air gun then clean the surface thoroughly with suitable solvent. If the moulding is to be refitted, clean the contact surfaces in the same manner.

Refitting

24 Fit the new tape to the moulding together with any new clips required.
25 Using the hot air gun, heat the door or wing to approximately 50°C.
26 Align the moulding with the clips and press firmly into position.
27 Refit the door inner trim panel or wheelarch liner as applicable.
28 Do not allow water to contact the moulding within 24 hours of refitting.

Wheelarch liners

29 The wheelarch liners are secured by a combination of screws and plastic clips, and the removal/refitting procedure is self-evident.

22 Seats - removal and refitting

Removal

Front seat

1 Slide the seat as far back as possible, then unbolt the seat runner forward ends (see illustration).
2 Slide the seat as far forward as possible, then remove the covers from the seat runner rear ends (see illustration).
3 Unbolt the seat runner rear ends from the floor, then remove the seat from inside the vehicle (see illustration). Where fitted, disconnect the wiring for the seat heaters and power height adjustment motor.

Rear seat cushion

4 The rear seat cushion is secured with a single bolt just left of centre on the rear edge, and hooks at the front edge. Unscrew the single rear bolt, then fold the cushion forwards and disconnect the front hooks (see illustration). Withdraw the seat from inside the vehicle.

Fixed rear seat back

5 To remove the rear seat back, unscrew the lower mounting bolts then lift the seat to release the upper hooks.
6 Move the seat belts to one side and withdraw the seat back from inside the vehicle.

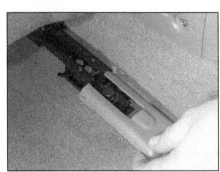

22.2 Remove the covers . . .

22.3 . . . and unscrew the rear mounting bolts

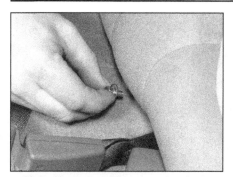

22.4a Unscrew and remove the single bolt . . .

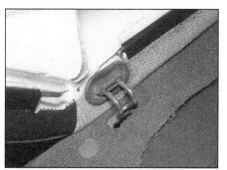

22.4b . . . and release the rear seat cushion from the front hooks

22.8 Removing the right-hand folding rear seat outer mounting bolt

7 If necessary, the armrest can be removed from the seat back by pulling out the plastic clip.

Folding rear seat back

8 To remove the right-hand seat back, first fold the seat forwards, then pull up the material covering and unscrew the bolts securing the seat to the hinge brackets **(see illustration)**. Withdraw the seat back from inside the vehicle.

9 To remove the left-hand seat back first remove the right-hand seat back as described in paragraph 8. Fold the seat forwards then unscrew the outer bolt securing the seat to the hinge. Unscrew the centre bolt and remove the centre pivot bracket, then withdraw the seat from inside the vehicle.

Remove the plastic cover if necessary **(see illustrations)**.

10 If necessary, the armrest can be removed from the left-hand seat back by removing the cover (one screw) and unscrewing the through-bolt.

Rear seat bolsters

11 The rear seat bolsters are removed by unscrewing the lower mounting bolt and lifting the bolster from the location pins **(see illustrations)**.

Refitting

12 Refitting is the reverse of the removal procedure, but tighten the mounting bolts to the specified torque. Make sure that the seat belts are not trapped behind the fixed seat back.

23 Seat belt components - removal and refitting

Note: *Note the positions of any washers and spacers on the seat belt anchors, and ensure that they are refitted in their original positions.*

Removal

Front

1 If the belt inner stalk is to be removed, remove the relevant front seat then unbolt the stalk from the seat **(see illustration)**.

2 If the outer belt is to be removed, first remove the centre pillar lower trim **(see illustration)**.

22.9a Removing the left-hand folding rear seat outer mounting bolt

22.9b Remove the left-hand folding rear seat centre bolt . . .

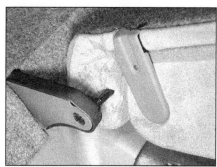

22.9c . . . and withdraw the seat

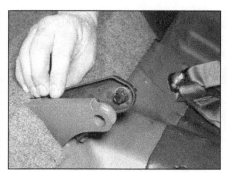

22.9d Removing the plastic cover

22.11a Remove the mounting bolt . . .

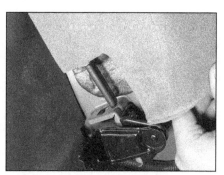

22.11b . . . and lift the rear seat bolster from the location pins

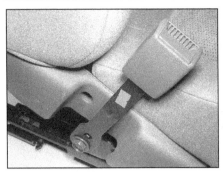

23.1 Front seat belt stalk

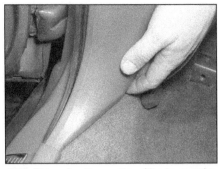

23.2 Removing the centre pillar lower trim

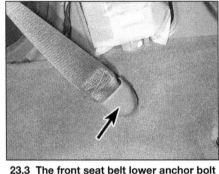

23.3 The front seat belt lower anchor bolt is located beneath the cover

3 Unscrew the lower anchor bolt securing the outer end of the seat belt to the inner sill panel **(see illustration)**.

4 Remove the trim from the shoulder adjustment on the centre pillar, then unscrew

the upper anchor bolt **(see illustration)**.

5 Unscrew the reel mounting bolt from the bottom of the centre pillar and withdraw the reel and seat belt from inside the vehicle **(see illustration)**.

6 If necessary, unbolt the adjustment mechanism from the centre pillar.

Rear

7 To remove the rear seat belt stalks, remove the rear seats as described in Section 22, then unscrew the anchor bolts and withdraw the stalks from inside the vehicle **(see illustration)**. Note that the centre lap belt buckle is located on the right-hand seat belt stalk.

8 To remove the rear seat belt reel, remove the rear seat bolster as described in Section 22, and also remove the trim from the roof rear quarter panel. Unscrew the anchor bolt from the front end of the seat belt, then unscrew the mounting bolts and remove the reel from the quarter panel **(see illustrations)**.

23.4 Removing the trim from the shoulder adjustment on the centre pillar

23.5 Front seat belt reel mounting bolt

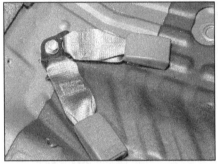

23.7 Rear seat belt stalks

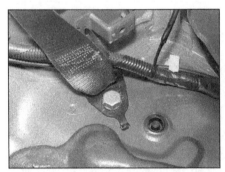

23.8a Rear seat belt front mounting bolt

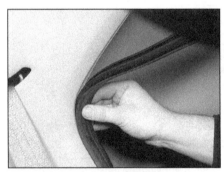

23.8b Remove the rubber strip . . .

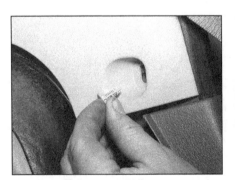

23.8c . . . and clips . . .

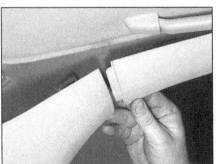

23.8d . . . then remove the trim panels . . .

23.8e . . . for access to the seat belt reel

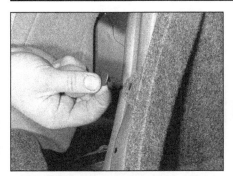

24.1 Removing a clip from the luggage compartment side trim

25.3a Remove the single front screw . . .

25.3b . . . and rear screws . . .

Refitting

9 Refitting is the reverse of the removal procedure, but make sure that the belts are correctly routed and tighten the mounting bolts to the specified torque. Note that the torque wrench setting for the smaller bolts is less than the main anchor bolts. Make sure that the rear side seat belts are routed through the guides on the cushion.

24 Interior trim panels - general information

Note: *Take extra care when removing plastic clips from interior trim panels, as the clips and panels are easily damaged or broken.*

1 Most interior trim panels are secured by clips **(see illustration)**; before attempting to

remove a panel always inspect it closely to check where all fasteners are located and to decide on the correct approach for removal. Remember that if the panel is being removed for access to another component, it may only be necessary to lift one end of the panel.

2 A wide variety of clip types are used, however most require the relevant panel to be prised free at the points where the clips enter the bodywork. When prising free a panel secured by hidden clips, always wrap tape around the blade of the tool used, to protect the paintwork.

3 When removing the front and centre pillar upper trim, remove the grab handle first.

4 When removing the rear shelf trim, remove the rear pillar trim first and note that the shelf rear clips are hooked into holes in the shelf body panel. Make sure these clips are engaged correctly before inserting the front clips.

5 It may be necessary to remove components, such as seats, handles, etc before a given panel can be removed. Refer to the relevant Section of this Chapter for details.

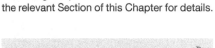
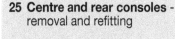

25 Centre and rear consoles - removal and refitting

Removal

1 Disconnect the battery negative lead.

2 Using a screwdriver, carefully prise the power window switch panel from the console - to do this, insert a screwdriver at one side on the rear of the panel then insert a further screwdriver at the front of the panel. Disconnect the wiring plug and remove the switch panel.

3 Remove the single front screw and two rear side screws, and withdraw the rear console. Move the front seats fully forwards for access to the side screws. The front screw is located through the switch aperture **(see illustrations)**.

4 Remove the single outer screw then use a screwdriver to prise the lower facia panel from under the steering column. Disconnect the wiring as applicable **(see illustrations)**.

5 Remove the hinge retaining screws from under the glovebox then withdraw the glovebox from the facia. Note that the hinges have locating pins on them **(see illustrations)**.

25.3c . . . then withdraw the rear console

25.4a Remove the screw . . .

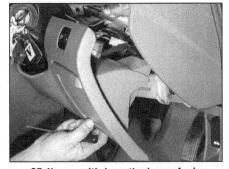

25.4b . . . withdraw the lower facia panel . . .

25.4c . . . and disconnect the wiring

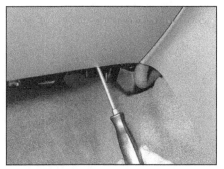

25.5a Unscrew the glovebox hinge screws . . .

25.5b ... and withdraw the glovebox from the facia

25.6 Removing the gear lever knob

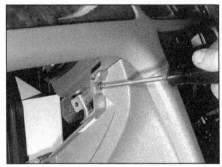
25.9a Unscrew the front screws ...

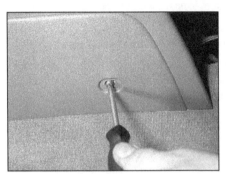
25.9b ... and side screws ...

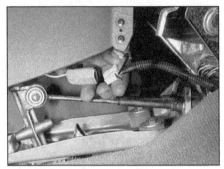
25.9c ... then withdraw the centre console and disconnect the wiring

6 On manual transmission models, pull down the gaiter then unscrew the knob from the top of the gear lever **(see illustration)**.
7 On automatic transmission models, wrap cloth around the selector lever and indicator panel to prevent damage to them as the console is being removed.
8 Apply the handbrake lever to provide additional working room.
9 Remove the retaining screws and use a screwdriver to release the front clips, then withdraw the centre console over the gear lever/selector lever. Remove the console from inside the vehicle **(see illustrations)**.
10 Remove the ashtray from the console.
11 Remove the screws securing the ashtray holder and gear lever surround panel to the console. Release the clips and remove the panels.

Refitting
12 Refitting is a reversal of removal.

26 Facia panel - removal and refitting

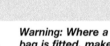

⚠️ **Warning: Where a passenger air bag is fitted, make sure that the safety recommendations given in Chapter 12 are followed, to prevent personal injury. Refer to Chapter 10 when removing the steering wheel and driver's air bag module.**

Removal
1 Disconnect the battery negative and positive leads, and **wait 10 minutes** (this is a safety requirement of the air bag system).

26.6a Removing the oddments pocket ...

26.6b ... and bracket from the facia

2 Remove the front seats as described in Section 22.
3 Remove the instrument panel as described in Chapter 12.
4 Remove the centre console as described in Section 25.
5 Remove the radio as described in Chapter 12.
6 Remove the screws (front and rear) and remove the oddments pocket and bracket from the facia **(see illustrations)**.
7 Remove the screws and withdraw the radio mounting bracket, disconnecting the wiring and aerial as it is being removed.
8 Remove the heater control panel as described in Chapter 3.
9 Disconnect the air vent control cable from the left-hand side of the heater unit. Depress the lower retaining clips and push out the vent assembly together with the cable from the facia.
10 Using a screwdriver, carefully prise out the side vents from the facia.
11 Unscrew the retaining bolts from under the glovebox then withdraw the glovebox from the facia.
12 Where a passenger air bag is fitted, remove the special red safety connector from its holder under the facia, then disconnect the air bag wiring from the main harness and fit the red connector to it. Unscrew the mounting nuts and withdraw the air bag module from the mounting bracket - keep the nuts with the module. Unscrew the nuts and remove the joint brackets and module brackets from the facia - keep the nuts with the joint brackets.
Caution: Note that the module bracket has the serial number of the air bag stamped on it, and must not be used for a different air bag module. Also note that the nuts for the module and joint brackets are different and require different torque settings - keep them separate and identified for position.
13 Lower the adjustable steering column to its lowest position, then remove the combination switches from the top of the steering column as described in Chapter 12.
14 Unscrew the crosshead screws and single bolt, and remove the facia bracket from under the steering column position.

26.16a Press from behind the facia . . .

26.16b . . . to remove the centre vent

26.17a Prise out the plastic covers . . .

15 Reach under the facia on the driver's side, and disconnect the wiring harness plugs from the fusebox.

16 Disconnect the heater control and air vent cables from the heater unit. Note the positions of the cables to aid refitting. If necessary, remove the centre vent (see illustrations).

17 Prise the plastic side covers from each end of the facia and unscrew the side mounting bolts (see illustrations).

18 Unscrew and remove the remaining mounting bolts at the front and sides of the facia (see illustration).

19 To prevent damage to the lower ends of the A pillar trim panels, cover them with tape.

20 With the help of an assistant, carefully withdraw the facia panel from the front location pin, and withdraw it from inside the vehicle.

Refitting

21 Refitting is a reversal of removal, but make sure that all electrical wiring is correctly reconnected to the relevant components and not trapped behind the facia. Tighten the facia mountings securely. On models fitted with a passenger air bag, before tightening the joint bracket mounting nuts, press the air bag module lightly downwards and forwards so that there are no gaps then fully tighten the nuts. Adjust the heater control cables with reference to Chapter 3.

 Warning: If a new passenger air bag is fitted, the old one should be disposed of by a Rover dealer using a special deployment tool. DO NOT attempt to deploy an air bag!

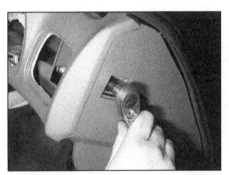

26.17b . . . and unscrew the facia side mounting bolts

26.18 Unscrewing the facia centre mounting bolts

Notes

Chapter 12
Body electrical systems

Contents

Degrees of difficulty

Easy, suitable for novice with little experience		Fairly easy, suitable for beginner with some experience		Fairly difficult, suitable for competent DIY mechanic		Difficult, suitable for experienced DIY mechanic		Very difficult, suitable for expert DIY or professional	

Specifications

Bulb ratings	Watts
Headlamp	55
Front sidelamp	5
Direction indicator	21
Front direction indicator side repeater	5
Stop/tail lamps	21/5
Rear foglamp	21
Reversing lamp	21
Number plate lamp	5
Interior lamp	5
Glovebox lamp	5
Luggage compartment lamp	10

Torque wrench setting	Nm	lbf ft
Radio aerial mast nut	2.3	1.7

1 General information and precautions

⚠ **Warning: Before carrying out any work on the electrical system, read through the precautions given in Safety first! at the beginning of this manual, and in Chapter 5. All models are equipped with an air bag system. When working on the** *electrical system, refer to the precautions given in Section 24, to avoid the possibility of personal injury.*

The electrical system is of 12-volt negative earth type. Power for the lights and all electrical accessories is supplied by a lead/acid type battery, which is charged by the alternator.

This Chapter covers repair and service procedures for the various electrical components not associated with the engine. Information on the battery, alternator and starter motor can be found in Chapter 5A.

It should be noted that, prior to working on any component in the electrical system, the battery negative terminal should first be disconnected, to prevent the possibility of electrical short-circuits and/or fires.

Caution: If the radio/cassette player fitted to the vehicle is one with an anti-theft security code, refer to the information given in the Reference Section at the rear of this manual before disconnecting the battery.

2 Electrical fault finding - general information

Note: *Refer to the precautions given in Safety first! and in Section 1 of this Chapter before starting work. The following tests relate to testing of the main electrical circuits, and should not be used to test delicate electronic circuits (such as anti-lock braking systems), particularly where an electronic control module is used.*

General

1 A typical electrical circuit consists of an electrical component, any switches, relays, motors, fuses, fusible links or circuit breakers related to that component, and the wiring and connectors which link the component to both the battery and the bodyshell. To help pinpoint a problem in an electrical circuit, wiring diagrams are included at the end of this Chapter.

2 Before attempting to diagnose an electrical fault, first study the appropriate wiring diagram, to obtain a more complete understanding of the components included in the particular circuit concerned. The possible sources of a fault can be narrowed down by noting whether other components related to the circuit are operating properly. If several components or circuits fail at one time, the problem is likely to be related to a shared fuse or earth connection.

3 Electrical problems usually stem from simple causes, such as loose or corroded connections, a faulty earth connection, a blown fuse, a melted fusible link, or a faulty relay (refer to Section 3 for details of testing relays). Visually inspect the condition of all fuses, wires and connections in a problem circuit before testing the components. Use the wiring diagrams to determine which terminal connections will need to be checked, in order to pinpoint the trouble-spot.

4 The basic tools required for electrical fault-finding include a circuit tester or voltmeter (a 12-volt bulb with a set of test leads can also be used for certain tests); a self-powered test light (sometimes known as a continuity tester); an ohmmeter (to measure resistance); a battery and set of test leads; and a jumper wire, preferably with a circuit breaker or fuse incorporated, which can be used to bypass suspect wires or electrical components. Before attempting to locate a problem with test instruments, use the wiring diagrams to determine where to make the connections.

5 To find the source of an intermittent wiring fault (usually due to a poor or dirty connection, or damaged wiring insulation), a wiggle test can be performed on the wiring. This involves wiggling the wiring by hand, to see if the fault occurs as the wiring is moved. It should be possible to narrow down the source of the fault to a particular section of wiring. This method of testing can be used in conjunction with any of the tests described in the following sub-Sections.

6 Apart from problems due to poor connections, two basic types of fault can occur in an electrical circuit - open-circuit, or short-circuit.

7 Open-circuit faults are caused by a break somewhere in the circuit, which prevents current from flowing. An open-circuit fault will prevent a component from working, but will not cause the relevant circuit fuse to blow.

8 Short-circuit faults are caused by a short somewhere in the circuit, which allows the current flowing in the circuit to escape along an alternative route, usually to earth. Short-circuit faults are normally caused by a breakdown in wiring insulation, which allows a feed wire to touch either another wire, or an earthed component such as the bodyshell. A short-circuit fault will normally cause the relevant circuit fuse to blow.

Finding an open-circuit

9 To check for an open-circuit, connect one lead of a circuit tester or voltmeter to either the negative battery terminal or a known good earth.

10 Connect the other lead to a connector in the circuit being tested, preferably nearest to the battery or fuse.

11 Switch on the circuit, bearing in mind that some circuits are live only when the ignition switch is moved to a particular position.

12 If voltage is present (indicated either by the test bulb lighting or a voltmeter reading, as applicable), this means that the section of the circuit between the relevant connector and the battery is problem-free.

13 Continue to check the remainder of the circuit in the same fashion.

14 When a point is reached at which no voltage is present, the problem must lie between that point and the previous test point with voltage. Most problems can be traced to a broken, corroded or loose connection.

Finding a short-circuit

15 To check for a short-circuit, first disconnect the load(s) from the circuit (loads are the components which draw current from a circuit, such as bulbs, motors, heating elements, etc).

16 Remove the relevant fuse from the circuit, and connect a circuit tester or voltmeter to the fuse connections.

17 Switch on the circuit, bearing in mind that some circuits are live only when the ignition switch is moved to a particular position.

18 If voltage is present (indicated either by the test bulb lighting or a voltmeter reading, as applicable), this means that there is a short-circuit.

19 If no voltage is present, but the fuse still blows with the load(s) connected, this indicates an internal fault in the load(s).

Finding an earth fault

20 The battery negative terminal is connected to earth - the metal of the engine/transmission and the car body - and most systems are wired so that they only receive a positive feed, the current returning via the metal of the car body. This means that the component mounting and the body form part of that circuit. Loose or corroded mountings can therefore cause a range of electrical faults, ranging from total failure of a circuit, to a puzzling partial fault. In particular, lights may shine dimly (especially when another circuit sharing the same earth point is in operation), motors (eg wiper motors or the radiator cooling fan motor) may run slowly, and the operation of one circuit may have an apparently-unrelated effect on another. Note that on many vehicles, earth straps are used between certain components, such as the engine/transmission and the body, usually where there is no metal-to-metal contact between components, due to flexible rubber mountings, etc.

21 To check whether a component is properly earthed, disconnect the battery, and connect one lead of an ohmmeter to a known good earth point. Connect the other lead to the wire or earth connection being tested. The resistance reading should be zero; if not, check the connection as follows.

22 If an earth connection is thought to be faulty, dismantle the connection, and clean back to bare metal both the bodyshell and the wire terminal or the component earth connection mating surface. Be careful to remove all traces of dirt and corrosion, then use a knife to trim away any paint, so that a clean metal-to-metal joint is made. On reassembly, tighten the joint fasteners securely; if a wire terminal is being refitted, use serrated washers between the terminal and the bodyshell, to ensure a clean and secure connection. When the connection is remade, prevent the onset of corrosion in the future by applying a coat of petroleum jelly or silicone-based grease, or by spraying on (at regular intervals) a proprietary ignition sealer.

3 Fuses and relays - general information

Fuses

1 Fuses are designed to break a circuit when a predetermined current is reached, in order to protect the components and wiring which could be damaged by excessive current flow. Any excessive current flow will be due to a fault in the circuit, usually a short-circuit.

2 The fuses and relays are located in the rear right-hand side of the engine compartment and below the driver's side of the facia **(see illustrations)**.

3 For access to the engine compartment fuses, open the bonnet then squeeze together the plastic clips and lift the cover from the fusebox **(see illustration)**. To access the fuses located inside the vehicle, turn the knob and swivel the cover away from the fusebox.

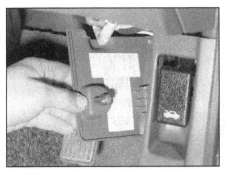

3.2a Open the cover for access to the fuses beneath the driver's side of the facia

3.2b Fuses located on the right-hand side of the driver's footwell (shown with facia removed)

3.3 Engine compartment fusebox with cover removed

4 A blown fuse can be recognised from its melted or broken wire. The main fuses (30, 40, 50 and 80 amp) look similar to relays and are plugged into the fusebox in a similar manner, however the standard fuses are smaller.

5 To remove a fuse, first ensure that the relevant circuit is switched off.

6 To remove a standard fuse, use the plastic tweezers supplied and pull the fuse from its location. To remove a main fuse, simply pull it directly from the fusebox.

7 Spare standard fuses are provided in the fusebox.

8 Before renewing a blown fuse, trace and rectify the cause, and always use a fuse of the correct rating (fuse ratings are specified on the inside of the fusebox cover). Never substitute a fuse of a higher rating, or make temporary repairs using wire or metal foil; more serious damage, or even fire, could result.

9 The radio/cassette player fuse is located in the rear of the unit, and can be accessed after removing the radio/cassette player.

Relays

10 A relay is an electrically-operated switch, which is used for the following reasons:
  a) *A relay can switch a heavy current remotely from the circuit in which the current is flowing, therefore allowing the use of lighter-gauge wiring and switch contacts.*
  b) *A relay can receive more than one control input, unlike a mechanical switch.*

  c) *A relay can have a timer function - for example, the intermittent wiper relay.*

11 The various relays are located on the fuseboxes both in the engine compartment and inside the passenger compartment.

12 If a circuit or system controlled by a relay develops a fault, and the relay is suspect, operate the system. If the relay is functioning, it should be possible to hear it click as it is energised. If this is the case, the fault lies with the components or wiring of the system. If the relay is not being energised, then either the relay is not receiving a main supply or a switching voltage, or the relay itself is faulty. Testing is by the substitution of a known good unit, but be careful - while some relays are identical in appearance and in operation, others look similar but perform different functions.

13 To remove a relay, first ensure that the relevant circuit is switched off. The relay can then simply be pulled out from the socket, and pushed back into position.

---

4 Switches - removal and refitting

Ignition switch

Removal

1 Disconnect the battery negative and positive leads, and **wait 10 minutes**. This is a

safety requirement of the air bag supplementary restraint system (see Section 24).

2 Remove the single screw then prise the lower facia panel from under the steering column. Disconnect the wiring as applicable.

3 Unscrew the screws and remove the upper and lower shrouds from the steering column.

4 Remove the cover from the fusebox in the drivers footwell, then disconnect the main wiring harness from the fusebox.

5 Turn the ignition key to position 0.

6 Unscrew the bolts, and remove the cover followed by the ignition switch and wiring.

Refitting

7 Refitting is a reversal of removal.

Steering column combination switches

Removal

8 Disconnect the battery negative and positive leads, and **wait 10 minutes**. This is a safety requirement of the air bag supplementary restraint system (see Section 24).

9 Remove the single screw then prise the lower facia panel from under the steering column. Disconnect the wiring as applicable.

10 Unscrew the screws and remove the upper and lower shrouds from the steering column.

11 Disconnect the wiring from the combination switch **(see illustration)**.

12 Unscrew the mounting screws and separate the switch from the base unit on the steering column **(see illustrations)**.

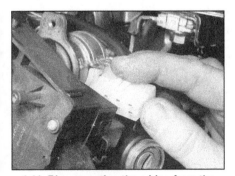

4.11 Disconnecting the wiring from the combination switch

4.12a Remove the screws . . .

4.12b . . . and separate the combination switch from the base unit

4.13a Remove the screws . . .

4.13b . . . and remove the slip ring . . .

4.13c . . . then unscrew the base unit screws

13 To remove the switch base unit it is necessary to remove the steering wheel then unscrew the screws and remove the slip ring or reel unit followed by the base unit over the top of the steering column (see illustrations).

Refitting

14 Refitting is a reversal of removal.

Headlight level adjuster

Removal

15 Remove the single screw then prise the lower facia panel from under the steering column. Disconnect the wiring as applicable.
16 Depress the plastic retainers and push out the adjuster from the rear of the lower facia panel.

Refitting

17 Refitting is a reversal of removal.

4.29 Remove the door grip screws from the inside of the door trim . . .

Hazard warning switch

Removal

18 Remove the centre console as described in Chapter 11.
19 Remove the heater control panel as described in Chapter 3.
20 Depress the plastic retainers and push out the hazard warning switch from the heater control panel.

Refitting

21 Refitting is a reversal of removal.

Instrument panel lighting rheostat

Removal

22 Remove the single screw then prise the lower facia panel from under the steering column. Disconnect the wiring as applicable.
23 Depress the plastic retainers and push out the rheostat from the rear of the lower facia panel.

Refitting

24 Refitting is a reversal of removal.

Heated rear window switch/cruise control main switch/foglight switch

Removal

25 Remove the upper screws from the instrument panel surround, and withdraw the surround. Disconnect the wiring from the switches.

26 Remove the retaining screws, and slide the switch from the surround.

Refitting

27 Refitting is a reversal of removal.

Electric exterior mirror switch

Removal

28 Remove the door inner trim panel as described in Chapter 11.
29 Remove the screws securing the front end of the door grip to the trim panel and move the door grip slightly away from the panel (see illustration).
30 Unscrew the switch mounting screws (see illustration).
31 Disconnect the wiring and withdraw the switch (see illustrations).

Refitting

32 Refitting is a reversal of removal.

Sunroof operating switch

Removal

33 Make sure that the front interior light switch is OFF, then use a screwdriver to prise off the interior light lens.
34 Unscrew the mounting bolts and withdraw the interior light housing from the headlining. Disconnect the wiring.
35 Press out the sunroof operating switch from the interior light housing.

Refitting

36 Refitting is a reversal of removal.

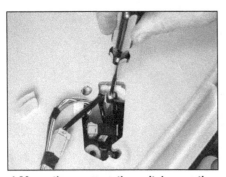

4.30 . . . then remove the switch mounting screws . . .

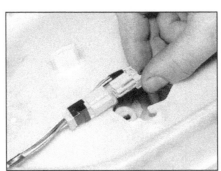

4.31a . . . disconnect the wiring . . .

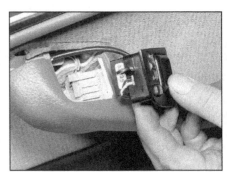

4.31b . . . and withdraw the switch

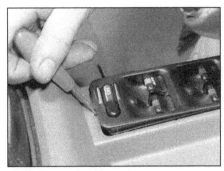

4.41a Prise the power window switch from the centre console . . .

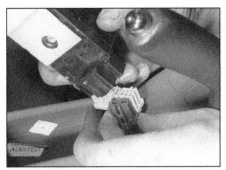

4.41b . . . and disconnect the wiring

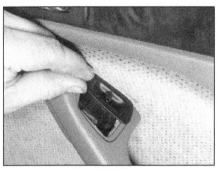

4.43 Remove the rear door power window switch . . .

Heated front seats switch

Removal

37 Make sure the ignition is switched off.
38 Using a small screwdriver, carefully prise out the switch from the centre console. Disconnect the wiring.

Refitting

39 Refitting is a reversal of removal.

Master power window switch

Removal

40 Make sure the ignition is switched off.
41 Using a screwdriver, carefully prise the power window switch panel from the centre console - to do this, insert a screwdriver at one side on the rear of the panel then insert a further screwdriver at the front of the panel. Disconnect the wiring plug and remove the switch panel **(see illustrations)**.

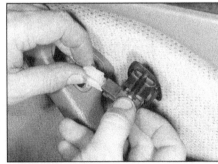

4.44 . . . and disconnect the wiring

Refitting

42 Refitting is a reversal of removal.

Rear door power window switch

Refitting

43 Remove the upper screw from the front of the door grip, then prise out the switch **(see illustration)**.
44 Disconnect the wiring and withdraw the switch **(see illustration)**.

Refitting

45 Refitting is a reversal of removal.

Power seat switch

Removal

46 Remove the seat as described in Chapter 11.
47 Prise out the cover, then remove the screw and remove the tilt adjust handle from the seat.
48 Remove the screws and remove the side cover from the seat.
49 Disconnect the wiring then undo the mounting screws and remove the switch from the side cover.

Refitting

50 Refitting is a reversal of removal.

Bonnet switch

Removal

51 Open the bonnet, then disconnect the wiring from the switch located on the engine compartment front cross panel.

52 Unscrew the mounting bolts and release the wiring connector support clip. Remove the switch from the cross panel.

Refitting

53 Refitting is a reversal of removal.

Courtesy light/door ajar warning switch

Note: *The switch does not provide a direct earth connection for the interior lights, this function being carried out by the interior light delay unit.*

Removal

54 Open the door to expose the switch in the door pillar.
55 Remove the screw and withdraw the switch from the door pillar. Disconnect the wiring **(see illustrations)**.

Refitting

56 Refitting is a reversal of removal.

> **HAYNES HINT** *Tape the wiring to the door pillar, or tie a length of string to the wiring, to retrieve it if it falls back into the door pillar.*

Glovebox illumination light switch

Removal

57 Open the glovebox, then remove the screws and withdraw the light switch from the facia. Disconnect the wiring **(see illustration)**.

Refitting

58 Refitting is a reversal of removal.

4.55a Remove the courtesy light/door ajar warning switch . . .

4.55b . . . and disconnect the wiring

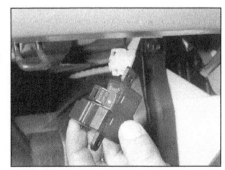

4.57 Removing the glovebox illumination switch

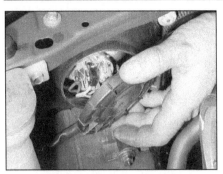

5.4a Removing the outer headlight cover . . .

5.4b . . . and inner headlight cover

5.5a Disconnect the wiring from the outer headlight bulb . . .

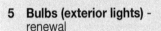

5 Bulbs (exterior lights) - renewal

General

1 Whenever a bulb is renewed, note the following points:

a) Make sure the electrical circuit is switched off.

b) Remember that, if the light has just been in use, the bulb may be extremely hot.

c) Always check the bulb contacts and holder, ensuring that there is clean metal-to-metal contact between the bulb and its live contact(s) and earth. Clean off any corrosion or dirt before fitting a new bulb.

d) Wherever bayonet-type bulbs are fitted, ensure that the live contact(s) bear firmly against the bulb contact.

e) Always ensure that the new bulb is of the correct rating (see Specifications), and that it is completely clean before fitting.

Headlight

2 Open the bonnet.

3 The outer bulb is for dipped beam and the inner bulb is for main beam. If removing the right-hand headlight main beam bulb, first lift the coolant expansion tank from its mounting and position to one side.

4 Unscrew the appropriate cover from the rear of the headlight (**see illustrations**).

5 Disconnect the wiring from the rear of the bulb (**see illustrations**).

6 Squeeze together the spring clip and pivot it away from the bulb (**see illustration**).

7 Remove the bulb from the bulbholder (**see illustrations**).

8 When handling the new bulb, use a tissue or clean cloth, to avoid touching the glass with the fingers; moisture and grease from the skin can cause blackening and rapid failure of this type of bulb. If the glass is accidentally touched, wipe it clean using methylated spirit.

9 Fit the new bulb using a reversal of the removal procedure; make sure that the bulb tabs are correctly located in the light unit cut-outs. When refitting the cover make sure that the cut-out on the rear lip is facing upwards.

10 Where necessary, refit the coolant expansion tank.

Front sidelight

11 Open the bonnet, then unscrew the outer cover from the rear of the headlight.

12 Disconnect the wiring from the front sidelight bulbholder.

13 Twist the bulbholder anti-clockwise and remove from the light unit (**see illustration**)

14 Pull the wedge-type bulb from the bulbholder (**see illustration**).

5.5b . . . and inner headlight bulb

5.6 Squeeze together the spring clip . . .

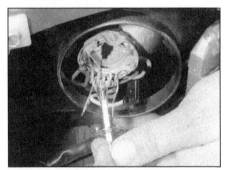

5.7a . . . and remove the outer headlight bulb

5.7b Removing the inner headlight bulb

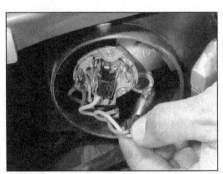

5.13 Remove the front sidelight bulbholder from the headlight . . .

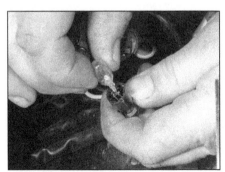

5.14 . . . then pull out the wedge-type bulb

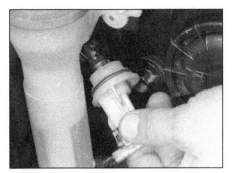

5.16 Disconnect the wiring . . .

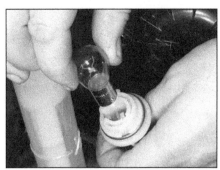

5.17 . . . then unscrew the front direction indicator bulbholder . . .

5.18 . . . and remove the bulb

15 Fit the new bulb using a reversal of the removal procedure.

Front direction indicator

16 Open the bonnet, then disconnect the wiring from the front direction indicator bulbholder in the headlight **(see illustration)**.
17 Twist the bulbholder anti-clockwise and remove it from the outer end of the headlight **(see illustration)**.
18 Depress and twist the bulb to remove it from the bulbholder **(see illustration)**. If necessary, disconnect the wiring from the bulbholder.
19 Fit the new bulb using a reversal of the removal procedure.

Front direction indicator side repeater

20 Push the front direction indicator side repeater lens forwards, and release the unit from the front wing **(see illustration)**.

21 Disconnect the wiring, then twist the bulbholder anti-clockwise and remove it from the light unit. Pull the wedge-type bulb from the bulbholder **(see illustrations)**.
22 Fit the new bulb using a reversal of the removal procedure.

Rear light cluster

23 Open the bootlid and lift the rear light cluster access cover in the rear corner of the luggage compartment **(see illustration)**.
24 Squeeze together the plastic tabs and withdraw the rear light cluster bulbholder from the light unit **(see illustration)**.
25 Depress and twist the relevant bulb to remove it from the bulbholder **(see illustration)**. The stop/tail bulb is at the top, the direction indicator bulb is at the middle outer position, the reversing light bulb is at the middle inner position, and the rear foglight bulb is at the bottom.

26 Fit the new bulb using a reversal of the removal procedure. Note that the stop/tail light bulb has offset pins, to ensure correct installation.

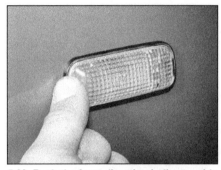

5.20 Push the front direction indicator side repeater lens forwards and remove the unit from the front wing . . .

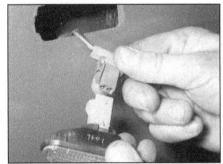

5.21a . . . then disconnect the wiring . . .

5.21b . . . remove the bulbholder . . .

5.21c . . . and pull out the wedge-type bulb

5.23 Lift the access cover . . .

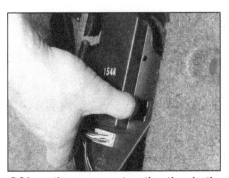

5.24 . . . then squeeze together the plastic tabs to remove the bulbholder

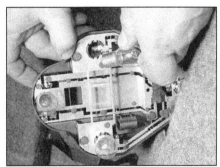

5.25 Removing a rear light cluster bulb

5.27a Remove the screws . . .

5.27b . . . and withdraw the rear number plate light unit

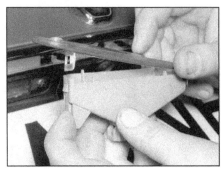

5.28a Remove the lens . . .

Rear number plate light

27 Open the bootlid then remove the screws and withdraw the appropriate rear number plate light unit until it is possible to disconnect the wiring (see illustrations).
28 Remove the lens, then pull out the wedge-type bulb (see illustrations).
29 Fit the new bulb using a reversal of the removal procedure.

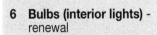

6 Bulbs (interior lights) -
renewal

General

1 Refer to Section 5, paragraph 1.

Roof front console light

2 Using a small screwdriver, prise the lens from the light unit (see illustration).
3 Remove the festoon-type bulb from the light contacts (see illustration).
4 Fit the new bulb using a reversal of the removal procedure, but make sure the bulb is held firmly between the contacts. Bend the contacts if necessary.

Interior and luggage compartment lights

5 Using a small screwdriver, prise the lens from the light unit (see illustration).
6 Remove the festoon-type bulb from the light contacts (see illustration).

7 Fit the new bulb using a reversal of the removal procedure, but make sure the bulb is held firmly between the contacts. Bend the contacts if necessary.

Door-mounted courtesy light

8 Using a small screwdriver, prise the lens from the light unit.
9 Remove the festoon-type bulb from the light contacts.
10 Fit the new bulb using a reversal of the removal procedure, but make sure the bulb is held firmly between the contacts. Bend the contacts if necessary.

Instrument panel lights

11 Remove the instrument panel, as described in Section 8.
12 Twist the relevant bulbholder anti-clockwise to remove it from the rear of the instrument panel (see illustration).

6.2 Prise off the roof front console light lens . . .

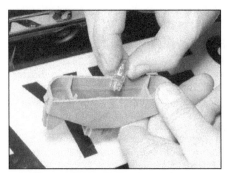

5.28b . . . then pull out the wedge-type bulb

13 Where applicable, pull the wedge-type bulb from the bulbholder.
14 Fit the new bulb using a reversal of the removal procedure, with reference to Section 8 when refitting the instrument panel.

6.3 . . . and remove the festoon-type bulb

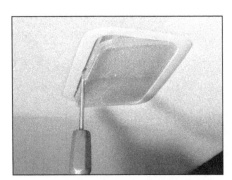

6.5 Prise the lens from the interior light . . .

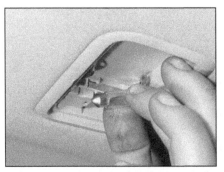

6.6 . . . and remove the festoon-type bulb

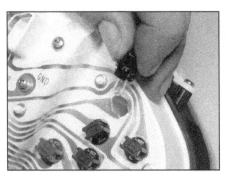

6.12 Removing a bulbholder from the instrument panel

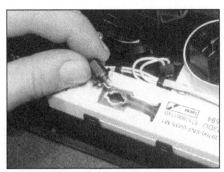

6.22 Removing the clock illumination bulb

6.32 Removing the bulbholder from the master power window switch

6.35 The two halves of the glovebox illumination light switch

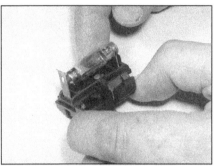

6.36 Removing the festoon-type bulb from the glovebox illumination light switch

Ashtray illumination bulb

15 Remove the centre console as described in Chapter 11.
16 Pull the bulbholder from the rear of the ashtray, and pull out the wedge-type bulb.
17 Fit the new bulb using a reversal of the removal procedure.

Cigarette lighter illumination bulb

18 Remove the centre console as described in Chapter 11.
19 Pull the bulbholder from the rear of the cigarette lighter, and pull out the wedge-type bulb.
20 Fit the new bulb using a reversal of the removal procedure.

Clock illumination bulb

21 Remove the heater control panel as described in Chapter 3.
22 Twist the bulbholder from the rear of the clock housing, then pull out the wedge-type bulb (see illustration).
23 Fit the new bulb using a reversal of the removal procedure.

Heater control panel illumination bulbs

24 Remove the heater control panel as described in Chapter 3.
25 Twist the relevant bulbholder anti-clockwise, and withdraw the bulbholder.
26 Pull the wedge-type bulb from the bulbholder.
27 Fit the new bulb using a reversal of the removal procedure.

Switch illumination bulb

28 Remove the switch as described in Section 4.
29 Twist the bulbholder anti-clockwise to remove it from the switch. The bulb is integral with the bulbholder.
30 Fit the new bulb using a reversal of the removal procedure.

Master power window switch illumination

Removal

31 Remove the master power window switch as described in Section 4.
32 Twist the bulbholder from the bottom of the switch (see illustration).

Refitting

33 Refitting is a reversal of removal.

Glovebox illumination light

Removal

34 Remove the switch as described in Section 4.
35 Using a small screwdriver, prise apart the two halves of the switch (see illustration).
36 Remove the festoon-type bulb from the light contacts (see illustration).

Refitting

37 Fit the new bulb using a reversal of the removal procedure, but make sure the bulb is held firmly between the contacts. Bend the contacts if necessary.

7 Exterior light units - removal and refitting

Headlight/direction indicator light

Removal

1 Remove the front bumper as described in Chapter 11.
2 Disconnect the wiring from the headlight and headlight adjuster (see illustration).
3 Unscrew the mounting bolts and withdraw the headlight unit from the front crossmember and body (see illustrations).

Refitting

4 Refitting is a reversal of removal, but if necessary have the headlight beam alignment adjusted.

7.2 Disconnecting the wiring from the rear of the headlight

7.3a Headlight lower mounting bolts . . .

7.3b . . . and upper mounting bolts

7.3c Removing the headlight unit

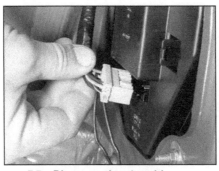

7.7a Disconnecting the wiring . . .

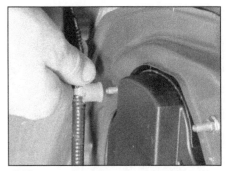

7.7b . . . and cable support from the rear light cluster

7.8a Unscrew the mounting nuts . . .

7.8b . . . and remove the rear light cluster

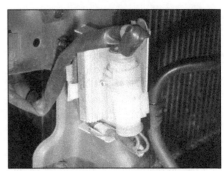

7.16 Headlight dim/dip resistor (front bumper removed)

Front direction indicator side repeater light

Removal and refitting

5 The procedure is described as part of the bulb renewal procedure in Section 5.

Rear light cluster

Removal

6 Open the bootlid and remove the trim from the rear corner of the luggage compartment.
7 Disconnect the wiring from the light and remove the cable support from the upper mounting stud **(see illustrations)**.
8 Unscrew the mounting nuts and withdraw the rear light unit from the body panel **(see illustrations)**.

Refitting

9 Refitting is a reversal of the removal procedure.

Rear number plate light

Removal

10 Open the bootlid then remove the screws and withdraw the lens from the appropriate rear number plate light unit.
11 Withdraw the light unit then disconnect the wiring.

Refitting

12 Refitting is a reversal of the removal procedure.

Headlight dim/dip resistor

Removal

13 The headlight dim/dip resistor is located behind the front bumper. The dim/dip control unit is located behind the lower facia trim panel inside the vehicle.
14 To remove the resistor, first remove the front bumper as described in Chapter 11.

15 Make sure that the dim/dip system is turned off.
Caution: The dim/dip resistor becomes very hot during use. Make sure it has cooled down before attempting to remove it.
16 Release the clip and disconnect the wiring connector **(see illustration)**.
17 Unbolt the resistor from the body.

Refitting

18 Refitting is a reversal of removal.

8 Instrument panel - removal and refitting

Removal

1 Disconnect the battery negative and positive leads, and **wait 10 minutes**. This is a safety requirement of the air bag supplementary restraint system (see Section 24).
2 Remove the two upper screws from the instrument panel surround, then withdraw the surround and disconnect the wiring from the two switches **(see illustrations)**. If required, the steering wheel may be removed to provide additional working room.
3 Tilt the steering column fully down. If required, remove the screws and withdraw the steering column upper and lower shrouds.
4 Unscrew the mounting screws then withdraw the instrument panel until the wiring connectors can be disconnected **(see illustrations)**.

8.2a Remove the instrument panel surround . . .

8.2b . . . and disconnect the wiring

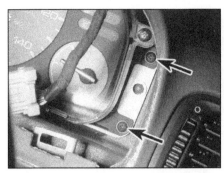

8.4a Instrument panel mounting screws

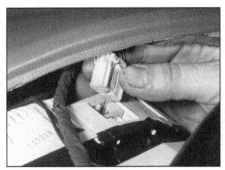

8.4b Disconnect the wiring . . .

8.4c . . . and withdraw the instrument panel to one side of the steering wheel

5 Carefully withdraw the instrument panel to one side of the steering wheel.

Refitting

6 Refitting is a reversal of removal, but make sure that the wiring connectors are fully engaged.

9 Instrument panel components - removal and refitting

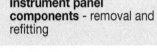

Caution: The instrument panel components are delicate and should be treated with care. Do not place gauges face down, as the needles may be bent and/or damaged resulting in them being inaccurate. Work in a clean environment to prevent dust and dirt entering the instrument panel.

Removal

1 Remove all bulbholders, then remove the screws and lift off the cover and sub-printed circuit board.
2 Separate the visor from the meter housing.
3 Remove the screws and lift off the main printed circuit board.
4 Remove the screws and detach the light case and wiring.
5 The instruments (coolant temperature gauge, fuel gauge, tachometer and speedometer) can now be removed after removing the relevant retaining screws.

11.2 Cigarette lighter mounted on the centre console

Refitting

6 Refitting is the reverse of the removal procedure, but make sure that the printed circuit board contact points are clean, and do not overtighten the screws into the plastic casing.

10 'Lights on' warning system - general information

1 On all models, a lights-on warning buzzer is fitted. The buzzer will sound if the driver's door is opened when the headlights or sidelights are switched on.
2 The buzzer unit is located behind the driver's side of the facia.

11 Cigarette lighter - removal and refitting

Removal

1 Remove the centre console as described in Chapter 11.
2 Remove the thermofuse housing from the cigarette lighter (see illustration).
3 Disconnect the illumination light bulbholder.
4 Unscrew the ring nut and release the cigarette lighter socket from the protector housing.
5 Recover the illumination ring from the centre console.

Refitting

6 Refitting is a reversal of removal, but align the lugs with the slot in the centre console and check the operation of the cigarette lighter before fully refitting the centre console.

12 Clock - removal and refitting

Removal

1 Disconnect the battery negative lead.

2 Remove the centre console (see Chapter 11) and heater control panel (see Chapter 3).
3 Undo the screws and separate the clock housing from the top of the heater control panel.
4 Using a small screwdriver, prise the hazard warning switch from the clock housing.

Refitting

5 Refitting is a reversal of removal.

13 Horn - removal and refitting

Removal

1 Disconnect the battery negative lead. On some models the horns are located behind the front bumper, however on most models they are located on the engine compartment front cross-panel below the bonnet lock.
2 Where necessary, remove the front bumper as described in Chapter 11.
3 Disconnect the wiring.
4 Unbolt and remove the horn from the mounting bracket. If necessary, also unbolt and remove the bracket (see illustration).

Refitting

5 Refitting is a reversal of removal. When replacing a horn, make sure the correct type is obtained to supplement the existing one.

13.4 Horn and mounting bracket

14 Speedometer speed sensor - removal and refitting

Removal

1 The speedometer speed sensor is located on the top of the power steering speed sensor on the transmission (see Chapter 10).
2 Disconnect the wiring, then unbolt the sensor and remove it from the engine compartment. Recover the drive link from the sensor.

Refitting

3 Refitting is a reversal of removal.

15 Wiper arm - removal and refitting

Removal

1 Operate the wiper motor, then switch it off so that the wiper arm returns to the parked position.
2 Stick a piece of tape along the edge of the wiper blade, to use as an alignment aid on refitting.
3 Unscrew and remove the spindle nut, then lift the blade off the glass and pull the wiper arm off its spindle **(see illustrations)**. If necessary, the arm can be levered off the spindle using a suitable flat-bladed screwdriver. If both windscreen wiper arms

15.3a Unscrew the spindle nut . . .

are removed, note their locations, as different arms are fitted to the driver's and passenger's sides.

Refitting

4 Refitting is a reversal of removal, but ensure that the wiper arm and spindle splines are clean and dry and align the blades with the tape fitted before removal.

16 Windscreen wiper motor and linkage - removal and refitting

Removal

1 Remove the wiper arms as described in Section 15.
2 Open the bonnet. Make sure the ignition is switched off.

16.4a Removing the windscreen lower moulding front clips . . .

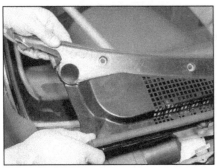
16.4c Removing the windscreen lower moulding

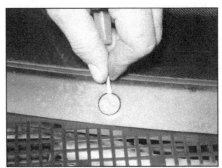
16.4b . . . and rear clips

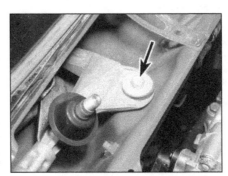
16.6a Wiper motor and linkage inner mounting bolt . . .

15.3b . . . and pull the wiper arm from the spindle

3 Pull the weatherstrip from the front edge of the bulkhead windscreen lower moulding.
4 Remove the screws and clips and remove the windscreen lower moulding for access to the wiper motor. Use a screwdriver to lever out the clips **(see illustrations)**.
5 Disconnect the wiring and release the connector from the bulkhead.
6 Unscrew the mounting bolts and withdraw the wiper motor and linkage **(see illustrations)**.
7 If necessary, unscrew and remove the nut and washer and disconnect the operating rod from the motor spindle.. The wiper motor may be unbolted from the linkage frame.

Refitting

8 Refitting is a reversal of removal, but refer to Section 15 when refitting the wiper arms.

17 Windscreen washer system components - removal and refitting

Washer fluid reservoir

Removal

1 The washer fluid reservoir filler neck is located on the left-hand side of the engine compartment, and the washer fluid reservoir is located behind the liner at the front of the left-hand wheelarch. Before removing the reservoir, syphon out all of the fluid using a suitable plastic tube.

16.6b . . . and outer mounting bolts

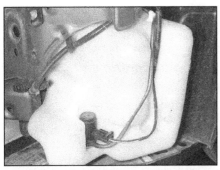

17.5 The washer fluid reservoir is mounted on the front left-hand corner of the vehicle

2 Jack up the front of the vehicle (see *Jacking and Vehicle Support*) and remove the left-hand front wheel.
3 Access to the washer fluid reservoir may be gained by either removing the front bumper or wheelarch liner as described in Chapter 11.
4 Remove the screw and withdraw the reservoir upper filler neck, then remove the lower filler neck from the rubber grommet in the top of the reservoir. Recover the float and grommet.
5 Disconnect the washer tubes and wiring connectors from the washer motors **(see illustration)**.
6 Unscrew the mounting bolts and remove the washer reservoir from the front valance.

Refitting

7 Refitting is a reversal of removal, but check the operation of the washers before refitting the bumper or liner.

Washer pump

Removal

8 Remove the washer reservoir as described in paragraphs 1 to 6.
9 Pull the washer pump from the reservoir, and recover the grommet **(see illustration)**.

Refitting

10 Refitting is a reversal of removal.

Windscreen washer nozzle

Removal

11 Open the bonnet.

18.6 Bolts securing the radio/cassette box to the bracket

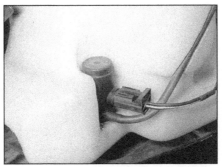

17.9 The washer pump, wiring and hose

12 Working under the bonnet, release the securing tabs using long-nosed pliers, then push the nozzle from the bonnet. Disconnect the fluid hose, and withdraw the nozzle.

Refitting

13 Refitting is a reversal of removal.

18 Radio/cassette player - removal and refitting

Note: *This Section describes the removal and refitting of the standard radio/cassette fitted as original equipment. The procedure may differ for non-standard equipment.*

Removal

1 Disconnect the battery negative lead.
2 Remove the facia lower trim panel and glovebox as described in Chapter 11.
3 Remove the surround from the front of the facia as described in Chapter 11.
4 The radio is secured in its mounting box with standard DIN fixings. Two special tools, obtainable from most car accessory shops, are required for removal. Alternatively, suitable tools can be fabricated from 3 mm diameter wire, such as welding rod.
5 Insert the tools into the two holes on each side of the radio and push them until they snap into place **(see illustration)**. The radio/cassette player can then be slid out of the mounting box. As the unit is withdrawn it is automatically disconnected from the wiring pins on the rear of the mounting box.

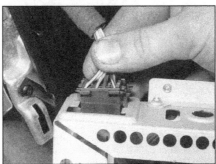

18.7a Disconnect the wiring . . .

6 If it is required to remove the mounting box, first remove the centre console as described in Chapter 11. Remove the heater control panel as described in Chapter 3, then reach under the radio/cassette mounting box and loosen the two bolts securing the box to the bracket **(see illustration)**.
7 Withdraw the mounting box and disconnect the wiring and aerial from the rear of it **(see illustrations)**.

Refitting

8 Refitting is a reversal of removal, but push the radio/cassette into its mounting box until the retaining lugs snap into place.

19 Loudspeakers - removal and refitting

Front door-mounted loudspeakers

Removal

1 Remove the door inner trim panel as described in Chapter 11.
2 Unscrew the retaining screws and withdraw the speaker a little way from the front door, then disconnect the wiring. Withdraw the speaker taking care not to damage its cone **(see illustration)**.

Refitting

3 Refitting is a reversal of removal.

18.5 Using the special tools to remove the radio/cassette

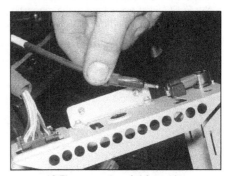

18.7b . . . and aerial from the radio/cassette mounting box

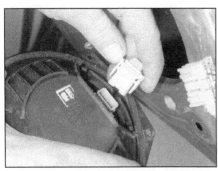

19.2 Disconnecting the wiring from the front door-mounted loudspeakers

Rear loudspeakers

Removal

4 Using a screwdriver, carefully prise the cover from the speaker.
5 Unscrew the retaining screws, withdraw the speaker, and disconnect the wiring. Withdraw the speaker taking care not to damage its cone (see illustration).

Refitting

6 Refitting is a reversal of removal.

Tweeter speakers

Removal

7 Using a screwdriver, carefully prise the tweeter speaker cover from the top of the facia.
8 Disconnect the wiring and remove the speaker from the facia.
9 If required, remove the screws and separate the speaker from the cover.

Refitting

10 Refitting is a reversal of removal.

20 Radio aerial - removal and refitting

Power aerial mast

Removal

1 The power aerial is located on the left-hand rear wing.
2 The aerial mast can be removed leaving the motor in situ. First apply tape to the rear wing to protect it against scratching.
3 Unscrew the nut and remove the spacer from the top of the aerial.
4 Have an assistant switch on the radio, then carefully withdraw the mast and cable as the motor extends it. Note which side of the cable the engagement teeth are on. Leave the radio switched on at this stage.

Refitting

5 Insert the cable into the aerial unit with the engagement teeth the correct way round. Check that the teeth are correctly engaged with the drive gear by moving the cable up and down.

19.5 The rear loudspeakers are mounted on the rear shelf

6 Have the assistant switch off the radio and allow the motor to pull the cable and mast into the housing.
7 Refit the spacer and nut and tighten the nut to the specified torque. Do not over-tighten the nut otherwise the mast may stick. Should this occur, back off the nut until the mast moves freely.

Power aerial unit

Removal

8 Remove the trim panel from the left-hand side of the luggage compartment with reference to Chapter 11 (see illustration).
9 Disconnect the motor wiring and the aerial lead.
10 Unscrew the nut from the top of the aerial unit taking care not to damage the rear wing, then unscrew the lower mounting nut securing the unit to the inner body. Withdraw the unit from inside the vehicle.

Refitting

11 Refitting is a reversal of removal, but tighten the upper mounting nut before tightening the lower one.

21 Cruise control system components - removal and refitting

1 The cruise control system is a vacuum operated system; the main components being a vacuum actuator unit, vacuum tank, vehicle speed sensor, electronic control unit (ECU),

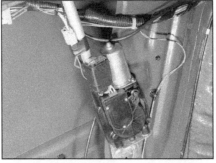

20.8 The power aerial unit is mounted on the left-hand side of the rear luggage compartment

auto gear position switch (automatic transmission models), clutch switch (manual transmission models), brake switch and set/resume switches on the steering wheel.

Electronic control unit (ECU)

Removal

2 Disconnect the battery negative and positive leads, and wait 10 minutes. This is a safety requirement of the air bag supplementary restraint system (see Section 24), and some of the cruise control system components are located near the SRS system components.
3 Remove the single screw then prise the lower facia panel from under the steering column. Disconnect the wiring as applicable.
4 Unscrew the mounting bolts securing the ECU beneath the facia, then disconnect the wiring and withdraw the unit.

Refitting

5 Refitting is a reversal of removal.

Set/resume switch

Removal

6 Disconnect the battery negative and positive leads, and wait 10 minutes. This is a safety requirement of the air bag supplementary restraint system (see Section 24), and some of the cruise control system components are located near the SRS system components.
7 Carefully prise the cover from the switch on the steering wheel.
8 Remove the screws and withdraw the switch from the steering wheel.

Refitting

9 Refitting is a reversal of removal.

Cruise control main switch

Removal and refitting

10 The procedure is described in Section 4.

Clutch pedal switch

Removal

11 Remove the single screw then prise the lower facia panel from under the steering column. Disconnect the wiring as applicable.
12 Disconnect the wiring from the clutch pedal switch.
13 Unscrew and remove the lower locknut, then remove the switch from the pedal bracket. Do not move the upper locknut if the switch is to be refitted, as this will retain the clutch pedal height position.

Refitting

14 Refitting is a reversal of removal, but check and if necessary adjust the clutch pedal height with reference to Chapter 6.

Auto selector position switch (automatic transmission models)

Removal

15 Remove the centre console as described in Chapter 11.

16 Disconnect the wiring, then unbolt the switch from the selector housing.

Refitting

17 Refitting is a reversal of removal.

Brake pedal switch

Removal

18 Remove the single screw then prise the lower facia panel from under the steering column. Disconnect the wiring as applicable.
19 Disconnect the wiring from the brake pedal switch.
20 Unscrew and remove the lower locknut, then remove the switch from the pedal bracket. Do not move the upper locknut if the switch is to be refitted, as this will retain the brake pedal height position.

Refitting

21 Refitting is a reversal of removal.

Actuator

Removal

22 Working in the engine compartment, pull back the boot then loosen the adjustment locknut (on the outside of the bracket) and disconnect the outer cable from the bracket.
23 Disconnect the inner cable from the actuator rod.
24 Disconnect the wiring.
25 Note the position of the vacuum hoses and vent hose, then disconnect them from the actuator.
26 Loosen the bolt securing the support bracket to the body.
27 Unscrew the remaining mounting bolt and withdraw the actuator from the engine compartment.
28 Unscrew the nuts and remove the bracket and mounting rubbers from the actuator.
29 If necessary, unscrew the screws and remove the filters, solenoid valves and O-rings. Obtain new components as necessary.

Refitting

30 Refitting is a reversal of removal, but adjust the cable as follows.

Adjustment

31 Manually operate the actuator cable and check that it moves freely without any signs of binding.
32 Run the engine at fast idle speed until the electric cooling fan operates and switches off.
33 Position a steel rule next to the actuator rod, then manually move the rod to the point where the engine speed starts to increase. This free play must be 11.0 ± 1.5 mm. If adjustment is required, loosen the locknuts then reposition the cable and tighten the locknuts. Check the free play adjustment again.

Vacuum tank

Removal

34 Jack up the front of the vehicle and support on axle stands (see *Jacking and Vehicle Support*).

35 Unscrew and remove the five outer screws retaining the underbody splash guard to the left-hand side of the vehicle.
36 Remove the front retaining screws from the left-hand front wheelarch, then pull out the liner for access to the vacuum tank.
37 Disconnect the vacuum hose from the tank.
38 Unbolt the vacuum tank from the body and withdraw from under the vehicle.

Refitting

39 Refitting is a reversal of removal.

22 Anti-theft alarm/immobiliser system - general information

Most models are fitted with an anti-theft alarm/immobiliser system which employs an infra-red handset and receiver unit. The vehicle can be locked by key without using the system, but in this case the engine is not immobilised and the internal movement sensor is inoperative. If the infra-red handset is used to lock the vehicle, it must also be used to disarm the system and disable the engine immobiliser.

Two batteries are located in the handset, and should they fail, they may be renewed by prising the handset apart using a small screwdriver. Make sure the new batteries are correctly located with their positive (+) sides facing downwards into the battery compartment.

If the handset fails to operate, the engine may be mobilised using the following procedure provided the four-digit key access code is known. First insert the key in the driver's door and unlock the door. With the door open, turn the key to the unlock position the number of times corresponding to the first digit of the key access code.

Turn the key to the lock position the number of times corresponding to the second digit of the key access code.

Turn the key to the unlock position the number of times corresponding to the third digit of the key access code.

Turn the key to the lock position the number of times corresponding to the fourth digit of the key access code.

Finally, turn the key once to the unlock position. The passenger's doors will now unlock and the engine will be fully mobilised. Note that if the incorrect number is entered three times, it will be necessary to wait 10 minutes before attempting to re-enter the number.

The anti-theft alarm/immobiliser system incorporates indicators in the front door inner trim panels, a bonnet switch, door actuators, alarm horn, security control switch (located in the rear luggage compartment side), bootlid switch, starter cut relay, receiver unit (located at the front of the roof), and door switches.

Any suspected faults with the system should be referred to a Rover dealer.

23 Heated front seat components - general information

Some models are fitted with heated front seats. The seats are heated by electrical elements built into the seat cushions. For access to the heating elements, the seats must be dismantled, and this work should be entrusted to a Rover dealer.

24 Air bag and supplementary restraint system - general information and precautions

General information

1 An air bag supplementary restraint system (SRS) is fitted to most models to prevent serious chest and head injuries during an accident. The driver's air bag is fitted in the steering wheel centre pad, and the optional passenger's air bag is fitted in the top of the facia panel. The air bag is inflated by a gas generator, which forces the bag out from its location in the steering wheel of facia.
2 The SRS system has been modified several times, and no attempt must be made to fit components from another vehicle.
3 The SRS system is armed when the ignition is switched on. The airbag warning light will illuminate for approximately 6 seconds when the ignition is switched on. If the light remains on after this period or if it illuminates with the engine running, there is a fault in the system and the vehicle should be taken to a Rover dealer for checking.

Precautions

 Warning: The following precautions must be observed when working on vehicles with an air bag system, to prevent the possibility of personal injury.

a) Do not attempt to test any of the air bag system circuits using test meters or any other test equipment.
b) Before working on the air bag and SRS related components (steering wheel and column), switch off the ignition, and disconnect the battery negative lead, then wait 10 MINUTES before carrying out any further work.
c) Do not attempt to turn the steering wheel or column with the steering gear removed.
d) If the air bag warning light comes on, or any fault in the system is suspected, consult a Rover dealer without delay. Do not attempt to carry out fault diagnosis, or any dismantling of the components.

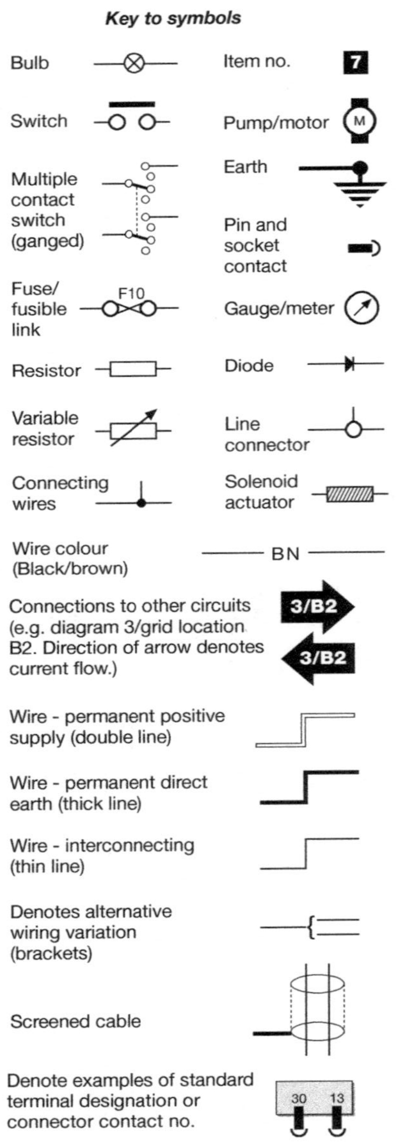

Key to symbols

	Bulb
	Switch
7	Item no.
M	Pump/motor
	Earth
	Pin and socket contact
	Multiple contact switch (ganged)
	Gauge/meter
F10	Fuse/fusible link
	Diode
	Resistor
	Line connector
	Variable resistor
	Solenoid actuator
	Connecting wires
— BN	Wire colour (Black/brown)
3/B2	Connections to other circuits (e.g. diagram 3/grid location B2. Direction of arrow denotes current flow.)
	Wire – permanent positive supply (double line)
	Wire – permanent direct earth (thick line)
	Wire – interconnecting (thin line)
	Denotes alternative wiring variation (brackets)
	Screened cable
30 13	Denote examples of standard terminal designation or connector contact no.

Earth locations

E1	Below engine compartment fusebox
E2	Below engine compartment fusebox
E3	Behind passenger's footwell trim panel
E4	Behind passenger's footwell trim panel
E5	Behind driver's footwell trim panel
E6	Behind driver's footwell trim panel
E7	Below driver's seat
E8	Below passenger's seat
E9	Below driver's seat
E10	Below passenger's seat
E11	RH side of engine
E12	Top LH front of engine, on valve cover
E13	Top LH front of engine
E14	LH side of engine compartment
E15	Behind centre of facia, near airbag control unit
E16	RH rear of luggage compartment
E17	LH rear of engine compartment
E18	RH rear of engine compartment
E19	Lower RH front of engine
E20	Bottom of LH 'C' pillar
E21	RH front of luggage compartment, behind rear seat
E22	LH front of engine compartment
E23	LH side of engine compartment
E24	RH rear of luggage compartment
E25	Below driver's seat
E26	Below rear of centre console

Typical passenger fusebox

Fuse	Rating	Circuit protected
F1	7.5A	Alarm
F2	15A	Engine management system
F3	10A	Airbag
F4	7.5A	Cruise control, alternator warning light
F5	7.5A	Electric windows, mirrors, sunroof
F6	30A	Wash/wipe
F7	7.5A	Heater and heated rear window
F8	10A	Direction indicators and reversing lights
F9	7.5A	Air conditioning
F10	7.5A	Dim/dip headlights
F11	10A	Electric aerial
F12	7.5A	Starting signal
F13	10A	Tail lights

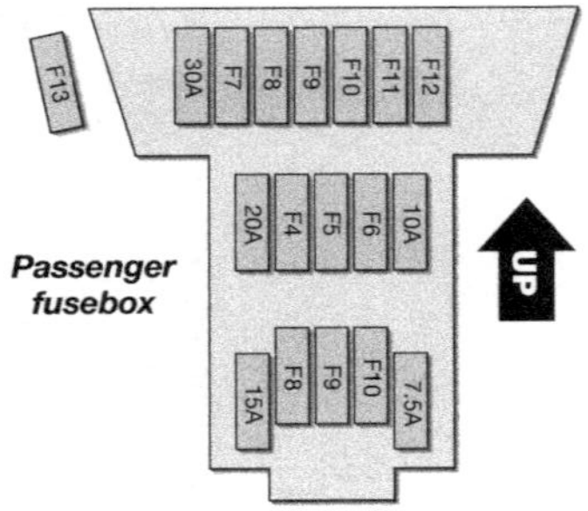

Typical engine fusebox

Fuse	Rating	Circuit protected
F1	10A	Dim/dip headlights
F2	20A	Central locking, alarm
F3	20A	Cooling fan
F4	30A	Sun roof
F5	10A	Lights
F6	30A	Headlight washers
F7	15A	Interior light
F8	15A	Cooling fan
F9	10A	Engine management system
F10	20A	Front seat height adjustment
F11	–	–
F12	7.5A	Radio/cassette
F13	20A	LH rear electric window
F14	20A	RH rear electric window
F15	20A	LH front electric window
F16	20A	RH front electric window
F17	20A	RH headlight
F18	20A	Stop lights, horn
F19	20A	LH headlight
F20	10A	Dim/dip headlights
F21	10A	Hazard warning lights
FA	80A	Main fuse (battery)
FB	50A	Main fuse (ignition)
FC	40A	Main fuse (heated rear window)
FD	30A	Main fuse (heater blower)
FE	30A	Main fuse (dash/parking lights)

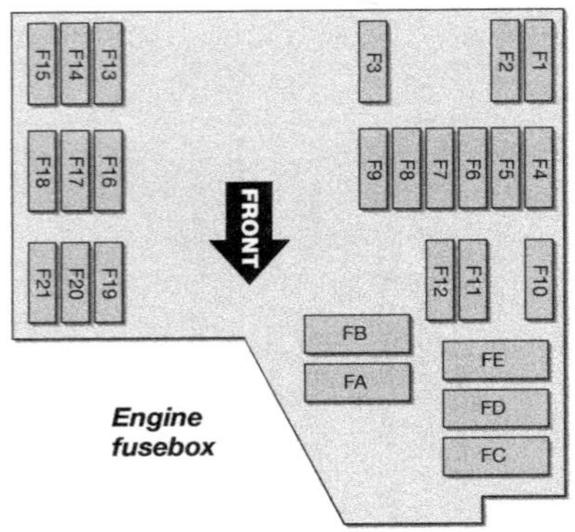

Engine fusebox

Passenger fusebox

Diagram 1 : Information for wiring diagrams

H29441
T.M.Marie

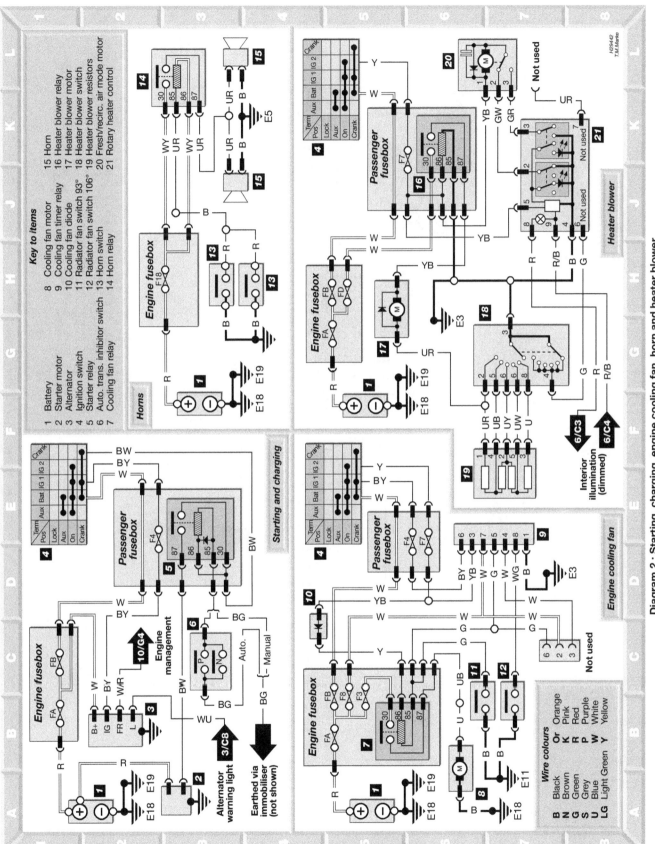

Diagram 2 : Starting, charging, engine cooling fan, horn and heater blower

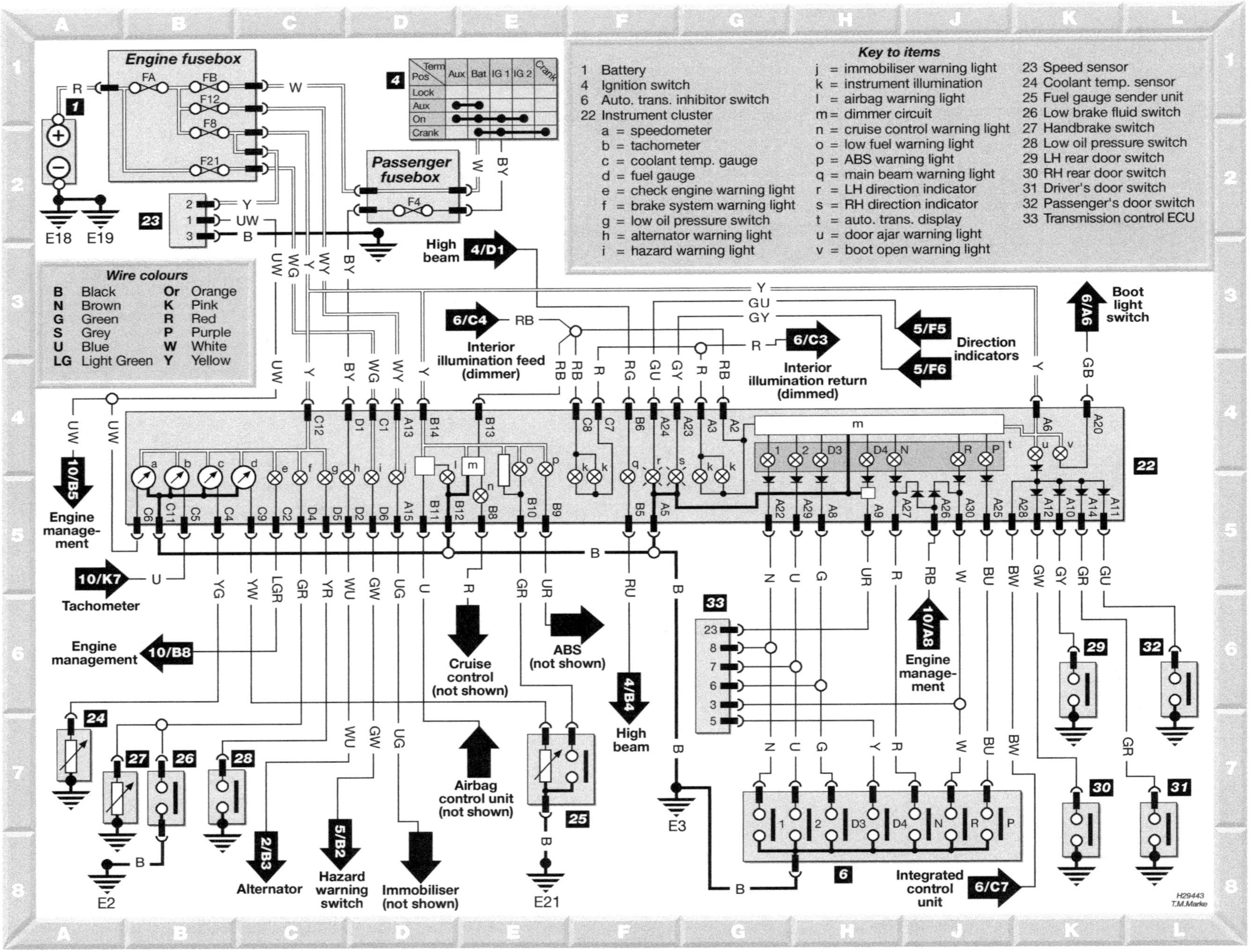

H29443
T.M.Marke

Key to items

1 Battery
4 Ignition switch
6 Auto. trans. inhibitor switch
22 Instrument cluster
  a = speedometer
  b = tachometer
  c = coolant temp. gauge
  d = fuel gauge
  e = check engine warning light
  f = brake system warning light
  g = low oil pressure switch
  h = alternator warning light
  i = hazard warning light
  j = immobiliser warning light
  k = instrument illumination
  l = airbag warning light
  m = dimmer circuit
  n = cruise control warning light
  o = low fuel warning light
  p = ABS warning light
  q = main beam warning light
  r = LH direction indicator
  s = RH direction indicator
  t = auto. trans. display
  u = door ajar warning light
  v = boot open warning light
23 Speed sensor
24 Coolant temp. sensor
25 Fuel gauge sender unit
26 Low brake fluid switch
27 Handbrake switch
28 Low oil pressure switch
29 LH rear door switch
30 RH rear door switch
31 Driver's door switch
32 Passenger's door switch
33 Transmission control ECU

Wire colours

B	Black	Or	Orange
N	Brown	K	Pink
G	Green	R	Red
S	Grey	P	Purple
U	Blue	W	White
LG	Light Green	Y	Yellow

Boot light switch

Direction indicators

Interior illumination return (dimmed)

Interior illumination feed (dimmer)

Engine management

ABS (not shown)

High beam

Cruise control (not shown)

Airbag control unit (not shown)

Immobiliser (not shown)

Hazard warning switch

Alternator

Engine management

Tachometer

Engine management

Integrated control unit

Passenger fusebox

Engine fusebox

Diagram 3 : Warning lights and gauges

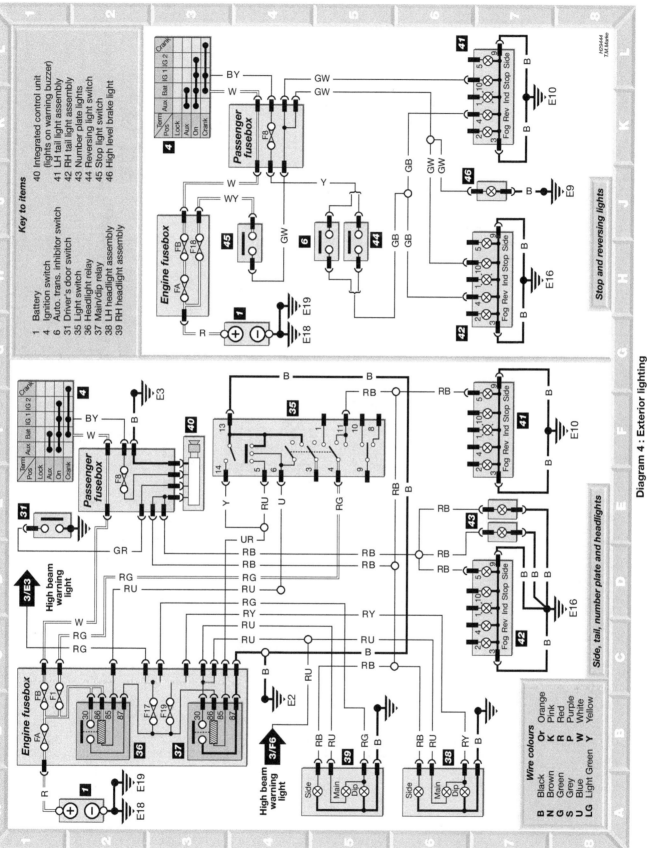

Diagram 4 : Exterior lighting

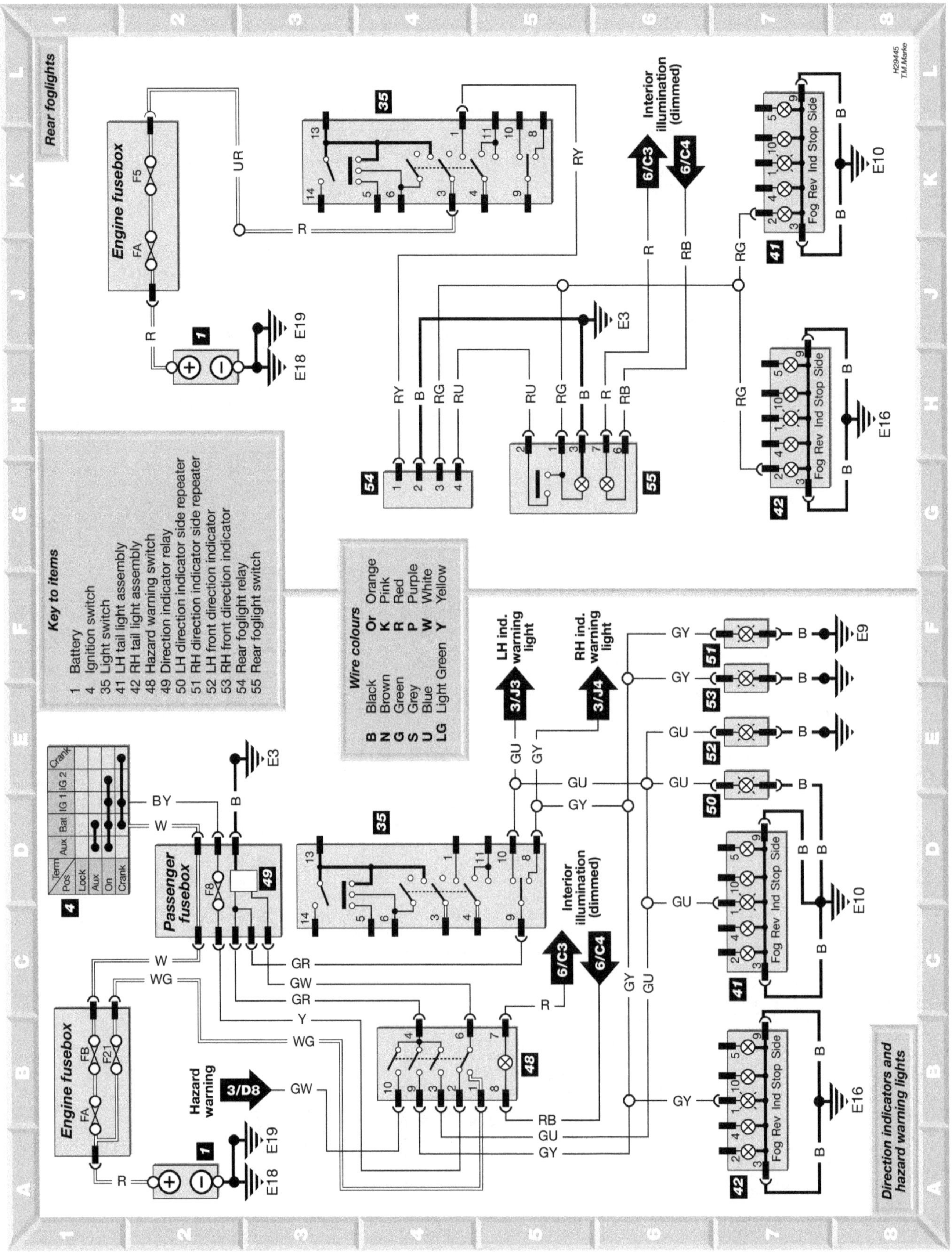

H29445
T.M.Marie

Rear foglights

Engine fusebox
F5
FA

35

Interior illumination (dimmed)
6/C3 6/C4

Fog Rev Ind Stop Side B E10
41

UR

R

R

1 E18 E19

RY

R RB RG

RY B RG RU RU RG B R RB RG

E3

Fog Rev Ind Stop Side B E16
42

54 55

Key to items

1 Battery
4 Ignition switch
35 Light switch
41 LH tail light assembly
42 RH tail light assembly
48 Hazard warning switch
49 Direction indicator relay
50 LH direction indicator side repeater
51 RH direction indicator side repeater
52 LH front direction indicator
53 RH front direction indicator
54 Rear foglight relay
55 Rear foglight switch

Wire colours

B Black   Or Orange
N Brown   K Pink
G Green   R Red
S Grey   P Purple
U Blue   W White
LG Light Green Y Yellow

LH ind. warning light
3/J3

RH ind. warning light
3/J4

GY E9
51
GY B
53
GU B
52
GU B
50
GU

GU GY

Crank
Term Aux Bat IG 1 IG 2
Pos
Lock
Aux
On
Crank
4

E3
B

BY
W

Passenger fusebox
F8 49

W
WG

Engine fusebox
FB F21
FA

Hazard warning
3/D8 GW

1 E18 E19

R

GR
GW
GR
Y
WG

35

Interior illumination (dimmed)
6/C3 6/C4

R

GY GU

Fog Rev Ind Stop Side B B E10
41

48

RB
GU
GY

GY Fog Rev Ind Stop Side B B E16
42

Direction indicators and hazard warning lights

Diagram 5 : Exterior lighting continued

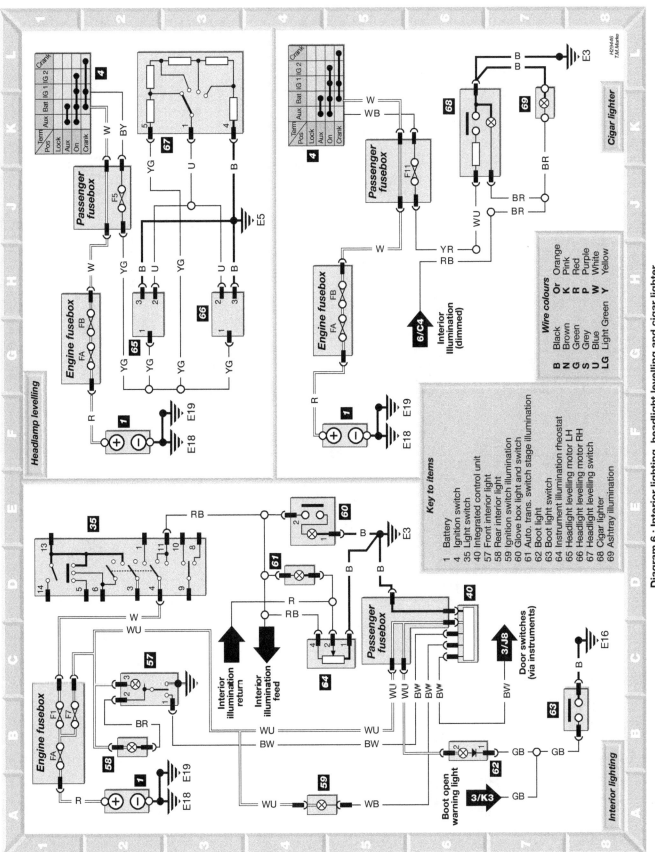

Wire colours

B	Black	**Or**	Orange
N	Brown	**K**	Pink
G	Green	**R**	Red
S	Grey	**P**	Purple
U	Blue	**W**	White
LG	Light Green	**Y**	Yellow

Key to items

1   Battery
4   Ignition switch
35 Light switch
40 Integrated control unit
57 Front interior light
58 Rear interior light
59 Ignition switch illumination
60 Glove box light and switch
61 Auto. trans. switch stage illumination
62 Boot light
63 Boot light switch
64 Instrument illumination rheostat
65 Headlight levelling motor LH
66 Headlight levelling motor RH
67 Headlight levelling switch
68 Cigar lighter
69 Ashtray illumination

Diagram 6 : Interior lighting, headlight levelling and cigar lighter

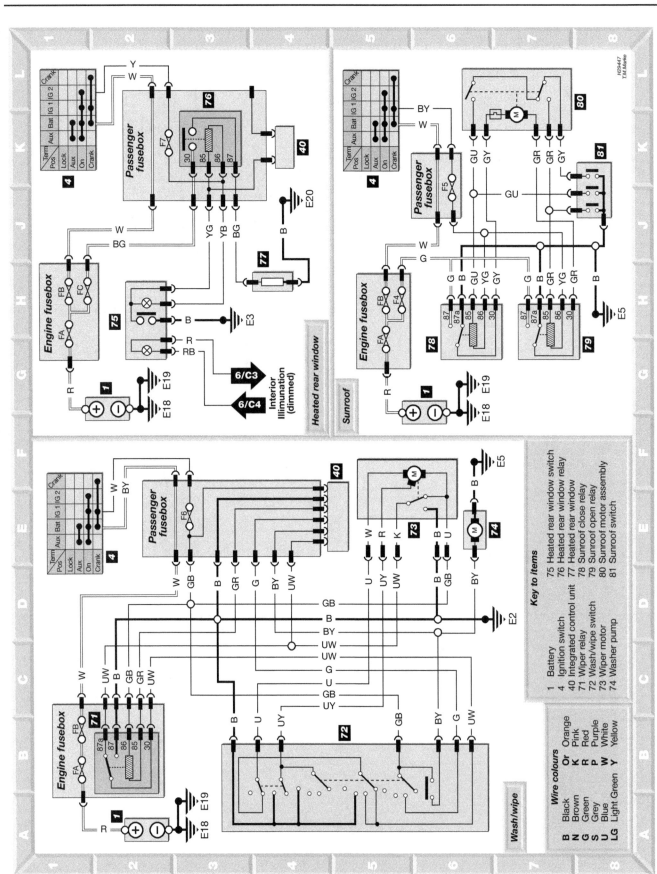

Diagram 7 : Wash/wipe, heated rear window and sunroof

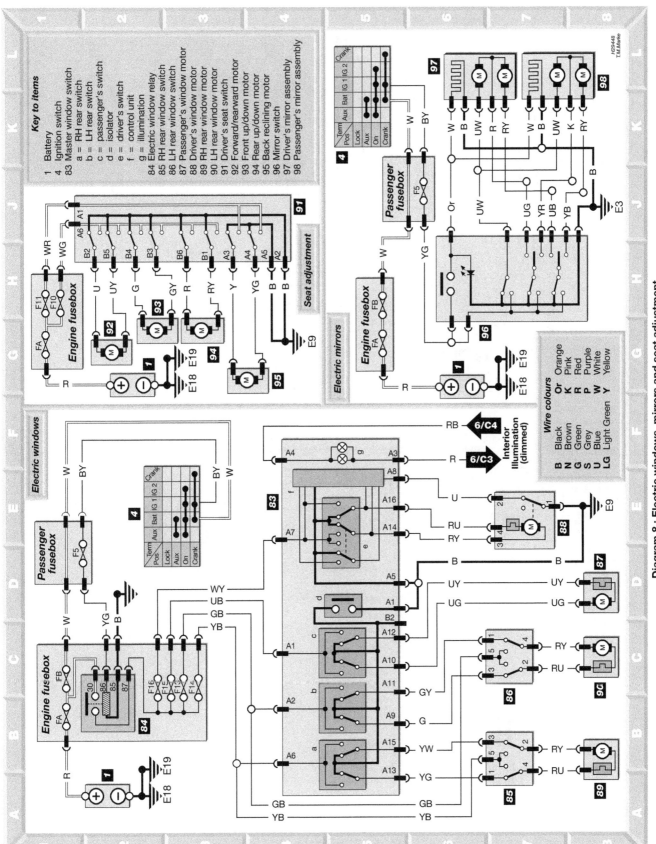

Key to items

1   Battery
4   Ignition switch
83 Master window switch
    a = RH rear switch
    b = LH rear switch
    c = passenger's switch
    d = isolator
    e = driver's switch
    f = control unit
    g = illumination
84 Electric window relay
85 RH rear window switch
86 LH rear window switch
87 Passenger's window motor
88 Driver's window motor
89 RH rear window motor
90 LH rear window motor
91 Driver's seat switch
92 Forward/rearward motor
93 Front up/down motor
94 Rear up/down motor
95 Back reclining motor
96 Mirror switch
97 Driver's mirror assembly
98 Passenger's mirror assembly

Seat adjustment

Electric mirrors

Electric windows

Wire colours

B	Black	Or	Orange
N	Brown	K	Pink
G	Green	R	Red
S	Grey	P	Purple
U	Blue	W	White
LG	Light Green	Y	Yellow

Diagram 8 : Electric windows, mirrors and seat adjustment

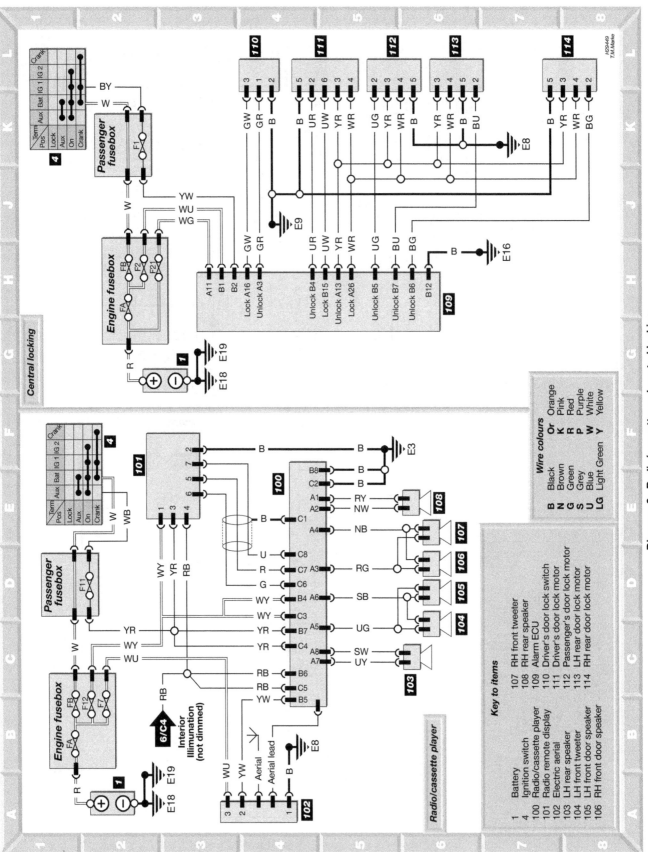

Diagram 9 : Radio/cassette and central locking

Central locking

Radio/cassette player

Wire colours

B	Black	Or	Orange
N	Brown	K	Pink
G	Green	R	Red
S	Grey	P	Purple
U	Blue	W	White
LG	Light Green	Y	Yellow

Key to items

1	Battery	107	RH front tweeter
4	Ignition switch	108	RH rear speaker
100	Radio/cassette player	109	Alarm ECU
101	Radio remote display	110	Driver's door lock switch
102	Electric aerial	111	Driver's door lock motor
103	LH rear speaker	112	Passenger's door lock motor
104	LH front tweeter	113	LH rear door lock motor
105	LH front door speaker	114	RH rear door lock motor
106	RH front door speaker		

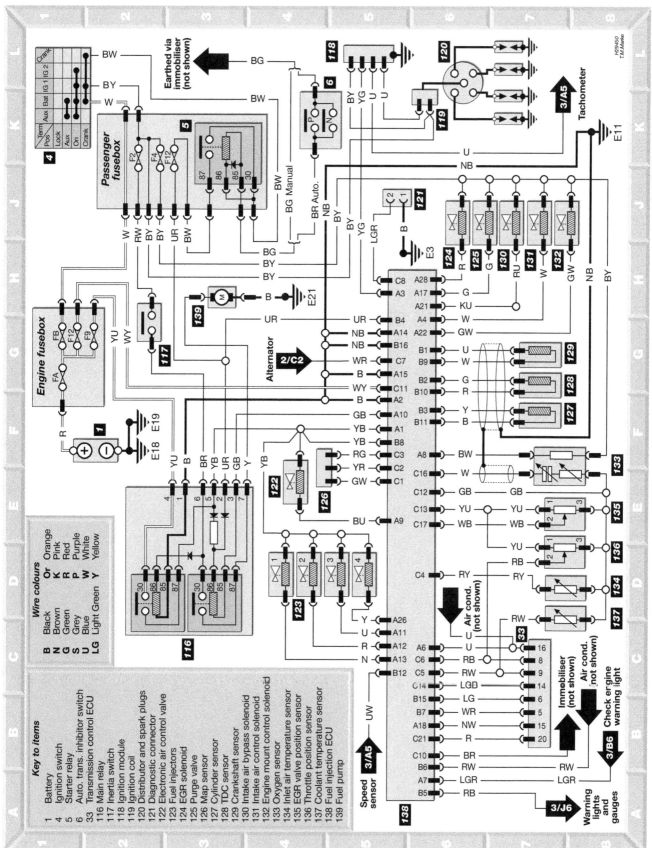

Diagram 10 : Engine management

Key to items
1 Battery
4 Ignition switch
5 Starter relay
6 Auto. trans. inhibitor switch
33 Transmission control ECU
116 Main relay
117 Inertia switch
118 Ignition module
119 Ignition coil
120 Distributor and spark plugs
121 Diagnostic connector
122 Electronic air control valve
123 Fuel injectors
124 EGR solenoid
125 Purge valve
126 Map sensor
127 Cylinder sensor
128 TDC sensor
129 Crankshaft sensor
130 Intake air bypass solenoid
131 Intake air control solenoid
132 Engine mount control solenoid
133 Oxygen sensor
134 Inlet air temperature sensor
135 EGR valve position sensor
136 Throttle position sensor
137 Coolant temperature sensor
138 Fuel injection ECU
139 Fuel pump

Wire colours
B Black   Or Orange
N Brown   K Pink
G Green   R Red
S Grey   P Purple
U Blue   W White
LG Light Green Y Yellow

Dimensions and weights

Note: *All figures are approximate, and may vary according to model. Refer to manufacturer's data for exact figures.*

Dimensions
Overall length . . . . .4645 mm
Overall width (including mirrors) . . . . .1950 mm
Overall height (unladen) . . . . .1380 mm
Wheelbase . . . . .2720 mm

Weights
Kerb weight*:
  618 models . . . . .1255 kg
  620 models:
    Si model . . . . .1255 kg
    SLi model . . . . .1285 kg
    GSi model . . . . .1310 kg
  623 models . . . . .1335 kg

Maximum gross vehicle weight*:
  618 models . . . . .1820 kg
  620 models:
    Si and SLi model . . . . .1820 kg
    GSi model . . . . .1850 kg
  623 models . . . . .1880 kg
Maximum towing weight (braked trailer):
  Manual transmission models:
    618 and 620 models:
      Single axle trailer . . . . .1220 kg
      Twin axle trailer . . . . .1400 kg
    623 models . . . . .1400 kg
  Automatic transmission models .1200 kg
Maximum rear axle load . . . . .950 kg
Maximum trailer nose weight . . . . .70 kg
Maximum roof rack load . . . . .75 kg
Automatic transmission models add 30 kg

Conversion factors

Length (distance)

Inches (in)	x 25.4	= Millimetres (mm)	x 0.0394	= Inches (in)
Feet (ft)	x 0.305	= Metres (m)	x 3.281	= Feet (ft)
Miles	x 1.609	= Kilometres (km)	x 0.621	= Miles

Volume (capacity)

Cubic inches (cu in; in³)	x 16.387	= Cubic centimetres (cc; cm³)	x 0.061	= Cubic inches (cu in; in³)
Imperial pints (Imp pt)	x 0.568	= Litres (l)	x 1.76	= Imperial pints (Imp pt)
Imperial quarts (Imp qt)	x 1.137	= Litres (l)	x 0.88	= Imperial quarts (Imp qt)
Imperial quarts (Imp qt)	x 1.201	= US quarts (US qt)	x 0.833	= Imperial quarts (Imp qt)
US quarts (US qt)	x 0.946	= Litres (l)	x 1.057	= US quarts (US qt)
Imperial gallons (Imp gal)	x 4.546	= Litres (l)	x 0.22	= Imperial gallons (Imp gal)
Imperial gallons (Imp gal)	x 1.201	= US gallons (US gal)	x 0.833	= Imperial gallons (Imp gal)
US gallons (US gal)	x 3.785	= Litres (l)	x 0.264	= US gallons (US gal)

Mass (weight)

Ounces (oz)	x 28.35	= Grams (g)	x 0.035	= Ounces (oz)
Pounds (lb)	x 0.454	= Kilograms (kg)	x 2.205	= Pounds (lb)

Force

Ounces-force (ozf; oz)	x 0.278	= Newtons (N)	x 3.6	= Ounces-force (ozf; oz)
Pounds-force (lbf; lb)	x 4.448	= Newtons (N)	x 0.225	= Pounds-force (lbf; lb)
Newtons (N)	x 0.1	= Kilograms-force (kgf; kg)	x 9.81	= Newtons (N)

Pressure

Pounds-force per square inch (psi; lbf/in²; lb/in²)	x 0.070	= Kilograms-force per square centimetre (kgf/cm²; kg/cm²)	x 14.223	= Pounds-force per square inch (psi; lbf/in²; lb/in²)
Pounds-force per square inch (psi; lbf/in²; lb/in²)	x 0.068	= Atmospheres (atm)	x 14.696	= Pounds-force per square inch (psi; lbf/in²; lb/in²)
Pounds-force per square inch (psi; lbf/in²; lb/in²)	x 0.069	= Bars	x 14.5	= Pounds-force per square inch (psi; lbf/in²; lb/in²)
Pounds-force per square inch (psi; lbf/in²; lb/in²)	x 6.895	= Kilopascals (kPa)	x 0.145	= Pounds-force per square inch (psi; lbf/in²; lb/in²)
Kilopascals (kPa)	x 0.01	= Kilograms-force per square centimetre (kgf/cm²; kg/cm²)	x 98.1	= Kilopascals (kPa)
Millibar (mbar)	x 100	= Pascals (Pa)	x 0.01	= Millibar (mbar)
Millibar (mbar)	x 0.0145	= Pounds-force per square inch (psi; lbf/in²; lb/in²)	x 68.947	= Millibar (mbar)
Millibar (mbar)	x 0.75	= Millimetres of mercury (mmHg)	x 1.333	= Millibar (mbar)
Millibar (mbar)	x 0.401	= Inches of water (inH₂O)	x 2.491	= Millibar (mbar)
Millimetres of mercury (mmHg)	x 0.535	= Inches of water (inH₂O)	x 1.868	= Millimetres of mercury (mmHg)
Inches of water (inH₂O)	x 0.036	= Pounds-force per square inch (psi; lbf/in²; lb/in²)	x 27.68	= Inches of water (inH₂O)

Torque (moment of force)

Pounds-force inches (lbf in; lb in)	x 1.152	= Kilograms-force centimetre (kgf cm; kg cm)	x 0.868	= Pounds-force inches (lbf in; lb in)
Pounds-force inches (lbf in; lb in)	x 0.113	= Newton metres (Nm)	x 8.85	= Pounds-force inches (lbf in; lb in)
Pounds-force inches (lbf in; lb in)	x 0.083	= Pounds-force feet (lbf ft; lb ft)	x 12	= Pounds-force inches (lbf in; lb in)
Pounds-force feet (lbf ft; lb ft)	x 0.138	= Kilograms-force metres (kgf m; kg m)	x 7.233	= Pounds-force feet (lbf ft; lb ft)
Pounds-force feet (lbf ft; lb ft)	x 1.356	= Newton metres (Nm)	x 0.738	= Pounds-force feet (lbf ft; lb ft)
Newton metres (Nm)	x 0.102	= Kilograms-force metres (kgf m; kg m)	x 9.804	= Newton metres (Nm)

Power

Horsepower (hp)	x 745.7	= Watts (W)	x 0.0013	= Horsepower (hp)

Velocity (speed)

Miles per hour (miles/hr; mph)	x 1.609	= Kilometres per hour (km/hr; kph)	x 0.621	= Miles per hour (miles/hr; mph)

Fuel consumption*

Miles per gallon (mpg)	x 0.354	= Kilometres per litre (km/l)	x 2.825	= Miles per gallon (mpg)

Temperature

Degrees Fahrenheit = (°C x 1.8) + 32   Degrees Celsius (Degrees Centigrade; °C) = (°F - 32) x 0.56

It is common practice to convert from miles per gallon (mpg) to litres/100 kilometres (l/100km), where mpg x l/100 km = 282

Spare parts are available from many sources, including makers appointed garages, accessory shops, and motor factors. To be sure of obtaining the correct parts, it will sometimes be necessary to quote the vehicle identification number. If possible, it can also be useful to take the old parts along for positive identification. Items such as starter motors and alternators may be available under a service exchange scheme - any parts returned should be clean.

Our advice regarding spare parts is as follows.

Officially appointed garages

This is the best source of parts which are peculiar to your car, and which are not otherwise generally available (eg, badges, interior trim, certain body panels, etc). It is also the only place at which you should buy parts if the vehicle is still under warranty.

Accessory shops

These are very good places to buy materials and components needed for the maintenance of your car (oil, air and fuel filters, light bulbs, drivebelts, greases, brake pads, touch-up paint, etc). Components of this nature sold by a reputable shop are usually of the same standard as those used by the car manufacturer.

Besides components, these shops also sell tools and general accessories, usually have convenient opening hours, charge lower prices, and can often be found close to home. Some accessory shops have parts counters where components needed for almost any repair job can be purchased or ordered.

Motor factors

Good factors will stock all the more important components which wear out quickly, and can sometimes supply individual components needed for the overhaul of a larger assembly (eg, brake seals and hydraulic parts, bearing shells, pistons, valves). They may also handle work such as cylinder block reboring, crankshaft regrinding, etc.

Tyre and exhaust specialists

These outlets may be independent, or members of a local or national chain. They frequently offer competitive prices when compared with a main dealer or local garage, but it will pay to obtain several quotes before making a decision. When researching prices, also ask what extras may be added - for instance fitting a new valve and balancing the wheel are sometimes charged on top of the price of a new tyre.

Other sources

Beware of parts or materials obtained from market stalls, car boot sales or similar outlets. Such items are not invariably sub-standard, but there is little chance of compensation if they do prove unsatisfactory. in the case of safety-critical components such as brake pads, there is the risk not only of financial loss, but also of an accident causing injury or death.

Second-hand components or assemblies obtained from a car breaker can be a good buy in some circumstances, but this sort of purchase is best made by the experienced DIY mechanic.

Vehicle identification

Modifications are a continuing and unpublicised process in vehicle manufacture, quite apart from major model changes. Spare parts manuals and lists are compiled upon a numerical basis, the individual vehicle identification numbers being essential to correct identification of the component concerned.

When ordering spare parts, always give as much information as possible. Quote the car model, year of manufacture and registration, chassis and engine numbers as appropriate.

The *Vehicle Identification Number (VIN)* plate is riveted to the left-hand wing valance and is visible once the bonnet has been opened. The vehicle identification (chassis) number is also stamped onto the top of the right-hand side of the engine compartment bulkhead and is also etched onto the windscreen and rear screen glass as an anti-theft deterrent **(see illustrations)**

The *trim code and paint code* are also stamped onto the VIN plate.

The *engine number* is stamped onto the front of the right-hand face of the cylinder block **(see illustration)**.

Vehicle Identification Number (VIN) plate location

The chassis number is also stamped onto the top right-hand side of the bulkhead

Engine number location

Whenever servicing, repair or overhaul work is carried out on the car or its components, it is necessary to observe the following procedures and instructions. This will assist in carrying out the operation efficiently and to a professional standard of workmanship.

Joint mating faces and gaskets

When separating components at their mating faces, never insert screwdrivers or similar implements into the joint between the faces in order to prise them apart. This can cause severe damage which results in oil leaks, coolant leaks, etc upon reassembly. Separation is usually achieved by tapping along the joint with a soft-faced hammer in order to break the seal. However, note that this method may not be suitable where dowels are used for component location.

Where a gasket is used between the mating faces of two components, ensure that it is renewed on reassembly, and fit it dry unless otherwise stated in the repair procedure. Make sure that the mating faces are clean and dry, with all traces of old gasket removed. When cleaning a joint face, use a tool which is not likely to score or damage the face, and remove any burrs or nicks with an oilstone or fine file.

Make sure that tapped holes are cleaned with a pipe cleaner, and keep them free of jointing compound, if this is being used, unless specifically instructed otherwise.

Ensure that all orifices, channels or pipes are clear, and blow through them, preferably using compressed air.

Oil seals

Oil seals can be removed by levering them out with a wide flat-bladed screwdriver or similar tool. Alternatively, a number of self-tapping screws may be screwed into the seal, and these used as a purchase for pliers or similar in order to pull the seal free.

Whenever an oil seal is removed from its working location, either individually or as part of an assembly, it should be renewed.

The very fine sealing lip of the seal is easily damaged, and will not seal if the surface it contacts is not completely clean and free from scratches, nicks or grooves. If the original sealing surface of the component cannot be restored, and the manufacturer has not made provision for slight relocation of the seal relative to the sealing surface, the component should be renewed.

Protect the lips of the seal from any surface which may damage them in the course of fitting. Use tape or a conical sleeve where possible. Lubricate the seal lips with oil before fitting and, on dual-lipped seals, fill the space between the lips with grease.

Unless otherwise stated, oil seals must be fitted with their sealing lips toward the lubricant to be sealed.

Use a tubular drift or block of wood of the appropriate size to install the seal and, if the seal housing is shouldered, drive the seal down to the shoulder. If the seal housing is unshouldered, the seal should be fitted with its face flush with the housing top face (unless otherwise instructed).

Screw threads and fastenings

Seized nuts, bolts and screws are quite a common occurrence where corrosion has set in, and the use of penetrating oil or releasing fluid will often overcome this problem if the offending item is soaked for a while before attempting to release it. The use of an impact driver may also provide a means of releasing such stubborn fastening devices, when used in conjunction with the appropriate screwdriver bit or socket. If none of these methods works, it may be necessary to resort to the careful application of heat, or the use of a hacksaw or nut splitter device.

Studs are usually removed by locking two nuts together on the threaded part, and then using a spanner on the lower nut to unscrew the stud. Studs or bolts which have broken off below the surface of the component in which they are mounted can sometimes be removed using a stud extractor. Always ensure that a blind tapped hole is completely free from oil, grease, water or other fluid before installing the bolt or stud. Failure to do this could cause the housing to crack due to the hydraulic action of the bolt or stud as it is screwed in.

When tightening a castellated nut to accept a split pin, tighten the nut to the specified torque, where applicable, and then tighten further to the next split pin hole. Never slacken the nut to align the split pin hole, unless stated in the repair procedure.

When checking or retightening a nut or bolt to a specified torque setting, slacken the nut or bolt by a quarter of a turn, and then retighten to the specified setting. However, this should not be attempted where angular tightening has been used.

For some screw fastenings, notably cylinder head bolts or nuts, torque wrench settings are no longer specified for the latter stages of tightening, "angle-tightening" being called up instead. Typically, a fairly low torque wrench setting will be applied to the bolts/nuts in the correct sequence, followed by one or more stages of tightening through specified angles.

Locknuts, locktabs and washers

Any fastening which will rotate against a component or housing during tightening should always have a washer between it and the relevant component or housing.

Spring or split washers should always be renewed when they are used to lock a critical component such as a big-end bearing retaining bolt or nut. Locktabs which are folded over to retain a nut or bolt should always be renewed.

Self-locking nuts can be re-used in non-critical areas, providing resistance can be felt when the locking portion passes over the bolt or stud thread. However, it should be noted that self-locking stiffnuts tend to lose their effectiveness after long periods of use, and should be renewed as a matter of course.

Split pins must always be replaced with new ones of the correct size for the hole.

When thread-locking compound is found on the threads of a fastener which is to be re-used, it should be cleaned off with a wire brush and solvent, and fresh compound applied on reassembly.

Special tools

Some repair procedures in this manual entail the use of special tools such as a press, two or three-legged pullers, spring compressors, etc. Wherever possible, suitable readily-available alternatives to the manufacturer's special tools are described, and are shown in use. In some instances, where no alternative is possible, it has been necessary to resort to the use of a manufacturer's tool, and this has been done for reasons of safety as well as the efficient completion of the repair operation. Unless you are highly-skilled and have a thorough understanding of the procedures described, never attempt to bypass the use of any special tool when the procedure described specifies its use. Not only is there a very great risk of personal injury, but expensive damage could be caused to the components involved.

Environmental considerations

When disposing of used engine oil, brake fluid, antifreeze, etc, give due consideration to any detrimental environmental effects. Do not, for instance, pour any of the above liquids down drains into the general sewage system, or onto the ground to soak away. Many local council refuse tips provide a facility for waste oil disposal, as do some garages. If none of these facilities are available, consult your local Environmental Health Department, or the National Rivers Authority, for further advice.

With the universal tightening-up of legislation regarding the emission of environmentally-harmful substances from motor vehicles, most current vehicles have tamperproof devices fitted to the main adjustment points of the fuel system. These devices are primarily designed to prevent unqualified persons from adjusting the fuel/air mixture, with the chance of a consequent increase in toxic emissions. If such devices are encountered during servicing or overhaul, they should, wherever possible, be renewed or refitted in accordance with the vehicle manufacturer's requirements or current legislation.

Note: It is antisocial and illegal to dump oil down the drain. To find the location of your local oil recycling bank, call this number free.

The jack supplied with the vehicle tool kit should only be used for changing the roadwheels - see *Wheel changing* at the front of this manual. When carrying out any other kind of work, raise the vehicle using a hydraulic (or trolley) jack, and always supplement the jack with axle stands positioned under the vehicle jacking points.

To raise the front of the vehicle, position the jack head underneath the towing eye/jacking bracket located at the front end of the crossmember, underneath the engine/transmission unit. Lift the vehicle to the required height and support it on axle stands positioned underneath the vehicle jacking points on the sills **(see illustration)**.

To raise the rear of the vehicle, position the jack head and position the towing eye/jacking bracket at the centre of the rear of the vehicle. Lift the vehicle to the required height and support it on axle stands positioned underneath the vehicle jacking points on the sills.

The jack supplied with the vehicle locates with the jacking points on the sills. Ensure that the jack head is correctly engaged before attempting to raise the vehicle.

Never work under, around, or near a raised vehicle, unless it is adequately supported in at least two places.

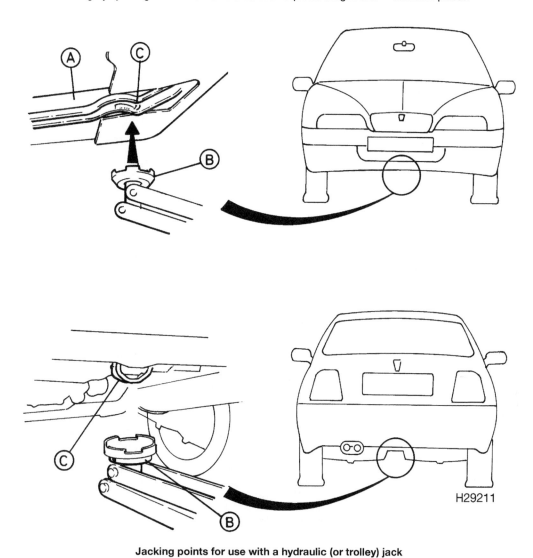

H29211

Jacking points for use with a hydraulic (or trolley) jack
A Engine crossmember   B Jack head   C Towing eye/jacking bracket

Radio/cassette unit anti-theft system - precaution

The radio/cassette/CD player/autochanger unit fitted as standard equipment by Rover is equipped with a built-in security code, to deter thieves. If the power source to the unit is cut, the anti-theft system will activate. Even if the power source is immediately reconnected, the radio/cassette unit will not function until the correct security code has been entered. Therefore if you do not know the correct security code for the unit, **do not** disconnect the battery negative lead, or remove the radio/cassette unit from the vehicle.

The procedure for reprogramming a unit that has been disconnected from its power supply varies from model to model - consult the handbook supplied with the unit for specific details or refer to your Rover dealer.

Introduction

A selection of good tools is a fundamental requirement for anyone contemplating the maintenance and repair of a motor vehicle. For the owner who does not possess any, their purchase will prove a considerable expense, offsetting some of the savings made by doing-it-yourself. However, provided that the tools purchased meet the relevant national safety standards and are of good quality, they will last for many years and prove an extremely worthwhile investment.

To help the average owner to decide which tools are needed to carry out the various tasks detailed in this manual, we have compiled three lists of tools under the following headings: *Maintenance and minor repair*, *Repair and overhaul*, and *Special*. Newcomers to practical mechanics should start off with the *Maintenance and minor repair* tool kit, and confine themselves to the simpler jobs around the vehicle. Then, as confidence and experience grow, more difficult tasks can be undertaken, with extra tools being purchased as, and when, they are needed. In this way, a *Maintenance and minor repair* tool kit can be built up into a *Repair and overhaul* tool kit over a considerable period of time, without any major cash outlays. The experienced do-it-yourselfer will have a tool kit good enough for most repair and overhaul procedures, and will add tools from the *Special* category when it is felt that the expense is justified by the amount of use to which these tools will be put.

Maintenance and minor repair tool kit

The tools given in this list should be considered as a minimum requirement if routine maintenance, servicing and minor repair operations are to be undertaken. We recommend the purchase of combination spanners (ring one end, open-ended the other); although more expensive than open-ended ones, they do give the advantages of both types of spanner.

☐ *Combination spanners:*
   Metric - 8 to 19 mm inclusive
☐ *Adjustable spanner - 35 mm jaw (approx.)*
☐ *Spark plug spanner (with rubber insert) - petrol models*
☐ *Spark plug gap adjustment tool - petrol models*
☐ *Set of feeler blades*
☐ *Brake bleed nipple spanner*
☐ *Screwdrivers:*
   Flat blade - 100 mm long x 6 mm dia
   Cross blade - 100 mm long x 6 mm dia
☐ *Combination pliers*
☐ *Hacksaw (junior)*
☐ *Tyre pump*
☐ *Tyre pressure gauge*
☐ *Oil can*
☐ *Oil filter removal tool*
☐ *Fine emery cloth*
☐ *Wire brush (small)*
☐ *Funnel (medium size)*

Repair and overhaul tool kit

These tools are virtually essential for anyone undertaking any major repairs to a motor vehicle, and are additional to those given in the *Maintenance and minor repair* list. Included in this list is a comprehensive set of sockets. Although these are expensive, they will be found invaluable as they are so versatile - particularly if various drives are included in the set. We recommend the half-inch square-drive type, as this can be used with most proprietary torque wrenches.

The tools in this list will sometimes need to be supplemented by tools from the *Special* list:

☐ *Sockets (or box spanners) to cover range in previous list (including Torx sockets)*
☐ *Reversible ratchet drive (for use with sockets)*
☐ *Extension piece, 250 mm (for use with sockets)*
☐ *Universal joint (for use with sockets)*
☐ *Torque wrench (for use with sockets)*
☐ *Self-locking grips*
☐ *Ball pein hammer*
☐ *Soft-faced mallet (plastic/aluminium or rubber)*
☐ *Screwdrivers:*
   Flat blade - long & sturdy, short (chubby), and narrow (electrician's) types
   Cross blade – Long & sturdy, and short (chubby) types
☐ *Pliers:*
   Long-nosed
   Side cutters (electrician's)
   Circlip (internal and external)
☐ *Cold chisel - 25 mm*
☐ *Scriber*
☐ *Scraper*
☐ *Centre-punch*
☐ *Pin punch*
☐ *Hacksaw*
☐ *Brake hose clamp*
☐ *Brake/clutch bleeding kit*
☐ *Selection of twist drills*
☐ *Steel rule/straight-edge*
☐ *Allen keys (inc. splined/Torx type)*
☐ *Selection of files*
☐ *Wire brush*
☐ *Axle stands*
☐ *Jack (strong trolley or hydraulic type)*
☐ *Light with extension lead*

Sockets and reversible ratchet drive

Valve spring compressor

Spline bit set

Piston ring compressor

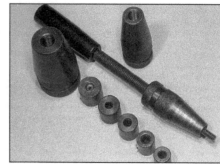

Clutch plate alignment set

Special tools

The tools in this list are those which are not used regularly, are expensive to buy, or which need to be used in accordance with their manufacturers' instructions. Unless relatively difficult mechanical jobs are undertaken frequently, it will not be economic to buy many of these tools. Where this is the case, you could consider clubbing together with friends (or joining a motorists' club) to make a joint purchase, or borrowing the tools against a deposit from a local garage or tool hire specialist. It is worth noting that many of the larger DIY superstores now carry a large range of special tools for hire at modest rates.

The following list contains only those tools and instruments freely available to the public, and not those special tools produced by the vehicle manufacturer specifically for its dealer network. You will find occasional references to these manufacturers' special tools in the text of this manual. Generally, an alternative method of doing the job without the vehicle manufacturers' special tool is given. However, sometimes there is no alternative to using them. Where this is the case and the relevant tool cannot be bought or borrowed, you will have to entrust the work to a dealer.

☐ Valve spring compressor
☐ Valve grinding tool
☐ Piston ring compressor
☐ Piston ring removal/installation tool
☐ Cylinder bore hone
☐ Balljoint separator
☐ Coil spring compressors (where applicable)
☐ Two/three-legged hub and bearing puller
☐ Impact screwdriver
☐ Micrometer and/or vernier calipers
☐ Dial gauge
☐ Stroboscopic timing light
☐ Dwell angle meter/tachometer
☐ Universal electrical multi-meter
☐ Cylinder compression gauge
☐ Hand-operated vacuum pump and gauge
☐ Clutch plate alignment set
☐ Brake shoe steady spring cup removal tool
☐ Bush and bearing removal/installation set
☐ Stud extractors
☐ Tap and die set
☐ Lifting tackle
☐ Trolley jack

Buying tools

Reputable motor accessory shops and superstores often offer excellent quality tools at discount prices, so it pays to shop around.

Remember, you don't have to buy the most expensive items on the shelf, but it is always advisable to steer clear of the very cheap tools. Beware of 'bargains' offered on market stalls or at car boot sales. There are plenty of good tools around at reasonable prices, but always aim to purchase items which meet the relevant national safety standards. If in doubt, ask the proprietor or manager of the shop for advice before making a purchase.

Care and maintenance of tools

Having purchased a reasonable tool kit, it is necessary to keep the tools in a clean and serviceable condition. After use, always wipe off any dirt, grease and metal particles using a clean, dry cloth, before putting the tools away. Never leave them lying around after they have been used. A simple tool rack on the garage or workshop wall for items such as screwdrivers and pliers is a good idea. Store all normal spanners and sockets in a metal box. Any measuring instruments, gauges, meters, etc, must be carefully stored where they cannot be damaged or become rusty.

Take a little care when tools are used. Hammer heads inevitably become marked, and screwdrivers lose the keen edge on their blades from time to time. A little timely attention with emery cloth or a file will soon restore items like this to a good finish.

Working facilities

Not to be forgotten when discussing tools is the workshop itself. If anything more than routine maintenance is to be carried out, a suitable working area becomes essential.

It is appreciated that many an owner-mechanic is forced by circumstances to remove an engine or similar item without the benefit of a garage or workshop. Having done this, any repairs should always be done under the cover of a roof.

Wherever possible, any dismantling should be done on a clean, flat workbench or table at a suitable working height.

Any workbench needs a vice; one with a jaw opening of 100 mm is suitable for most jobs. As mentioned previously, some clean dry storage space is also required for tools, as well as for any lubricants, cleaning fluids, touch-up paints etc, which become necessary.

Another item which may be required, and which has a much more general usage, is an electric drill with a chuck capacity of at least 8 mm. This, together with a good range of twist drills, is virtually essential for fitting accessories.

Last, but not least, always keep a supply of old newspapers and clean, lint-free rags available, and try to keep any working area as clean as possible.

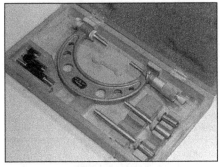
Micrometer set

Dial test indicator ("dial gauge")

Stroboscopic timing light

Compression tester

Stud extractor set

This is a guide to getting your vehicle through the MOT test. Obviously it will not be possible to examine the vehicle to the same standard as the professional MOT tester. However, working through the following checks will enable you to identify any problem areas before submitting the vehicle for the test.

Where a testable component is in borderline condition, the tester has discretion in deciding whether to pass or fail it. The basis of such discretion is whether the tester would be happy for a close relative or friend to use the vehicle with the component in that condition. If the vehicle presented is clean and evidently well cared for, the tester may be more inclined to pass a borderline component than if the vehicle is scruffy and apparently neglected.

It has only been possible to summarise the test requirements here, based on the regulations in force at the time of printing. Test standards are becoming increasingly stringent, although there are some exemptions for older vehicles. For full details obtain a copy of the Haynes publication Pass the MOT! (available from stockists of Haynes manuals).

An assistant will be needed to help carry out some of these checks.

The checks have been sub-divided into four categories, as follows:

1 Checks carried out **FROM THE DRIVER'S SEAT**

2 Checks carried out **WITH THE VEHICLE ON THE GROUND**

3 Checks carried out **WITH THE VEHICLE RAISED AND THE WHEELS FREE TO TURN**

4 Checks carried out on **YOUR VEHICLE'S EXHAUST EMISSION SYSTEM**

---

1 Checks carried out **FROM THE DRIVER'S SEAT**

Handbrake

☐ Test the operation of the handbrake. Excessive travel (too many clicks) indicates incorrect brake or cable adjustment.

☐ Check that the handbrake cannot be released by tapping the lever sideways. Check the security of the lever mountings.

Footbrake

☐ Depress the brake pedal and check that it does not creep down to the floor, indicating a master cylinder fault. Release the pedal, wait a few seconds, then depress it again. If the pedal travels nearly to the floor before firm resistance is felt, brake adjustment or repair is necessary. If the pedal feels spongy, there is air in the hydraulic system which must be removed by bleeding.

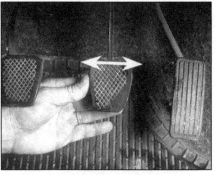

☐ Check that the brake pedal is secure and in good condition. Check also for signs of fluid leaks on the pedal, floor or carpets, which would indicate failed seals in the brake master cylinder.

☐ Check the servo unit (when applicable) by operating the brake pedal several times, then keeping the pedal depressed and starting the engine. As the engine starts, the pedal will move down slightly. If not, the vacuum hose or the servo itself may be faulty.

Steering wheel and column

☐ Examine the steering wheel for fractures or looseness of the hub, spokes or rim.

☐ Move the steering wheel from side to side and then up and down. Check that the steering wheel is not loose on the column, indicating wear or a loose retaining nut. Continue moving the steering wheel as before, but also turn it slightly from left to right.

☐ Check that the steering wheel is not loose on the column, and that there is no abnormal

movement of the steering wheel, indicating wear in the column support bearings or couplings.

Windscreen and mirrors

☐ The windscreen must be free of cracks or other significant damage within the driver's field of view. (Small stone chips are acceptable.) Rear view mirrors must be secure, intact, and capable of being adjusted.

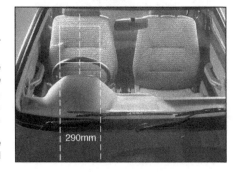

290mm

Seat belts and seats

Note: *The following checks are applicable to all seat belts, front and rear.*

☐ Examine the webbing of all the belts (including rear belts if fitted) for cuts, serious fraying or deterioration. Fasten and unfasten each belt to check the buckles. If applicable, check the retracting mechanism. Check the security of all seat belt mountings accessible from inside the vehicle.

☐ The front seats themselves must be securely attached and the backrests must lock in the upright position.

Doors

☐ Both front doors must be able to be opened and closed from outside and inside, and must latch securely when closed.

2 Checks carried out WITH THE VEHICLE ON THE GROUND

Vehicle identification

☐ Number plates must be in good condition, secure and legible, with letters and numbers correctly spaced – spacing at (A) should be twice that at (B).

☐ The VIN plate and/or homologation plate must be legible.

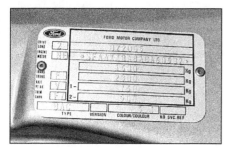

Electrical equipment

☐ Switch on the ignition and check the operation of the horn.

☐ Check the windscreen washers and wipers, examining the wiper blades; renew damaged or perished blades. Also check the operation of the stop-lights.

☐ Check the operation of the sidelights and number plate lights. The lenses and reflectors must be secure, clean and undamaged.

☐ Check the operation and alignment of the headlights. The headlight reflectors must not be tarnished and the lenses must be undamaged.

☐ Switch on the ignition and check the operation of the direction indicators (including the instrument panel tell-tale) and the hazard warning lights. Operation of the sidelights and stop-lights must not affect the indicators - if it does, the cause is usually a bad earth at the rear light cluster.

☐ Check the operation of the rear foglight(s), including the warning light on the instrument panel or in the switch.

Footbrake

☐ Examine the master cylinder, brake pipes and servo unit for leaks, loose mountings, corrosion or other damage.

☐ The fluid reservoir must be secure and the fluid level must be between the upper (A) and lower (B) markings.

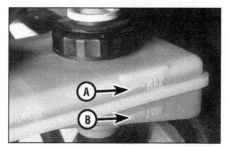

☐ Inspect both front brake flexible hoses for cracks or deterioration of the rubber. Turn the steering from lock to lock, and ensure that the hoses do not contact the wheel, tyre, or any part of the steering or suspension mechanism. With the brake pedal firmly depressed, check the hoses for bulges or leaks under pressure.

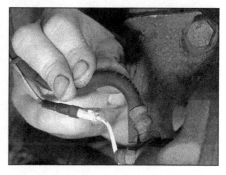

Steering and suspension

☐ Have your assistant turn the steering wheel from side to side slightly, up to the point where the steering gear just begins to transmit this movement to the roadwheels. Check for excessive free play between the steering wheel and the steering gear, indicating wear or insecurity of the steering column joints, the column-to-steering gear coupling, or the steering gear itself.

☐ Have your assistant turn the steering wheel more vigorously in each direction, so that the roadwheels just begin to turn. As this is done, examine all the steering joints, linkages, fittings and attachments. Renew any component that shows signs of wear or damage. On vehicles with power steering, check the security and condition of the steering pump, drivebelt and hoses.

☐ Check that the vehicle is standing level, and at approximately the correct ride height.

Shock absorbers

☐ Depress each corner of the vehicle in turn, then release it. The vehicle should rise and then settle in its normal position. If the vehicle continues to rise and fall, the shock absorber is defective. A shock absorber which has seized will also cause the vehicle to fail.

Exhaust system

☐ Start the engine. With your assistant holding a rag over the tailpipe, check the entire system for leaks. Repair or renew leaking sections.

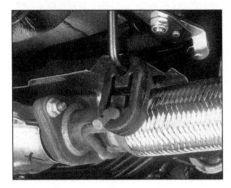

3 Checks carried out
WITH THE VEHICLE RAISED AND THE WHEELS FREE TO TURN

Jack up the front and rear of the vehicle, and securely support it on axle stands. Position the stands clear of the suspension assemblies. Ensure that the wheels are clear of the ground and that the steering can be turned from lock to lock.

Steering mechanism

☐ Have your assistant turn the steering from lock to lock. Check that the steering turns smoothly, and that no part of the steering mechanism, including a wheel or tyre, fouls any brake hose or pipe or any part of the body structure.
☐ Examine the steering rack rubber gaiters for damage or insecurity of the retaining clips. If power steering is fitted, check for signs of damage or leakage of the fluid hoses, pipes or connections. Also check for excessive stiffness or binding of the steering, a missing split pin or locking device, or severe corrosion of the body structure within 30 cm of any steering component attachment point.

Front and rear suspension and wheel bearings

☐ Starting at the front right-hand side, grasp the roadwheel at the 3 o'clock and 9 o'clock positions and shake it vigorously. Check for free play or insecurity at the wheel bearings, suspension balljoints, or suspension mountings, pivots and attachments.
☐ Now grasp the wheel at the 12 o'clock and 6 o'clock positions and repeat the previous inspection. Spin the wheel, and check for roughness or tightness of the front wheel bearing.

☐ If excess free play is suspected at a component pivot point, this can be confirmed by using a large screwdriver or similar tool and levering between the mounting and the component attachment. This will confirm whether the wear is in the pivot bush, its retaining bolt, or in the mounting itself (the bolt holes can often become elongated).

☐ Carry out all the above checks at the other front wheel, and then at both rear wheels.

Springs and shock absorbers

☐ Examine the suspension struts (when applicable) for serious fluid leakage, corrosion, or damage to the casing. Also check the security of the mounting points.
☐ If coil springs are fitted, check that the spring ends locate in their seats, and that the spring is not corroded, cracked or broken.
☐ If leaf springs are fitted, check that all leaves are intact, that the axle is securely attached to each spring, and that there is no deterioration of the spring eye mountings, bushes, and shackles.

☐ The same general checks apply to vehicles fitted with other suspension types, such as torsion bars, hydraulic displacer units, etc. Ensure that all mountings and attachments are secure, that there are no signs of excessive wear, corrosion or damage, and (on hydraulic types) that there are no fluid leaks or damaged pipes.
☐ Inspect the shock absorbers for signs of serious fluid leakage. Check for wear of the mounting bushes or attachments, or damage to the body of the unit.

Driveshafts
(fwd vehicles only)

☐ Rotate each front wheel in turn and inspect the constant velocity joint gaiters for splits or damage. Also check that each driveshaft is straight and undamaged.

Braking system

☐ If possible without dismantling, check brake pad wear and disc condition. Ensure that the friction lining material has not worn excessively, (A) and that the discs are not fractured, pitted, scored or badly worn (B).

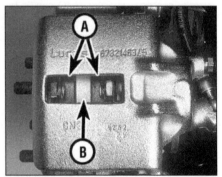

☐ Examine all the rigid brake pipes underneath the vehicle, and the flexible hose(s) at the rear. Look for corrosion, chafing or insecurity of the pipes, and for signs of bulging under pressure, chafing, splits or deterioration of the flexible hoses.
☐ Look for signs of fluid leaks at the brake calipers or on the brake backplates. Repair or renew leaking components.
☐ Slowly spin each wheel, while your assistant depresses and releases the footbrake. Ensure that each brake is operating and does not bind when the pedal is released.

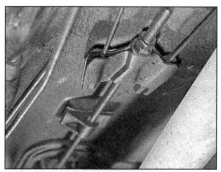

☐ Examine the handbrake mechanism, checking for frayed or broken cables, excessive corrosion, or wear or insecurity of the linkage. Check that the mechanism works on each relevant wheel, and releases fully, without binding.

☐ It is not possible to test brake efficiency without special equipment, but a road test can be carried out later to check that the vehicle pulls up in a straight line.

Fuel and exhaust systems

☐ Inspect the fuel tank (including the filler cap), fuel pipes, hoses and unions. All components must be secure and free from leaks.

☐ Examine the exhaust system over its entire length, checking for any damaged, broken or missing mountings, security of the retaining clamps and rust or corrosion.

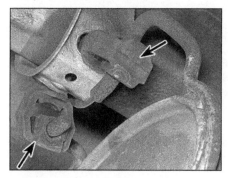

Wheels and tyres

☐ Examine the sidewalls and tread area of each tyre in turn. Check for cuts, tears, lumps, bulges, separation of the tread, and exposure of the ply or cord due to wear or damage. Check that the tyre bead is correctly seated on the wheel rim, that the valve is sound and

properly seated, and that the wheel is not distorted or damaged.

☐ Check that the tyres are of the correct size for the vehicle, that they are of the same size and type on each axle, and that the pressures are correct.

☐ Check the tyre tread depth. The legal minimum at the time of writing is 1.6 mm over at least three-quarters of the tread width. Abnormal tread wear may indicate incorrect front wheel alignment.

Body corrosion

☐ Check the condition of the entire vehicle structure for signs of corrosion in load-bearing areas. (These include chassis box sections, side sills, cross-members, pillars, and all suspension, steering, braking system and seat belt mountings and anchorages.) Any corrosion which has seriously reduced the thickness of a load-bearing area is likely to cause the vehicle to fail. In this case professional repairs are likely to be needed.

☐ Damage or corrosion which causes sharp or otherwise dangerous edges to be exposed will also cause the vehicle to fail.

4 Checks carried out on YOUR VEHICLE'S EXHAUST EMISSION SYSTEM

Petrol models

☐ Have the engine at normal operating temperature, and make sure that it is in good tune (ignition system in good order, air filter element clean, etc).

☐ Before any measurements are carried out, raise the engine speed to around 2500 rpm, and hold it at this speed for 20 seconds. Allow

the engine speed to return to idle, and watch for smoke emissions from the exhaust tailpipe. If the idle speed is obviously much too high, or if dense blue or clearly-visible black smoke comes from the tailpipe for more than 5 seconds, the vehicle will fail. As a rule of thumb, blue smoke signifies oil being burnt (engine wear) while black smoke signifies unburnt fuel (dirty air cleaner element, or other carburettor or fuel system fault).

☐ An exhaust gas analyser capable of measuring carbon monoxide (CO) and hydrocarbons (HC) is now needed. If such an instrument cannot be hired or borrowed, a local garage may agree to perform the check for a small fee.

CO emissions (mixture)

☐ At the time of writing, the maximum CO level at idle is 3.5% for vehicles first used after August 1986 and 4.5% for older vehicles. From January 1996 a much tighter limit (around 0.5%) applies to catalyst-equipped vehicles first used from August 1992. If the CO level cannot be reduced far enough to pass the test (and the fuel and ignition systems are otherwise in good condition) then the carburettor is badly worn, or there is some problem in the fuel injection system or catalytic converter (as applicable).

HC emissions

☐ With the CO emissions within limits, HC emissions must be no more than 1200 ppm (parts per million). If the vehicle fails this test at idle, it can be re-tested at around 2000 rpm; if the HC level is then 1200 ppm or less, this counts as a pass.

☐ Excessive HC emissions can be caused by oil being burnt, but they are more likely to be due to unburnt fuel.

Diesel models

☐ The only emission test applicable to Diesel engines is the measuring of exhaust smoke density. The test involves accelerating the engine several times to its maximum unloaded speed.

Note: *It is of the utmost importance that the engine timing belt is in good condition before the test is carried out.*

☐ Excessive smoke can be caused by a dirty air cleaner element. Otherwise, professional advice may be needed to find the cause.

Engine 1

- ☐ Engine fails to rotate when attempting to start
- ☐ Engine rotates, but will not start
- ☐ Engine difficult to start when cold
- ☐ Engine difficult to start when hot
- ☐ Starter motor noisy or excessively-rough in engagement
- ☐ Engine starts, but stops immediately
- ☐ Engine idles erratically
- ☐ Engine misfires at idle speed
- ☐ Engine misfires throughout the driving speed range
- ☐ Engine hesitates on acceleration
- ☐ Engine stalls
- ☐ Engine lacks power
- ☐ Engine backfires
- ☐ Oil pressure warning light illuminated with engine running
- ☐ Engine runs-on after switching off
- ☐ Engine noises

Cooling system 2

- ☐ Overheating
- ☐ Overcooling
- ☐ External coolant leakage
- ☐ Internal coolant leakage
- ☐ Corrosion

Fuel and exhaust systems 3

- ☐ Excessive fuel consumption
- ☐ Fuel leakage and/or fuel odour
- ☐ Excessive noise or fumes from exhaust system

Clutch 4

- ☐ Pedal travels to floor - no pressure or very little resistance
- ☐ Clutch fails to disengage (unable to select gears).
- ☐ Clutch slips (engine speed increases, with no increase in vehicle speed)
- ☐ Judder as clutch is engaged
- ☐ Noise when depressing or releasing clutch pedal

Manual transmission 5

- ☐ Noisy in neutral with engine running
- ☐ Noisy in one particular gear
- ☐ Difficulty engaging gears
- ☐ Jumps out of gear
- ☐ Vibration
- ☐ Lubricant leaks

Automatic transmission 6

- ☐ Fluid leakage
- ☐ Transmission fluid brown, or has burned smell
- ☐ General gear selection problems
- ☐ Transmission will not downshift (kickdown) with accelerator pedal fully depressed
- ☐ Engine will not start in any gear, or starts in gears other than Park or Neutral
- ☐ Transmission slips, shifts roughly, is noisy, or has no drive in forward or reverse gears

Driveshafts 7

- ☐ Vibration when accelerating or decelerating
- ☐ Clicking or knocking noise on turns (at slow speed on full-lock)

Braking system 8

- ☐ Vehicle pulls to one side under braking
- ☐ Noise (grinding or high-pitched squeal) when brakes applied
- ☐ Excessive brake pedal travel
- ☐ Brake pedal feels spongy when depressed
- ☐ Excessive brake pedal effort required to stop vehicle
- ☐ Judder felt through brake pedal or steering wheel when braking
- ☐ Brakes binding
- ☐ Rear wheels locking under normal braking

Suspension and steering 9

- ☐ Vehicle pulls to one side
- ☐ Wheel wobble and vibration
- ☐ Excessive pitching and/or rolling around corners, or during braking
- ☐ Wandering or general instability
- ☐ Excessively-stiff steering
- ☐ Excessive play in steering
- ☐ Lack of power assistance
- ☐ Tyre wear excessive

Electrical system 10

- ☐ Battery will not hold a charge for more than a few days
- ☐ Ignition/no-charge warning light remains illuminated with engine running
- ☐ Ignition/no-charge warning light fails to come on
- ☐ Lights inoperative
- ☐ Instrument readings inaccurate or erratic
- ☐ Horn inoperative, or unsatisfactory in operation
- ☐ Windscreen wipers inoperative, or unsatisfactory in operation
- ☐ Windscreen washers inoperative, or unsatisfactory in operation
- ☐ Electric windows inoperative, or unsatisfactory in operation
- ☐ Central locking system inoperative, or unsatisfactory in operation

Introduction

The vehicle owner who does his or her own maintenance according to the recommended service schedules should not have to use this section of the manual very often. Modern component reliability is such that, provided those items subject to wear or deterioration are inspected or renewed at the specified intervals, sudden failure is comparatively rare. Faults do not usually just happen as a result of sudden failure, but develop over a period of time. Major mechanical failures in particular are usually preceded by characteristic symptoms over hundreds or even thousands of miles. Those components which do occasionally fail without warning are often small and easily carried in the vehicle.

With any fault-finding, the first step is to decide where to begin investigations. Sometimes this is obvious, but on other occasions, a little detective work will be necessary. The owner who makes half a dozen haphazard adjustments or replacements may be successful in curing a fault (or its symptoms), but will be none the wiser if the fault recurs, and ultimately may have spent more time and money than was necessary. A calm and logical approach will be found to be more satisfactory in the long run. Always take into account any warning signs or abnormalities that may have been noticed in the period preceding the fault - power loss, high or low gauge readings, unusual smells, etc - and remember that failure of components such as fuses or spark plugs may only be pointers to some underlying fault.

The pages which follow provide an easy-reference guide to the more common problems which may occur during the operation of the vehicle. These problems and their possible causes are grouped under headings denoting various components or systems, such as Engine, Cooling system, etc. The Chapter and/or Section which deals with the problem is also shown in brackets. Whatever the fault, certain basic principles apply. These are as follows:

Verify the fault. This is simply a matter of being sure that you know what the symptoms are before starting work. This is particularly important if you are investigating a fault for someone else, who may not have described it very accurately.

Dont overlook the obvious. For example, if the vehicle wont start, is there fuel in the tank? (Dont take anyone elses word on this particular point, and dont trust the fuel gauge either!) If an electrical fault is indicated, look for loose or broken wires before digging out the test gear.

Cure the disease, not the symptom. Substituting a flat battery with a fully-charged one will get you off the hard shoulder, but if the underlying cause is not attended to, the new battery will go the same way. Similarly, changing oil-fouled spark plugs for a new set will get you moving again, but remember that the reason for the fouling (if it wasnt simply an incorrect grade of plug) will have to be established and corrected.

Dont take anything for granted. Particularly, dont forget that a new component may itself be defective (especially if its been rattling around in the boot for months), and dont leave components out of a fault diagnosis sequence just because they are new or recently-fitted. When you do finally diagnose a difficult fault, youll probably realise that all the evidence was there from the start.

1 Engine

Engine fails to rotate when attempting to start

☐ Battery terminal connections loose or corroded (Chapter 1)
☐ Battery discharged or faulty (Chapter 5)
☐ Broken, loose or disconnected wiring in the starting circuit (Chapter 5)
☐ Defective starter solenoid or switch (Chapter 5)
☐ Defective starter motor (Chapter 5)
☐ Starter pinion or flywheel ring gear teeth loose or broken (Chapters 2 and 5)
☐ Engine earth strap broken or disconnected (Chapter 5)

Engine rotates, but will not start

☐ Fuel tank empty
☐ Battery discharged (engine rotates slowly) (Chapter 5)
☐ Battery terminal connections loose or corroded (Chapter 1)
☐ Ignition components damp or damaged (Chapters 1 and 5)
☐ Broken, loose or disconnected wiring in the ignition circuit (Chapters 1 and 5)
☐ Worn, faulty or incorrectly-gapped spark plugs (Chapter 1)
☐ Fuel injection system fault (Chapter 4)
☐ Major mechanical failure (eg camshaft drive) (Chapter 2)

Engine difficult to start when cold

☐ Battery discharged (Chapter 5)
☐ Battery terminal connections loose or corroded (Chapter 1)
☐ Worn, faulty or incorrectly-gapped spark plugs (Chapter 1)
☐ Fuel injection system fault (Chapter 4)
☐ Other ignition system fault (Chapters 1 and 5)
☐ Low cylinder compressions (Chapter 2)

Engine difficult to start when hot

☐ Air filter element dirty or clogged (Chapter 1)
☐ Fuel injection system fault (Chapter 4)
☐ Low cylinder compressions (Chapter 2)

Starter motor noisy or excessively-rough in engagement

☐ Starter pinion or flywheel ring gear teeth loose or broken (Chapters 2 and 5)
☐ Starter motor mounting bolts loose or missing (Chapter 5)
☐ Starter motor internal components worn or damaged (Chapter 5)

Engine starts, but stops immediately

☐ Loose or faulty electrical connections in the ignition circuit (Chapters 1 and 5)
☐ Vacuum leak at the throttle housing or inlet manifold (Chapter 4)
☐ Blocked injector/fuel injection system fault (Chapter 4)

Engine idles erratically

☐ Air filter element clogged (Chapter 1)
☐ Vacuum leak at the throttle housing, inlet manifold or associated hoses (Chapter 4)
☐ Worn, faulty or incorrectly-gapped spark plugs (Chapter 1)
☐ Uneven or low cylinder compressions (Chapter 2)
☐ Camshaft lobes worn (Chapter 2)
☐ Timing belt incorrectly fitted (Chapter 2)
☐ Blocked injector/fuel injection system fault (Chapter 4)

Engine misfires at idle speed

☐ Worn, faulty or incorrectly-gapped spark plugs (Chapter 1)
☐ Faulty spark plug HT leads (Chapter 1)
☐ Vacuum leak at the throttle housing, inlet manifold or associated hoses (Chapter 4)
☐ Blocked injector/fuel injection system fault (Chapter 4)
☐ Distributor cap cracked or tracking internally (Chapter 1).
☐ Uneven or low cylinder compressions (Chapter 2)
☐ Disconnected, leaking, or perished crankcase ventilation hoses (Chapter 4)

Engine misfires throughout the driving speed range

☐ Fuel filter choked (Chapter 1)
☐ Fuel pump faulty, or delivery pressure low (Chapter 4)
☐ Fuel tank vent blocked, or fuel pipes restricted (Chapter 4)
☐ Vacuum leak at the throttle housing, inlet manifold or associated hoses (Chapter 4)
☐ Worn, faulty or incorrectly-gapped spark plugs (Chapter 1)
☐ Faulty spark plug HT leads (Chapter 1)
☐ Distributor cap cracked or tracking internally (Chapter 1)
☐ Faulty ignition coil (Chapter 5)
☐ Uneven or low cylinder compressions (Chapter 2)
☐ Blocked injector/fuel injection system fault (Chapter 4)

Engine hesitates on acceleration

☐ Worn, faulty or incorrectly-gapped spark plugs (Chapter 1)
☐ Vacuum leak at the throttle housing, inlet manifold or associated hoses (Chapter 4)
☐ Blocked injector/fuel injection system fault (Chapter 4)

Engine stalls

☐ Vacuum leak at the throttle housing, inlet manifold or associated hoses (Chapter 4)
☐ Fuel filter choked (Chapter 1)
☐ Fuel pump faulty, or delivery pressure low (Chapter 4)
☐ Fuel tank vent blocked, or fuel pipes restricted (Chapter 4)
☐ Blocked injector/fuel injection system fault (Chapter 4)

1 Engine (continued)

Engine lacks power

- ☐ Timing belt incorrectly fitted (Chapter 2)
- ☐ Fuel filter choked (Chapter 1)
- ☐ Fuel pump faulty, or delivery pressure low (Chapter 4)
- ☐ Uneven or low cylinder compressions (Chapter 2)
- ☐ Worn, faulty or incorrectly-gapped spark plugs (Chapter 1)
- ☐ Vacuum leak at the throttle housing, inlet manifold or associated hoses (Chapter 4)
- ☐ Blocked injector/fuel injection system fault (Chapter 4)
- ☐ Brakes binding (Chapters 1 and 9)
- ☐ Clutch slipping (Chapter 6)

Engine backfires

- ☐ Timing belt incorrectly fitted (Chapter 2)
- ☐ Vacuum leak at the throttle housing, inlet manifold or associated hoses (Chapter 4)
- ☐ Blocked injector/fuel injection system fault (Chapter 4)

Oil pressure warning light illuminated with engine running

- ☐ Low oil level, or incorrect oil grade (Chapter 1)
- ☐ Faulty oil pressure sensor (Chapter 5)
- ☐ Worn engine bearings and/or oil pump (Chapter 2)
- ☐ High engine operating temperature (Chapter 3)
- ☐ Oil pressure relief valve defective (Chapter 2)
- ☐ Oil pick-up strainer clogged (Chapter 2)

Engine runs-on after switching off

- ☐ Excessive carbon build-up in engine (Chapter 2)
- ☐ High engine operating temperature (Chapter 3)
- ☐ Fuel injection system fault (Chapter 4)

Engine noises

Pre-ignition (pinking) or knocking during acceleration or under load

- ☐ Ignition timing incorrect/ignition system fault (Chapters 1 and 5)
- ☐ Incorrect grade of spark plug (Chapter 1)
- ☐ Incorrect grade of fuel (Chapter 1)
- ☐ Vacuum leak at the throttle housing, inlet manifold or associated hoses (Chapter 4)
- ☐ Excessive carbon build-up in engine (Chapter 2)
- ☐ Blocked injector/fuel injection system fault (Chapter 4)

Whistling or wheezing noises

- ☐ Leaking inlet manifold or throttle housing gasket (Chapter 4)
- ☐ Leaking exhaust manifold gasket or pipe-to-manifold joint (Chapter 4)
- ☐ Leaking vacuum hose (Chapters 4, 5 and 9)
- ☐ Blowing cylinder head gasket (Chapter 2)

Tapping or rattling noises

- ☐ Worn valve gear or camshaft (Chapter 2)
- ☐ Ancillary component fault (water pump, alternator, etc) (Chapters 3, 5, etc)

Knocking or thumping noises

- ☐ Worn big-end bearings (regular heavy knocking, perhaps less under load) (Chapter 2)
- ☐ Worn main bearings (rumbling and knocking, perhaps worsening under load) (Chapter 2)
- ☐ Piston slap (most noticeable when cold) (Chapter 2)
- ☐ Ancillary component fault (water pump, alternator, etc) (Chapters 3, 5, etc)

2 Cooling system

Overheating

- ☐ Insufficient coolant in system ('Weekly checks')
- ☐ Thermostat faulty (Chapter 3)
- ☐ Radiator core blocked, or grille restricted (Chapter 3)
- ☐ Cooling fan circuit fault (Chapter 3)
- ☐ Inaccurate temperature gauge sender unit (Chapter 3)
- ☐ Airlock in cooling system (Chapter 3)
- ☐ Pressure cap faulty (Chapter 3)

Overcooling

- ☐ Thermostat faulty (Chapter 3)
- ☐ Inaccurate temperature gauge sender unit (Chapter 3)
- ☐ Cooling fan circuit fault (Chapter 3)

External coolant leakage

- ☐ Deteriorated or damaged hoses or hose clips (Chapter 1)
- ☐ Radiator core or heater matrix leaking (Chapter 3)
- ☐ Pressure cap faulty (Chapter 3)
- ☐ Coolant pump internal seal leaking (Chapter 3)
- ☐ Coolant pump-to-block seal leaking (Chapter 3)
- ☐ Boiling due to overheating (Chapter 3)
- ☐ Core plug leaking (Chapter 2)

Internal coolant leakage

- ☐ Leaking cylinder head gasket (Chapter 2)
- ☐ Cracked cylinder head or cylinder block (Chapter 2)

Corrosion

- ☐ Infrequent draining and flushing (Chapter 1)
- ☐ Incorrect coolant mixture or inappropriate coolant type (Chapter 1)

3 Fuel and exhaust systems

Excessive fuel consumption

- ☐ Air filter element dirty or clogged (Chapter 1)
- ☐ Fuel injection system fault (Chapter 4)
- ☐ Ignition timing incorrect/ignition system fault (Chapters 1 and 5)
- ☐ Tyres under-inflated (Chapter 1)

Fuel leakage and/or fuel odour

- ☐ Damaged or corroded fuel tank, pipes or connections (Chapter 4)

Excessive noise or fumes from exhaust system

- ☐ Leaking exhaust system or manifold joints (Chapters 1 and 4)
- ☐ Leaking, corroded or damaged silencers or pipe (Chapters 1 and 4)
- ☐ Broken mountings causing body or suspension contact (Chapter 1)

4 Clutch

Pedal travels to floor - no pressure or very little resistance

☐ Hydraulic fluid level low/air in the hydraulic system (Chapter 6)
☐ Broken clutch release bearing or fork (Chapter 6)
☐ Broken diaphragm spring in clutch pressure plate (Chapter 6)

Clutch fails to disengage (unable to select gears)

☐ Hydraulic fluid level too high
☐ Clutch disc sticking on gearbox input shaft splines (Chapter 6)
☐ Clutch disc sticking to flywheel or pressure plate (Chapter 6)
☐ Faulty pressure plate assembly (Chapter 6)
☐ Clutch release mechanism worn or badly assembled (Chapter 6)

Clutch slips (engine speed increases, with no increase in vehicle speed)

☐ Hydraulic fluid level too high
☐ Clutch disc linings excessively worn (Chapter 6)
☐ Clutch disc linings contaminated with oil or grease (Chapter 6)
☐ Faulty pressure plate or weak diaphragm spring (Chapter 6)

Judder as clutch is engaged

☐ Clutch disc linings contaminated with oil or grease (Chapter 6)
☐ Clutch disc linings excessively worn (Chapter 6)
☐ Faulty or distorted pressure plate or diaphragm spring (Chapter 6).
☐ Worn or loose engine or gearbox mountings (Chapter 2)
☐ Clutch disc hub or gearbox input shaft splines worn (Chapter 6)

Noise when depressing or releasing clutch pedal

☐ Worn clutch release bearing (Chapter 6)
☐ Worn or dry clutch pedal bushes (Chapter 6)
☐ Faulty pressure plate assembly (Chapter 6)
☐ Pressure plate diaphragm spring broken (Chapter 6)
☐ Broken clutch disc cushioning springs (Chapter 6)

5 Manual transmission

Noisy in neutral with engine running

☐ Input shaft bearings worn (noise apparent with clutch pedal released, but not when depressed) (Chapter 7)*
☐ Clutch release bearing worn (noise apparent with clutch pedal depressed, possibly less when released) (Chapter 6)

Noisy in one particular gear

☐ Worn, damaged or chipped gear teeth (Chapter 7)*

Difficulty engaging gears

☐ Clutch fault (Chapter 6)
☐ Worn or damaged gearchange cables (Chapter 7)
☐ Worn synchroniser units (Chapter 7)*

Jumps out of gear

☐ Worn or damaged gearchange cables (Chapter 7)
☐ Worn synchroniser units (Chapter 7)*
☐ Worn selector forks (Chapter 7)*

Vibration

☐ Lack of oil (Chapter 1)
☐ Worn bearings (Chapter 7)*

Lubricant leaks

☐ Leaking differential output oil seal (Chapter 7)
☐ Leaking housing joint (Chapter 7)*
☐ Leaking input shaft oil seal (Chapter 7)*

Although the corrective action necessary to remedy the symptoms described is beyond the scope of the home mechanic, the above information should be helpful in isolating the cause of the condition, so that the owner can communicate clearly with a professional mechanic.

6 Automatic transmission

Note: *Due to the complexity of the automatic transmission, it is difficult for the home mechanic to properly diagnose and service this unit. For problems other than the following, the vehicle should be taken to a dealer service department or automatic transmission specialist. Do not be too hasty in removing the transmission if a fault is suspected, as most of the testing is carried out with the unit still fitted.*

Fluid leakage

☐ Automatic transmission fluid is usually dark in colour. Fluid leaks should not be confused with engine oil, which can easily be blown onto the transmission by airflow.
☐ To determine the source of a leak, first remove all built-up dirt and grime from the transmission housing and surrounding areas using a degreasing agent, or by steam-cleaning. Drive the vehicle at low speed, so airflow will not blow the leak far from its source. Raise and support the vehicle, and determine where the leak is coming from. The following are common areas of leakage:

a) Oil pan (Chapter 1 and 7)
b) Dipstick tube (Chapter 1 and 7)
c) Transmission-to-fluid cooler pipes/unions (Chapter 7)

Transmission fluid brown, or has burned smell

☐ Transmission fluid level low, or fluid in need of renewal (Chapter 1)

General gear selection problems

☐ Chapter 7B deals with checking and adjusting the selector cable on automatic transmissions. The following are common problems which may be caused by a poorly-adjusted cable:

a) Engine starting in gears other than Park or Neutral.
b) Indicator panel indicating a gear other than the one actually being used.
c) Vehicle moves when in Park or Neutral.
d) Poor gear shift quality or erratic gear changes.

☐ Refer to Chapter 7B for the selector cable adjustment procedure.

6 Automatic transmission (continued)

Transmission will not downshift (kickdown) with accelerator pedal fully depressed

☐ Low transmission fluid level (Chapter 1)
☐ Incorrect selector cable adjustment (Chapter 7)

Engine will not start in any gear, or starts in gears other than Park or Neutral

☐ Incorrect selector lever position switch adjustment (Chapter 7)
☐ Incorrect selector cable adjustment (Chapter 7)

Transmission slips, shifts roughly, is noisy, or has no drive in forward or reverse gears

☐ There are many probable causes for the above problems, but the home mechanic should be concerned with only one possibility - fluid level. Before taking the vehicle to a dealer or transmission specialist, check the fluid level and condition of the fluid as described in Chapter 1. Correct the fluid level as necessary, or change the fluid and filter if needed. If the problem persists, professional help will be necessary.

7 Driveshafts

Vibration when accelerating or decelerating

☐ Worn inner constant velocity joint (Chapter 8)
☐ Bent or distorted driveshaft (Chapter 8)
☐ Worn intermediate shaft bearing (Chapter 8)

Clicking or knocking noise on turns (at slow speed on full-lock)

☐ Worn outer constant velocity joint (Chapter 8)
☐ Lack of constant velocity joint lubricant, possibly due to damaged gaiter (Chapter 8)
☐ Worn intermediate shaft bearing (Chapter 8)

8 Braking system

Note: *Before assuming that a brake problem exists, make sure that the tyres are in good condition and correctly inflated, that the front wheel alignment is correct, and that the vehicle is not loaded with weight in an unequal manner. Apart from checking the condition of all pipe and hose connections, any faults occurring on the anti-lock braking system should be referred to a Rover dealer for diagnosis.*

Vehicle pulls to one side under braking

☐ Worn, defective, damaged or contaminated brake pads on one side (Chapters 1 and 9)
☐ Seized or partially-seized brake caliper piston (Chapters 1 and 9)
☐ A mixture of brake pad lining materials fitted between sides (Chapters 1 and 9)
☐ Brake caliper mounting bolts loose (Chapter 9)
☐ Worn or damaged steering or suspension components (Chapters 1 and 10)

Noise (grinding or high-pitched squeal) when brakes applied

☐ Brake pad friction lining material worn down to metal backing (Chapters 1 and 9)
☐ Excessive corrosion of brake disc (may be apparent after the vehicle has been standing for some time (Chapters 1 and 9)
☐ Foreign object (stone chipping, etc) trapped between brake disc and shield (Chapters 1 and 9)

Excessive brake pedal travel

☐ Faulty master cylinder (Chapter 9)
☐ Air in hydraulic system (Chapters 1 and 9)
☐ Faulty vacuum servo unit (Chapter 9)

Brake pedal feels spongy when depressed

☐ Air in hydraulic system (Chapters 1 and 9)
☐ Deteriorated flexible rubber brake hoses (Chapters 1 and 9)
☐ Master cylinder mounting nuts loose (Chapter 9)
☐ Faulty master cylinder (Chapter 9)

Excessive brake pedal effort required to stop vehicle

☐ Faulty vacuum servo unit (Chapter 9)
☐ Disconnected, damaged or insecure brake servo vacuum hose (Chapter 9)
☐ Primary or secondary hydraulic circuit failure (Chapter 9)
☐ Seized brake caliper piston (Chapter 9)
☐ Brake pads incorrectly fitted (Chapters 1 and 9)
☐ Incorrect grade of brake pads fitted (Chapters 1 and 9)
☐ Brake pad linings contaminated (Chapters 1 and 9)

Judder felt through brake pedal or steering wheel when braking

☐ Excessive run-out or distortion of discs (Chapters 1 and 9)
☐ Brake pad linings worn (Chapters 1 and 9)
☐ Brake caliper mounting bolts loose (Chapter 9)
☐ Wear in suspension or steering components or mountings (Chapters 1 and 10)

Brakes binding

☐ Seized brake caliper piston (Chapter 9)
☐ Incorrectly-adjusted parking brake mechanism (Chapter 9)
☐ Faulty master cylinder (Chapter 9)

Rear wheels locking under normal braking

☐ Rear brake pad linings contaminated (Chapters 1 and 9)
☐ Rear brake discs warped (Chapters 1 and 9)

9 Suspension and steering

Note: *Before diagnosing suspension or steering faults, be sure that the trouble is not due to incorrect tyre pressures, mixtures of tyre types, or binding brakes.*

Vehicle pulls to one side

- ☐ Defective tyre (*'Weekly checks'*)
- ☐ Excessive wear in suspension or steering components (Chapters 1 and 10)
- ☐ Incorrect front wheel alignment (Chapter 10)
- ☐ Accident damage to steering or suspension components (Chapter 1)

Wheel wobble and vibration

- ☐ Front roadwheels out of balance (vibration felt mainly through the steering wheel) (Chapters 1 and 10)
- ☐ Rear roadwheels out of balance (vibration felt throughout the vehicle) (Chapters 1 and 10)
- ☐ Roadwheels damaged or distorted (Chapters 1 and 10)
- ☐ Faulty or damaged tyre (*'Weekly checks'*)
- ☐ Worn steering or suspension joints, bushes or components (Chapters 1 and 10)
- ☐ Wheel bolts loose (Chapters 1 and 10)

Excessive pitching and/or rolling around corners, or during braking

- ☐ Defective shock absorbers (Chapters 1 and 10)
- ☐ Broken or weak spring and/or suspension component (Chapters 1 and 10)
- ☐ Worn or damaged anti-roll bar or mountings (Chapter 10)

Wandering or general instability

- ☐ Incorrect front wheel alignment (Chapter 10)
- ☐ Worn steering or suspension joints, bushes or components (Chapters 1 and 10)
- ☐ Roadwheels out of balance (Chapters 1 and 10)
- ☐ Faulty or damaged tyre (*'Weekly checks'*)
- ☐ Wheel bolts loose (Chapters 1 and 10)
- ☐ Defective shock absorbers (Chapters 1 and 10)

Excessively-stiff steering

- ☐ Seized steering linkage balljoint or suspension balljoint (Chapters 1 and 10)
- ☐ Broken or incorrectly-adjusted drivebelt - power steering (Chapter 1)
- ☐ Incorrect front wheel alignment (Chapter 10)
- ☐ Steering box or linkage damaged (Chapter 10)

Excessive play in steering

- ☐ Worn steering column intermediate shaft coupling joint (Chapter 10)
- ☐ Worn steering linkage balljoints (Chapters 1 and 10)
- ☐ Worn steering box (Chapter 10)
- ☐ Worn steering or suspension joints, bushes or components (Chapters 1 and 10)

Lack of power assistance

- ☐ Broken or incorrectly-adjusted auxiliary drivebelt (Chapter 1)
- ☐ Incorrect power steering fluid level (*'Weekly checks'*)
- ☐ Restriction in power steering fluid hoses (Chapter 1)
- ☐ Faulty power steering pump (Chapter 10)
- ☐ Faulty steering gear (Chapter 10)

Tyre wear excessive

Tyres worn on inside or outside edges

- ☐ Tyres under-inflated (wear on both edges) (*'Weekly checks'*)
- ☐ Incorrect camber or castor angles (wear on one edge only) (Chapter 10)
- ☐ Worn steering or suspension joints, bushes or components (Chapters 1 and 10)
- ☐ Excessively-hard cornering
- ☐ Accident damage

Tyre treads exhibit feathered edges

- ☐ Incorrect toe setting (Chapter 10)

Tyres worn in centre of tread

- ☐ Tyres over-inflated (*'Weekly checks'*)

Tyres worn on inside and outside edges

- ☐ Tyres under-inflated (*'Weekly checks'*)

Tyres worn unevenly

- ☐ Tyres/wheels out of balance (Chapter 1)
- ☐ Excessive wheel or tyre run-out (Chapter 1)
- ☐ Worn shock absorbers (Chapters 1 and 10)
- ☐ Faulty tyre (*'Weekly checks'*)

10 Electrical system

Note: *For problems associated with the starting system, refer to the faults listed under Engine earlier in this Section.*

Battery will not hold a charge for more than a few days

- ☐ Battery defective internally (Chapter 5)
- ☐ Battery terminal connections loose or corroded (*'Weekly checks'*)
- ☐ Auxiliary drivebelt worn or incorrectly adjusted (Chapter 1)
- ☐ Alternator not charging at correct output (Chapter 5)
- ☐ Alternator or voltage regulator faulty (Chapter 5)
- ☐ Short-circuit causing continual battery drain (Chapters 5 and 12)

Ignition/no-charge warning light remains illuminated with engine running

- ☐ Auxiliary drivebelt broken, worn, or incorrectly adjusted (Chapter 1)
- ☐ Alternator brushes worn, sticking, or dirty (Chapter 5)
- ☐ Alternator brush springs weak or broken (Chapter 5)
- ☐ Internal fault in alternator or voltage regulator (Chapter 5)
- ☐ Broken, disconnected, or loose wiring in charging circuit (Chapter 5)

Ignition/no-charge warning light fails to come on

- ☐ Warning light bulb blown (Chapter 12)
- ☐ Broken, disconnected, or loose wiring in warning light circuit (Chapter 12)
- ☐ Alternator faulty (Chapter 5)

10 Electrical system (continued)

Lights inoperative

- ☐ Bulb blown (Chapter 12)
- ☐ Corrosion of bulb or bulbholder contacts (Chapter 12)
- ☐ Blown fuse (Chapter 12)
- ☐ Faulty relay (Chapter 12)
- ☐ Broken, loose, or disconnected wiring (Chapter 12)
- ☐ Faulty switch (Chapter 12)

Instrument readings inaccurate or erratic

Instrument readings increase with engine speed

- ☐ Faulty voltage regulator (Chapter 12)

Fuel or temperature gauges give no reading

- ☐ Faulty gauge sender unit (Chapters 3 and 4)
- ☐ Wiring open-circuit (Chapter 12)
- ☐ Faulty gauge (Chapter 12)

Fuel or temperature gauges give continuous maximum reading

- ☐ Faulty gauge sender unit (Chapters 3 and 4)
- ☐ Wiring short-circuit (Chapter 12)
- ☐ Faulty gauge (Chapter 12)

Horn inoperative, or unsatisfactory in operation

Horn operates all the time

- ☐ Horn push either earthed or stuck down (Chapter 12)
- ☐ Horn cable-to-horn push earthed (Chapter 12)

Horn fails to operate

- ☐ Blown fuse (Chapter 12)
- ☐ Cable or cable connections loose, broken or disconnected (Chapter 12)
- ☐ Faulty horn (Chapter 12)

Horn emits intermittent or unsatisfactory sound

- ☐ Cable connections loose (Chapter 12)
- ☐ Horn mountings loose (Chapter 12)
- ☐ Faulty horn (Chapter 12)

Windscreen wipers inoperative, or unsatisfactory in operation

Wipers fail to operate, or operate very slowly

- ☐ Wiper blades stuck to screen, or linkage seized or binding (Chapters 1 and 12)
- ☐ Blown fuse (Chapter 12)
- ☐ Cable or cable connections loose, broken or disconnected (Chapter 12)
- ☐ Faulty relay (Chapter 12)
- ☐ Faulty wiper motor (Chapter 12)

Wiper blades sweep over too large or too small an area of the glass

- ☐ Wiper arms incorrectly positioned on spindles (Chapter 1)
- ☐ Excessive wear of wiper linkage (Chapter 12)
- ☐ Wiper motor or linkage mountings loose or insecure (Chapter 12)

Wiper blades fail to clean the glass effectively

- ☐ Wiper blade rubbers worn or perished (*'Weekly checks'*)
- ☐ Wiper arm tension springs broken, or arm pivots seized (Chapter 12)
- ☐ Insufficient windscreen washer additive to adequately remove road film (*'Weekly checks'*)

Windscreen washers inoperative, or unsatisfactory in operation

One or more washer jets inoperative

- ☐ Blocked washer jet (Chapter 1)
- ☐ Disconnected, kinked or restricted fluid hose (Chapter 12)
- ☐ Insufficient fluid in washer reservoir (*'Weekly checks'*)

Washer pump fails to operate

- ☐ Broken or disconnected wiring or connections (Chapter 12)
- ☐ Blown fuse (Chapter 12)
- ☐ Faulty washer switch (Chapter 12)
- ☐ Faulty washer pump (Chapter 12)

Washer pump runs for some time before fluid is emitted from jets

- ☐ Faulty one-way valve in fluid supply hose (Chapter 12)

Electric windows inoperative, or unsatisfactory in operation

Window glass will only move in one direction

- ☐ Faulty switch (Chapter 12)

Window glass slow to move

- ☐ Regulator seized or damaged, or in need of lubrication (Chapter 11)
- ☐ Door internal components or trim fouling regulator (Chapter 11)
- ☐ Faulty motor (Chapter 11)

Window glass fails to move

- ☐ Blown fuse (Chapter 12)
- ☐ Faulty relay (Chapter 12)
- ☐ Broken or disconnected wiring or connections (Chapter 12)
- ☐ Faulty motor (Chapter 11)

Central locking system inoperative, or unsatisfactory in operation

Complete system failure

- ☐ Blown fuse (Chapter 12)
- ☐ Faulty relay (Chapter 12)
- ☐ Broken or disconnected wiring or connections (Chapter 12)
- ☐ Faulty motor (Chapter 11)

Latch locks but will not unlock, or unlocks but will not lock

- ☐ Faulty master switch (Chapter 12)
- ☐ Broken or disconnected latch operating rods or levers (Chapter 11)
- ☐ Faulty relay (Chapter 12)
- ☐ Faulty motor (Chapter 11)

One solenoid/motor fails to operate

- ☐ Broken or disconnected wiring or connections (Chapter 12)
- ☐ Faulty operating assembly (Chapter 11)
- ☐ Broken, binding or disconnected latch operating rods or levers (Chapter 11)
- ☐ Fault in door latch (Chapter 11)

A

ABS (Anti-lock brake system) A system, usually electronically controlled, that senses incipient wheel lockup during braking and relieves hydraulic pressure at wheels that are about to skid.

Air bag An inflatable bag hidden in the steering wheel (driver's side) or the dash or glovebox (passenger side). In a head-on collision, the bags inflate, preventing the driver and front passenger from being thrown forward into the steering wheel or windscreen.

Air cleaner A metal or plastic housing, containing a filter element, which removes dust and dirt from the air being drawn into the engine.

Air filter element The actual filter in an air cleaner system, usually manufactured from pleated paper and requiring renewal at regular intervals.

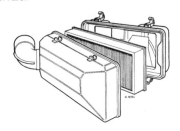
Air filter

Allen key A hexagonal wrench which fits into a recessed hexagonal hole.

Alligator clip A long-nosed spring-loaded metal clip with meshing teeth. Used to make temporary electrical connections.

Alternator A component in the electrical system which converts mechanical energy from a drivebelt into electrical energy to charge the battery and to operate the starting system, ignition system and electrical accessories.

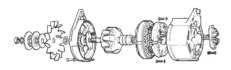
Alternator (exploded view)

Ampere (amp) A unit of measurement for the flow of electric current. One amp is the amount of current produced by one volt acting through a resistance of one ohm.

Anaerobic sealer A substance used to prevent bolts and screws from loosening. Anaerobic means that it does not require oxygen for activation. The Loctite brand is widely used.

Antifreeze A substance (usually ethylene glycol) mixed with water, and added to a vehicle's cooling system, to prevent freezing of the coolant in winter. Antifreeze also contains chemicals to inhibit corrosion and the formation of rust and other deposits that would tend to clog the radiator and coolant passages and reduce cooling efficiency.

Anti-seize compound A coating that reduces the risk of seizing on fasteners that are subjected to high temperatures, such as exhaust manifold bolts and nuts.

Anti-seize compound

Asbestos A natural fibrous mineral with great heat resistance, commonly used in the composition of brake friction materials. Asbestos is a health hazard and the dust created by brake systems should never be inhaled or ingested.

Axle A shaft on which a wheel revolves, or which revolves with a wheel. Also, a solid beam that connects the two wheels at one end of the vehicle. An axle which also transmits power to the wheels is known as a live axle.

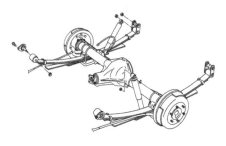
Axle assembly

Axleshaft A single rotating shaft, on either side of the differential, which delivers power from the final drive assembly to the drive wheels. Also called a driveshaft or a halfshaft.

B

Ball bearing An anti-friction bearing consisting of a hardened inner and outer race with hardened steel balls between two races.

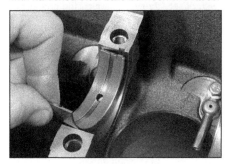
Bearing

Bearing The curved surface on a shaft or in a bore, or the part assembled into either, that permits relative motion between them with minimum wear and friction.

Big-end bearing The bearing in the end of the connecting rod that's attached to the crankshaft.

Bleed nipple A valve on a brake wheel cylinder, caliper or other hydraulic component that is opened to purge the hydraulic system of air. Also called a bleed screw.

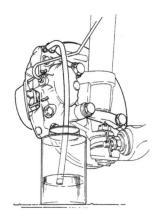
Brake bleeding

Brake bleeding Procedure for removing air from lines of a hydraulic brake system.

Brake disc The component of a disc brake that rotates with the wheels.

Brake drum The component of a drum brake that rotates with the wheels.

Brake linings The friction material which contacts the brake disc or drum to retard the vehicle's speed. The linings are bonded or riveted to the brake pads or shoes.

Brake pads The replaceable friction pads that pinch the brake disc when the brakes are applied. Brake pads consist of a friction material bonded or riveted to a rigid backing plate.

Brake shoe The crescent-shaped carrier to which the brake linings are mounted and which forces the lining against the rotating drum during braking.

Braking systems For more information on braking systems, consult the *Haynes Automotive Brake Manual*.

Breaker bar A long socket wrench handle providing greater leverage.

Bulkhead The insulated partition between the engine and the passenger compartment.

C

Caliper The non-rotating part of a disc-brake assembly that straddles the disc and carries the brake pads. The caliper also contains the hydraulic components that cause the pads to pinch the disc when the brakes are applied. A caliper is also a measuring tool that can be set to measure inside or outside dimensions of an object.

Camshaft A rotating shaft on which a series of cam lobes operate the valve mechanisms. The camshaft may be driven by gears, by sprockets and chain or by sprockets and a belt.

Canister A container in an evaporative emission control system; contains activated charcoal granules to trap vapours from the fuel system.

Canister

Carburettor A device which mixes fuel with air in the proper proportions to provide a desired power output from a spark ignition internal combustion engine.

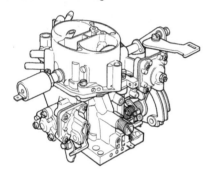

Carburettor

Castellated Resembling the parapets along the top of a castle wall. For example, a castellated balljoint stud nut.

Castellated nut

Castor In wheel alignment, the backward or forward tilt of the steering axis. Castor is positive when the steering axis is inclined rearward at the top.

Catalytic converter A silencer-like device in the exhaust system which converts certain pollutants in the exhaust gases into less harmful substances.

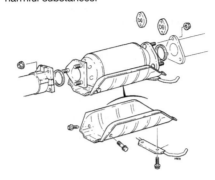

Catalytic converter

Circlip A ring-shaped clip used to prevent endwise movement of cylindrical parts and shafts. An internal circlip is installed in a groove in a housing; an external circlip fits into a groove on the outside of a cylindrical piece such as a shaft.

Clearance The amount of space between two parts. For example, between a piston and a cylinder, between a bearing and a journal, etc.

Coil spring A spiral of elastic steel found in various sizes throughout a vehicle, for example as a springing medium in the suspension and in the valve train.

Compression Reduction in volume, and increase in pressure and temperature, of a gas, caused by squeezing it into a smaller space.

Compression ratio The relationship between cylinder volume when the piston is at top dead centre and cylinder volume when the piston is at bottom dead centre.

Constant velocity (CV) joint A type of universal joint that cancels out vibrations caused by driving power being transmitted through an angle.

Core plug A disc or cup-shaped metal device inserted in a hole in a casting through which core was removed when the casting was formed. Also known as a freeze plug or expansion plug.

Crankcase The lower part of the engine block in which the crankshaft rotates.

Crankshaft The main rotating member, or shaft, running the length of the crankcase, with offset "throws" to which the connecting rods are attached.

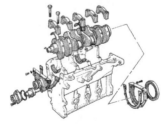

Crankshaft assembly

Crocodile clip See Alligator clip

D

Diagnostic code Code numbers obtained by accessing the diagnostic mode of an engine management computer. This code can be used to determine the area in the system where a malfunction may be located.

Disc brake A brake design incorporating a rotating disc onto which brake pads are squeezed. The resulting friction converts the energy of a moving vehicle into heat.

Double-overhead cam (DOHC) An engine that uses two overhead camshafts, usually one for the intake valves and one for the exhaust valves.

Drivebelt(s) The belt(s) used to drive accessories such as the alternator, water pump, power steering pump, air conditioning compressor, etc. off the crankshaft pulley.

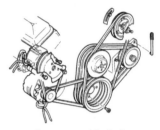

Accessory drivebelts

Driveshaft Any shaft used to transmit motion. Commonly used when referring to the axleshafts on a front wheel drive vehicle.

Driveshaft

Drum brake A type of brake using a drum-shaped metal cylinder attached to the inner surface of the wheel. When the brake pedal is pressed, curved brake shoes with friction linings press against the inside of the drum to slow or stop the vehicle.

Drum brake assembly

E

EGR valve A valve used to introduce exhaust gases into the intake air stream.

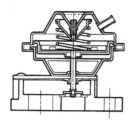

EGR valve

Electronic control unit (ECU) A computer which controls (for instance) ignition and fuel injection systems, or an anti-lock braking system. For more information refer to the *Haynes Automotive Electrical and Electronic Systems Manual.*

Electronic Fuel Injection (EFI) A computer controlled fuel system that distributes fuel through an injector located in each intake port of the engine.

Emergency brake A braking system, independent of the main hydraulic system, that can be used to slow or stop the vehicle if the primary brakes fail, or to hold the vehicle stationary even though the brake pedal isn't depressed. It usually consists of a hand lever that actuates either front or rear brakes mechanically through a series of cables and linkages. Also known as a handbrake or parking brake.

Endfloat The amount of lengthwise movement between two parts. As applied to a crankshaft, the distance that the crankshaft can move forward and back in the cylinder block.

Engine management system (EMS) A computer controlled system which manages the fuel injection and the ignition systems in an integrated fashion.

Exhaust manifold A part with several passages through which exhaust gases leave the engine combustion chambers and enter the exhaust pipe.

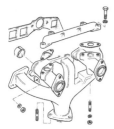

Exhaust manifold

F

Fan clutch A viscous (fluid) drive coupling device which permits variable engine fan speeds in relation to engine speeds.

Feeler blade A thin strip or blade of hardened steel, ground to an exact thickness, used to check or measure clearances between parts.

Feeler blade

Firing order The order in which the engine cylinders fire, or deliver their power strokes, beginning with the number one cylinder.

Flywheel A heavy spinning wheel in which energy is absorbed and stored by means of momentum. On cars, the flywheel is attached to the crankshaft to smooth out firing impulses.

Free play The amount of travel before any action takes place. The "looseness" in a linkage, or an assembly of parts, between the initial application of force and actual movement. For example, the distance the brake pedal moves before the pistons in the master cylinder are actuated.

Fuse An electrical device which protects a circuit against accidental overload. The typical fuse contains a soft piece of metal which is calibrated to melt at a predetermined current flow (expressed as amps) and break the circuit.

Fusible link A circuit protection device consisting of a conductor surrounded by heat-resistant insulation. The conductor is smaller than the wire it protects, so it acts as the weakest link in the circuit. Unlike a blown fuse, a failed fusible link must frequently be cut from the wire for replacement.

G

Gap The distance the spark must travel in jumping from the centre electrode to the side

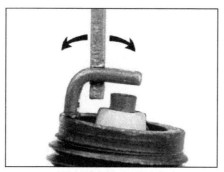

Adjusting spark plug gap

electrode in a spark plug. Also refers to the spacing between the points in a contact breaker assembly in a conventional points-type ignition, or to the distance between the reluctor or rotor and the pickup coil in an electronic ignition.

Gasket Any thin, soft material - usually cork, cardboard, asbestos or soft metal - installed between two metal surfaces to ensure a good seal. For instance, the cylinder head gasket seals the joint between the block and the cylinder head.

Gasket

Gauge An instrument panel display used to monitor engine conditions. A gauge with a movable pointer on a dial or a fixed scale is an analogue gauge. A gauge with a numerical readout is called a digital gauge.

H

Halfshaft A rotating shaft that transmits power from the final drive unit to a drive wheel, usually when referring to a live rear axle.

Harmonic balancer A device designed to reduce torsion or twisting vibration in the crankshaft. May be incorporated in the crankshaft pulley. Also known as a vibration damper.

Hone An abrasive tool for correcting small irregularities or differences in diameter in an engine cylinder, brake cylinder, etc.

Hydraulic tappet A tappet that utilises hydraulic pressure from the engine's lubrication system to maintain zero clearance (constant contact with both camshaft and valve stem). Automatically adjusts to variation in valve stem length. Hydraulic tappets also reduce valve noise.

I

Ignition timing The moment at which the spark plug fires, usually expressed in the number of crankshaft degrees before the piston reaches the top of its stroke.

Inlet manifold A tube or housing with passages through which flows the air-fuel mixture (carburettor vehicles and vehicles with throttle body injection) or air only (port fuel-injected vehicles) to the port openings in the cylinder head.

J

Jump start Starting the engine of a vehicle with a discharged or weak battery by attaching jump leads from the weak battery to a charged or helper battery.

L

Load Sensing Proportioning Valve (LSPV) A brake hydraulic system control valve that works like a proportioning valve, but also takes into consideration the amount of weight carried by the rear axle.

Locknut A nut used to lock an adjustment nut, or other threaded component, in place. For example, a locknut is employed to keep the adjusting nut on the rocker arm in position.

Lockwasher A form of washer designed to prevent an attaching nut from working loose.

M

MacPherson strut A type of front suspension system devised by Earle MacPherson at Ford of England. In its original form, a simple lateral link with the anti-roll bar creates the lower control arm. A long strut - an integral coil spring and shock absorber - is mounted between the body and the steering knuckle. Many modern so-called MacPherson strut systems use a conventional lower A-arm and don't rely on the anti-roll bar for location.

Multimeter An electrical test instrument with the capability to measure voltage, current and resistance.

N

NOx Oxides of Nitrogen. A common toxic pollutant emitted by petrol and diesel engines at higher temperatures.

O

Ohm The unit of electrical resistance. One volt applied to a resistance of one ohm will produce a current of one amp.

Ohmmeter An instrument for measuring electrical resistance.

O-ring A type of sealing ring made of a special rubber-like material; in use, the O-ring is compressed into a groove to provide the sealing action.

O-ring

Overhead cam (ohc) engine An engine with the camshaft(s) located on top of the cylinder head(s).

Overhead valve (ohv) engine An engine with the valves located in the cylinder head, but with the camshaft located in the engine block.

Oxygen sensor A device installed in the engine exhaust manifold, which senses the oxygen content in the exhaust and converts this information into an electric current. Also called a Lambda sensor.

P

Phillips screw A type of screw head having a cross instead of a slot for a corresponding type of screwdriver.

Plastigage A thin strip of plastic thread, available in different sizes, used for measuring clearances. For example, a strip of Plastigage is laid across a bearing journal. The parts are assembled and dismantled; the width of the crushed strip indicates the clearance between journal and bearing.

Plastigage

Propeller shaft The long hollow tube with universal joints at both ends that carries power from the transmission to the differential on front-engined rear wheel drive vehicles.

Proportioning valve A hydraulic control valve which limits the amount of pressure to the rear brakes during panic stops to prevent wheel lock-up.

R

Rack-and-pinion steering A steering system with a pinion gear on the end of the steering shaft that mates with a rack (think of a geared wheel opened up and laid flat). When the steering wheel is turned, the pinion turns, moving the rack to the left or right. This movement is transmitted through the track rods to the steering arms at the wheels.

Radiator A liquid-to-air heat transfer device designed to reduce the temperature of the coolant in an internal combustion engine cooling system.

Refrigerant Any substance used as a heat transfer agent in an air-conditioning system. R-12 has been the principle refrigerant for many years; recently, however, manufacturers have begun using R-134a, a non-CFC substance that is considered less harmful to the ozone in the upper atmosphere.

Rocker arm A lever arm that rocks on a shaft or pivots on a stud. In an overhead valve engine, the rocker arm converts the upward movement of the pushrod into a downward movement to open a valve.

Rotor In a distributor, the rotating device inside the cap that connects the centre electrode and the outer terminals as it turns, distributing the high voltage from the coil secondary winding to the proper spark plug. Also, that part of an alternator which rotates inside the stator. Also, the rotating assembly of a turbocharger, including the compressor wheel, shaft and turbine wheel.

Runout The amount of wobble (in-and-out movement) of a gear or wheel as it's rotated. The amount a shaft rotates "out-of-true." The out-of-round condition of a rotating part.

S

Sealant A liquid or paste used to prevent leakage at a joint. Sometimes used in conjunction with a gasket.

Sealed beam lamp An older headlight design which integrates the reflector, lens and filaments into a hermetically-sealed one-piece unit. When a filament burns out or the lens cracks, the entire unit is simply replaced.

Serpentine drivebelt A single, long, wide accessory drivebelt that's used on some newer vehicles to drive all the accessories, instead of a series of smaller, shorter belts. Serpentine drivebelts are usually tensioned by an automatic tensioner.

Serpentine drivebelt

Shim Thin spacer, commonly used to adjust the clearance or relative positions between two parts. For example, shims inserted into or under bucket tappets control valve clearances. Clearance is adjusted by changing the thickness of the shim.

Slide hammer A special puller that screws into or hooks onto a component such as a shaft or bearing; a heavy sliding handle on the shaft bottoms against the end of the shaft to knock the component free.

Sprocket A tooth or projection on the periphery of a wheel, shaped to engage with a chain or drivebelt. Commonly used to refer to the sprocket wheel itself.

Starter inhibitor switch On vehicles with an

automatic transmission, a switch that prevents starting if the vehicle is not in Neutral or Park.

Strut See MacPherson strut.

T

Tappet A cylindrical component which transmits motion from the cam to the valve stem, either directly or via a pushrod and rocker arm. Also called a cam follower.

Thermostat A heat-controlled valve that regulates the flow of coolant between the cylinder block and the radiator, so maintaining optimum engine operating temperature. A thermostat is also used in some air cleaners in which the temperature is regulated.

Thrust bearing The bearing in the clutch assembly that is moved in to the release levers by clutch pedal action to disengage the clutch. Also referred to as a release bearing.

Timing belt A toothed belt which drives the camshaft. Serious engine damage may result if it breaks in service.

Timing chain A chain which drives the camshaft.

Toe-in The amount the front wheels are closer together at the front than at the rear. On rear wheel drive vehicles, a slight amount of toe-in is usually specified to keep the front wheels running parallel on the road by offsetting other forces that tend to spread the wheels apart.

Toe-out The amount the front wheels are closer together at the rear than at the front. On front wheel drive vehicles, a slight amount of toe-out is usually specified.

Tools For full information on choosing and using tools, refer to the *Haynes Automotive Tools Manual*.

Tracer A stripe of a second colour applied to a wire insulator to distinguish that wire from another one with the same colour insulator.

Tune-up A process of accurate and careful adjustments and parts replacement to obtain the best possible engine performance.

Turbocharger A centrifugal device, driven by exhaust gases, that pressurises the intake air. Normally used to increase the power output from a given engine displacement, but can also be used primarily to reduce exhaust emissions (as on VW's "Umwelt" Diesel engine).

U

Universal joint or U-joint A double-pivoted connection for transmitting power from a driving to a driven shaft through an angle. A U-joint consists of two Y-shaped yokes and a cross-shaped member called the spider.

V

Valve A device through which the flow of liquid, gas, vacuum, or loose material in bulk may be started, stopped, or regulated by a movable part that opens, shuts, or partially obstructs one or more ports or passageways. A valve is also the movable part of such a device.

Valve clearance The clearance between the valve tip (the end of the valve stem) and the rocker arm or tappet. The valve clearance is measured when the valve is closed.

Vernier caliper A precision measuring instrument that measures inside and outside dimensions. Not quite as accurate as a micrometer, but more convenient.

Viscosity The thickness of a liquid or its resistance to flow.

Volt A unit for expressing electrical "pressure" in a circuit. One volt that will produce a current of one ampere through a resistance of one ohm.

W

Welding Various processes used to join metal items by heating the areas to be joined to a molten state and fusing them together. For more information refer to the *Haynes Automotive Welding Manual*.

Wiring diagram A drawing portraying the components and wires in a vehicle's electrical system, using standardised symbols. For more information refer to the *Haynes Automotive Electrical and Electronic Systems Manual*.

Note: *References throughout this index are in the form - "Chapter number" • "page number"*

Preserving Our Motoring Heritage

< The Model J Duesenberg Derham Tourster. Only eight of these magnificent cars were ever built – this is the only example to be found outside the United States of America

Almost every car you've ever loved, loathed or desired is gathered under one roof at the Haynes Motor Museum. Over 300 immaculately presented cars and motorbikes represent every aspect of our motoring heritage, from elegant reminders of bygone days, such as the superb Model J Duesenberg to curiosities like the bug-eyed BMW Isetta. There are also many old friends and flames. Perhaps you remember the 1959 Ford Popular that you did your courting in? The magnificent 'Red Collection' is a spectacle of classic sports cars including AC, Alfa Romeo, Austin Healey, Ferrari, Lamborghini, Maserati, MG, Riley, Porsche and Triumph.

A Perfect Day Out

Each and every vehicle at the Haynes Motor Museum has played its part in the history and culture of Motoring. Today, they make a wonderful spectacle and a great day out for all the family. Bring the kids, bring Mum and Dad, but above all bring your camera to capture those golden memories for ever. You will also find an impressive array of motoring memorabilia, a comfortable 70 seat video cinema and one of the most extensive transport book shops in Britain. The Pit Stop Cafe serves everything from a cup of tea to wholesome, home-made meals or, if you prefer, you can enjoy the large picnic area nestled in the beautiful rural surroundings of Somerset.

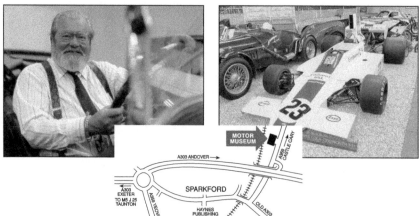

> John Haynes O.B.E., Founder and Chairman of the museum at the wheel of a Haynes Light 12.

< Graham Hill's Lola Cosworth Formula 1 car next to a 1934 Riley Sports.

The Museum is situated on the A359 Yeovil to Frome road at Sparkford, just off the A303 in Somerset. It is about 40 miles south of Bristol, and 25 minutes drive from the M5 intersection at Taunton.
Open 9.30am - 5.30pm (10.00am - 4.00pm Winter) 7 days a week, *except Christmas Day, Boxing Day and New Years Day*
Special rates available for schools, coach parties and outings Charitable Trust No. 292048